# So, What's the Deal with the Rapture?

By Mark Harvey

*Pro 18:13 He that answereth a matter before he heareth it, it is folly and shame unto him.*

© 2020 by Mark Harvey
Updated and edited December 2021
ISBN: 9781654775261

# So, What's the Deal with the Rapture?

## By Mark Harvey

| | |
|---|---|
| Introduction | 3 |
| Chapter 1. The Smartest Man in the World | 9 |
| Chapter 2. Blind Men Describing an Elephant | 25 |
| Chapter 3. The Man Who Knew Too Much | 79 |
| Chapter 4. The Key to All Future Prophecy | 123 |
| Chapter 5. Carpe Diem | 205 |
| Chapter 6. A House Divided | 271 |
| Chapter 7. The Day of Reckoning for the Church | 343 |
| Chapter 8. The Hockey Sticks of the Revelation | 364 |
| Chapter 9. Obviously... | 410 |
| Chapter 10. Anticipation | 456 |

*Isa 28:9 Whom shall he teach knowledge? and whom shall he make to understand doctrine? them that are weaned from the milk, and drawn from the breasts.*

*10 For precept must be upon precept, precept upon precept; line upon line, line upon line; here a little, and there a little:*

# Introduction

Back in 1987 the pre-tribulation rapture was frequently on the lips of many, many conservative, fundamentalist, and evangelical Christians. Preachers preached it over and over. Home Bible studies were all over it. Christian literature was full of articles on it. Hal Lindsay's best-selling book *"The Late Great Planet Earth"* had been out since 1970. It had become a popular movie by 1978 and was responsible for a flood of books by many other authors on the subject. The New York Times declared that Lindsay's book was the number one non-fiction best seller of the decade of the seventies.

I started with 1987 because that was the year I was adopted into the family of God. I was saved from my sins and eternity in hellfire by the grace of God. It was a time of great excitement for the Christians I associated with. Rapture fever had swept through the conservative wing of Christianity and may have been peaking just about the time I came to Christ. I was enthralled at the very idea and since the day of the rapture was assuredly very, very close I was happy to have made it into the kingdom of God just in time.

In 1988, Edgar C. Whisenant put out a booklet entitled *"88 Reasons Why the Rapture Will Be In 1988"*. I read it over several times and learned a lot from that little booklet, but sadly it was unconvincing. Rapture theory had quickly become my passion, and by this time I had already read several books on the subject. My knowledge and sophistication in the subject were rapidly expanding. It had gotten to the point where I could understand the arguments well enough to see where they were flawed. And there were always flaws.

But I wasn't ready to give up on the pre-trib rapture. I doubled down and began researching the scriptures on my own. At the same time, I kept reading more books on the rapture hoping for a breakthrough from some different author. Unfortunately, the number of problems I found was only growing. I finally abandoned all the books. They were too disappointing. I was convinced that the truth was in the scriptures, and I determined to find it there.

By now it was deep into the 1990's and most of my Christian friends, and the preachers, and the home Bible studies, and the Christian periodicals seemed to have moved on. The rapture was supposed to have occurred, but it just hadn't. That was deflating but I was beginning to have breakthroughs in my personal studies. I realized that the things that had been holding me back were preconceived notions that I had not fully abandoned.

Once I recognized those preconceived notions and abandoned them the light started pouring through. The study was great because the volume of scriptures that spoke to the subject was great. But I was on my way. So, now I am writing this, after 32 years of digging and learning.

This book follows the line of doctrinal development called for in the book of Isaiah.

*Isa 28:9 Whom shall he teach knowledge? and whom*

*shall he make to understand doctrine? them that are weaned from the milk, and drawn from the breasts.*

*10 For precept must be upon precept, precept upon precept; line upon line, line upon line; here a little, and there a little:*

We will establish the premise and the problems associated with the various rapture positions in the first two chapters and then begin developing the solution in the following chapters. Our study passages will range from the book of Isaiah to the book of the Revelation. Hopefully, it will be built precept upon precept and line upon line, here a little and there a little until the solution will seem unavoidable.

That means there will be repetition. Lots of repetition of critical points of doctrine. But each time, they will come from a different perspective or from different scriptures and will often include additional proofs. Hopefully, they will grow on you and bring you to an understanding that they are entirely biblical and necessary for full understanding of the rapture of the Church.

Additionally, there are scripture quotations. Lots of scripture quotations. There are two reasons for this. One is that the ideas in this book, although not necessarily new, are seldom found or written about thoroughly in other works. They are a little less simplistic and thus less accepted in the smug and scripturally apathetic Church we find around us in so many places today. The second reason for so much scripture quotation is simply this. That is where the full truth is. Anything I write that doesn't line up with the scriptures is just wrong.

Beyond all this, the scriptures I quote are generally high-powered passages. They say things that are wonderful and fascinating and terrifying. They are wonderful to a saved person longing to be with God in eternity. They are fascinating to a person interested in how all this will develop over the next few years and months. Yes, you read that right. We will examine scriptures that seem to imply we are now in the correct timeframe for much prophecy fulfillment. And finally, they are terrifying to an unsaved person who realizes he or she might be facing massive geological and judgmental events without God. Hopefully, any such people reading this book will come to a saving knowledge of the only true God and His Christ.

My advice is to slow down when you come to a scripture quotation. Read it carefully, trying to appreciate the amazing things it describes. I believe that, because they are quoted from the King James Bible, Authorized Version of 1611, they are the very words God Himself has chosen to speak to you in the English language.

In this work, I hope to maintain fidelity solely to those inspired, God-breathed, inerrant, infallible Words of the living God. By admitting to this stance, I have bound myself to accept and believe every word in my Bible. I cannot fudge a passage to make my doctrine work. I cannot go back to some non-extant, long-dead original language to select a different meaning for a word from a questionable dictionary for that language. I cannot pretend to have some arcane knowledge that is not readily apparent to anybody with an open heart and mind. I must go with what is written in its context and with a justifiable, normal understanding. This is the method for studying prophecy insisted upon by the Apostle Peter:

*2Pe 1:20 Knowing this first, that **no prophecy** of the scripture **is of any private interpretation**.*
*21 For the prophecy came not in old time by the will of man: but holy men of God spake as they were moved by the Holy Ghost.*

My hope and prayer here is that those who are not convinced that we have the very words of God in the English language, will find what I have discovered. The powerful continuity and stunning homogeneity and exquisite doctrinal purity and precise accuracy of every prophecy in the King James Bible could only come from God Himself. The specially developed and elegant language of the King James Bible Authorized Version of 1611 is far more aesthetically pleasing than the so-called easier-to-understand modern versions. The King James Bible is the pinnacle of literary achievement in the entire history of the world. Nearly every literary device available in the English language can be found multiple times within its pages. No other author can come close to this achievement. Why would you consider using something lesser, especially when all other modern English versions are filled with proven doctrinal errors. (There are lists and lists of these that can be easily found if you care to look.) And further, only this Bible has the unique internal Bible study aid by following the same word or phrase throughout the entire 66 book omnibus written by one Author.

We have been encouraged to turn away from this magnificent work in favor of the simplistic, unremarkable, impossible-to-memorize works of modern revision committees that have no problem inserting their own doctrinal preferences in favor of the doctrines given by God. We have been convinced we should force God down to our low grammatical level rather than rising to the soaring literary level more becoming to His grandeur. Let's afford to God the glory and honor His position deserves and requires.

I urge modern version readers to pay special attention to the scriptures quoted in this work. By the time you get halfway through, I believe you will begin to agree with me that these passages are authoritative and understandable and much more exciting to read than some of the bland aftermarket replacement wording in the versions you may have been reading. Hopefully by the end you will have developed a greater appreciation for the greatest literary work ever.

Never forget the Church has a powerful enemy who wants nothing more than to turn you away from the truth unto fables.

"The Word of God well understood and religiously obeyed is the shortest route to spiritual perfection. And we must not select a few favorite passages to the exclusion of others. Nothing less than a whole Bible can make a whole Christian." -A.W. Tozer

## Chapter 1. The Smartest Man in the World, or…
### (The Plain Biblical Fact of Rapture)

There is a joke that has been around for a while now. You may have heard it, but it goes well with this chapter. Here is one version of it.

A rocket scientist, a brain surgeon, an elderly pastor, and a young boy all went on an excursion in a small private plane. As they were watching the beautiful scenery below, the engine started to make unusual noises. Soon, the pilot came out of the cockpit and said the plane was going to crash. He put on a parachute and as he was jumping out, he advised them to do the same. They got out the parachutes and found there were only three of them.

The brain surgeon immediately grabbed a chute and said, "I've got lots of patients who depend on me. I have to live." So, he took a parachute and jumped out.

The rocket scientist spoke up next and explained that he was the smartest man in the world. The world needed him, so he too had to live. He also grabbed a chute and jumped out.

The elderly pastor then said to the young boy, "I have lived a long, good life and I'm prepared to die, while you are just getting started. Take the chute and jump, son. I will go down with the plane."

But the boy answered and said, "There is no problem here, sir. We both have a chute because the smartest man in the world just jumped out with my backpack."

So, here's the application to this chapter. We will see that one quarter of protestant pastors don't believe in a rapture for one reason or another. Most of those simply don't believe it should be taken literally. However, in First Corinthians chapter 15, the Apostle Paul described a very straightforward event that some of us have chosen to call a rapture. If you don't believe such a plainly described event should be taken literally, what in the world should be taken literally? This is a chapter where Paul describes the major events of the Church Age. If you don't believe this, then to be consistent you shouldn't believe in the death, burial, and resurrection of Christ which starts this listing of events. If you don't believe in those events, you simply cannot believe in Christianity.

There is no doubt many of these pastors are highly educated, brilliant men just as the rocket scientist was. But perhaps some should examine their parachute more closely. The Bible was written to a special class of people, and their kind may have problems with it. Consider these verses:

*1 Cor 1:26 For ye see your calling, brethren, how that not many wise men after the flesh, not many mighty, not many noble, are called:*
*27 But God hath chosen the foolish things of the world to confound the wise; and God hath chosen the weak things of the world to confound the things which are mighty;*
*28 And base things of the world, and things which are despised, hath God chosen, yea, and things which are not,*

*to bring to nought things that are:*
*29 That no flesh should glory in his presence.*

Plus, there's this:

*Luk 10:21 In that hour Jesus rejoiced in spirit, and said, I thank thee, O Father, Lord of heaven and earth, that thou hast hid these things from the wise and prudent, and hast revealed them unto babes: even so, Father; for so it seemed good in thy sight.*

So, who do you think the scriptures were written to? The head in the clouds and minds filled with soaring philosophically and theologically pleasing scripture renderings types? Not so much. They were written to simple folks who can read a verse and believe what it says. By doing that, we are going to find some amazing truths that some of those other guys would never believe. So, let's go!

There is probably less consensus on the fact and timing of the rapture of the Church in Protestant Christianity than on any other doctrine. For those who may not know, the rapture is a moment in time when the righteous are removed from the Earth directly to Heaven by the Lord Jesus Christ, allowing them to escape physical death. This is believed, by most, to occur at the end of the current age, just before Christ returns to peacefully reign over the whole Earth for the final one thousand years of its history, a period known as the **millennial reign of Christ**. It is hotly debated among churchmen whether there even is a rapture in the scriptures, and among those who believe in the rapture, its timing is even more hotly debated. The theological term for study of this period is called eschatology, but it is more commonly referred to as the end-times or last days.

In April of 2016, Lifeway Research did a survey of 1000 senior Protestant pastors on their view of end-times theology. This study verified what many probably already suspected – that the Church is a long way from consensus on this doctrine. It presented:

1. four possibilities for the rapture,

2. the option not to take the rapture literally from the text,

3. Preterism – a belief that most or all future prophecies were fulfilled by the time the second temple was destroyed in 70 AD,

4. and none of these.

Before giving the statistical findings, let's quickly review the four rapture possibilities mentioned. The first is a Pre-tribulation rapture. This position states that the rapture will occur sometime prior to the start of a **seven-year tribulation** period when great and terrifying plagues or judgments will rain down upon all the people on Earth. The **thousand-year millennium of peace and rest under the direct, physical, and present reign of Christ**, they believe, immediately follows this seven-year period.

The second option is for a Post-tribulation rapture. This, as the name implies, occurs immediately after the tribulation and immediately before the millennial reign of Christ begins.

The final two positions are the Mid-tribulation Rapture, which can be taken exactly as the name implies and the Pre-wrath rapture. The Pre-wrath rapture is a more recent position and is said to occur during the tribulation but prior to the start of the seven vial judgments recorded in the book of Revelation, chapter 16, which are specifically said to be the vials of the wrath of God in the text.

There is one more position that has been overlooked in the survey. That is a position where more than one rapture position could be correct. That is the position that allows more than one of these positions to have the correct timing. We will delve deeply into that possibility in this work. All four of these rapture positions are part of a doctrine called **Premillennialism**. Premillennialists all believe the Lord Jesus will come back to Earth and reign in His physical body for 1000 years. They only vary on whether and when there will be a rapture event.

So, the survey found that 25% of responding pastors didn't believe the rapture event was meant to be taken literally. Additionally, 8% of the pastors didn't believe any of the offered positions were correct. That is fully one third of all these pastors don't believe in any of the most common rapture positions put forth. Beyond that, Preterism was the favored position of another 1%. So, just over a third of all pastors rejected the four rapture positions completely.

Among the rapture positions, pre-tribulationism was favored by 36% of the pastors surveyed. Post-tribulationism was championed by 18%. The mid-tribulation and pre-wrath positions trailed at 4% each.

So, what is a new Christian, or one who has not been carefully taught about the end-times, to believe? Considering the disarray of this particular doctrinal mudpuddle, these Christians may have the best opportunity to find the full truth of the matter. Many, likely most, adherents of the above positions have become very hardened in their stances and are not very open to challenges from competing schools of thought. Yet, we will see in this work, that all have serious weaknesses and scriptural conflicts that scream for resolution.

It is a great mystery to me why this is the case, but some of it may have to do with loyalty to the teacher or mentor who first showed these pastors the position they hold. Bible school and seminary professors have a great interest in seeing their students maintain fidelity to the systematic theologies they have been taught. That helps to preserve the doctrinal peculiarities of their particular denomination or institution for the next generation. Thus, they are expert in generating loyalty among their students, very frequently for a lifetime. Additionally, their preachers are then very eager to teach these truths to those Christians they are privileged to shepherd.

Although over 25% of the pastors surveyed reject a rapture completely, I believe that the fact of a rapture can be demonstrated in the scriptures quite easily. That is, it can be demonstrated for anyone who takes the scriptures literally. As presented in the survey, the majority of those pastors who don't accept a rapture, do not always take the scriptures literally.

This presents a serious problem for the Church as a whole. If some of the scriptures are not to be taken literally, who is the arbiter of which passages to take literally? If no passages are to be taken literally, how can we ever trust that we have the right interpretation? Is it only for the clergy of a specific denomination? This kind of esoteric thinking led to the doctrine of the Nicolaitans which God explicitly says he hates in Rev. 2:5. Therefore, in this work, we will accept only literal interpretations **or** widely agreed upon analogies, usually where scripture indicates internally that they are meant to be so understood, so that we can all stay on the same page. In no case will we accept allegories not so announced in the scriptures or arcane interpretations. So, let's go step by step and demonstrate the truth and necessity of the rapture. After that, we can more readily place it in its proper timeframe.

Although the term rapture is not found in the Bible, a description of the event is found in scriptures. Simply by calling an event clearly found in scriptures a 'rapture' event, we can use the simplest form of logic to prove its existence. The definition is taken from Bible events; therefore, the concept is in the Bible. Any term could have been used but rapture is the one that has been widely accepted. In fact, the Bible does give us a word for this event, but it just never found popularity. Hebrews 11:5 uses the word "translation" when describing the same event as it happened to Enoch.

Under this logic, the rapture absolutely exists for anyone who takes the scriptures literally. In the following passage, we find a rapture tied to the resurrection of the righteous dead in Christ. It is rather lengthy, but you need to read it very carefully to understand several truths about the rapture.

*1Co 15:35 But some man will say, How are the dead raised up? and with what body do they come?*

*36 Thou fool, that which thou sowest is not quickened, except it die:*

*37 And that which thou sowest, thou sowest not that body that shall be, but bare grain, it may chance of wheat, or of some other grain:*

*38 But God giveth it a body as it hath pleased him, and to every seed his own body.*

*39 All flesh is not the same flesh: but there is one kind of flesh of men, another flesh of beasts, another of fishes, and another of birds.*

*40 There are also celestial bodies, and bodies terrestrial: but the glory of the celestial is one, and the glory of the terrestrial is another.*

*41 There is one glory of the sun, and another glory of the moon, and another glory of the stars: for one star differeth from another star in glory.*

*42 So also is the resurrection of the dead. It is sown in corruption; it is raised in incorruption:*

*43 It is sown in dishonour; it is raised in glory: it is sown in weakness; it is raised in power:*

*44 It is sown a natural body; it is raised a spiritual body. There is a natural body, and there is a spiritual body.*

OK. So, in ten verses, we find a question about the physical, fleshly body of a resurrected saint. (Understand, a saint is anybody who has been born again according to the biblical plan of salvation.) After several examples, we end with the answer in verse 44. There is a natural body and there is a spiritual body, but both are a type of flesh. The natural body is corruptible so it will decay over time. The spiritual body is incorruptible and will never decay (v. 42). It is a body suitable for eternal life. This is the body we will need for eternity so, if we are never to see death due to being raptured, we must exchange bodies or have our current body changed at the moment we become eternal beings. Continuing:

*45 And so it is written, The first man Adam was made a living soul; the last Adam was made a quickening spirit.*

*46 Howbeit that was not first which is spiritual, but that which is natural; and afterward that which is spiritual.*

*47 The first man is of the earth, earthy: the second man is the Lord from heaven.*

*48 As is the earthy, such are they also that are earthy: and as is the heavenly, such are they also that are heavenly.*

*49 And as we have borne the image of the earthy, we shall also bear the image of the heavenly.*

This truth is testified to by the apostle John:

*1Jn 3:2 Beloved, now are we the sons of God, and it doth not yet appear what we shall be: but we know that, when he shall appear, we shall be like him; for we shall see him as he is.*

Back to the rapture:

*50 Now this I say, brethren, that flesh and blood cannot inherit the kingdom of God; neither doth corruption inherit incorruption.*

*51 Behold, I shew you a mystery; We shall not all sleep, but we shall all be changed,*

*52 In a moment, in the twinkling of an eye, at the last trump: for the trumpet shall sound, and the dead shall be raised incorruptible, and we shall be changed.*

*53 For this corruptible must put on incorruption, and this mortal must put on immortality.*

*54 So when this corruptible shall have put on incorruption, and this mortal shall have put on immortality, then shall be brought to pass the saying that is written, Death is swallowed up in victory.*

*55 O death, where is thy sting? O grave, where is thy victory?*

*56 The sting of death is sin; and the strength of sin is the law.*

*57 But thanks be to God, which giveth us the victory through our Lord Jesus Christ.*

So, we find here scriptural proof that not all of us will "sleep", a biblical term for death. At some point, living saints will be instantly changed from a flesh and blood body to a spiritual body that cannot die. That is the first step of a rapture event for saints living at that time. There is more. To find it out we need to look at a related passage.

*1 Th 4:13 But I would not have you to be ignorant, brethren, concerning them which are asleep, that ye sorrow not, even as others which have no hope.*

*14 For if we believe that Jesus died and rose again, even so them also which sleep in Jesus will God bring with him.*

*15 For this we say unto you by the word of the Lord, that we which are alive and remain unto the coming of the Lord shall not prevent them which are asleep.*

*16 For the Lord himself shall descend from heaven with a shout, with the voice of the archangel, and with the trump of God: and the dead in Christ shall rise first:*

*17 Then we which are alive and remain shall be caught up together with them in the clouds, to meet the Lord in the air: and so shall we ever be with the Lord.*

*18 Wherefore comfort one another with these words.*

In verses 13-15 of the above passage, we see two classes of saints. Those who sleep in Jesus (the righteous dead in Christ), and those who are alive and remain until the coming of the Lord. In verse 16, Christ resurrects His righteous dead, and in verse 17, He catches up those that are alive and remain to be with Him forever. As we saw in the previous passage, these people must be changed into a spiritual body in order to live forever. So, this is the second part of a rapture event. To summarize, a rapture event requires:

1. A change from a natural (mortal) body to a spiritual (immortal) body, and

2. Being "caught up" from the Earth to be with the Lord for eternity without dying.

The resurrection of the righteous dead in Christ ties these two scriptures together. We are meant to understand that these two passages speak of the same event. Simply because we are naming this two-part event a 'rapture', we can conclude that a rapture is a biblical fact. People who claim that rapture is not supported by scriptures, simply haven't looked at this logically, or literally, or don't really understand what we mean by the term rapture.

As we will see, the scriptures we have examined tell us not only that there is a rapture, but also give enough information to tell us when it will occur. But wait, there's more. There are a number of scriptures that detail returns of Jesus Christ to this Earth for several reasons. For instance, we find a return at the end of the tribulation in Rev. 19. The passage indicates that He will come as King of kings and Lord of lords to defeat His enemies and in the next chapter we see His millennial reign. There is some evidence in the passage to indicate that this coming is preceded by a rapture.

There is another set of scriptures that describe an additional coming. This time He comes upon His Church as a Thief in the night. We will investigate later whether this coming includes a rapture event. It is first hinted at in:

*Zep 2:3 Seek ye the LORD, all ye meek of the earth, which have wrought his judgment; seek righteousness, seek meekness: it may be ye shall be hid in the day of the LORD'S anger.*

The entire book of Zephaniah is devoted to a time period known as "the day of the LORD". We will study this day in detail later in this book. Suffice it to say for now, that it includes the seven-year tribulation and the thousand-year millennial reign of Christ. This verse applies to all the meek of the Earth. It says there is a possibility of being "hid" or escaping the wrath of God in the tribulation. Obviously, it applies to people living at that time. This fact opens up the possibility of a rapture event. Now, moving on to scriptures that seem to offer the same possibility, we find:

*Rev 3:3 Remember therefore how thou hast received and heard, and hold fast, and repent. If therefore thou shalt not watch, I will come on thee as a thief, and thou shalt not know what hour I will come upon thee.*

In this verse as well as in Rev. 16:15 we find the Lord Jesus declaring that He will come as a Thief upon His Church. Further, we see in 1 Thes. 5:2 and in the following passage that the day of the Lord will also come as a thief in the night.

*2Pe 3:10 But the day of the Lord will come as a thief in the night; in the which the heavens shall pass away with a great noise, and the elements shall melt with fervent heat, the earth also and the works that are therein shall be burned up.*

## Scriptural instructions for developing doctrines

The King James Bible has been divinely arranged so that words used repeatedly in the same context are meant to tie ideas together. That is because the design of this book is such that we must gather scriptures referring to a single doctrine from many passages throughout the entire 66 book collection of scriptures. Although the Bible was penned by many men over a long period of time, it clearly has only one Author (2 Tim. 3:16) and therefore every passage of the book is completely homogeneous with all other passages. To review, this principle is described thusly here:

*Isa 28:9 Whom shall he teach knowledge? and whom shall he make to understand doctrine? them that are weaned from the milk, and drawn from the breasts.*
*10 For precept must be upon precept, precept upon*

*precept; line upon line, line upon line; here a little, and there a little:*

So, applying this principle, we can understand that the coming of the Lord as a Thief and the coming of the day of the Lord as a thief in the night are meant to be tied together. The Thief comes in His own day. Finally, applying this principle one more time, in Luke 12 and in the following passage from Matthew, we find a thief coming in which a house is broken up. Here, the goodman of the house is the person watching over the household of the Son of man, meaning Jesus Christ. The house is broken up by the Thief who is, in fact, the Son of man. In verses 40-41, we find examples where some are taken away and some are left behind. This is exactly what happens in a rapture event. Only the righteous living people are removed while the unrighteous are not. There is severe punishment later in the chapter for the goodman of the house found not doing his Lord's will.

*Mat 24:40 Then shall two be in the field; the one shall be taken, and the other left.*

*41 Two women shall be grinding at the mill; the one shall be taken, and the other left.*

*42 Watch therefore: for ye know not what hour your Lord doth come.*

*43 But know this, that if the goodman of the house had known in what watch the thief would come, he would have watched, and would not have suffered his house to be broken up.*

*44 Therefore be ye also ready: for in such an hour as ye think not the Son of man cometh.*

So, the Lord comes back as a Thief for His servants and steals some of them to the surprise of the others. The previous verses we have looked at tie this time to the start of the day of the LORD. These people are escaping the tribulation without dying just as Zeph. 2:3 said it could happen. We must therefore conclude that this is likely a rapture event. We should also conclude that raptures remove God's people from the time of tribulation to a safe haven above. This is their primary purpose and benefit. Much more on this later.

The possibility of a rapture should be a source of comfort and a blessed hope for the people of God. It is important to be found living for Jesus at the time of the rapture. One of my favorite passages speaks to this very fact.

*Tit 2:11 For the grace of God that bringeth salvation hath appeared to all men,*
*12 Teaching us that, denying ungodliness and worldly lusts, we should live soberly, righteously, and godly, in this present world;*
*13 Looking for that blessed hope, and the glorious appearing of the great God and our Saviour Jesus Christ;*
*14 Who gave himself for us, that he might redeem us from all iniquity, and purify unto himself a peculiar people, zealous of good works.*

It is also a purifying hope. If God's people are looking for and expecting a rapture, they will tend to reject any sin in their lives.

*1Jn 3:2 Beloved, now are we the sons of God, and it doth not yet appear what we shall be: but we know that, when he shall appear, we shall be like him; for we shall see him as he is.*

*3 And every man that hath this hope in him purifieth himself, even as he is pure.*

Also consider:

*Php 3:20 For our conversation is in heaven; from whence also we look for the Saviour, the Lord Jesus Christ:*

*21 Who shall change our vile body, that it may be fashioned like unto his glorious body, according to the working whereby he is able even to subdue all things unto himself.*

So, again, we will exchange a vile body for a glorious body on that great day.

# Chapter 2. Blind Men Describing an Elephant, or...

## (The Popular Rapture Positions and Their Problems)

The parable of the blind men and the elephant is a very ancient story of Indian origin. There are many variations, but broadly it goes as follows:

A group of blind men heard that a strange animal, called an elephant, had been brought to the town, but none of them were aware of its shape and form. Out of curiosity, they asked a sighted man to lead them to it. So, when they found it, they groped about it. In the case of the first person, whose hand landed on the trunk, he reported that an elephant is like a thick snake. Another one, who touched its ear, said it seemed like a kind of fan. Another blind man, whose hand landed on its leg, said the elephant is a pillar like a tree-trunk. The one who placed his hand upon its side said an elephant is like a wall. Another who felt its tail, described it as a rope. The last felt its tusk and stated that the elephant is that which is hard, smooth and like a spear.

The parable tells us that men can speak truth about a subject but fail to account for the full truth and thus ultimately be wrong in their conclusions. This is what we will find to be the case in all the following rapture positions.

**Pre-tribulationism**

Having conclusively demonstrated that a rapture is called for in the scriptures, we are now ready to examine the basic rapture positions and determine whether any of them are viable in their currently most popular constructs. We will start with the most prevalent position, the pre-tribulation rapture.

The pre-tribulation rapture theory states that the rapture will occur at some indeterminable point before or concurrent with the start of the seven-year tribulation, and the concurrent 70$^{th}$ week of Daniel 9:24-27. Christians, they say, are not appointed to wrath, so they will not face the terrible judgments of the tribulation.

The pre-tribulation rapture was introduced to the Church in the 1830's by a preacher and prolific writer named John Nelson Darby (1800-1882). There is some evidence that others believed in this rapture before Darby, but to the vast majority of the true Church it was something entirely new. Pre-trib detractors love to point out that Darby got his inspiration by dubious methods but that is a weak and ultimately toothless argument. If a doctrine is found in the scriptures, then it is a scriptural doctrine. It is utterly unimportant how it was first introduced to the Church.

Darby faced many challenges to his work from important contemporaries, including Baptist preacher Charles Spurgeon, considered one of the greatest preachers of his time. But Darby was a forceful and persistent and persuasive and compelling man and was able to start two entirely new Protestant denominations based on his teachings. Eventually, his rapture theory found its way into many mainstream denominations.

Darby's rapture theory was readily accepted by an influential preacher named C. I. Scofield (1843-1921). Scofield produced an annotated reference bible that promoted the pre-trib rapture in his notes. This Bible took off and became exceedingly popular throughout the next century and is still a big seller today. Another preacher who ran with Darby's rapture model was Clarence Larkin (1850-1924). He drew many graphical and artistic timelines that he included in several books on the subject. They were also well received in the Evangelical and Fundamentalist movements. These efforts moved the pre-trib rapture into the limelight and as mentioned, it became the most popular end-times model of our present day.

The pre-tribulation rapture theory is based on three major tenets. These are the doctrine of Imminence, the desire to place the rapture at Rev. 4:1, and the doctrine of Antichrist taken from Daniel 9:26-27. Two of them contradict each other and the third is based on an improper reading of the scriptures. You have to wonder how it became so popular, even in the face of Charles Spurgeon's opposition.

**Imminence**

So, now I am going to do great harm to the pre-trib rapture position. Yet, I want the reader to understand, we are going to come full circle to demonstrate a pre-trib rapture in this book. It absolutely exists in scriptures but not in the way that it is currently widely taught. A crucial element has been overlooked that places specific responsibilities on the people of God. And that is very important to understand. This rapture is hinted at in an oddly placed verse, probably as a reminder that the then-current situation might have been avoided. Here, Jesus Christ is the speaker: We will see why in chapter 9.

*Rev 16:15 Behold, I come as a thief. Blessed is he that watcheth, and keepeth his garments, lest he walk naked, and they see his shame.*

Compare this verse to the following and you will see at least two distinct comings of Christ yet to occur:

*Mat 24:30 And then shall appear the sign of the Son of man in heaven: and then shall all the tribes of the earth mourn, and they shall see the Son of man coming in the clouds of heaven with power and great glory.*

This, definitely, is not the way a Thief comes! People don't mourn when they see a thief coming. They lock the doors and arm themselves. But mostly they never see him coming. Thus, these must be viewed as two separate comings.

Chapter 4 of this book will deal more exhaustively with much of what follows here regarding Daniel 9:24-27. So, if you don't get it all this time, you will see it all again. I'm sorry to be repetitive but that is one of the most important chapters in the Bible for laying a foundation to understanding end-times events. If you get that straight, end-times doctrines go from almost unintelligible to straightforward and logical and chronological. So, please bear with me. The current rapture doctrine of each of the four positions mentioned here is so convoluted and confusing that many who try to teach it don't seem to really understand it all themselves.

The pre-trib rapture argument starts with a very strange but much cherished doctrine. It is known as the doctrine of imminence. The doctrine of imminence holds that Christ can rapture His saints at any moment, without the need for any prophetic event to happen first, and this has been true for the entire Church Age. They believe they will be taken completely by surprise (as by a Thief), even possibly in the very next moment of time. The other rapture theories require the tribulation to have started so there is no possibility of imminence until after some of the very specific judgments of the tribulation have occurred. It is therefore used as a central tenet to prove that the rapture must be pre-trib. This doctrine faces one major obstacle, however. And that obstacle is that it is not found anywhere in the King James Bible.

**The first argument for imminence**

The proponents of imminence use two basic arguments for the doctrine. Both are quite easily defeated. The first argument uses scriptures that speak of the Lord coming soon or quickly in addition to scriptures that encourage us to be waiting and watching for our Lord's return. Dr. Thomas Ice of Liberty University has put together a list of verses to prove imminence. Here is his list: 1 Cor. 1:7; 16:22; Phil. 3:20; 4:5; 1 Thess. 1:10; Tit. 2:13; Heb. 9:28; Jam. 5:7–9; 1 Pet. 1:13; Jude 21: Rev. 3:11; 22:7, 12, 17, 20. If you go through these verses, you will see there is no concrete support for imminence. Rather, the doctrine must be inferred from the language of the verses. Some of these verses could be argued with equal aplomb for all four rapture positions because they only affirm that Christ will indeed return. They only appear to support imminence if you are predisposed to believe in imminence.

Darby was at least a stepfather of the imminence doctrine if not *the* father. But apparently, he had trouble proving it from the King James Bible which was in common usage at that time. He also found, as we will study later, the KJV to be a hindrance to his doctrine of The Antichrist. So, he set about producing his own translation of the scriptures. This is reminiscent of the Jehovah's Witness movement which also had to produce their own translation of the scriptures because their teachings were incompatible with the KJV.

Darby altered a number of passages in the New Testament where he inserted the words 'about to', apparently to prove his position on imminence. Here is an example. It is hard to imagine that he actually found any manuscript evidence on which to base these alterations.

Darby translation:

*1 Peter 5:1 The elders which [are] among you I exhort, who [am their] fellow-elder and witness of the sufferings of the Christ, who also [am] partaker of the glory **about to** be revealed:*

The KJV reads:

*1Pe 5:1 The elders which are among you I exhort, who am also an elder, and a witness of the sufferings of Christ, and also a partaker of the glory that shall be revealed:*

There are other self-patronizing changes to the scriptures Darby made to prove his doctrinal theory. The point here is that Darby himself apparently couldn't find imminence in the KJV. So, he created an abomination of the words of God to get around the problem. Most KJV believers seem to be entirely unaware of these very serious issues with the pre-trib doctrine. They seem to believe in imminence more out of necessity than because they can actually prove the doctrine.

The argument Thomas Ice has made is that, because some of these verses imply we should be **eagerly** watching for the return of the Lord, there could not be any intervening event that we should be watching for first. That seems logical enough, but it utterly fails as a proof. It only rises to the level of speculation which is a very poor standard to build doctrine upon.

Many pre-trib adherents use the following passage as an incentive to encourage church attendance and holy living.

*Heb 10:24 And let us consider one another to provoke unto love and to good works:*
*25 Not forsaking the assembling of ourselves together, as the manner of some is; but exhorting one another: and so much the more, as ye see the day approaching.*

In addition to this being another encouragement to watch for the Lord, this is a refutation of imminence. It strongly implies that we can and must see the day (of the Lord as they believe) approaching before it overtakes us. Something, according to this verse, gives us the ability to see the day getting closer. Imminence insists on no advance warning of any kind. It can always happen in the very next instant of time.

Continuing the theme of the passage in Hebrews just shown, we can find scriptures that insist there must be intervening events before His coming. We will show some events later in this book which still must happen before Jesus comes and an event which happens concurrently with the Thief rapture. But for now, we will show one that has already happened which destroys imminence at least early-on in the Church Age.

*Joh 21:18 Verily, verily, I say unto thee, When thou wast young, thou girdedst thyself, and walkedst whither thou wouldest: but when thou shalt be old, thou shalt stretch forth thy hands, and another shall gird thee, and carry thee whither thou wouldest not.*

*19 This spake he, signifying by what death he should glorify God. And when he had spoken this, he saith unto him, Follow me.*

Pre-trib rapture proponents believe all living saints will be caught up at the same time to be with the Lord when the rapture occurs. However, in the above passage, Christ is telling Peter that he will die. Thus, if the rapture occurred before the death of Peter, he would not die, and Christ would have been a false prophet. Oh, what a tangled web. This is not the only example we could have given. This is a big fail for the doctrine of imminence and puts a dent in the pre-trib rapture position.

**The second argument for imminence**

The second argument for imminence is based on scriptures such as this:

*Mar 13:32 But of that day and that hour knoweth no man, no, not the angels which are in heaven, neither the Son, but the Father.*

Here, they say, Jesus is specifically saying that no man knoweth the day and the hour of His return. So, if it occurred after the tribulation had started, it would be fairly easy to pin down at least a narrow time for it to happen. Thus, it must be before the tribulation. Some go so far as to say that the day has not been pinned down yet by God Himself. Thus, they will often say: "If the Lord tarries, we will do this and thus." There are at least two verses in scriptures that specifically say He or 'it' will NOT tarry (Hab. 2:3 and Heb. 10:37). Additionally, our text verse above assures us that the Father absolutely does know the day and hour, so the day and hour are already set in heaven.

It gets worse for them. 1 Thes. 5:4 tells us that the very day should not overtake us as a "thief". In other words, we should know what day the Thief (Rev. 16:15) will come! Going even further, The Lord Himself declares in Rev. 3:3, that **we** will **not** know the very hour of His return **only if** we are **not** watching for Him.

So why the discrepancy between Mark 13:32 and the two passages just referenced? It is really quite simple. Jesus told His disciples that no man, including Himself in His role as the God/Man, knoweth (present tense!) the day or the hour. He never said, "can know" or "will know". He specifically said "knoweth". He didn't speak to whether that would still be true in the future. When Jesus spoke those words, He was still presenting Himself to the Jews as their potential King. This is generally the case in all other passages with similar wording.

Had the Jews accepted Him, He would still have gone to the cross, but at the hands of the Romans rather than the Jews. After His resurrection, all remaining unfulfilled prophecy would have been fulfilled in the next few years and the kingdom would have been established right then.

Because the Jews, in fact, rejected their Messiah, the Church Age was instituted, and the kingdom was postponed until the end of the Church Age. Thus, there were two possible dates for His return. God the Father preplanned all of this (see 1 Cor. chapter 2) but kept it from all others, including His Son, so that the kingdom offer would be genuine. We will provide more proof of this later in the chapter but understand that this pre-trib argument is another fail.

**The pre-tribulation rapture 'at the last Church'**

Another vitally important position of pre-trib adherents is found in Rev. 4:1:

*Rev 4:1 After this I looked, and, behold, a door was opened in heaven: and the first voice which I heard was as it were of a trumpet talking with me; which said, Come up hither, and I will shew thee things which must be hereafter.*

Pre-trib adherents almost invariably argue that the command to "come up hither" given to John in this verse, is also given to the whole Church at that time. If you are not well versed in pre-trib doctrine, this may seem shocking to you. But this is a major part of the doctrine so let's take a closer look.

The major reason posited is that, because the Church is mentioned in Rev. chapters 2-3 and then never mentioned again, the Church must have been raptured at Rev.4:1. Just a little attempt at humor here. Please bear with me. Chapters 2-3 go through a list of specific messages from Christ to seven specific churches. It is believed broadly among pre-trib adherents that the churches represent consecutive time periods throughout the Church Age. Thus, the Church of Laodicea (Rev. 3:14-22) is the seventh and last church period. So, apparently those pre-trib adherents believe that the rapture occurs 'at the last Church' of seven churches, but not 'at the last trump' of seven trumpets (see 1 Cor 15:51-52).

(To be fair, some pre-trib adherents believe all seven churches have existed simultaneously at all times throughout the Church Age. Still, there was the need for this information to be presented to the churches since the prophecies and warnings were given to and for them. Thus, there could be no rapture before John wrote the Revelation in about 90 AD.)

To claim that this last mention of the Church puts us into the tribulation period is very odd indeed. First of all, it blows imminence right out of the water again. Although the Lord can rapture us out at any time in the Church Age, He cannot rapture us out until all the seven ages of the Church are finished. Now that's an oxymoron for you.

The major tenet of imminence is that the rapture can happen at any time with no need for any prophesied events to occur first. Yet this verse starts with the words "After this"! That immediately puts a time requirement involving prophetic events on the pre-trib rapture. Many pre-trib adherents seem able to compartmentalize their beliefs. That is, when they teach imminence, they ignore the timing of the rapture. Then, when they teach the time of the rapture, they ignore imminence. This alone should be enough to cause serious doubt about this position. There is a curious but true phenomenon. Pre-trib adherents often point to world events or conditions and say they are signs that the coming of the Lord is drawing nearer. Yet, by definition, imminence is never nearer at one time than another. Remember, there are no signs or preconditions allowed to stand in the way of the Lord's return.

There is, in reality, no compelling reason to presume the Church is gone just because it isn't mentioned in the rest of the book. This is quite common in other books of the New Testament. For instance, Galatians mentions the Church three times, all in chapter 1. Does the rest of the book deal only with post Church Age events? Of course not. 1 Thes. mentions the Church only once in chapter 1 and once in chapter 2. That's it. 2 Thes. mentions the Church only in verses 1 and 4 of chapter 1. Finally, the books of 2 Peter, 1 John, 2 John, and Jude never mention the Church at all. Are we to believe all of these are post-Church Age scriptures?

Rev. 4:1 is reminiscent of another verse in the Bible:

*2Co 12:2 I knew a man in Christ above fourteen years ago, (whether in the body, I cannot tell; or whether out of the body, I cannot tell: God knoweth;) such an one caught up to the third heaven.*

In this verse, the Apostle Paul is recalling a similar event. He was taken directly to heaven where he was shown and taught the doctrines he would need to take the gospel to the Gentiles. There was nobody taken with him, and he was returned to Earth when it was over. In Rev. 4:1, John is taken to heaven to show him things that would come hereafter. Then, he was returned to Earth where he wrote the book of the Revelation. Nobody is mentioned accompanying him. This is another fail for pre-tribulationism.

## Who is "he" in Dan. 9:27?

We will delve more deeply into this question later and will show that almost all the end-times doctrinal problems stem from an incorrect reading of the following single passage of scripture.

*Dan 9:24 Seventy weeks are determined upon thy people and upon thy holy city, to finish the transgression, and to make an end of sins, and to make reconciliation for iniquity, and to bring in everlasting righteousness, and to seal up the vision and prophecy, and to anoint the most Holy.*

*25 Know therefore and understand, that from the going forth of the commandment to restore and to build Jerusalem unto the Messiah the Prince shall be seven weeks, and threescore and two weeks: the street shall be built again, and the wall, even in troublous times.*

*26 And after threescore and two weeks shall Messiah be cut off, but not for himself: and the people of the prince that shall come shall destroy the city and the sanctuary; and the end thereof shall be with a flood, and unto the end of the war desolations are determined.*

*27 And he shall confirm the covenant with many for one week: and in the midst of the week he shall cause the sacrifice and the oblation to cease, and for the overspreading of abominations he shall make it desolate, even until the consummation, and that determined shall be poured upon the desolate.*

Most of the error in all the current rapture positions comes from reading verse 26 incorrectly from a grammatical perspective. We will give a more exhaustive argument in chapter 4, but some commentary is necessary here.

The majority of people educated in modern US schools have no idea how to read the complicated sentence structure in the King James Bible. We no longer make the fine distinctions in meanings that the much more sophisticated language skills of the 1600's enabled. So, let's look closely at the single sentence in verse 26. It is a compound sentence containing three clauses separated by a colon and a semi-colon. It is necessary to understand the use of colons to know how to read this sentence. Stay with me here because this is a little tedious but necessary to arrive at the scriptural truth.

According to Richard Hughes in his book *"An English Grammar for the Study of Scripture"*:

"The colon (:) has one primary use in scriptures: it separates independent clauses where the second clause helps explain the first clause."

So, in verse 26, the clause: "and the people of the prince that shall come shall destroy the city and the sanctuary" has a sole purpose of adding information about the clause: "And after threescore and two weeks shall Messiah be cut off, but not for himself". Messiah is clearly the subject of the sentence and everything after the first clause could be safely dropped without changing the narrative continuing in the next sentence.

Moving to the next verse we find a third person, male, singular pronoun which requires a male, singular antecedent: *"And he shall confirm the covenant with many for one week"*. There are two singular males in the previous sentence that could fit the bill. They are Messiah and the prince. In simple grammar, this verse would be broken into two or more sentences and since we usually choose the closest possible antecedent, in this case, that would be the prince. In fact, most recent theologians have read the passage as if it were simple grammar. It is not. It is a compound sentence including a colon.

Many modern versions replace the colon with a semi-colon, or a comma, or a period. All these cases would require the prince to be the antecedent for "he" in verse 27. End of argument.

However, the far more accurate KJV uses a colon. The colon tells us that the information from there to the end of the sentence is not necessary to understand the overall narrative. Rather, it is additional information about a particular result of Messiah being cut off. There are many more results but this one is mentioned at this point because it is a punishment to Israel specifically for 'cutting off' her Messiah. Therefore, we are still speaking of Messiah when we start the next sentence. The colon requires Messiah to be the antecedent of "he" in verse 27.

**If "he" refers to the prince...**

Darby and the pre-trib adherents insist that this prince is a character called 'The Antichrist'. Antichrist is another product of Darby's version of the Old Testament. Darby never produced an English version of the Old Testament, but he did produce the OT in several other languages. After his death, his students translated his OT into English based on his foreign translations. They fully understood his teaching on the subject of Antichrist, so the Darby Old Testament carefully reflects that teaching in Daniel 9:26-27. Full disclosure: Although, we will find Darby's Antichrist to be an entirely fictional character in chapter 4 of this work, we will still find a powerful antichrist at the beginning of the tribulation. He just won't match the deeds of Darby's Antichrist and he won't be 'The Antichrist'.

So, now we need to see how our doctrines will differ based on the two interpretations. In the case where "he" refers to the prince, we find the prince confirming a covenant for one week. Verse 9:24 above refers to a period of 70 weeks. It is historically demonstrable and almost universally accepted that these are each a week of years, so we are talking about 490 years here. Verse 25 of our passage in Daniel speaks of 7 weeks and 62 weeks for a total of 69 out of 70 weeks of years. The week of verse 27 then, would logically be the 70th week of the 70 weeks mentioned above. Pre-trib adherents will argue that there is a break in the weeks at that 69 weeks point. The final week must wait until the character called Antichrist appears to confirm the covenant.

Here is the reason for the break between the 69th and 70th weeks mentioned above. The Jews had a conditional Covenant of the Law with God, known as the Mosaic Covenant. Once they broke the covenant, God had the right to withdraw His responsibility to it at any time. God was exceedingly longsuffering for the Israelites, as they broke the covenant again and again over 1600 years. However, when they murdered His Son, their Messiah, His longsuffering ended. His exclusive Mosaic Covenant with the Jews ended before the 70 weeks ended. A new age had begun. The offer of a physical kingdom with Messiah as their King was also temporarily withdrawn and the kingdom moved to the spiritual realm. This new age must now run its course before God finishes His dealings with Israel. That last statement will be demonstrated from scripture in the next section, but it can also be observed from history.

It is important to see the scriptures that confirm these arguments:

*Zec 11:10 And I took my staff, even Beauty, and cut it asunder, that I might* **break my covenant** *which I had made with all the people.*
*11 And it was broken in that day: and so the poor of the flock that waited upon me knew that it was the word of the LORD.*
*12 And I said unto them, If ye think good, give me my price; and if not, forbear. So they weighed for my price thirty pieces of silver.*
*13 And the LORD said unto me, Cast it unto the potter: a goodly price that I was prised at of them. And I took the thirty pieces of silver, and cast them to the potter in the house of the LORD.*

This is obviously a prophecy of the death of Christ when Judas betrayed Him for thirty pieces of silver. The money was used by the priests to buy the potter's field. It establishes the time when the covenant will be broken. Continuing:

*Rom 11:11 I say then, Have they stumbled that they should fall? God forbid: but rather through their fall salvation is come unto the Gentiles, for to provoke them to jealousy.*

Recapping, the Church Age was instituted when Israel rejected her messianic kingdom. Pre-trib adherents teach that the first 69 weeks or 483 years of the prophecy were completed just days before the crucifixion. They conclude that, because all Bible prophecy must be fulfilled, there remains one week of years or 7 years for God to deal with

Israel. The 70 weeks of years did not happen consecutively because the Mosaic covenant with Israel was broken before it ended. That covenant was conditional and at the death of Christ, God ended it and turned to the Gentiles, changing His interactions with mankind from physical to spiritual applications.

Now, the prince of Dan. 9:26 in our passage is said to be the Antichrist mentioned in 1 John 2:18. The pre-trib adherents believe that Antichrist is a powerful character who will come at the start of the 7-year tribulation and establish a covenant with Israel while, by mid-trib, establishing himself as the ruler of the whole world. In the middle of the tribulation, according to our passage, he will turn on Israel and break his covenant per: *"And he shall confirm the covenant with many for one week: and in the midst of the week he shall cause the sacrifice and the oblation to cease"*.

Some pre-trib adherents have argued that the covenant confirmed with Israel by the Antichrist will be the Mosaic Covenant. Scriptures clearly state that covenant has been broken and replaced with the Church. The next covenant God will make with Israel is the New Covenant which will begin in the millennium (Heb. 8:8-13). Therefore, Antichrist will be deceiving Israel with this covenant.

This all seems to tie together in a very neat package, but it makes some pretty big assumptions. For instance, there is no scripture to tie this to the Antichrist of 1 John. Pre-trib adherents believe this prince makes a covenant with Israel. If he is not their Antichrist, they don't have a fallback verse for the covenant. In scriptures, it is rare for a doctrine to be built on only one verse or passage (review Isa. 28:9-10).  Also, pre-trib adherents tend to ignore the fact that this prophecy of the prince was fulfilled completely when Titus, prince of Rome, destroyed the city and the sanctuary in 70 AD.  Finally, and just as importantly, no qualifying 483-year period ending at the crucifixion really fits the historical time for the appearance of Messiah and the start of His ministry.

Dan. 9:25 requires that the 70 weeks start from the going forth of the commandment to restore and rebuild Jerusalem.  There are four such commandments in scriptures so choosing the right one is important for the count of years to arrive at the right time relative to the ministry of Messiah and thus validate the prophecy.

In a very tortured attempt, Scotland Yard Chief Inspector Sir Robert Anderson in his book *The Coming Prince* (1894) tried to demonstrate exactly 483 years from the commandment of Artaxerxes 1 to Nehemiah in about 445 BC (Neh. 2:6) until, according to Anderson, the triumphal entry of Jesus into Jerusalem in 32 AD, just days before His crucifixion.  Anderson used a 360-day year as a "prophetic" year and then adjusted the time to 173,880 days.  Later he added in too few leap years by jumping around to different calendars.  This was necessary to get the right number of days. He also used an arbitrary start day and some other questionable devices to make it all work.  As you can see, it is very important for pre-trib adherents to have the 483-year period end at the point of the crucifixion.  More on this later.

Finally, for the record I must point out that in the wording of many modern bible versions "he" is logically Antichrist. But most modern versions have thousands of changes from the KJV and thousands of differences between each other. If you can live with that kind of confusion, there is no reason to accept the accuracy of any passage of scripture, no logic in discussing the merit and meaning of any particular passage, and little reason to believe we have any accurate and meaningful word from God (1 Cor. 14:33). Modern version readers normally accept almost all versions as having merit (except sometimes the KJV) so for them to discuss fine points of doctrine is utter nonsense. In the KJV, however, there is more reason to doubt "he" refers to the prince than there is reason to accept it.

**If "he" refers to Messiah...**

In the case where "he" is accepted as a reference to Messiah, we find quite a different scenario. To refresh our memory:

*"And he shall confirm the covenant with many for one week: and in the midst of the week he shall cause the sacrifice and the oblation to cease, and for the overspreading of abominations he shall make it desolate, even until the consummation, and that determined shall be poured upon the desolate."*

Here Messiah confirms a covenant with many for one week and causes the sacrifice and oblation to cease after 3.5 years. As it turns out, this fits the scriptures precisely. If we start counting the 70 weeks from the commandment to Ezra to restore the temple and build Jerusalem (per verse 9:25 above), we find that the first 69 weeks or 483 years take us from about 458 BC when king Artaxerxes made his decree to about 26 AD when, historically, Jesus began His public ministry at age 30 (subtract 1 year when changing from BC to AD). Jesus ministered for 3.5 years before He was crucified. That is exactly the 'midst' of a week of 7 years. So, at this point we have completed 69.5 weeks out of 70. The sacrifice and oblation ceased in that they were of no effect or value once Jesus became the final sacrifice for our salvation. Messiah Jesus caused the sacrifice and the oblation to cease, not Antichrist! The Mosaic Covenant is now long dead and there is no reason to sacrifice animals for sins anymore. (I will reveal the covenant that Messiah confirmed in a later chapter.)

Thus, there were only 3.5 years of the 490 years left for God to deal with Israel before the Church Age intervened. We will fully demonstrate in this work that the *general* rapture of the Church occurs at the middle of the tribulation, leaving the required 3.5 years for God to finish all His prophecies concerning Israel.

I should point out here that, although the Mosaic Covenant of the Law was broken, God still has an unconditional covenant with Israel. This is known as the Abrahamic Covenant and preserved for all history in:

*Gen 13:14 And the LORD said unto Abram, after that Lot was separated from him, Lift up now thine eyes, and look from the place where thou art northward, and southward, and eastward, and westward:*

*15 For all the land which thou seest, to thee will I give it, and to thy seed for ever.*

*16 And I will make thy seed as the dust of the earth: so*

*that if a man can number the dust of the earth, then shall thy seed also be numbered.*

*17 Arise, walk through the land in the length of it and in the breadth of it; for I will give it unto thee.*

As you can see, God will never stop dealing with Israel in a special way. Although He no longer requires the deeds of the Law from them, He will always honor His promise regarding the land of Israel. Historically, the Abrahamic Covenant was interrupted for most of the Church Age but is now being re-established. This is an often overlooked but important point of our text in Daniel.

*Dan 9:27 And he shall confirm the covenant with many for one week: and in the midst of the week he shall cause the sacrifice and the oblation to cease, and for the overspreading of abominations he shall make it desolate, even until the* **consummation**, *and that determined shall be poured upon the desolate.* (Bold print mine.)

The pronoun "it" here refers to Jerusalem as mentioned in the previous verse. So, Jerusalem was to be made desolate until the consummation. Indeed, Jerusalem has been desolate for much of the last 1800 years but has now been repopulated and rebuilt. By this we should understand that we are in the time of the **consummation! We are now in the time of completion or the time of the end according to this passage.** The actual last 3.5-year period of the 70 weeks does not begin, however, until the 666 Beast of Revelation 13 appears for the final 42 months which is 3.5 years:

*Rev 13:4 And they worshipped the dragon which gave power unto the beast: and they worshipped the beast, saying, Who is like unto the beast? who is able to make war with him?*

*5 And there was given unto him a mouth speaking great things and blasphemies; and power was given unto him to continue forty and two months.*

*6 And he opened his mouth in blasphemy against God, to blaspheme his name, and his tabernacle, and them that dwell in heaven.*

*7 And it was given unto him to make war with the saints, and to overcome them: and power was given him over all kindreds, and tongues, and nations.*

*8 And all that dwell upon the earth shall worship him, whose names are not written in the book of life of the Lamb slain from the foundation of the world.*

Although the case for the prince making and breaking a covenant seems to offer a very tidy package, the case for Messiah is actually much tidier. The 70 weeks continue chronologically for 69.5 weeks or 486.5 years until Messiah is "cut off" (verse 26) and therefore the sacrifice and the oblation cease (to have efficacy). Virtually all Christians believe that Christ the Messiah became the final sacrifice for sins immediately when He shed His blood on the cross of Calvary. Virtually all Christians believe that Christ the Messiah was "cut off, but not for Himself" when He shed His blood on the cross at Calvary. This all happened right on time according to corroborating secular history. And all precisely as the passage requires. Why fight such wonderful harmony of scripture with observed history?

**More proof verses for the pre-trib position**

In another attempt to create their Antichrist, pre-trib adherents will point to this passage:

*2Th 2:3 Let no man deceive you by any means: for that day shall not come, except there come a falling away first, and that man of sin be revealed, the son of perdition;*

*4 Who opposeth and exalteth himself above all that is called God, or that is worshipped; so that he as God sitteth in the temple of God, shewing himself that he is God.*

Here they claim that the man of sin is the Antichrist. This passage further bolsters their claim that the rapture is pre-trib because the falling away is a reference to the rapture and it happens before Antichrist is revealed. And, since Antichrist comes at the start of the tribulation, the rapture is necessarily pre-trib. That's perfect if the man of sin is their Antichrist and if the event described happens at the start of the tribulation. But from verse 4 we see that this is actually the Beast of Rev. 13 who comes out of the bottomless pit at mid-trib to slay the two witnesses of Rev. 11 and then commits the abomination of desolation which is described thusly in the verse: *"so that he as God sitteth in the temple of God, shewing himself that he is God."* See also Matt. 24:15 with Dan. 12:9-11 which can both be demonstrated to be a mid-trib event. This actually works as a proof for a mid-trib rapture.

Pre-trib adherents often then point to the white horse rider of Rev. 6:2 as proof that Antichrist will come at the start of the tribulation. This rider compares favorably with a character in Daniel chapters 7, 8, and 11. He also has characteristics similar to Christ, but in fact, he is not Christ. Thus, he is Antichrist in their view. I will demonstrate that they are close to the truth in a later chapter, but for now I will just point out that this presents a problem of consistency of interpretation. If the white horse rider is a specific person, then the red horse rider and the black horse rider and the pale horse rider should also be specific persons in that chapter. They have no candidates for these riders. In fact, we will find that none of them are specific persons. Rather, they are all spirits. Also, they do not come at the start of the tribulation. I don't want to give anything more away at this time, but a later chapter will reveal the truth about this character.

There is one more thing that pre-trib adherents are guilty of and perhaps it is their most grievous mistake. That is, ignoring scriptures that challenge their position. The Bible tells us:

*1Co 2:11 For what man knoweth the things of a man, save the spirit of man which is in him? even so the things of God knoweth no man, but the Spirit of God.*
*12 Now we have received, not the spirit of the world, but the spirit which is of God; that we might know the things that are freely given to us of God.*

There are many things in the scriptures that are freely given to us. For instance, 1 Cor. 15:52 clearly states that the rapture occurs at the last trump. The fact that there are 7 trumpet judgments in the Revelation, and it can be demonstrated that all the other events associated with that rapture are found in the same time period as that last trumpet judgment does not sway them one bit. The fact that a compilation of scriptures clearly shows when the day of the Lord starts in the Revelation events doesn't move them at all. We will see there are more of such ignorations in pre-tribulationism.

Before completing this section, there is one more passage we need to look at so that I won't appear to be a hypocrite based on that last point. By this time, many pre-trib adherents are probably casting about for a way to scripturally salvage their position. There are some even less helpful verses they will go to, hoping they will help their cause. Probably the most heavily relied on is this one:

*1Th 5:9 For God hath not appointed us to wrath, but to obtain salvation by our Lord Jesus Christ,*
*10 Who died for us, that, whether we wake or sleep, we should live together with him.*

The phrase "whether we wake or sleep" ties this passage to a rapture scenario. Pre-trib adherents will argue that since we are not appointed to wrath, we cannot enter the tribulation. But the verse does not say that at all. If that were the point of the passage, it would no doubt have been stated something like "we will not experience God's special outpouring of wrath". It does not say anything like that. It uses the word "appointed". This is introducing the possibility for two outcomes. Appointments can be made or missed. What it implies is that, while we don't have to experience wrath, we may do that anyway. To help us better understand the word "appointment", let's look at another passage:

*Heb 9:27 And as it is appointed unto men once to die, but after this the judgment:*
*28 So Christ was once offered to bear the sins of many; and unto them that look for him shall he appear the second time without sin unto salvation.*

Although "it is appointed unto men once to die", pre-trib adherents universally agree that all saints who are raptured will never die. That is part of the definition of a rapture. So, the word "appointed" here does not mean we will definitely die. We will not die if we miss this appointment due to the rapture intervening before our appointment. The precision of the language of the KJV must always be accounted for when developing doctrines. For an interesting study, compare Heb. 9:28 above with Rev. 3:3. That might help you see where I am heading here as well as anything I may write.

**Conclusion for the pre-trib rapture position**

The Darby et al. pre-trib position on the rapture fails miserably in three key areas. One, it requires the unsound and unproveable doctrine of imminence. A second problem occurs when the rapture is assigned to Rev. 4:1. This not only says nothing resembling a rapture of all saints, but it is also in direct conflict with imminence. The third problem is the need to present the prince of Dan. 9:26 as John's Antichrist without a single scripture to tie them together and then tie the prince to the pronoun "he" in verse 27. Daniel chapters 7,8, 11, and 12 offer no good solution to the problem of identifying Antichrist either, as they deal with a little horn that, in one form is Antiochus IV Epiphanes, and in the other form is clearly the Beast of Revelation 13.

It is clear from John's epistles that many antichrists were already on the scene before he penned those books, and it is scripturally impossible from these passages to place

Darby's Antichrist at the start of the tribulation.  So, although these Daniel passages speak of a very powerful end-times character, there is no compelling reason for him to be identified as the Antichrist of the pre-trib adherents. This artificial creation of Antichrist, we will see, completely destroys the simple chronology of the Revelation and creates much confusion.

**Mid-tribulationism**

By now you may have surmised that I find the mid-trib position to have some merit.  That is true, but I find serious fault with the way mid-trib adherents arrive at their conclusions.  The greatest problem I see is that mid-trib adherents tend to argue the position very poorly. They rarely go to the heart of the matter.  Mid-trib adherents tend to overwhelm the reader with a large volume of scriptures that they believe hint at their point. We will get to the heart of the matter in chapter 4.

I should point out that mid-trib is not a popular terminology with many of its adherents.  They often claim that they are pre-trib because the rapture occurs before the "great tribulation" as specified in Matt. 24:21.  This is said to be the last half of Daniels 70$^{th}$ week.  So, it is still 3.5 years before the return of Christ for the final battle of Armageddon that ends the 70$^{th}$ week.  Others call it the mid-week rapture in order to sharpen the distinction between the tribulation and Daniel's 70$^{th}$ week.  It is primarily called the mid-trib rapture by pre-trib adherents and post-trib adherents who insist on a 7-year tribulation. I will continue to use the term mid-trib because that is what the survey used and because in my view it is an adequate one.

The major tenet of mid-tribulationism is that the rapture occurs at the last trumpet of the 7 trumpet judgments. They believe this corresponds with the verses:

*1 Co 15:51 Behold, I shew you a mystery; We shall not all sleep, but we shall all be changed,*
*52 In a moment, in the twinkling of an eye, at the last trump: for the trumpet shall sound, and the dead shall be raised incorruptible, and we shall be changed.*

We used this passage earlier to prove the fact of rapture and it surely speaks of a last trump. There is much debate over what the last trump is because this verse imperils all the other rapture positions. It connects a very specific event to the rapture. It is a poison pill for many that results in some rather strained explanations.

Pre-trib adherents often claim the last trump is merely the only trumpet the Church will hear on Earth. It is one of the most important reasons they claim Rev. 4:1 is the time of the rapture. To review:

*Rev 4:1 After this I looked, and, behold, a door was opened in heaven: and the first voice which I heard was as it were of a trumpet talking with me; which said, Come up hither, and I will shew thee things which must be hereafter.*

In order to make this the last trump, they connect it to the trump Israel heard at Mt. Sinai, when the Law was given (Exo. 19:16). Those, they say, are both specifically the trump of God. Thus, they explain, the last trump of the trumpet judgments is not the one referenced by the term "last trump". It does not seem too important that Rev. 4:1 gives a description of a voice that sounds like a trumpet. It is not a trumpet. Oh, well. Post-trib adherents at least have a real trumpet found in Matt. 24:31. Since the post-trib rapture occurs immediately before the second coming of Christ, any trumpet that sounds would, of necessity, be the last trump.

The major errors of the mid-trib position closely mirror those of the pre-trib adherents. That should not be surprising since they sometimes see themselves as pre-trib. There is no need to further expound on what we have already covered. They still misinterpret Daniel 9:24-27. Thus, they still have the prince as Antichrist. They still argue that Christians cannot face the wrath of God per 1 Thes. 5:9. Mid-trib adherents often argue for relative tranquility for Israel under the reign of Antichrist for the first 3.5 years. This, even though the 7 seals (according to some) and the first six trumpet judgments are occurring. This makes their position appear to be utter nonsense and belittles the mighty judgments that are falling on all the Earth. There has been an attempt to spiritualize the judgments up to the 7th trump and then take the following vial judgments as literal. Thus, some adherents, at one time, argued that some of the seal judgments had already occurred in World Wars I and II.

As is readily apparent to those who are not mid-trib, the argument fails the test of consistency. Mid-trib adherents fail to apply 2 Peter 1:20 to their exegetics.

*2Pe 1:20 Knowing this first, that no prophecy of the scripture is of any private interpretation.*

Mid-trib adherents sometimes tend to make themselves the arbiter of which scriptures to spiritualize and which to take literally. This puts them in a state as serious to God as the men who alter the scriptures to their own hurt in the modern translations. (See Rev. 22:18-19).

There is not a large volume of work done on this rapture because it is only accepted by about 4% of protestant pastors according to our study mentioned in chapter 1. Additionally, some of those who do write about the mid-trib rapture use modern versions of the bible for their exegesis. Their proof verses have the wrong words and they sometimes come up with wrong and weak conclusions because, ummm, different words have different meanings! Some will go back to their Greek and Hebrew language versions as if that gives them an advantage. That allows them to vary even farther from the correct English text and win an argument on some imagined linguistic technicality. Usually, nobody else will accept such an effort.

Another problem mid-trib adherents tend to have is the opposite of one of the pre-trib adherents' problems. They gamely but ineffectively try to deal with passages that seem to weaken their position, so they fail to offer a coherent doctrine that is homogeneous with the whole counsel of God. This leaves them open to attack by the much more popular and plentiful pre- and post-trib adherents. It is no wonder that the position can't gain any traction against those opposing positions.

Finally, there are proponents of the mid-trib rapture from many theologically variant sectors of the Church. Arminian believers will try to protect their doctrinal preferences as will Baptists and Charismatics, etc. With so few adherents and with so many different doctrinal starting points, there is no clear voice for mid-tribulationism.

**Mid-trib Summary**

As you might suspect, it is very hard to refute a doctrine that is very loosely defined. It has myriad minor problems as well as the major problems that we have already dealt with. Those being the misinterpretation of Daniel 9:24-27 regarding the Antichrist and misinterpretation of 1 Thes. 5:9 regarding not being appointed to wrath. Nevertheless, it has one major tenet that must be refuted by competing positions. That is, the rapture at the seventh and last trumpet of a series of trumpet judgments. And this some have vigorously attempted. Pre-tribulationist John F. Walvoord, one-time president of Dallas Theological Seminary argued that the seventh trump is sounded well past the middle of the tribulation, and therefore is within the great tribulation of Matt. 24:21. This seems to be a common argument so let's deal with it.

In Rev. chapter 11, we find the death of the two witnesses after ministering for 1260 days within the tribulation (11:3) and the seventh trump sounding (11:15). Then in

Rev. 13:5 the beast, who ascended from the bottomless pit to murder the witnesses is said to continue for 42 months. We know from many passages that the beast continues until Armageddon at the end of the tribulation when he is thrown into the Lake of Fire (Rev. 19:20). So, the beast reigns for the last 3.5 years of the tribulation. One of the most prominently mentioned powers of the beast Is his special power over the saints of God.

*Rev 13:7 And it was given unto him to make war with the saints, and to overcome them: and power was given him over all kindreds, and tongues, and nations.*

This power is verified in Dan 12:7 where we find the phrase "time, times, and the dividing of time" denoting 3.5 years of power over the holy people. It is important to recognize this special power in order to place the entire 3.5 years of the two witness's ministry before the time of the beast. Had there been an overlap of their time periods, the beast would have killed them earlier.

The two witnesses continue for 3.5 years until the beast kills them. So, we have 3.5 years for the two witnesses and 3.5 years from their death for the beast, for a total of seven years – the length of the entire tribulation. And right in the middle of those two time periods the seventh trumpet sounds according to Rev. 11:3-15. It is very difficult to place the seventh trumpet anywhere but the middle of the tribulation. So, let's give the mid-trib adherents a win on this point if nothing else.

**The pre-wrath rapture position**

The pre-wrath rapture theory exploded into the rapture discussion when author and founder of Zion's Hope ministry, Marv Rosenthal switched from the pre-trib to the pre-wrath position. Rosenthal used his Jewish heritage to advantage as he was able to shed additional light on many scriptures (or so some thought). This came at a time when Messianic Jews and the organization, Jews for Jesus, moved into the spotlight. His 1990 book *"The Pre-wrath Rapture of the Church"* was widely read and put the theory on the religious map. Four percent of the protestant pastors surveyed support the pre-wrath position.

The pre-wrath position proposed to take what was 'provably' true from each of the other three positions and combine them into one harmonious theory of the rapture. The result was the pre-wrath rapture. This rapture is said to occur before the wrath of God would fall on the world during the tribulation, but after the wrath of Antichrist/Satan and/or man had fallen in the first half of the tribulation.

Similar to mid-tribulationism, the entire theory is built around a single phrase of scripture, "the wrath of God", as in this verse:

*Rev 16:1 And I heard a great voice out of the temple saying to the seven angels, Go your ways, and pour out the vials of the wrath of God upon the earth.*

The argument is that the seal and trumpet judgments of Rev. 6-11 are all judgments of Satan or of man, but the vial judgments are specifically called "the wrath of God". We will examine what was retained from each of the other three positions to see if there is reason for hope in this position.

From pre-tribulationism, the pre-wrath position takes the Church's exemption from the wrath of God. The argument starts with this verse:

*1Th 5:9 For God hath not appointed us to wrath, but to obtain salvation by our Lord Jesus Christ,*

We have demonstrated above why this argument is a total fail. Even if this were a valid argument, it would only serve to give a last possible moment for the rapture. It seems the pre-wrath people have made the leap to say this forces the rapture to occur immediately before the vial judgments. But it just doesn't.

From mid-tribulationism, Mr. Rosenthal took the distinction between the great tribulation and the entire 70th week of Daniel 9. The wrath of God, they say, occurs in the great tribulation within the second half of the week of years. Thus, pre-wrath is closer to mid-trib than it is to the other two.

From post-tribulationism the distinction is made between the "great tribulation" and the "day of the Lord". Post-trib adherents tend to place the day of the Lord starting with the millennium. Post-trib adherents believe Christ will rapture His Church just before the battle of Armageddon and then bring them back with Him to begin His millennial kingdom. It is hard to see how pre-wrath offers any consolation to post-trib adherents but maybe the pre-wrath people just think they are ungrateful.

There seems to be a split where some pre-wrath people believe only the vial judgments of Rev. 16 occur after the rapture while others believe that all the trumpet and vial judgments occur after the rapture. This is because the sixth seal judgment ends with this statement:

*Rev 6:16 And said to the mountains and rocks, Fall on us, and hide us from the face of him that sitteth on the throne, and from the wrath of the Lamb:*
*Rev 6:17 For the great day of his wrath is come; and who shall be able to stand?*

Following this statement, the trumpet judgments are found in Rev. 8-11 and the vials in Rev.16.

So, in another concession to post-trib, some pre-wrath people believe that the persecution by Antichrist will be cut short just before the end of the 70th week, providing an interval between the rapture and Christ's descent for the battle of Armageddon, during which time all the trumpet and vial judgments will occur.

**Pre-wrath Summary**

Wow! Who knew doctrine by compromise could be this difficult? So, what have we got here? We've got three groups who feel cheated out of some of their pet doctrines such as imminence, the last trump, and a single coming of Christ, rather than two. We've still got Antichrist in Daniel 9. We're still misreading and abusing scriptures that say we are not appointed to wrath. And, for some, we've got

14 judgments with one as long as 5 months squeezed into days or weeks (see Rev. 9:5).  Finally, we have no compelling scriptural reason, beyond a single phrase, to accept this doctrine.  And that phrase of scripture only matters if "we are not appointed unto wrath" means we will not experience the wrath of God *in the tribulation*!  Pre-wrath is a great big fail on that point alone.

**Post-tribulationism**

*Mat 24:13 But he that shall endure unto the end, the same shall be saved.*

Post-tribulationism has one overriding tenet that all in this camp insist on.  There is only one return of Christ!  Post-trib adherents insist that no scripture allows for more than a one-event second coming.  Therefore, all Church Age Christians alive at the start of the tribulation must survive (!!!) the entire 7-year tribulation to be raptured.  They claim that all saints will rise to meet the Lord in the air and then turn around and descend with Him for the battle of Armageddon.  From that point, Christ will remain on Earth with them and establish His 1000-year kingdom.  Proof verses:

*Act 1:11 Which also said, Ye men of Galilee, why stand ye gazing up into heaven? this same Jesus, which is taken up from you into heaven, shall so come in like manner as ye have seen him go into heaven.*

And:

*Mat 24:29 Immediately after the tribulation of those days shall the sun be darkened, and the moon shall not give her light, and the stars shall fall from heaven, and the powers of the heavens shall be shaken:*

*30 And then shall appear the sign of the Son of man in heaven: and then shall all the tribes of the earth mourn, and they shall see the Son of man coming in the clouds of heaven with power and great glory.*

*31 And he shall send his angels with a great sound of a trumpet, and they shall gather together his elect from the four winds, from one end of heaven to the other.*

This is a very powerful statement of the return of Christ. It matches well to Rev. 19:11-21 at the battle of Armageddon. When tied to the next passage, you can see the power of the post-trib argument.

*1Th 4:16 For the Lord himself shall descend from heaven with a shout, with the voice of the archangel, and with the trump of God: and the dead in Christ shall rise first:*

*17 Then we which are alive and remain shall be caught up together with them in the clouds, to meet the Lord in the air: and so shall we ever be with the Lord.*

Chronologically, the trumpet of Matt. 24:31 is the last trumpet to occur in the scriptures so the post-trib adherents have a strong argument for the last trump. Certainly, more than the lame last trump of the pre-trib adherents.

We will see later that the 1 Thessalonians passage works best, and really only, for the mid-trib position although all four positions try to claim it. If all the events in the passage hadn't already occurred all together, and if it did not have the phrase "and remain" in the passage, then the position would seem almost unassailable **to this point** in the argument.

There are more problems for the two-event return of Christ proponents.  Rev. chapter 19 lays out a powerful argument for one return of Christ.  When the chapter starts, Babylon has been judged and destroyed.  Virtually all the events of the tribulation, including the 7 seal, trumpet, and vial judgments have been completed.  The wicked of the world have all been gathered together for the final battle.  In fact, all that remains is the actual battle of Armageddon culminating in victory for our Lord before the start of the millennial kingdom.  We will look at that chapter next.

*Rev 19:1 And after these things I heard a great voice of much people in heaven, saying, Alleluia; Salvation, and glory, and honour, and power, unto the Lord our God:*

Clearly, our post-trib friends will say, the "much people" shouting and glorifying God are those just raptured from the Earth.

*2 For true and righteous are his judgments: for he hath judged the great whore, which did corrupt the earth with her fornication, and hath avenged the blood of his servants at her hand.*

*3 And again they said, Alleluia. And her smoke rose up for ever and ever.*

*4 And the four and twenty elders and the four beasts fell down and worshipped God that sat on the throne, saying, Amen; Alleluia.*

*5 And a voice came out of the throne, saying, Praise our God, all ye his servants, and ye that fear him, both small and great.*

Verses three to five are very reminiscent of Rev. 7:9-17, which two of the other rapture positions often lay claim to as raptured saints. Then:

### The Marriage Supper of the Lamb

*6 And I heard as it were the voice of a great multitude, and as the voice of many waters, and as the voice of mighty thunderings, saying, Alleluia: for the Lord God omnipotent reigneth.*

*7 Let us be glad and rejoice, and give honour to him: for the marriage of the Lamb is come, and his wife hath made herself ready.*

*8 And to her was granted that she should be arrayed in fine linen, clean and white: for the fine linen is the righteousness of saints.*

*9 And he saith unto me, Write, Blessed are they which are called unto the marriage supper of the Lamb. And he saith unto me, These are the true sayings of God.*

*10 And I fell at his feet to worship him. And he said unto me, See thou do it not: I am thy fellowservant, and of thy brethren that have the testimony of Jesus: worship God: for the testimony of Jesus is the spirit of prophecy.*

Obviously, the saints are now in heaven. In verse 7 the Church is finally called the "wife" of Christ rather than the bride of Christ. They are given white robes and called to the marriage supper.

Continuing:

### The Rider on a White Horse

*11 And I saw heaven opened, and behold a white horse; and he that sat upon him was called Faithful and True, and in righteousness he doth judge and make war.*

*12 His eyes were as a flame of fire, and on his head were many crowns; and he had a name written, that no man knew, but he himself.*

*13 And he was clothed with a vesture dipped in blood: and his name is called The Word of God.*

*14 And the armies which were in heaven followed him upon white horses, clothed in fine linen, white and clean.*

*15 And out of his mouth goeth a sharp sword, that with it he should smite the nations: and he shall rule them with a rod of iron: and he treadeth the winepress of the fierceness and wrath of Almighty God.*

*16 And he hath on his vesture and on his thigh a name written, KING OF KINGS, AND LORD OF LORDS.*

*17 And I saw an angel standing in the sun; and he cried with a loud voice, saying to all the fowls that fly in the midst of heaven, Come and gather yourselves together unto the supper of the great God;*

*18 That ye may eat the flesh of kings, and the flesh of captains, and the flesh of mighty men, and the flesh of horses, and of them that sit on them, and the flesh of all men, both free and bond, both small and great.*

*19 And I saw the beast, and the kings of the earth, and their armies, gathered together to make war against him that sat on the horse, and against his army.*

*20 And the beast was taken, and with him the false prophet that wrought miracles before him, with which he deceived them that had received the mark of the beast, and them that worshipped his image. These both were cast alive into a lake of fire burning with brimstone.*

*21 And the remnant were slain with the sword of him that sat upon the horse, which sword proceeded out of his mouth: and all the fowls were filled with their flesh.*

This matches well with Matt. 24:29-31. Verses 11-21 here describe the battle of Armageddon and the judgment of the beast and the false prophet. The next chapter goes right to the millennial reign of Christ. Now we can find in Rev. 16:14-16, the wicked separated from the righteous. Remember, the righteous do not participate in the battle of Armageddon. So, the wicked are separated from the righteous while both are still on earth.

*Rev 16:14 For they are the spirits of devils, working miracles, which go forth unto the kings of the earth and of the whole world, to gather them to the battle of that great day of God Almighty.*
*Rev 16:15 Behold, I come as a thief. Blessed is he that watcheth, and keepeth his garments, lest he walk naked, and they see his shame.*
*Rev 16:16 And he gathered them together into a place called in the Hebrew tongue Armageddon.*

Then, back to chapter 19, we find the rapture, the marriage, the second coming of Christ, and the end of the tribulation all in the final chapter of The Revelation before the millennium. So, the order of events post-trib adherents insist on is evident. What a neat and tidy package!

Of course, the package doesn't take into account many other passages that present some serious problems. To counter that issue, post-trib adherents present some passages they believe defeat the other positions. The idea is to be the last man standing even if they haven't dealt with their true problem passages.

I'm quite sure there are other proofs given for the timing of the post-trib rapture, most especially Matt. 24:29-31, but I am going to provide here the one that I see in scriptures that actually delivers a post-trib rapture!

## The post-trib rapture in scripture

Revelation chapter 14 also indicates a third rapture.

*Rev 14:14 And I looked, and behold a white cloud, and upon the cloud one sat like unto the Son of man, having on his head a golden crown, and in his hand a sharp sickle.*

*15 And another angel came out of the temple, crying with a loud voice to him that sat on the cloud, Thrust in thy sickle, and reap: for the time is come for thee to reap; for the harvest of the earth is ripe.*

*16 And he that sat on the cloud thrust in his sickle on the earth; and the earth was reaped.*

*17 And another angel came out of the temple which is in heaven, he also having a sharp sickle.*

*18 And another angel came out from the altar, which had power over fire; and cried with a loud cry to him that had the sharp sickle, saying, Thrust in thy sharp sickle, and gather the clusters of the vine of the earth; for her grapes are fully ripe.*

*19 And the angel thrust in his sickle into the earth, and gathered the vine of the earth, and cast it into the great winepress of the wrath of God.*

*20 And the winepress was trodden without the city, and blood came out of the winepress, even unto the horse bridles, by the space of a thousand and six hundred furlongs.*

This passage describes the battle of Armageddon from a different perspective and with additional information beyond what we find in chapter 19. But look at the elements of the passage. The Son of man reaps the harvest because it is finally fully ripe. He is wearing a golden crown at this point, having taken his kingdom back in Rev. 11:17. So, this is the explanation for the appearance of raptured people in Rev. 19:1-5. It is, in fact, a third rapture. There is one more element we should see here. Notice that the four and twenty elders and the four beasts are present at each rapture, Rev.7:11, 11:16, and 19:4. Interestingly, these raptured folks arrive in time for the marriage supper of the Lamb in the next several verses. It is not readily apparent to me whether these people are part of the bride, or guests at the wedding, although I lean toward the latter status. We will not dwell on this rapture because those being raptured are not part of the Church Age. But the passage does tell us that men will turn to JEHOVAH even in the Great Tribulation when the penalty, if caught, is certain and swift death.

## A supposed problem passage for those who argue for a two-part second coming of Christ

Post-trib adherents have brought forth several passages that they believe make the pre-trib position unscriptural and logically untenable. The first of these we will discuss is Jesus' parable of the tares among the wheat here presented:

*Mat 13:24 Another parable put he forth unto them, saying, The kingdom of heaven is likened unto a man which sowed good seed in his field:*

*25 But while men slept, his enemy came and sowed tares among the wheat, and went his way.*

*26 But when the blade was sprung up, and brought forth fruit, then appeared the tares also.*

*27 So the servants of the householder came and said unto him, Sir, didst not thou sow good seed in thy field? from whence then hath it tares?*

*28 He said unto them, An enemy hath done this. The servants said unto him, Wilt thou then that we go and gather them up?*

*29 But he said, Nay; lest while ye gather up the tares, ye root up also the wheat with them.*

*30 Let both grow together until the harvest: and in the time of harvest I will say to the reapers, Gather ye together first the tares, and bind them in bundles to burn them: but gather the wheat into my barn.*

This must be compared to its explanation given by our Lord Himself:

*Mat 13:36 Then Jesus sent the multitude away, and went into the house: and his disciples came unto him, saying, Declare unto us the parable of the tares of the field.*

*37 He answered and said unto them, He that soweth the good seed is the Son of man;*

*38 The field is the world; the good seed are the children of the kingdom; but the tares are the children of the wicked one;*

*39 The enemy that sowed them is the devil; the harvest is the end of the world; and the reapers are the angels.*

*40 As therefore the tares are gathered and burned in the fire; so shall it be in the end of this world.*

*41 The Son of man shall send forth his angels, and they shall gather out of his kingdom all things that offend, and them which do iniquity;*

*42 And shall cast them into a furnace of fire: there shall be wailing and gnashing of teeth.*

*43 Then shall the righteous shine forth as the sun in the kingdom of their Father. Who hath ears to hear, let him hear.*

The point of contention is that this passage clearly states that the tares, or wicked ones are gathered before the wheat, or righteous sons of God, whereas pre-trib theology requires the righteous are resurrected and raptured out of the world much earlier. At first glance, based on Rev. 16:14-16, this may seem to be a valid argument for the post-trib crowd. However, let's take a closer look.

This gathering is at the end of this world (v. 40). Post-trib adherents contend that it is in conjunction with the rapture, just prior to the millennial reign of Christ. I find no evidence of a rapture event at all in these passages, but I do clearly see they occur at the end of this world. As it happens, we can find an event that duplicates the situation described here at the end of the millennial reign of Christ:

*Rev 20:7 And when the thousand years are expired, Satan shall be loosed out of his prison,*

*8 And shall go out to deceive the nations which are in the four quarters of the earth, Gog and Magog, to gather them together to battle: the number of whom is as the sand of the sea.*

*9 And they went up on the breadth of the earth, and compassed the camp of the saints about, and the beloved city: and fire came down from God out of heaven, and devoured them.*

*10 And the devil that deceived them was cast into the lake of fire and brimstone, where the beast and the false prophet are, and shall be tormented day and night for ever and ever.*

*11 And I saw a great white throne, and him that sat on it, from whose face* **the earth and the heaven fled**

*away; and there was found no place for them.*
(bolding added)

As we see here, there are still wicked people and righteous people on the Earth at the end of Christ's thousand-year reign. At this final defeat of Satan, the wicked tares are gathered together and disposed of while the righteous wheat remains. Verse 11 then clearly indicates the end of this world just as the parable claims. This gathering occurs 1000 years after the post-trib adherents rapture and thus the passage does not defeat pre-tribulationism.

One final, important point must be made. In the parable we find God's angels gathering them which do iniquity whereas in the Revelation account we find Satan inciting wicked people to gather together. However, Satan is not omnipresent and therefore cannot do such a great job alone. We are told that Satan deceives the nations in order to gather them. It does not say that he gathers them personally. There is much room here to presume the holy angels may have part in bringing the wicked to the place of judgment, thus fulfilling the parable more fully. It seems likely that, no matter how hopeful for the post-trib adherents' case, all camps have placed this parable in the wrong timeframe.

**Post-trib rapture conflicts**

Of course, the greatest conflict that post-trib adherents face is the fact that two prior raptures can be demonstrated in the scriptures. Their best defense is to say: "I don't accept your proofs based on Matt. 24:29-31 and 1 Thes. 4:16-17." That is just not a strong argument.

Another passage that only **seems** to help the post-trib adherents is this:

*Rev 16:15 Behold, I come as a thief. Blessed is he that watcheth, and keepeth his garments, lest he walk naked, and they see his shame.*

This verse is presented just as the followers of the Beast are being gathered for the battle of Armageddon. Since the speaker is Jesus, the Thief rapture is in view here.

The major problem is that a coming as a Thief simply doesn't fit the context at this point in time. There is no possibility of a surprise here because prophecy is quite clear as to when this will happen. The great darkness of the fifth vial and the drying up of the Euphrates which had just occurred, plus the gathering of the unrighteous for Armageddon would be obvious signs of the times.

If the rapture happened at this point, then the righteous would be gathered out well before the wicked. That is a no-no for most post-trib adherents. Although we find a rapture here, it just is not as a Thief. This verse is here to warn us that the Thief rapture is the one we should be striving for.

**Post-tribulationism's greatest fail**

A much more powerful argument can be made against a post-tribulation rapture for the Church is based on certain events that occur during the tribulation. One is the special power given to the 666 Beast who appears at mid-trib to kill the two witnesses of Rev. chapter 11. Scriptures tell us:

*Rev 11:3 And I will give power unto my two witnesses, and they shall prophesy a thousand two hundred and threescore days, clothed in sackcloth.*

*Rev 11:7 And when they shall have finished their testimony, the beast that ascendeth out of the bottomless pit shall make war against them, and shall overcome them, and kill them.*

And:

*Rev 13:4 And they worshipped the dragon which gave power unto the beast: and they worshipped the beast, saying, Who is like unto the beast? who is able to make war with him?*

*5 And there was given unto him a mouth speaking great things and blasphemies; and power was given unto him to continue forty and two months.*

*Rev 13:7 And it was given unto him to make war with the saints, and to overcome them: and power was given him over all kindreds, and tongues, and nations.*

So, the Beast has absolute power to overcome the saints, and:

*Dan 7:25 And he shall speak great words against the most High, and shall wear out the saints of the most High, and think to change times and laws: and they shall be given into his hand until a time and times and the dividing of time.*

The saints shall be **given** into his hand.

So according to these passages, Jesus will leave His Church without protection for 3.5 years while the Beast is free to hunt them down and kill them. This is the same Church that He has loved and protected for over two thousand years and declared to her:

*Heb 13:5 ... for he hath said, I will never leave thee, nor forsake thee.*

There are other passages that promise good and protection to the Church corporately. Consider this passage:

*Mat 16:18 And I say also unto thee, That thou art Peter, and upon this rock I will build my church; and the gates of hell shall not prevail against it.*

Surely the Beast qualifies here as the gates of hell prevailing since he came out of the bottomless pit. From the midpoint of the tribulation, he has had power to prevail over the saints for 42 months. If the Church is still on Earth at that time, God has reneged on this promise.

In spite of this, there have always been individuals who were asked to give up their lives for the cause of Christ. Martyrdom has existed throughout the Church Age. However, post-tribulational doctrine implies that Christ has gone back on His promises to the entire Church. This goes beyond martyrdom to a complete abandonment of the promises Christ made to the Church, and this in her most desperate hour. On this point alone, the post-trib theory utterly falls apart. Although there will be "elect" saints saved in the Great Tribulation, they do not have the promises and protections afforded to the Church.

Another issue post-tribulationism creates is the need to store up wealth and property for the tribulation. Since no man can buy or sell anything during the last 3.5 years without the mark of the Beast (Rev. 13:17), and further, since taking the mark immediately damns one's soul to hell (Rev. 14:8-11), the Church must survive on savings for barter, stored goods, and old-fashioned foraging and gardening.

The cynic in me makes me notice an issue here. It seems to me that more than one former preacher of pre-tribulationism has changed to post-tribulationism after making a lot of money from speaking gigs and book sales. After all, preaching the soon return of Christ makes accumulation of great wealth a shameful thing for those 'in the know' considering the needs of the Church, the number of lost people remaining, and the lateness of the hour, and the uselessness of money in the kingdom of God. The book of James has some choice words for people like this:

*Jas 5:1 Go to now, ye rich men, weep and howl for your miseries that shall come upon you.*
*2 Your riches are corrupted, and your garments are motheaten.*
*3 Your gold and silver is cankered; and the rust of them shall be a witness against you, and shall eat your flesh as it were fire. Ye have heaped treasure together for the last days.*

## Conclusions regarding the four positions on the rapture

Based on the information we have discussed so far; all these positions have some truth but none of these positions has any advantage over the other three. However, the problem is found in that statement. The information all these positions put forth is incomplete. None of them seems to have considered all the available scriptures. And in some cases, they have not fully accepted what the scriptures plainly and freely give us.

*1Co 2:12 Now we have received, not the spirit of the world, but the spirit which is of God; that we might know the things that are freely given to us of God.*

We have demonstrated some of the serious conflicts with the scriptures that remain unresolved for each theory. In fact, we have shown outright contradictions and even a degree of heresy in standing by provably false doctrine.

Those that hold to the pre-, mid-, and post-tribulation rapture positions we have studied all have a couple things in common. First, there is definitely a rapture associated with each position, so they are partly right. But second, they are like the blind men describing the elephant. They never consider that there might be more than one rapture, and this requires assigning the appropriate scriptures to each position. They stubbornly cling to their preconceived notions about what the elephant must look like and go to great lengths to prove they are right. Finally, all of them claim that 1 Cor.15:51-52 and 1 Thes. 4:14-17 apply to the rapture they champion.

So how can this problem be resolved? The rest of this work will be dedicated to finding a solution that harmonizes all pertinent scriptures and ultimately arrives at inescapable conclusions.

## Chapter 3.  The Man Who Knew Too Much, or… (What We Can Learn from the Prophet Daniel)

The prophet Daniel is one of the most amazing characters in the Old Testament.  His prophecies are so detailed and the fulfillments so precise that even some churchmen cannot accept his story.  They insist that he never existed, or he must have lived many years after the Babylonian captivity of Judah.  These men believe the prophecy had to have been written after the procession of empires he described had occurred.  However, Jesus gave testimony to his existence and one of his contemporaries, the prophet Ezekiel, called him out by name in his prophetic book written during the Babylonian captivity.

The title of this chapter is a little facetious because it implies that Daniel will get himself in trouble for being such a great prophet.  Daniel is a man of impeccable character and when he is called to serve again (in the next few years), he will do it without hesitation.  You may be wondering what I am babbling about now, but I am going to throw in a little freebie here.  A freebie in the sense that it is not necessary information for this study.  In Daniel chapter 12 we read:

*Dan 12:8  And I heard, but I understood not: then said I, O my Lord, what shall be the end of these things?*
*9  And he said, Go thy way, Daniel: for the words are closed up and sealed till the time of the end.*
*Dan 12:13  But go thou thy way till the end be: for thou*

*shalt rest, and stand in thy lot at the end of the days.*

Daniel will stand in his lot at the end of days. His lot is to be a prophet of God, so he is going to stand and prophesy at the end of days.

Now, let's look at another man. The Apostle John wrote the book of the Revelation and in that book, he was told:

*Rev 10:8 And the voice which I heard from heaven spake unto me again, and said, Go and take the little book which is open in the hand of the angel which standeth upon the sea and upon the earth.*
*9 And I went unto the angel, and said unto him, Give me the little book. And he said unto me, Take it, and eat it up; and it shall make thy belly bitter, but it shall be in thy mouth sweet as honey.*
*10 And I took the little book out of the angel's hand, and ate it up; and it was in my mouth sweet as honey: and as soon as I had eaten it, my belly was bitter.*
*11 And he said unto me, Thou must prophesy again before many peoples, and nations, and tongues, and kings.*

Here we see that John will also prophesy again. So, what we have here is the two greatest experts in the scriptures on future prophecy scheduled to come back and prophesy again. Folks, these are the two witnesses of Revelation chapter 11. When I wrote that Daniel knew too much, I was referring to the death that awaits the two witnesses. They must prophesy exactly 1260 days and then be murdered by the Beast of Rev. 13.

Many people want to make Elijah out to be one of these witnesses, but Elijah is specifically prophesied to come before the day of the LORD starts. Beyond this, we will see in a later chapter that Elijah does not have a partner. We will also see that it is reasonable to believe all three of these men are alive and walking among us today. Each will be revealed when the time is right.

Some of this is a bit premature for some readers because so much scripture remains to be studied. But those who already know some bible prophecy will understand and for the rest, just keep this in mind. You will understand it all by and by.

As a book of prophecy, Daniel is just as important to the Old Testament as the book of the Revelation is to the New Testament. Both contain the most definitive prophetic statements to be found in all the scriptures. Each is completely indispensable for understanding end-times prophecy and each complements the other perfectly.

The book of Daniel gives the historical procession of kings and kingdoms beginning with the Babylonian kingdom but eventually splitting into two separate lines that finally reunite in the final millennial kingdom of Christ. The book of the Revelation primarily elaborates on the very end-times of Daniel's prophecy but also presents some important history of the period from the cross of Christ to His crown. That kingdom begins as a spiritual kingdom in the hearts of His believers and ends in His triumph over the physical kingdoms of the world.

We will be looking at chapters 2, 7, 8, 11, and 12 of Daniel's incredible book where we will discover seven kingdoms and eight kings variously described as amazing beasts. By understanding who and what these beasts represent we can discover where we are on the prophetic calendar and what to expect in the immediate future. The progression of kingdoms is repeated three times from three different perspectives. From verse 4 of chapter 2 through chapter 7, Daniel writes in Aramaic, the Chaldean language. These passages chronicle the remaining history of the Gentile world up to the millennial reign of Christ from a Gentile perspective, in a Gentile language. The rest of the book of Daniel is written in Hebrew, detailing the remaining history of the world up to the end of the tribulation as it relates to the Jewish people.

Chapter 2 gives a broad overview of history from the time of Nebuchadnezzar, king of Babylon up to the eternal kingdom of our Lord. In this chapter, the king has had a dream that he cannot remember. He has required of his wise men that they reveal this dream to him or die if they fail. Daniel was one who would have died but God revealed the matter to him, and the king was pacified. This is Daniel's description of the vision and God's explanation of it.

*Dan 2:32 This image's head was of fine gold, his breast and his arms of silver, his belly and his thighs of brass,*

*33 His legs of iron, his feet part of iron and part of clay.*

*34 Thou sawest till that a stone was cut out without hands, which smote the image upon his feet that were of iron and clay, and brake them to pieces.*

*35 Then was the iron, the clay, the brass, the silver, and the gold, broken to pieces together, and became like the chaff of the summer threshingfloors; and the wind carried them away, that no place was found for them: and the stone that smote the image became a great mountain, and filled the whole earth.*

*36 This is the dream; and we will tell the interpretation thereof before the king.*

*37 Thou, O king, art a king of kings: for the God of heaven hath given thee a kingdom, power, and strength, and glory.*

*38 And wheresoever the children of men dwell, the beasts of the field and the fowls of the heaven hath he given into thine hand, and hath made thee ruler over them all. Thou art this head of gold.*

*39 And after thee shall arise another kingdom inferior to thee, and another third kingdom of brass, which shall bear rule over all the earth.*

*40 And the fourth kingdom shall be strong as iron: forasmuch as iron breaketh in pieces and subdueth all things: and as iron that breaketh all these, shall it break in pieces and bruise.*

*41 And whereas thou sawest the feet and toes, part of potters' clay, and part of iron, the kingdom shall be divided; but there shall be in it of the strength of the iron, forasmuch as thou sawest the iron mixed with miry clay.*

*42 And as the toes of the feet were part of iron, and part of clay, so the kingdom shall be partly strong, and partly broken.*

*43 And whereas thou sawest iron mixed with miry clay, they shall mingle themselves with the seed of men: but they shall not cleave one to another, even as iron is not mixed with clay.*

*44 And in the days of these kings shall the God of heaven set up a kingdom, which shall never be destroyed: and the kingdom shall not be left to other people, but it shall break in pieces and consume all these kingdoms, and it shall stand for ever.*

*45 Forasmuch as thou sawest that the stone was cut out of the mountain without hands, and that it brake in pieces the iron, the brass, the clay, the silver, and the gold; the great God hath made known to the king what shall come to pass hereafter: and the dream is certain, and the interpretation thereof sure.*

We can conclude from later chapters as well as secular history what these kingdoms were. Nebuchadnezzar, we are told, was the head of gold and the kingdom of the head was Babylonia. The kingdom represented by the breast and arms was Medo-Persia. The brass kingdom of the belly and thighs was Grecia. Finally, the fourth kingdom, the iron kingdom will be a divided kingdom. From secular history, we know that Rome succeeded Greece and further that Rome was eventually divided into the Eastern and Western Roman Empires. This is usually given as the explanation for this fourth kingdom, but it is not without problems. Both the Eastern and Western empires eventually fell apart and lost their relevance. However, Daniel's narrative does not allow for this. Therefore, either this prophecy is incorrect, or our common interpretation is incorrect. I favor the latter explanation.

Before launching into this explanation, I need to caution any Roman Catholics who may be reading this. This is by no means meant to denigrate any individual Catholic or their personal relationship with God. There are many

Catholics who don't go along with everything their church has done or is doing in the world. Many have little or no idea of the true history of their Church. But the simple facts are that, after having endured horrific persecution from the state of Rome, the Church happily embraced the state when the Emperor Constantine converted and made Christianity the state religion in the 4th century AD. There was a complete capitulation to the state at that time and the upshot of it was this. The Churches in the empire deposed Jesus Christ as their head and replaced Him with the Roman Empire and eventually a Pope wielding all the power of the state. Using this clever device, Satan was able to produce a church where strict adherence to her doctrines actually prevents eternal salvation. Back to our narrative.

Although the secular Roman Empire has passed from the scene, it left in its wake a religious kingdom that has held sway over its subjects with more power than the secular kingdom ever possessed. As the Roman Emperors began to lose their grip, the Popes of the Roman Catholic Church began to replace them. This vicious and apostate church set up its headquarters in Rome and became fiercer and crueler than the empire had ever dreamed of being. She set up Inquisitions which she used to murder her enemies and steal their fortunes. She ruthlessly rooted out all the true Christians she could find, calling them heretics and slaughtering entire towns and villages. To understand the horrors of the trail of blood left by this church, you need to research the history of the Anabaptists and the Albigenses, and the Waldenses, and the Huguenots, and many other groups of Christians. Also read *'Foxe's Book of Martyrs'*.

She pursued and slaughtered the Jewish people, calling them Christ-killers. The holocaust of World War 2 was mild by comparison. She fits the fierceness required of this fourth kingdom, as more fully described in chapter 7, far better than secular Rome did. In addition, she continues to exert great influence over a large part of the world population to this day. The Roman Catholic Church, as a continuation of the secular kingdom, fits perfectly the description of one leg of this fourth kingdom.

What then of the other leg? Chapters 8 through 11 of Daniel revert to the Hebrew language and a history more pertinent to the Jews. Those chapters speak of oppression by the Greeks from the time of Alexander the Great until deep into the Roman Empire era. By the time the iron foot of Rome descended upon the neck of the Jewish people, they had been heavily influenced or Hellenized by Greek culture. This caused a great division among the people between those who chose loyalty to their God and His laws and the more secular Hellenists. Although they became subjects of Rome, their culture was not forced to change. Thus, it was the Grecian cultural influence that was always the real danger to the Jewish people. This continued right up until the time that Rome broke up the Jewish nation and scattered them in the final Diaspora.

Chapter 11 describes this other leg of the fourth kingdom. The Grecian empire reached its zenith during the reign of Alexander the Great. Upon his death, the kingdom was divided between four of his generals. These four kingdoms were eventually consolidated into just two kingdoms. They were the kingdoms of the Seleucids and the Ptolemys. They are generically described in this chapter as the king of the north (Seleucids) and the king of the south (Ptolemys). The king of the north eventually ruled most of the original kingdom of Alexander while the king of the south ruled over Egypt and North Africa. It will become apparent that the line of this king of the north is the other leg of the vision of chapter 2

Greece and Rome coexisted for many hundreds of years although the power of the former was generally in decline and the power of the latter generally was rising. During this entire period, the Seleucids and the Ptolemy's battled for control of the original kingdom of Grecia. Israel found herself geographically right in the middle of this conflict. She was claimed by both sides and forced into tribute and service. In battle after battle the armies passed through Israel, raping and pillaging and destroying the land and the people. Many of the Jews became loyal to the Grecians and adopted their culture in order to curry favor and survive. Thus, while the rest of the world was being crushed by Rome, Israel was being crushed by the Greeks. Both kingdoms were legs of iron, but one was so to the Gentile world while the other was so to the Jews.

Although these two empires battled each other for supremacy in the political realm, the Greek, or Hellenist, culture continued to grow and heavily influenced Roman culture as well as that of the rest of the world. Rome finally won the supremacy from a military standpoint but culturally the Greeks were the clear victors. In fact, the majority of the New Testament was written in the Greek language. This book had more influence on Roman history and, in fact, world history than any other factor from that era.

During the time when the Seleucids and the Ptolemys were mightily oppressing Israel, a particularly evil Seleucid king rose to prominence. We will deal more fully this king, Antiochus IV Epiphanes, in the discussion of chapter 11. He outlawed Jewish religious rites, committed an 'abomination of desolation' in the temple and slaughtered or sold into slavery a large portion of the population of Jerusalem between 175 and 164 years before Christ. Interestingly, the text of our current King James Bible can be traced back to Antioch, the capital city of Antiochus IV Epiphanes. It was there that the followers of Christ were first called Christians over 200 years later. The text was faithfully copied and divinely protected for accuracy through succeeding generations. It was translated into successive languages as it made its way through Europe and into England where it finally culminated in the divinely preserved King James text.

At the same time, the text also moved south into Egypt where the scholars of the day sifted through it, took it apart, and reconstituted it into something they felt a higher intellect could be comfortable with. The abomination they created influenced the texts that the Roman Catholic Church used and produced many corrupt manuscripts that survive to the present day. All English texts, other than the KJV, have these variant and corrupted textual readings found frequently in their translations. God promised to preserve His Words perfectly in a number of places throughout the scriptures.

However, Satan has understood the importance of preserving the Words of God and produced his own versions in an attempt to drown out the true Words of God.

Just as the secular Roman kingdom was eventually replaced by a false religious kingdom, the Hellenic Seleucid kingdom was also eventually replaced by a false religious kingdom. The Muslim religion has grown as large and as influential as the Roman Catholic religion. This religion reigns supreme in much of the territories ruled by the Seleucids and the Ptolemys. It is also divided along the lines of the kingdoms of the king of the north and the king of the south. Many of the Arabic and southern Muslims, especially the Egyptians, are Sunnis or Sunni type sects whereas the Muslims of the north, especially the Persians, are largely Shiites. Both sects have as an ultimate goal, the establishment of a worldwide caliphate under Sharia law. That is, a kingdom where the Koran and the religious leadership are the final authority over secular as well as religious practices. The king of the north and the king of the south are still at war in this regard as both intend to have their version of Islam rule the world. Both Islam and Roman Catholicism are iron kingdoms with long records of mercilessly crushing their enemies. Both kingdoms will produce a fierce last-days king about whom the scriptures have much to say. Finally, both kingdoms are spiritual kingdoms ruled by the same spiritual ruler, Satan. It is in this sense that the two legs are treated as a single, fourth kingdom in chapter 2.

The ten toes in this chapter show up just before the final kingdom of Christ (the stone cut out of the mountain without hands) appears on the scene. They are further described in Revelation 17:12-14 and in Daniel chapter 7 as ten horns. These are ten leaders of Catholic-leaning nations that will form a confederation to destroy Rome and transfer the papal authority and power to the final Beast. They will then seek to defeat the Lamb of God in the final battle. The chapter ends with the assurance that the God of heaven will set up a final kingdom that will never be destroyed.

Chapter 2 gives us a complete historical picture which is broken down and further developed in chapters 7 through 12. In summary, the head represents king Nebuchadnezzar and his kingdom of Babylon. The breast and two arms of silver represent Darius and Cyrus, both of whom are mentioned by name in the book of Daniel, as well as their kingdoms of Media and Persia which were brought together under Cyrus. The belly and thighs of brass represent Alexander the Great and his kingdom of Grecia.

The two legs of iron are special cases. They started out as the kingdoms of Rome and Seleucia. However, they crossed over into the time when God has changed His method of dealing with man. After the crucifixion of Christ, God ceased from dealing with man in the physical realm. The kingdom of God became the kingdom of the heart, a spiritual kingdom. The promises to Israel were all based in the physical realm. They were promised things such as wealth, good health, long life, victory in battle, fertility of man and beast and so on. Deuteronomy 28 details these promises quite explicitly. The promises after the cross were victory over sin, joy, peace with God and all good things for the heart and soul. The book of Galatians was written to specifically address this difference. Seeking the promises to Israel has created major problems for the church. The song that claims 'every promise in the book is mine' is simply not scriptural and should be abandoned despite its catchy tune.

Thus, the two legs of iron which started as physical kingdoms have now moved into the spiritual realm. They now continue as the two great false religions of Roman Catholicism and Islam. This is temporary however as they will be reinstituted in the physical realm as the kingdom of the final king of the north found in Daniel 11 and the kingdom of the Beast in Revelation 13.

**Daniel 7**

Chapter 7, as we have noted, provides a history of the world from a Gentile perspective. The beasts found in this chapter are all carnivorous and aggressive wild animals. There are four beasts which represent four kings of four of the kingdoms of chapter two. This chapter ignores one of the legs of the image of chapter 2. It is the Gentile account and deals with the empires that most affect the Gentile world.

The first beast is like a lion with eagle's wings.

*Dan 7:3 And four great beasts came up from the sea, diverse one from another.*

*4 The first was like a lion, and had eagle's wings: I beheld till the wings thereof were plucked, and it was lifted up from the earth, and made stand upon the feet as a man, and a man's heart was given to it.*

This is quite obviously a reference to Nebuchadnezzar who actually grew characteristics of an animal and lived as an animal for seven years according to chapter 4:

*Dan 4:33 The same hour was the thing fulfilled upon Nebuchadnezzar: and he was driven from men, and did eat grass as oxen, and his body was wet with the dew of heaven, till his hairs were grown like eagles' feathers, and his nails like birds' claws.*

The second beast of Daniel 7 was like a bear with three ribs in its mouth.

*Dan 7:5 And behold another beast, a second, like to a bear, and it raised up itself on one side, and it had three ribs in the mouth of it between the teeth of it: and they said thus unto it, Arise, devour much flesh.*

The kingdom of this king isn't specifically identified until chapter 8 but there is enough evidence in the text to identify him. Babylonia was conquered by Cyrus, king of Persia. Cyrus had already combined Media and Persia, probably by marrying the daughter of Darius, king of Media. When he conquered Babylonia, he was too busy waging military campaigns to rule it properly, so he made his father-in-law Darius co-regent until Darius died three years later. At that time, Cyrus became king of the three kingdoms of Babylonia, Media, and Persia which are indicated by the three ribs in the mouth of the bear.

The third beast of chapter 7 was like a leopard with four wings and four heads.

*Dan 7:6 After this I beheld, and lo another, like a leopard, which had upon the back of it four wings of a fowl; the beast had also four heads; and dominion was given to it.*

Again, the kingdom of this beast is identified in chapter 8 as Grecia but there is evidence in this text to help with identification. When Alexander the Great died, his kingdom was split up between his four generals which is depicted in the four wings and four heads. We know from history that there was a significant time gap between the kingdom of Alexander the Great and the kingdom of Rome which is the fourth kingdom described in this chapter. The time gap is dealt with very specifically in chapters 8 and 11 as a separate entity. However, in this chapter it is also properly treated as a continuation of Grecia. This era was dominated by the line of one of Alexander's four generals. We have seen that this is the Seleucid kingdom, named after the family line, that dominated the northern part of Alexander's kingdom.

The fourth beast was diverse from all the other beasts according to the text and in fact was very complex.

*Dan 7:7 After this I saw in the night visions, and behold a fourth beast, dreadful and terrible, and strong exceedingly; and it had great iron teeth: it devoured and brake in pieces, and stamped the residue with the feet of it: and it was diverse from all the beasts that were before it; and it had ten horns.*

*8 I considered the horns, and, behold, there came up among them another little horn, before whom there were three of the first horns plucked up by the roots: and, behold, in this horn were eyes like the eyes of man, and a mouth speaking great things.*

*9 I beheld till the thrones were cast down, and the Ancient of days did sit, whose garment was white as snow, and the hair of his head like the pure wool: his throne was like the fiery flame, and his wheels as burning fire.*

*10 A fiery stream issued and came forth from before him: thousand thousands ministered unto him, and ten thousand times ten thousand stood before him: the judgment was set, and the books were opened.*

*11 I beheld then because of the voice of the great words which the horn spake: I beheld even till the beast was slain, and his body destroyed, and given to the burning flame.*

Although this kingdom devoured the others and acted like a wild carnivore, it had horns like an herbivorous animal. It is this difference that makes this fourth beast diverse from the rest. The first three are strictly carnivores, but this beast is a carnivore with some attributes of an herbivore. It is important to understand that horns in scripture denote spiritual power, whether good or evil. We find that out in these scriptures:

*Hab 3:3 God came from Teman, and the Holy One from mount Paran. Selah. His glory covered the heavens, and the earth was full of his praise.*

*4 And his brightness was as the light; he had horns coming out of his hand: and there was the hiding of his power.*

*Dan 8:7 And I saw him come close unto the ram, and he was moved with choler against him, and smote the ram, and brake his two horns: and there was no power in the ram to stand before him...*

The kingdom of this beast continues from its establishment until the kingdom of our Lord is finally established. Interestingly, not much information is given about any specific king of this kingdom until its very last king. The kingdom continues over a very long period of time.

Comparing verse 11 above with Rev. 19:20 we can see that the manner of death provides strong proof that this horn is the final Beast of Rev. 13. In fact, he is called a beast rather than a horn at the end of this verse. Here the cause of his death and destruction is the burning flame. In the Revelation we see that the flame is the Lake of Fire.

*Rev 19:20 And the beast was taken, and with him the false prophet that wrought miracles before him, with which he deceived them that had received the mark of the beast, and them that worshipped his image. These both were cast alive into a lake of fire burning with brimstone.*

There is an apparent contradiction here as the one beast was cast into the Lake of Fire alive whereas the other was slain first. It is a minor point because all beings in hell are alive to the torture of the flames but spiritually dead to God. So, both are dead in one sense and alive in another at the same time. The terminology deals with different perspectives of the same outcome. The volume of the scriptures assures us they are the same person. When we look at the Lake of Fire, we will see this beast could be transported to the edge of this lake by truck in an hour or so from his location at the end of the final war in the tribulation.

All these kingdoms can be identified by historical perspective. This fourth beast kingdom continues until the kingdom of the little horn, the final Beast, which occurs just before the millennial kingdom, a fact easily discovered by reading Revelation chapters 17-20. That being the case, we realize from history that this is the last kingdom that claimed the right and the power to rule the entire world, the kingdom of Rome.

*Dan 7:19 Then I would know the truth of the fourth beast, which was diverse from all the others, exceeding dreadful, whose teeth were of iron, and his nails of brass; which devoured, brake in pieces, and stamped the residue with his feet;*

*20 And of the ten horns that were in his head, and of the other which came up, and before whom three fell; even of that horn that had eyes, and a mouth that spake very great things, whose look was more stout than his fellows.*

*21 I beheld, and the same horn made war with the saints, and prevailed against them;*

*22 Until the Ancient of days came, and judgment was given to the saints of the most High; and the time came that the saints possessed the kingdom.*

*23 Thus he said, The fourth beast shall be the fourth kingdom upon earth, which shall be diverse from all kingdoms, and shall devour the whole earth, and shall tread it down, and break it in pieces.*

*24 And the ten horns out of this kingdom are ten kings that shall arise: and another shall rise after them; and he shall be diverse from the first, and he shall subdue three kings.*

*25 And he shall speak great words against the most High, and shall wear out the saints of the most High, and think to change times and laws: and they shall be given into his hand until a time and times and the dividing of time.*

*26 But the judgment shall sit, and they shall take away his dominion, to consume and to destroy it unto the end.*

*27 And the kingdom and dominion, and the greatness of the kingdom under the whole heaven, shall be given to the people of the saints of the most High, whose kingdom is an everlasting kingdom, and all dominions shall serve and obey him.*

Verses 21-25 of chapter 7 identify this little horn precisely. This beast speaks great blasphemies against the Most High, and further, is given specific power to overcome the saints. Comparing this with Rev 13:4-7 below, we see that he is the final beast whose number is 666. It is most important to understand that this beast comes from the Roman kingdom and can thus be differentiated from the little horn of chapter 8.

*Rev 13:4 And they worshipped the dragon which gave power unto the beast: and they worshipped the beast, saying, Who is like unto the beast? who is able to make war with him?*

*5 And there was given unto him a mouth speaking great things and blasphemies; and power was given unto him to continue forty and two months.*

*6 And he opened his mouth in blasphemy against God, to blaspheme his name, and his tabernacle, and them that dwell in heaven.*

*7 And it was given unto him to make war with the saints, and to overcome them: and power was given him over all kindreds, and tongues, and nations.*

**Daniel 8**

Daniel 8 begins in the last year of Belshazzar, king of Babylon. Babylon is literally months away from being conquered by Cyrus the Great of the Medo-Persians and therefore is not mentioned here. This passage deals primarily with the second and third kingdoms of chapters 2 and 7, and then, ignoring the fourth (Roman) kingdom of chapter 7, deals primarily with the Seleucid kingdom after the death of Alexander the Great. It follows the line of the other leg of the image of chapter 2.

The beasts in this chapter are domesticated herbivores. Herbivores are not hunters and only aggressive under rare circumstances, thus we see an emphasis on their horns which is their only instrument of aggression. This is meant to indicate their true power is in the spirit world. The horns on these beasts always refer to a specific king or his spiritual representative. The beasts in this passage, excepting the little horn, are what God has described as clean animals. That means they can be eaten and used for sacrifices. This brings in a spiritual dimension to the danger they present to the people of God.

Whereas the beasts in chapter 7 present a physical danger to the entire world, these beasts represent the danger of wooing the Jews away from worship of the true God. This proved to be the case for those in captivity in Babylon. When Cyrus the Persian conquered Babylon, he encouraged the Jews to return to Jerusalem, yet the majority of the people chose to stay. It was even more evident when the descendants of the Jews that did return, turned to Hellenism in large numbers during the wars of the Ptolemys and the Seleucids. Thus, while both legs of the image of chapter 2 speak of actual worldwide physical oppression, in a stronger sense they refer to the two separate lines or legs of physical and spiritual oppression for the people of God. In order to make this plain to His people, God ordained that Daniel should write chapter 7 in a Gentile language and chapter 8 in the Hebrew language.

Chapter 8 begins with a description of the reign of two kings combined in one beast.

*Dan 8:1 In the third year of the reign of king Belshazzar a vision appeared unto me, even unto me Daniel, after that which appeared unto me at the first.*

*2 And I saw in a vision; and it came to pass, when I saw, that I was at Shushan in the palace, which is in the province of Elam; and I saw in a vision, and I was by the river of Ulai.*

*3 Then I lifted up mine eyes, and saw, and, behold, there stood before the river a ram which had two horns: and the two horns were high; but one was higher than the other, and the higher came up last.*

*4 I saw the ram pushing westward, and northward, and southward; so that no beasts might stand before him, neither was there any that could deliver out of his hand; but he did according to his will, and became great.*

Later in the chapter, the interpretation is made quite plain.

*Dan 8:19 And he said, Behold, I will make thee know what shall be in the last end of the indignation: for at the time appointed the end shall be.*

*20 The ram which thou sawest having two horns are the kings of Media and Persia.*

Here we see that the ram represents both Media and Persia and the two horns are the two kings mentioned by name in Daniel's book, Darius and Cyrus. Daniel was foreseeing the conquest of Babylonia as well as most of the rest of the known world.

*Dan 8:5 And as I was considering, behold, an he goat came from the west on the face of the whole earth, and touched not the ground: and the goat had a notable horn between his eyes.*

*6 And he came to the ram that had two horns, which I had seen standing before the river, and ran unto him in the fury of his power.*

*7 And I saw him come close unto the ram, and he was moved with choler against him, and smote the ram, and brake his two horns: and there was no power in the ram to stand before him, but he cast him down to the ground, and stamped upon him: and there was none that could deliver the ram out of his hand.*

*8 Therefore the he goat waxed very great: and when he was strong, the great horn was broken; and for it came up four notable ones toward the four winds of heaven.*

The he-goat advanced quickly and at the height of his power, he died. This so aptly describes the explosive but brief reign of Alexander the Great that it is almost universally accepted that Grecia is this he-goat and Alexander is the notable horn. The text leaves no doubt about the kingdom.

*Dan 8:21 And the rough goat is the king of Grecia: and the great horn that is between his eyes is the first king.*

The four notable horns of verse 8 above then can only be Alexander's four generals among whom his kingdom was divided. It will become obvious that the little horn is the real subject of this chapter. The rest of the chapter is primarily meant to show where the little horn came from so that he can be differentiated from the little horn of chapter 7. This king commits a 'transgression of desolation' giving both the sanctuary and the host to be trodden underfoot. He also caused the daily sacrifice to be taken away. This tells us that the daily sacrifice had been reestablished at this time and the temple worship had been reinstated. By comparing history to Daniel 11, we see that this has already occurred and been thoroughly documented in the reign of Antiochus IV Epiphanes, one in the line of Seleucid kings who ruled the northern part of Alexander's kingdom. As we shall see, this is not the only occurrence of this type of event that Daniel prophesied.

Before further discussion of this chapter, we should note that Daniel gives us important insight on some elements of the spiritual realm. We can conclude from Daniel chapter 10 that at least some events in the physical realm have a counterpart in the spiritual realm. In chapter 10 we find that Daniel mourned and fasted and prayed for three full weeks. At the end of the three weeks, an angel appeared to him. He was able to see and hear the angel but the men that were with him could not. Even so, they were filled with terror and hid themselves. Daniel was enabled to see into the soulish side of the spirit kingdom.

*Dan 10:12 Then said he unto me, Fear not, Daniel: for from the first day that thou didst set thine heart to understand, and to chasten thyself before thy God, thy words were heard, and I am come for thy words.*

*13 But the prince of the kingdom of Persia withstood me one and twenty days: but, lo, Michael, one of the chief princes, came to help me; and I remained there with the kings of Persia.*

*14 Now I am come to make thee understand what shall befall thy people in the latter days: for yet the vision is for many days.*

*Dan 10:20 Then said he, Knowest thou wherefore I come unto thee? and now will I return to fight with the prince of Persia: and when I am gone forth, lo, the prince of Grecia shall come.*

*21 But I will shew thee that which is noted in the scripture of truth: and there is none that holdeth with me in these things, but Michael your prince.*

Michael in this passage is a reference to Michael the Archangel referenced in Daniel chapter 12 and again in the book of Jude. The angel that appeared to Daniel had to get Michael's help to get past the spirit world representative of Cyrus, king of Persia. He informs Daniel that he has to go back and fight the spiritual prince of Persia until the spiritual prince of Grecia comes on the scene. Michael, here is identified as the prince of the Jewish people.

Returning to chapter 8, we can now understand the text more fully.

*Dan 8:10 And it waxed great, even to the host of heaven; and it cast down some of the host and of the stars to the ground, and stamped upon them.*

*11 Yea, he magnified himself even to the prince of the host, and by him the daily sacrifice was taken away, and the place of his sanctuary was cast down.*

*12 And an host was given him against the daily sacrifice by reason of transgression, and it cast down the truth to the ground; and it practised, and prospered.*

*13 Then I heard one saint speaking, and another saint said unto that certain saint which spake, How long shall be the vision concerning the daily sacrifice, and the transgression of desolation, to give both the sanctuary and the host to be trodden under foot?*

*14 And he said unto me, Unto two thousand and three hundred days; then shall the sanctuary be cleansed.*

The little horn that waxed great, even to the host of heaven was the spiritual counterpart to a physical king.

The prince of the host here is Michael the Archangel who fights for the Jewish people in the spiritual realm. The stars are angelic warriors. The host of heaven refers to all beings in the soulish realm who serve JEHOVAH God.

Concurrently with this war in the spiritual realm, the physical little horn is taking away the daily sacrifice in the temple and committing the transgression of desolation of verse 13. (This transgression of desolation has historical fulfillment as well as future fulfillment.) The host that was given to the little horn in the physical realm was the host of Hellenized Jews, who during the reign of Antiochus IV Epiphanes, were anxious to abolish the worship of JEHOVAH in order to curry favor with their Greek masters. Verses 13 and 14 tell us there will be 2300 days between the transgression of abomination and the cleansing of the sanctuary. There is historical evidence that the 2300-day period was the actual time until the sanctuary was cleansed in the historical fulfillment of this prophecy.

Daniel's description of this beast and the attendant events have been fulfilled historically. However, Gabriel's interpretation of this prophecy is specifically aimed at the time of the end:

*Dan 8:15 And it came to pass, when I, even I Daniel, had seen the vision, and sought for the meaning, then, behold, there stood before me as the appearance of a man.*

*16 And I heard a man's voice between the banks of Ulai, which called, and said, Gabriel, make this man to understand the vision.*

*17 So he came near where I stood: and when he came, I was afraid, and fell upon my face: but he said unto me,*

*Understand, O son of man: for at the time of the end shall be the vision.*

This prophecy has an obvious double application. In verse 11 of this chapter the little horn magnified himself to the prince (small p) of the host or Michael. Later, in the interpretation, verse 25 says he will stand up to the Prince (capital P) of princes or the Lord Jesus Christ.

Applying the double application, we can see that in the future there will be another abomination of desolation 2300 days before the end of the tribulation when the sanctuary will be finally cleansed. Thus, we know that this little horn will survive until at least 2300 days before the end of the tribulation. This abomination of desolation should then occur about 220 days or 7 plus months after the tribulation begins.

These abominations of desolation are not the ones spoken of in the New Testament by Jesus and by the Apostle Paul. That one is prophesied in Daniel 12:11 and will occur 1290 days before the end of the tribulation. That is the one from which the Jews of Judea are advised to flee to the mountains immediately. At that point, the Beast will declare himself to be the only true God and almost assuredly pronounce a death sentence on those who worship any other God. The 1290 days present a very definite schedule for the Jews of that time to go by and further, present evidence that every detail of prophecy has a precise time at which it will occur. That doctrinal point is verified by verse 19 of this chapter.

*Dan 8:18 Now as he was speaking with me, I was in a deep sleep on my face toward the ground: but he touched me, and set me upright.*

*19 And he said, Behold, I will make thee know what shall be in the last end of the indignation: for* **at the time appointed the end shall be**.

Moving ahead to the interpretation of the prophecy:

*Dan 8:22 Now that being broken, whereas four stood up for it, four kingdoms shall stand up out of the nation, but not in his power.*

*23 And in the latter time of their kingdom, when the transgressors are come to the full, a king of fierce countenance, and understanding dark sentences, shall stand up.*

*24 And his power shall be mighty, but not by his own power: and he shall destroy wonderfully, and shall prosper, and practise, and shall destroy the mighty and the holy people.*

*25 And through his policy also he shall cause craft to prosper in his hand; and he shall magnify himself in his heart, and by peace shall destroy many: he shall also stand up against the Prince of princes; but he shall be broken without hand.*

Verses 23-25 here jump ahead to the latter time or end-times of the kingdoms of the north and the south. In verse 11 of this chapter the spiritual representative of this little horn stood up to Michael the Archangel. That was as far as he went in the past fulfillment of this prophecy. Here, as we have seen, in the final fulfillment, he will even stand against the Prince of princes who is Jesus Christ himself. At that point, he will be broken without hand or without help.

Verse 24 here gives us a special insight to this man. He will be mighty, and his every effort will prosper for a time but not by his own power. We will discuss this other power in a later chapter where we will see that it is the spirit of antichrist that is driving him. This is the same spirit that has empowered and driven many men like Stalin and Hitler and many popes over the last 2000 years. This spirit specifically drives the 'beasts of the Earth' to destroy the holy people, that is, the servants of the true God

Verse 25 tells us this man will be a skillful politician. Honest people are guided by principles and plans, but true politicians have policies. His policy will be peace, but his practice will be war and violence.

There is one more bonus I would like to add to close out this discussion on Daniel 8. Not because of the need to know this, but rather to demonstrate the homogeneity of the scriptures and the proof of a single Author working through many different men. We saw in our discussion of Daniel 7 that horns represent spiritual power, whether good or evil. Then we saw four horns here in Daniel 8 that represented men with spiritual as well as physical power over Israel. These **four** horns represented Darius, Cyrus, Alexander the Great, and the little horn. The little horn is a special case who represents Antiochus 4 Epiphanes, the final king of the north and the Beast of Rev. 11 and 13-20.

In 519 BC, three years before the second temple was completed, and 189 years before the "notable horn" known as Alexander the Great conquered the known world, the prophet Zechariah saw this vision:

*Zec 1:18 Then lifted I up mine eyes, and saw, and behold **four** horns.*

*19 And I said unto the angel that talked with me, What be these? And he answered me, These are the horns which have **scattered** Judah, Israel, and Jerusalem.*

*20 And the LORD shewed me four carpenters.*

*21 Then said I, What come these to do? And he spake, saying, These are the horns which have **scattered** Judah, so that no man did lift up his head: but these are come to fray them, to cast out the horns of the Gentiles, which lifted up their horn over the land of Judah to **scatter** it.*

Zechariah here verified that there would be four horns, or four great leaders of the Gentiles that would **scatter** Judah, Israel, and Jerusalem. Now look up Dan. 11:24 and 12:7 to see that the term scatter is consistent with the workings of the little horn. Many books, many men, ONE Author! This is how correct Bible study is done, but it works only in the KJV where the omniscient AUTHOR placed English words strategically to help **sincere** truth-seekers find the truth. Precept upon precept, precept upon precept, line upon line, line upon line, here a little and there a little. (see Isa. 28:13)

### Daniel 11

Chapter 11 starts by recapping the prophecies of the kingdoms of Media and Persia and Grecia, calling them out by name. It then prophesies the reign and death of

Alexander the Great.  We are told that the kingdom would not pass to Alexander's heirs, but to four others.  We know from secular history that the kingdom was split between four of his generals.  Among these generals only two lines gained any great power, the Ptolemys of the southern kingdom, of which Egypt is the chief nation, and the northern kingdom Seleucids of which Persia was initially the chief nation.

The chapter can be divided into three sections.  Verses 1-28 give the history of the kingdoms from Darius to the early part of the reign of the Seleucid king Antiochus IV Epiphanes with most emphasis on the post-Alexander the Great wars between the king of the south (the Ptolemys) and the king of the north (the Seleucids).  This was a time of great oppression for Israel.  The kings of the north and the south passed through the land on their way to the wars and as they went, they murdered and plundered the people.  The chapter states it rather matter-of-factly:

*Dan 11:16  But he that cometh against him shall do according to his own will, and none shall stand before him: and he shall stand in the glorious land, which by his hand shall be consumed.*

The succession of kings continued until an especially evil and prophetically significant king named Antiochus IV Epiphanes came to power.  He was the son of Antiochus III the Great and was originally named Mithridates.  When he came to power, he took his new name which tells us much about his character.  Epiphanes translates as God Manifest and indeed, he saw himself as deity.

By the time he arrived on the scene many of the Jews had already become Hellenists and turned away from Jewish rites and traditions. They believed this would help them gain favor with the oppressive kings of the Ptolemys and Seleucids. The Greeks despised the Jewish religion and sought to convert the Jews to worship Zeus and his pantheon of gods.

Verses 29-39 of chapter 11 explain how vile and evil Antiochus IV Epiphanes was and describe the abomination of desolation and related events. Finally, verses 40-45 jump ahead to "the time of the end" and chronicle the final war of the king of the north when he defeats the king of the south and then comes to his end.

We see then that there are two prominent kings mentioned in verses 29-45 of this chapter. Both are called the king of the north. One, we know as Antiochus IV Epiphanes. The other we know as a still future king only by the terminology of 'king of the North'. His actual name will not be known until he appears on the scene as history unfolds before us. His reign will be quite short but extremely significant.

Antiochus IV conspired with the Hellenists and deposed the High Priest Jason, replacing him with his own man, Menelaus. This conspiracy is mentioned in verse 30:

*Dan 11:30 For the ships of Chittim shall come against him: therefore he shall be grieved, and return, and have indignation against the holy covenant: so shall he do; he shall even return, and have intelligence with them that forsake the holy covenant.*

In 168 BC, Antiochus IV undertook another of his campaigns in Egypt. This attack aroused the ire of the Romans who were well on their way to world domination by this time. The threat of war with the Romans forced him to withdraw. This resulted in a rumor of his death back in Jerusalem. The traditionalist Jews then rose up and restored Jason as High Priest. Upon being turned back and humiliated by the Romans he returned to Jerusalem and ruthlessly sacked the city massacring young and old, women and children, for three days.

In 167 BC Antiochus IV entered the temple, erected an image of, and altar to, Zeus and sacrificed a pig on it. He then outlawed Jewish worship and ordered the worship of Zeus as the supreme god. The Bible states it thusly:

*Dan 11:31 And arms shall stand on his part, and they shall pollute the sanctuary of strength, and shall take away the daily sacrifice, and they shall place the abomination that maketh desolate.*

Daniel had prophesied this abomination of desolation back in chapter 8 where we dealt with it more thoroughly.

*Dan 8:12 And an host was given him against the daily sacrifice by reason of transgression, and it cast down the truth to the ground; and it practised, and prospered.*

*13 Then I heard one saint speaking, and another saint said unto that certain saint which spake, How long shall be the vision concerning the daily sacrifice, and the transgression of desolation, to give both the sanctuary and the host to be trodden under foot?*

*14 And he said unto me, Unto two thousand and three hundred days; then shall the sanctuary be cleansed.*

Such desecration prompted the Maccabean revolt by the Hasmoneans which ended in their eventual victory and cleansing of the temple 2300 days later. It is an event still celebrated by the Jews today as the festival of Hanukkah.

The climate of that time is captured in verses 32-35:

*Dan 11:32 And such as do wickedly against the covenant shall he corrupt by flatteries: but the people that do know their God shall be strong, and do exploits.*

*33 And they that understand among the people shall instruct many: yet they shall fall by the sword, and by flame, by captivity, and by spoil, many days.*

*34 Now when they shall fall, they shall be holpen with a little help: but many shall cleave to them with flatteries.*

*35 And some of them of understanding shall fall, to try them, and to purge, and to make them white, even to the time of the end: because it is yet for a time appointed.*

As mentioned, Antiochus IV began to see himself more and more as a god and began to demonstrate eccentric behavior. Some of his contemporaries began calling him Antiochus IV *Epimanes* which roughly translates as Mad Man. Verses 36-39 describe how exceedingly evil and perverted Antiochus IV actually was:

*Dan 11:36 And the king shall do according to his will; and he shall exalt himself, and magnify himself above every god, and shall speak marvellous things against the God of gods, and shall prosper till the indignation be accomplished: for that that is determined shall be done.*

*37 Neither shall he regard the God of his fathers, nor the desire of women, nor regard any god: for he shall magnify himself above all.*

*38 But in his estate shall he honour the God of forces: and a god whom his fathers knew not shall he honour with gold, and silver, and with precious stones, and pleasant things.*

*39 Thus shall he do in the most strong holds with a strange god, whom he shall acknowledge and increase with glory: and he shall cause them to rule over many, and shall divide the land for gain.*

This description has a double application with the little horn of Daniel 8, who, as the last days king of the north is the subject of the rest of the chapter.

*Dan 11:40 And at the time of the end shall the king of the south push at him: and the king of the north shall come against him like a whirlwind, with chariots, and with horsemen, and with many ships; and he shall enter into the countries, and shall overflow and pass over.*

*41 He shall enter also into the glorious land, and many countries shall be overthrown: but these shall escape out of his hand, even Edom, and Moab, and the chief of the children of Ammon.*

*42 He shall stretch forth his hand also upon the countries: and the land of Egypt shall not escape.*

*43 But he shall have power over the treasures of gold and of silver, and over all the precious things of Egypt: and the Libyans and the Ethiopians shall be at his steps.*

*44 But tidings out of the east and out of the north shall trouble him: therefore he shall go forth with great fury to destroy, and utterly to make away many.*

*45 And he shall plant the tabernacles of his palace between the seas in the glorious holy mountain; yet he shall come to his end, and none shall help him.*

The final king of the north will win his battle with Egypt and then overthrow many countries (vv. 41-42). He will also enter the land of Israel and plant the tabernacles of his palace on the Temple Mount. There is no mention of a war with Israel so we must assume he has some sort of pact with the Jews. We will see in a later chapter that the lands that escape out of his hand will be held by Israel by that time.

Because the last days king of the north will be from a Muslim nation, it is logical to assume he could only come to such great power if he were also a Muslim. This would explain his attraction to the temple mount since it is the third holiest site in Islam. By this time, according to Daniel 12, the tribulation will have begun and thus the tribulation temple will likely have been built. This would then be a second Abomination of Desolation.

As in many examples of prophecy, this Abomination of Desolation prophecy has a past as well as a future fulfillment. We have pointed out that both Christ and Paul prophesied 200 plus years after Antiochus IV that it would occur again at the time of the end.

It should be noted that this little horn comes to an entirely different end than the little horn of chapter 7. That little horn is the Beast of Revelation 13 and he is cast alive into the Lake of Fire (Rev.19:20). This little horn will die alone with none to help Him. This death matches to Daniel 8:25:

*Dan 8:25 And through his policy also he shall cause craft to prosper in his hand; and he shall magnify himself in his heart, and by peace shall destroy many: he shall also stand up against the Prince of princes; but he shall be broken without hand.*

**Daniel 12 is a continuation of chapter 11.**

*Dan 12:1 And at that time shall Michael stand up, the great prince which standeth for the children of thy people: and there shall be a time of trouble, such as never was since there was a nation even to that same time: and at that time thy people shall be delivered, every one that shall be found written in the book.*

*2 And many of them that sleep in the dust of the earth shall awake, some to everlasting life, and some to shame and everlasting contempt.*

Chapter 12 starts, as we shall see, right **at the middle of the tribulation.** Verse 2 clearly speaks of **the resurrection of the just** since they are the only ones who receive everlasting life. The general resurrection of the wicked dead is at the end of the millennial reign of Christ according to Rev. chapter 20.

*Rev 20:4 And I saw thrones, and they sat upon them, and judgment was given unto them: and I saw the souls of them that were beheaded for the witness of Jesus, and for the word of God, and which had not worshipped the beast, neither his image, neither had received his mark upon their foreheads, or in their hands; and they lived and reigned with Christ a thousand years.*

*5 But the rest of the dead lived not again until the thousand years were finished. This is the first resurrection.*

Rev. 20:4 represents the end of the first resurrection. This resurrection of the righteous dead starts at the end of the Church Age and includes almost all the saved dead from the entire history of the world to that point right at mid-tribulation. The resurrection of the righteous is not completed until those who were saved during the last three and a half years of the tribulation are added in time to reign during the millennium with Christ. This resurrection also includes a special class of martyrs of Jesus who were beheaded for their faith. These are the saints spoken of in the fifth seal judgment:

*Rev 6:9 And when he had opened the fifth seal, I saw under the altar the souls of them that were slain for the word of God, and for the testimony which they held:*

*10 And they cried with a loud voice, saying, How long, O Lord, holy and true, dost thou not judge and avenge our blood on them that dwell on the earth?*

*11 And white robes were given unto every one of them; and it was said unto them, that they should rest yet for a little season, until their fellowservants also and their brethren, that should be killed as they were, should be fulfilled.*

Daniel 12:2 also mentions a curious class of people who are resurrected with the saints at mid-tribulation. These are resurrected to shame and everlasting contempt. The passage seems to match up with a parable of Jesus told in Matt. 22. This is a parable of the marriage supper of the Lamb. It is obvious that there will be at least some unsaved people resurrected with the righteous dead. These are apparently a class of hypocrites that will receive their punishment early.

*Mat 22:11 And when the king came in to see the guests, he saw there a man which had not on a wedding garment:*

*12 And he saith unto him, Friend, how camest thou in hither not having a wedding garment? And he was speechless.*

*13 Then said the king to the servants, Bind him hand and foot, and take him away, and cast him into outer darkness; there shall be weeping and gnashing of teeth.*

*14 For many are called, but few are chosen.*

There are other scriptures that deal with special treatment for hypocrites such as Matt. 24:51 and Matt. 25:14-46. The point is that verse 2 of Daniel 12 occurs at mid-tribulation and not at the end of the millennium as the final phrase of the verse might suggest. There is no conflict here.

Chapter 12 picks up right at the middle of the 7-year tribulation. This can be determined from verses 6-7 in which the time remaining is described as a time, times and half a time. Here a time stands for one year, times is two years, and a half time is half a year. Thus, we have the final three and a half years of the tribulation.

*Dan 12:6 And one said to the man clothed in linen, which was upon the waters of the river, How long shall it be to the end of these wonders?*

*7 And I heard the man clothed in linen, which was upon the waters of the river, when he held up his right hand and his left hand unto heaven, and sware by him that liveth for ever that it shall be for a time, times, and an half; and when he shall have accomplished to scatter the power of the holy people, all these things shall be finished.*

Verse 7 is particularly interesting in its use of the pronoun 'he': Dan 12:7b . . . and when **he** shall have accomplished to scatter the power of the holy people, all these *things* shall be finished. This logically seems to refer to the king of the north of chapter 11:45 who was killed before this time and therefore in the first half of the tribulation. However, it also describes the reign of the final Beast as described in Rev. chapter 13. Now consider the following passage:

*Rev 17:8 The beast that thou sawest was, and is not; and shall ascend out of the bottomless pit, and go into perdition: and they that dwell on the earth shall wonder, whose names were not written in the book of life from the foundation of the world, when they behold the beast that was, and is not, and yet is.*

*Rev 17:10 And there are seven kings: five are fallen, and one is, and the other is not yet come; and when he cometh, he must continue a short space.*

*11 And the beast that was, and is not, even he is the eighth, and is of the seven, and goeth into perdition.*

John wrote this passage during the reign of the sixth king and noted that the final Beast was a man that had already lived and died by that time in the form of one of the earlier kings. This passage opens the possibility that Antiochus IV Epiphanes, the final king of the north, and the final beast are all three the same person. Antiochus, the final king of the north, and the Beast are all three identified by Daniel as a little horn. Additionally, Antiochus and the final king of the north are mentioned consecutively in Daniel 11 as **the** king of the north. Each of these three commits an abomination of desolation. Finally, Rev. 13:3 tells us that the beast was someone who suffered a death blow to the head which was so miraculously healed that all the world wondered at him. If the king of the north died before mid-trib and was resurrected as the Beast all the world would certainly wonder at him. We shall see in a later chapter that this concept of three appearances of the same person on Earth in three different lives has biblical precedent in the three appearances of Elijah.

This resurrection creates a conundrum since the 666 beast has also been presented in this work as a Roman Catholic. I believe the solution is that the beast declares Romanism to be the true religion gone wrong due to knowledge gained after death. He becomes the spiritual and physical leader of both Catholics and Muslims as well as the rest of the world.

Verses 11-13 below have important information regarding the end of the tribulation. First of all, we see that there is definitely an abomination of desolation in the second half of the tribulation. This is accompanied by an end to daily sacrifice for the Jews - again. In addition, there are at least 65 days beyond the 42 months given to the Beast's reign before the start of the millennial reign. Finally, we see that Daniel will return sometime during the tribulation as a prophet.

*Dan 12:11 And from the time that the daily sacrifice shall be taken away, and the abomination that maketh desolate set up, there shall be a thousand two hundred and ninety days.*

*12 Blessed is he that waiteth, and cometh to the thousand three hundred and five and thirty days.*

*13 But go thou thy way till the end be: for thou shalt rest, and stand in thy lot at the end of the days.*

### Summary of Daniel's prophecies of the nations

In summary, the book of Daniel presents the history of the world from his time until sin is defeated and righteousness reigns in the millennial reign of Christ in three presentations. Chapter 2 chronicles, in the image of a man, the kingdoms of Babylonia, Medo-Persia, and Grecia from the head to the thighs. At that point, it splits into two legs or lines of dominion. One leg is the next world military empire after Alexander the Great, that is, Rome. This kingdom initially shares power with what is left of Alexander's (the other leg) kingdom. Between them they dominate the known world. Over time, the Roman leg begins to dominate the world militarily, while the Grecian leg begins to dominate the world culturally. It is this cultural domination that presents the greatest danger to Jews as it threatens to swallow them up and destroy their existence as a distinct people of God.

The leg that leads to the militarily superior Roman Empire is detailed in chapter 7 in the Gentile language of Babylon. This line is of greatest interest to the Gentile world. The leg that details the culturally superior Greek line is written in Hebrew in chapters 8-12. This is the line that most affects the nation of Israel. Daniel chapter 9 describes a particularly important 490-year period in the history of that leg which introduces the timing of the ministry of Messiah. We will look at this period in the next chapter.

Chapter 11 introduces the reign of the king(s) of the North out of the Grecian leg. All but one of these kings appear before Rome reaches the peak of her power. The last one appears at the time of the end and comes out of an evil spiritual power.

Chapters 7 and 8 both present a king at the end of the time of Gentile domination in the form of a little horn. The horn indicates that both kings come out of a spiritual entity. In the case of the Roman leg, this entity is the Roman Catholic Church. In the case of the Grecian leg, this entity is the Muslim religion which controls the majority of the land claimed by the Seleucids and the Ptolemys. Thus, we see that the power moved from the physical realm to the spiritual realm in both legs. This is because the battle between righteousness and evil moved from the physical realm to the spiritual realm when the Church Age was instituted. The city of Revelation 17 and 18 demonstrates this change from a physical to a spiritual kingdom. Revelation 17 describes the destruction of spiritual Rome or the Vatican whereas Revelation 18 describes the physical city of Rome of the Apostle John's Day. These two kingdoms are finally combined into the kingdom of the final Beast in Daniel 12. At this point, the Church Age ends, and the final world kingdom becomes both a spiritual and a physical kingdom. Thus, when Christ defeats the Beast, He conquers both the physical and spiritual kingdoms and becomes Lord of all.

So, Daniel prophesies eight worldly kings and seven worldly kingdoms, the fifth of which continues and runs concurrently with the sixth kingdom. The seven kingdoms are Babylonia, Media, Persia, Grecia, Seleucia, Rome, and the kingdom of the beast of Rev. 13. The kings referred to are Nebuchadnezzar, Darius, Cyrus, Alexander the Great, Antiochus IV Epiphanes (a Seleucid), the emperor (Domitian?) of Rome, the final king of the north (a Seleucid), and the Beast of Rev.13. The final king from the Seleucid kingdom is called in Daniel 11 by the generic name of king of the north. The kingdom of this king is strengthened at the time of the end and is concurrent with the latter stages of the Roman kingdom. Both of these last two kingdoms are religious in nature. This matches perfectly to Rev. 17:10-11.

*Rev 17:10 And there are seven kings: five are fallen, and one is, and the other is not yet come; and when he cometh, he must continue a short space.*

*Rev 17:11 And the beast that was, and is not, even he is the eighth, and is of the seven, and goeth into perdition.*

# Chapter 4. The Key to All Future Prophecy, or...
## (What We Can Learn from Daniel Chapter 9)

Refer to this chart for dates or events mentioned in this chapter. All dates considered historically accurate within 1 or 2 years by many secular historians.

| Gentile Rulers Over the Jews and Notable Jewish Events - 626 BC to 138 AD |||
|---|---|---|
| Year(s) | Name/Event | Remarks |
| 626-605 BC | Nabopolassar | First King of Babylonian Empire. Father of Nebuchadnezzar |
| 608-597 BC | Jehoiakim | King of Judah. Birth name was Eliakim |
| 605 BC | Daniel | Daniel carried to Babylon in 3rd year of Jehoiakim, king of Judah |
| 605-562 BC | Nebuchadnezzar | Besieged Jerusalem 605 BC. Took captives in 597 BC (including Ezekiel), 586 BC, and 582 BC. Destroyed city walls and temple in 586 BC. Book of Daniel. |
| 597-586 BC | Zedekiah | Last king of Judah. |
| 586 BC | Temple | Temple destroyed |
| 562-560 BC | Evil-Merodach | Released Jeconiah after 37 years in prison. |
| 560-556 BC | Nergalsharezer | Son-in-law to Nebuchadnezzar |
| 556-539 BC | Nabonidus/ | Ruled with son, |

| | Belshazzar | Belshazzar as co-regent |
|---|---|---|
| 539-530 BC | Cyrus the Great | Conquered Babylon, assigned uncle, Darius the Mede, as regent over Babylon in 539 BC |
| 539-537 BC | Darius the Mede | King of the Medes, ruled Babylon for Cyrus. Daniel 6, 9-12. |
| 539/ 538 BC | Cyrus the Great | Released Jews. Commanded them to rebuild temple and city of Jerusalem. Prophesied in Isa. 44:28 |
| 537 BC | Second Temple | Second temple started. |
| 530-522 BC | Cambyses II | Son of Cyrus the Great. AKA Artaxerxes in Ezra 4,6 |
| 521-486 BC | Darius 1 the Great | Son-in-law of Cyrus the Great |
| 516 BC | Second Temple | Temple completed after 21 years in building. 70 years after destruction of Solomon's Temple. |
| 485-465 BC | Xerxes 1 the Great | Possibly Ahasuerus of Book of Esther |
| 465-425 BC | Artaxerxes 1 | Sent Ezra and later Nehemiah to Jerusalem to beautify temple, rebuild city and wall. |
| 458 BC | Ezra | Sent from Babylon as Priest to beautify temple/city |
| 445 BC | Nehemiah | Sent from Babylon as |

|  |  | Governor to rebuild city/wall |
|---|---|---|
| 425-424 BC | Xerxes II |  |
| 423-404 BC | Darius II |  |
| 409 BC | Jerusalem | Presumably, the year that Jerusalem rebuild was completed per Neh. 7:4 which states the houses had not yet been built. First 7 weeks of years, Dan. 9:25 |
| 404-359 BC | Artaxerxes II |  |
| 359-338 BC | Artaxerxes III |  |
| 338-336 BC | Arses |  |
| 336-330 BC | Darius III | Last of Persian kings governing Jews |
| 330-323 BC | Alexander the Great | Alexander took the Persian empire in 330 BC |
| 323-175 BC | Seluecids and Ptolemys | Various kings of the north and the south ruled or held the Jews to tribute per Daniel chapter 11 |
| 175-163 BC | Antiochus IV Epiphanes | Prominently mentioned in Dan. 11:21-39 and Dan 8:9-12. He committed the first "abomination that maketh desolate" in 167 BC |
| 167 BC | Temple | Antiochus IV Epiphanes |

| | | |
|---|---|---|
| | | desecrated the temple |
| 163-63 BC | Seleucids and Ptolemys | Various Greek kings of the north and kings of the south ruled the Jews until Rome shut the Seleucids down. |
| 63-27 BC | Roman Republic | Various Roman leaders including Pompey, Julius Caesar, Crassus, Mark Antony, and Octavian |
| 45 BC | Julian Calendar | Julius Caesar's Calendar in effect as of Jan. 1 of 45 BC |
| 27 BC – 14 AD | Augustus Caesar Roman Empire | Octavian became Emperor Augustus Caesar Start of Roman Empire |
| 5 BC | Jesus Christ | Jesus born in Bethlehem, possibly on Feast of Trumpets, Oct. 2 |
| 14-37 AD or (12-37 AD) | Tiberius Caesar | Caesar during ministry of Christ. Received Tribunician power 4 AD, Co-Princeps 12 AD, reigned solely in 14 AD |
| 26 AD | Jesus Christ | Began public ministry near 30th birthday. (Remember to subtract 1 year when going from BC to AD because of no zero year.) End of 7 weeks plus 62 weeks of years or 483 years, Dan |

| | | |
|---|---|---|
| | | 9:25 |
| 30 AD | Jesus Christ | Died on Passover, April 3 at age 33 ½. Midst of 70th week of years, Dan 9:27 (486.5 years from commandment to Ezra in 458 BC) |
| 37-41 AD | Caligula | |
| 41-54 AD | Claudius | |
| 54-68 AD | Nero | |
| 68-69 AD | Various | Galba, Otho, Vitellius |
| 69-79 AD | Vespasian | Emperor during fall of Jerusalem to Titus, 70 AD |
| 70 AD | Jerusalem | Titus (prince of Rome) defeated, sacked Jerusalem. Destroyed temple. Killed possibly in excess of 1.1 million people |
| 79-81 AD | Titus | Son of Vespasian. The "prince" of Daniel 9:26 |
| 81-96 AD | Domitian | Probable Emperor when the Revelation was written by John the Apostle. Referenced in Rev. 17:10 as the one that 'is' |
| 96-98 AD | Nerva | Appointed by the senate |
| 98-117 AD | Trajan | Adopted son of Nerva |
| 117-138 AD | Hadrian | Adopted son of Trajan |
| 135 AD | Jewish nation | 2nd diaspora. All Jews |

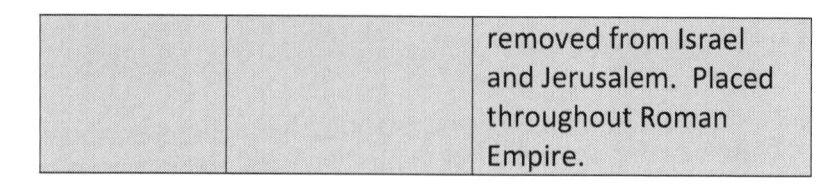

|  |  | removed from Israel and Jerusalem. Placed throughout Roman Empire. |
|---|---|---|

*Pro 18:13 He that answereth a matter before he heareth it, it is folly and shame unto him.*

I have started this chapter with the verse above to encourage the reader to read this entire chapter before discarding it or tossing away the book. This chapter will cause stress, anxiety, or outright anger to many readers. Yet, if read to the very end, it should set a new premillennial paradigm that can erase all of the previously examined (chapter 2) premillennial systems with all their faults and weaknesses in favor of one that eventually solves all the problem scriptures those systems face. This new understanding will preserve the expected homogeneity of the (KJV) scriptures and finally open up the exquisite simplicity of end-times prophecy.

Daniel chapter 9 is the most widely mis-interpreted chapter for end-times prophecy in the Old Testament. It is the proof scripture for the Darby Antichrist fallacy, twisted tribulation timetables, and many rapture-theory errors. It is frequently tied to end-times scenarios all through the Bible by prophecy teachers without credible evidence to show why it should apply.

Despite all this, it is not a difficult chapter to understand at all. It is quite straightforward and if you get the right starting point for the prophecy within, you end up with much already fulfilled prophecy that does not require a second fulfillment. If you get the wrong starting point, however, you end up denying much already fulfilled prophecy.

We will present here the full understanding that the King James Bible requires and then try to determine how prophecy experts managed to get it so twisted and wrong.

The chapter begins with Daniel's prayer for the restoration of an independent Jewish state complete with its capital in Jerusalem, a new temple for Levitical worship, and a king from the line of David.

*Dan 9:1 In the first year of Darius the son of Ahasuerus, of the seed of the Medes, which was made king over the realm of the Chaldeans;*

Referring to our chronological chart at the beginning of this chapter, we see this prayer was offered in about 539 BC, the very year that Cyrus released the Jews with orders to rebuild the city and the temple in Jerusalem.

*Dan 9:2 In the first year of his reign I Daniel understood by books the number of the years, whereof the word of the LORD came to Jeremiah the prophet, that he would accomplish seventy years in the desolations of Jerusalem.*

Daniel was reading the prophecy of one of his contemporaries, Jeremiah. This was found in the book of Jeremiah, chapter 25:11-12 and chapter 29:10. Part of

Jeremiah's prophecy remains to be fulfilled to this day. Jeremiah prophesied that the land of the Chaldeans (Babylonians) would become perpetual desolations. This is also prophesied in Isa. 13 and Jer. 50 among other places. In these passages, Babylon's final destruction is clearly scheduled within the tribulation.

Daniel's summation of the prophecy of Jeremiah deals specifically with Jerusalem whereas the original prophecy was directed at the whole land of Israel. It is likely he was influenced by the prayer of Solomon at the dedication of the original temple found in 1 Kings 8:46-50.

In fact, it is probable that his observance of the instructions in that prayer would land him, or had landed him, in the lion's den (as chronicled in Daniel chapter 6) in this same year. It is not clear whether this prayer of Daniel was made before or after Cyrus the Great released the Jews. But, if it was made before, it was answered very quickly.

**Daniel intercedes for his people**

*Dan 9:3 And I set my face unto the Lord God, to seek by prayer and supplications, with fasting, and sackcloth, and ashes:*

*4 And I prayed unto the LORD my God, and made my confession, and said, O Lord, the great and dreadful God, keeping the covenant and mercy to them that love him, and to them that keep his commandments;*

*5 We have sinned, and have committed iniquity, and have done wickedly, and have rebelled, even by departing from thy precepts and from thy judgments:*

*6 Neither have we hearkened unto thy servants the prophets, which spake in thy name to our kings, our princes, and our fathers, and to all the people of the land.*

*16 O Lord, according to all thy righteousness, I beseech thee, let thine anger and thy fury be turned away from thy city Jerusalem, thy holy mountain: because for our sins, and for the iniquities of our fathers, Jerusalem and thy people are become a reproach to all that are about us.*

*17 Now therefore, O our God, hear the prayer of thy servant, and his supplications, and cause thy face to shine upon thy sanctuary that is desolate, for the Lord's sake.*

*18 O my God, incline thine ear, and hear; open thine eyes, and behold our desolations, and the city which is called by thy name: for we do not present our supplications before thee for our righteousnesses, but for thy great mercies.*

*19 O Lord, hear; O Lord, forgive; O Lord, hearken and do; defer not, for thine own sake, O my God: for thy city and thy people are called by thy name.*

## Gabriel Brings an Answer

*Dan 9:20 And whiles I was speaking, and praying, and confessing my sin and the sin of my people Israel, and presenting my supplication before the LORD my God for the holy mountain of my God;*

*21 Yea, whiles I was speaking in prayer, even the man Gabriel, whom I had seen in the vision at the beginning, being caused to fly swiftly, touched me about the time of the evening oblation.*

*22 And he informed me, and talked with me, and said, O Daniel, I am now come forth to give thee skill and understanding.*

*23 At the beginning of thy supplications the commandment came forth, and I am come to shew thee; for thou art greatly beloved: therefore understand the matter, and consider the vision.*

Gabriel was the special angel used to announce, here, the coming of Messiah and later, the birth of Jesus Christ. This dual announcement by the same angel was purposefully done to prove that Jesus was the promised Messiah.

**The Seventy Weeks**

*Dan 9:24 Seventy weeks are determined upon thy people and upon thy holy city, to finish the transgression, and to make an end of sins, and to make reconciliation for iniquity, and to bring in everlasting righteousness, and to seal up the vision and prophecy, and to anoint the most Holy.*

*25 Know therefore and understand, that from the going forth of the commandment to restore and to build Jerusalem unto the Messiah the Prince shall be seven weeks, and threescore and two weeks: the street shall be built again, and the wall, even in troublous times.*

*26 And after threescore and two weeks shall Messiah be cut off, but not for himself: and the people of the prince that shall come shall destroy the city and the sanctuary; and the end thereof shall be with a flood, and unto the end of the war desolations are determined.*

*27 And he shall confirm the covenant with many for one week: and in the midst of the week he shall cause the sacrifice and the oblation to cease, and for the overspreading of abominations he shall make it desolate, even until the consummation, and that determined shall be poured upon the desolate.*

These last four verses incorporate a history of the Jews from the commandment of verse 25 until the final fulfillment of the six points laid out in verse 24. All the prophecies of these four verses would be completed over a period of "seventy weeks". As a practical matter, none of them were completely fulfilled within seventy actual weeks which, in hindsight, we now understand refers to weeks of years. Thus there were 490 years of history remaining for Daniel's people and for the holy city, that is, Jerusalem until they would "finish the transgression, and to make an end of sins, and to make reconciliation for iniquity, and to bring in everlasting righteousness, and to seal up the vision and prophecy, and to anoint the most Holy."

So, we know what the completion of the prophecy looks like, but we don't yet know where it starts. Verse 25 here tells us there will be a specific commandment to restore and to build Jerusalem that will start the 490-year clock. Scriptures give four similar commandments so we must determine which one is the intended start time. The first such commandment was made by Cyrus the Great shortly after he conquered the city of Babylon and took over the empire in 539 BC. It is a grand commandment and worthy of inclusion here because it gives great glory to our God.

*Ezr 1:1 Now in the first year of Cyrus king of Persia, that the word of the LORD by the mouth of Jeremiah might be fulfilled, the LORD stirred up the spirit of Cyrus king of Persia, that he made a proclamation throughout all his kingdom, and put it also in writing, saying,*

This proclamation was necessary "that the word of the LORD by the mouth of Jeremiah might be fulfilled". Jeremiah's prophecy of 70 years of desolations in Israel could only be fulfilled by the rebuilding of the temple. Therefore, the Jews had to be back in their land to build it. And indeed, in the next two verses, we see a commandment to do exactly that.

*2 Thus saith Cyrus king of Persia, The LORD God of heaven hath given me all the kingdoms of the earth; and he hath charged me to build him an house at Jerusalem, which is in Judah.*

*3 Who is there among you of all his people? his God be with him, and let him go up to Jerusalem, which is in Judah, and build the house of the LORD God of Israel, (he is the God,) which is in Jerusalem.*

This, however, is not the commandment Gabriel was speaking of per verse 25 of the prophecy of seventy weeks. In that case, the seventy weeks would have ended in 49 BC. But, at that time Messiah had not yet come and none of the conditions of verse 24 had been fulfilled. The second possible start point for the 70 weeks of years was the decree of Darius 1 the Great in about 520 BC to continue the work of the temple which had ceased due to complaints to the king from the enemies of the Jews. This was described in Ezra chapters 4-6. It does not work for the same reasons the first commandment couldn't work.

We will look at the fourth possibility, chronologically, before the third because it is probably the most widely accepted commandment date, and the reasoning is so bogus it is shocking that anyone has accepted it. After that we will look at the correct (third) commandment date and demonstrate that it precisely fits the prophecy as given in the King James Bible. Here is that fourth commandment:

*Neh 2:1 And it came to pass in the month Nisan, in the twentieth year of Artaxerxes the king, that wine was before him: and I took up the wine, and gave it unto the king. Now I had not been beforetime sad in his presence.*

*Neh 2:4 Then the king said unto me, For what dost thou make request? So I prayed to the God of heaven.*

*5 And I said unto the king, If it please the king, and if thy servant have found favour in thy sight, that thou wouldest send me unto Judah, unto the city of my fathers' sepulchres, that I may build it.*

*6 And the king said unto me, (the queen also sitting by him,) For how long shall thy journey be? and when wilt thou return? So it pleased the king to send me; and I set him a time.*

Here we have a commandment to rebuild the city of Jerusalem, just as the prophecy required. But we have a chronology issue. The count of years takes us well beyond the time of Messiah. So, an explanation was proposed which found wide and overly eager acceptance.

From verses 24-27 of Daniel 9, we can see that the important point in the life of Messiah for the purposes of this prophecy is the point at which He is cut off or, as we now know, crucified. So that is the point toward which some prophetic scholars direct this prophecy. However, the verse specifically states that He is cut off after 69 weeks. Additionally, it does not specify how long afterwards it is that He is cut off.

There is a widely held belief (first proposed by Sir Robert Anderson) that the first 69 weeks, or 483-year period, points to the Triumphal Entry into Jerusalem recorded in passages such as Mark 11 and Luke 19 in which Jesus openly accepted the title of King from the multitudes. This was only days before His crucifixion. This argument demands that the commandment to Nehemiah in the 20th year of Artaxerxes 1 is the commandment intended for this prophecy.

Although I have not personally read Sir Robert Anderson's book, *"The Coming Prince"*, it has been summarized so many times by so many others that we can reproduce their work here with a high level of confidence. That position goes like this.

Secular history places the twentieth year of Artaxerxes in 445 or 444 BC. Counting from the more commonly accepted year 445 BC would end the 483 years at 37 AD (subtracting one year for the lack of a year zero between BC and AD). This date would seem too late since, *if our calendar were correct*, Christ the Messiah would have died around 33 or 34 AD. However, few, if any, historians believe our Gregorian calendar is dependable enough on that point in history to be used with precision. Many events from the period we are dealing with are given a variety of dates by various historians, but most frequently within a range of about 2 years. But the birth and death years of Christ are not even that precise. The important point to take from this, however, is that we are very much in the right ballpark to presume that Messiah the Prince is the same person as Jesus the Christ.

**Sir Robert Anderson's calculation**

Sir Robert Anderson (1841-1918), in his work *"The Coming Prince"*, proposed using 360-day "prophetic" years as the basis for the 483-year count. This would have the effect of moving the actual year on our calendar back to a more historically acceptable year for the crucifixion of Christ. On the ancient (pre- Babylonian captivity) Jewish calendar, a month was always 30 days, and a year was normally 12 months. Thus, a year was nominally 360 days. This counting method is used in at least one other prophecy where three and a half years are given also as 1260 days in Revelation 11:2-3. Thus, Anderson felt justified in assigning the nomenclature "prophetic year" to a 360-day year.

Anderson broke the years down into days and thus 483 years of 360 days came out to 173,880 days. The Bible states that the decree of Artaxerxes to rebuild Jerusalem, made in his twentieth year, was given in the month of Nisan. Anderson believed (hoped?) that it would have been on the first day of Nisan and calculated that day would have been March 14, 445 BC on the **Julian** calendar. (Understand, the Julian calendar did not exist until the first century BC.) He then calculated, using the secular date for the start of the reign of Tiberius in 14 AD plus the 15 years given in Luke 3:1, that Jesus began his ministry in 29 AD. He further believed that Jesus celebrated four Passovers in His ministry so the final one would have been in AD 32. Using lunar charts, he calculated the date for Passover in AD 32 and then counted back to place the Triumphal Entry on April 6, 32 AD. This comes out to 476 years of 365 days plus an additional 24 days between March 14 and April 6, apparently including March 14. This gave him a total of 173,764 days.

Having the start and end dates defined, he added back in the number of days (116) for leap years and came up with exactly 173,880 days or exactly 483 prophetic years to the day of the Triumphal Entry. This is all so neatly tied together, and it sounds so amazing, that there is strong temptation to just accept it and go with it. Unfortunately, upon further examination, it is not without problems.

**Problems with Anderson's calculations**

The first and most noticeable problem with Anderson's system is that he used differing calendars to arrive at the number of leap-days to add. The fact is that his 476 years of 365 days produce 119 leap-days rather than the 116 he found. But that would not equal 173,880 days!

It may be that the actual writing was so detailed, and the calculations so spread out that this wasn't obvious to many pre-trib prophecy teachers from casually reading the book. It may be that only by summarizing all the calculations as above that it becomes apparent.

But look! 483 consecutive 360-day years don't have leap-days. We should merely have 483 years of 360 days or 173,880 from Mar 14, 445 BC to April 6, 32 AD on a modern calendar. So, what is all this leap-day talk about? Why break it down to days if the years works perfectly?

Here is why. 476 years of 365.25 days equals 173,859 days. Adding in the additional 24 days from March 14 to April 6 yields 173,883 days. So, the 360 day-year actually did not work exactly. It merely took us up to a point in the middle of the pre-crucifixion week. I believe it was all about blowing smoke in our eyes.

It seems painfully obvious that when his prophetic year failed to work out using a significant start date, Anderson was merely casting about to find a way to save his theory. He felt like he desperately needed Nisan 1. His original intention likely was to arrive at the day of the crucifixion, but he couldn't make it happen. So, he found the closest important day and used that. He found the day of the Triumphal Entry into Jerusalem and disappeared three leap-days via calendar gymnastics to get there. Sound disingenuous? I think so.

The Triumphal Entry is never mentioned in the original prophecy and has no meaningful place in the narrative. It wasn't a real solution at all, but he managed to sell his story to an overwilling Church that was falling head-over-heels in love with Darby's Antichrist.

A better solution would have been to simply start on Nisan 6, or March 19, 445 BC to arrive at his preferred day of the crucifixion and then say it works within an acceptable timeframe, so it *could* be true. Easy, but so banal!

But who would have accepted March 19, 445 BC and April 6, 32 AD with such poor justification? He had a big problem with his 32 AD year, which not many secular historians would accept. Plus, as we shall see, he had a problem with a more historically accurate alternative commandment. His whole purpose was to find 7 years remaining of Daniel's 70 weeks prophecy at the point of the crucifixion of Christ which is not the case with the alternative commandment. If he could not arrive at 7 years remaining, Darby's entire postulation would be a failure.

The second problem this calculation faces is that the ancient Jewish calendar was quite complicated. Because they only used 30-day months they came up short about five and a quarter days per year based on the solar solstices. By strictly continuing with that calendar, feast days tied to the harvest would have soon begun occurring at the wrong time of the year. In fact, all the feast days tied to a particular month would have moved far away from their original purpose. The Jews compensated with additional months in certain years. Although the system appears to be somewhat complicated, we can see that, on average, a month would have to be added about every 6 years. Thus, for short periods such as the three and a half years previously mentioned, a 360-day year is completely appropriate. However, beyond a decade or so, continuous 360-day years simply don't work and there is no biblical evidence of this kind of counting method over a long period of time anywhere else in scriptures. It is obvious that none of the Gregorian, or the Julian, or the Jewish calendars give us 483 years in that time frame. It would seem inconsistent of God to change His counting of years in just this one instance of scripture without telling us He did it. In God's economy, in every case, the facts of the physical world turn out to match His prophecies. In Anderson's economy we seem to have a case of contriving to force the prophecy to fit the facts as he wanted them to be.

The third major problem with Anderson's work is that it absolutely counts on secular history being correct on the twentieth year of Artaxerxes and the beginning of the reign of Tiberius. It is well established that ancient historians, just like modern ones, changed and embellished history to enhance the image and legacy of their rulers. In addition, our current calendar has been changed and revised from time to time. Beyond that, we don't know enough about the accuracy of many of the ancient calendars which we use for dates and time periods. Calendars are not to be accepted on blind faith. For instance, our Gregorian calendar, as of this year, counts 2020 years since the birth of Christ but almost no historians accept that. In actuality, the likelihood of a secular date or time span being correct to the very day in that time period is far too low to accept. Just to illustrate, the Russian delegation to the 1908 Olympics was two weeks late because they were still using the Julian calendar while the other nations were using our Gregorian calendar. So, you can see the problems associated with changing from calendar to calendar.

Perhaps even more significantly, the start point for the reign of Tiberius Caesar is open for discussion. He was given Tribunician powers as early as 4 AD and then became a Co-Princeps with his stepfather, Augustus Caesar, in 12 AD. The scriptures actually say Tiberius was **in** his 15th year before John the Baptist began his ministry. That means that he had reigned for 14 years plus some days or months, which causes another issue in that Mr. Anderson assumed 15 full years. This seems to be another point of doubt. It was this presumption that allowed Anderson to get his vitally necessary 29 AD for the start of Messiah's ministry. It would seem most reasonable to believe the scriptural count of years began from the point that Tiberius became equal in power with Augustus rather than from the death of Augustus. This most closely fits the secular dates promoted for the birth year of Jesus.

A lesser problem is that Anderson presumed 1 Nisan with neither scriptural nor secular justification. And lastly, some have found evidence to indicate that Anderson placed Nisan 1 thirty days too early in the year. All in all, we can say that although it sounds very impressive, there are just too many problems with Anderson's calculations.

So, we conclude that the 360-day year doesn't work for timing the 483 years from the going forth of the commandment in 445 BC until Messiah the Prince. Further, using normal solar years takes us from 445 BC to 37 AD. 37 AD is well beyond any reckoning for the death of Messiah. The belief is nearly unanimous that He died several to many years before that.

All the rapture positions we reviewed in chapter 2 of this book rely on the 483 years ending **at the crucifixion** of Messiah. Their interpretation of the Daniel 9 passage requires that the entire 70$^{th}$ week of 7 years remains after the death of Messiah. In fact, all these positions completely collapse if anything more or less than a week of seven years remains of the 70 weeks of years. In truth, since Anderson's calculations are completely necessary to their position, it is little wonder the rapture teachers of our times have not challenged his work. They have found no other way to make the chronology work out in their favor.

I should point out before moving on, that the wording of the prophecy fits this 20$^{th}$ year of Artaxerxes much better, aesthetically, than the commandment I will be presenting as correct. For comparison, I will present the verses here.

*Dan 9:25 Know therefore and understand, that from the going forth of the commandment to restore and to build Jerusalem unto the Messiah the Prince shall be seven weeks, and threescore and two weeks: the street shall be built again, and the wall, even in troublous times.*

As compared to

*Neh 2:5 And I said unto the king, If it please the king, and if thy servant have found favour in thy sight, that thou wouldest send me unto Judah, unto the city of my fathers' sepulchres, that I may build it.*
*6 And the king said unto me, (the queen also sitting by him,) For how long shall thy journey be? and when wilt thou return? So it pleased the king to send me; and I set him a time.*

As you can see from these verses, and indeed from much of the book of Nehemiah, the building of the wall in troublous times was the central theme of Nehemiah's governorship. You should notice that the commandment of Dan. 9:25 was specifically to restore and to build the city of Jerusalem, whereas the one I will show you next is much more specifically aimed at upgrading the second temple in Jerusalem. For most, that makes this 20th year of Artaxerxes commandment a lock for the one referred to in Dan. 9:25. It is only the fact that it doesn't work chronologically that makes us seek another alternative to that commandment of Artaxerxes. There is, in fact, one for which the chronological timing actually matches the 70 weeks of years perfectly.

It is worth noting before we move on that it appears Nehemiah returned to serve the king for a time before the city of Jerusalem was finally rebuilt. He set the process in motion but did not fully see it through as he requested to do in Neh. 2:5. So, this commandment did not fulfill the requirement in Dan. 9:25 fully because Nehemiah had a firm return date of less than 49 years.

This problem is not unlike other problems with prophetic interpretations. For instance, many have tried to tie the 70 years of desolations mentioned in Jeremiah and referenced in Daniel 9:2 from the point of Daniel's captivity in 605 BC to the decree of Cyrus the Great in 539 BC to the Jews regarding rebuilding the house of their God. As you can see, this is only 66 years so fudge factors have been applied. There were at least three other possible starting points for the prophecy when captives were taken to Babylon in 597 BC, 586 BC, and 582 BC. But history shows us that the correct starting point for the 70 years was 586 BC when Jerusalem was finally sacked, and the temple destroyed. It was exactly 70 years from that point until the second temple was completed in 516 BC. This was, chronologically, the third of four possibilities for the starting point of the 70 years prophesied by Jeremiah. Scriptures, as usual, provide help with this discussion:

*Zec 1:7 Upon the four and twentieth day of the eleventh month, which is the month Sebat, in the second year of Darius, came the word of the LORD unto Zechariah, the son of Berechiah, the son of Iddo the prophet, saying,*

*Zec 1:12 Then the angel of the LORD answered and said, O LORD of hosts, how long wilt thou not have mercy on Jerusalem and on the cities of Judah, against which thou hast had indignation these threescore and ten years?*

Here we can see that the angel of the LORD claims that the 70 years were still ongoing in 519 BC (see chronology chart). According to verse 12 here, the LORD had not yet had mercy on Jerusalem. The temple was completed three years after this vision of Zechariah.

## The commandments to Ezra and Nehemiah

Interestingly, of the four possible dates for the starting point of the 70 weeks of Daniel 9:25, it is also the third possibility that is the correct one from an historical or chronological perspective. To accept this date, we must justify the wording problems we discussed earlier between the commandments to rebuild the city in Daniel 9 and the commandment of Cyrus the Great, stated here:

*Ezr 1:2 Thus saith Cyrus king of Persia, The LORD God of heaven hath given me all the kingdoms of the earth; and he hath charged me to build him an house at Jerusalem, which is in Judah.*

This verse is the main thrust for all the commandments we are examining. All of them received their legitimacy from Cyrus' original commandment. I contend, however, that rebuilding the city and its walls around the temple was always a given as part of that commandment. Where would the glory be in building a beautiful temple in the midst of a pile of rubble? What kind of legacy would that be for a man who called himself Cyrus the Great?

Intuitively, we understand this, but the scriptures themselves also give us a couple clues.

The first clue, or set of clues, is found in the scriptures regarding the actual building of the temple. In Ezra 4:4,12 and 5:3,9 we see the building of the wall being challenged by the adversaries of the Jews. These verses describe the situation 70-85 years before Nehemiah ever went to Jerusalem. Consider the language used:

*Ezr 4:4 Then the people of the land weakened the hands of the people of Judah, and troubled them in building,*

*Ezr 4:12 Be it known unto the king, that the Jews which came up from thee to us are come unto Jerusalem, building the rebellious and the bad city, and have set up the walls thereof, and joined the foundations.*

*Ezr 5:3 At the same time came to them Tatnai, governor on this side the river, and Shetharboznai, and their companions, and said thus unto them, Who hath commanded you to build this house, and to make up this wall?*

*Ezr 5:9 Then asked we those elders, and said unto them thus, Who commanded you to build this house, and to make up these walls?*

These verses tell the story of the building of the temple, the city, and the wall many years before Ezra and Nehemiah came on the scene. The work was stopped under Cambyses II and restarted in the second year of Darius I the Great. You should note that the Artaxerxes mentioned in Nehemiah 4 is called Cambyses II in secular history. Artaxerxes was believed to be a common title of Persian kings at that time. The Artaxerxes that sent Ezra and Nehemiah to Jerusalem should be more properly called Artaxerxes 1 from secular history. He was the first Persian king to make the title Artaxerxes his formal name when on the throne.

So, referring back to Ezra 4:12, we see that the Jews were building the city, and the walls were set up and the foundation joined. It is obvious that the very work mentioned in Daniel 9:25 had already been started long before Nehemiah came on the scene to finish the walls. Also, the question in Ezra 5:3, *"Who hath commanded you to build this house, and to make up this wall?"* indicates an understanding that the Jews claimed to have a commandment to build the wall.

There is one more passage of scripture that ties much of this together. This one is a prophecy spoken by Isaiah around 711 BC or about 166 years before Cyrus released the Jews in 539 BC. Isaiah prophesied the as-yet-unborn Cyrus by name which, no doubt, Cyrus became aware of. That can be determined by his release statement in the verses above.

In Isaiah 44:21-45:13, we find a story of the restoration of Jerusalem and the temple by a man named Cyrus. Neither of these had been destroyed as yet so the hearers of this message must have wondered what in the world Isaiah was talking about. The last verse of this passage is very telling that part of the commandment of Cyrus was **to rebuild the city of Jerusalem.**

*Isa 44:28 That saith of Cyrus, He is my shepherd, and*

*shall perform all my pleasure:* **even saying to Jerusalem, Thou shalt be built; and to the temple, Thy foundation shall be laid.**

*Isa 45:1 Thus saith the LORD to his anointed, to Cyrus, whose right hand I have holden, to subdue nations before him; and I will loose the loins of kings, to open before him the two leaved gates; and the gates shall not be shut;*

*Isa 45:4 For Jacob my servant's sake, and Israel mine elect, I have even called thee by thy name: I have surnamed thee, though thou hast not known me.*

*Isa 45:13 I have raised him up in righteousness, and I will direct all his ways:* **he shall build my city***, and he shall let go my captives, not for price nor reward, saith the LORD of hosts.*

God says that: "He (Cyrus) shall build my city". If you believe the Bible, then you must accept that the commandments to rebuild the temple and Jerusalem and the street and the wall were in the original commandment given by Cyrus the Great in 539 BC. Every commandment thereafter was based on this original commandment and there is no reason to prefer the commandment given to Nehemiah based on the slightly more precise wording of the scriptures in that passage. Ezra 4:4 was careful to mention the troublous times that occurred many years earlier. In fact, the troubles mentioned in the book of Ezra are possibly as dire as those mentioned in Nehemiah's book. We conclude then that the commandment in Daniel 9:25 can and must be extended to all four of the commandments that are possibilities for the starting point of the prophecy of 70 weeks.

The second clue is found in the reaction Nehemiah had in learning the wall and structures had not been rebuilt. Nehemiah was well aware that his king, Artaxerxes 1, had commissioned Ezra to go up to Jerusalem and both teach the law and beautify the temple in the 7$^{th}$ year of his reign. So, when his brother and other acquaintances returned to Shushan 13 years later, he was emotionally distraught when they reported the condition of the city and the walls. Here's how it was stated in the scriptures:

*Neh 1:1 The words of Nehemiah the son of Hachaliah. And it came to pass in the month Chisleu, in the twentieth year, as I was in Shushan the palace,*

*2 That Hanani, one of my brethren, came, he and certain men of Judah; and I asked them concerning the Jews that had escaped, which were left of the captivity, and concerning Jerusalem.*

*3 And they said unto me, The remnant that are left of the captivity there in the province are in great affliction and reproach: the wall of Jerusalem also is broken down, and the gates thereof are burned with fire.*

*4 And it came to pass, when I heard these words, that I sat down and wept, and mourned certain days, and fasted, and prayed before the God of heaven,*

It is clear from these verses that Nehemiah's expectation was that the rest of the city would have been rebuilt and repaired by Ezra by that time. He was so upset that he immediately requested permission from the king to go and rectify the situation. Understanding all this, we are ready to dissect verses 24-27 and come to the full truth of the prophecy of 70 weeks. Restating our verses:

*Dan 9:24 Seventy weeks are determined upon thy people and upon thy holy city, to finish the transgression, and to make an end of sins, and to make reconciliation for iniquity, and to bring in everlasting righteousness, and to seal up the vision and prophecy, and to anoint the most Holy.*

As pointed out repeatedly, the 70 weeks of verse 24 are almost universally understood to be weeks of years for a total of 490 years. Six conditions follow that will be the markers for the end of the 490 years. Perhaps the reconciliation for iniquity was made by our Lord on the cross of Calvary, but the other five conditions remain to be fulfilled. So, this four-verse prophecy has never been completely fulfilled. On the other hand, some parts have been fulfilled in stunning detail.

*Dan 9:25 Know therefore and understand, that from the going forth of the commandment to restore and to build Jerusalem unto the Messiah the Prince shall be seven weeks, and threescore and two weeks: the street shall be built again, and the wall, even in troublous times.*

This verse breaks the weeks down into three distinct parts. It is critical to know that God has placed divisions in this prophecy. In verse 27, we will see that the 70th week is further divided into two halves so that there are four total sections to this prophecy. It is the chronological placement of the third section that has caused all the problems with rapture theology.

Verse 25 above deals with the first two sections of the

prophecy. The first is a period of seven weeks or 49 years. It clearly starts with the going forth of the commandment to restore and build Jerusalem, which includes building the street again and the wall in troublous times. The street here probably refers to housing and other structures in orderly rows to provide an easy thoroughfare for all the people to use, as in every city. The wall was built in 52 days under extreme duress because the neighboring Gentiles and Samaritans had threatened to physically stop the construction out of jealousy.

We will show that the 49 years here are to be reckoned from the 7th year of Artaxerxes in 458 BC until 409 BC. Ezra the priest was sent in 458 BC with several tasks. He was sent to be a teaching priest because, since the second temple was completed some 79 years earlier in 516 BC, the people had become careless and had ceased to practice their faith properly. It seems the Persian kings, including Artaxerxes 1, took comfort in the knowledge that godly men were praying for their prosperity and the prosperity of the empire to the God of Israel in the temple in Jerusalem. It was worthwhile to them to spend great resources on that comfort.

In addition, Ezra was sent with the power to levy taxes for needed materials on all the people round about Israel. His taxing power included levies of silver and gold and all things necessary to accomplish his mission.

Finally, we see in Ezra 7:27 that Ezra felt his primary duty was to beautify the temple of God. This is also an indication that rebuilding the city and the wall were implied in Ezra's mission. The city had been reduced to rubble and burned-out structures back in 586 BC, some 128 years ago. Attempts were made to clear it up, but obviously, according to Nehemiah, had not gotten very far.

As a priest, it seems, Ezra concentrated his efforts on the temple.

Perhaps he intended to eventually turn to the rest of the city, since prophetically he had 49 years and access to funding for the task, but it was too frustratingly slow for Nehemiah to put up with. The job required a civil leader and Nehemiah became that man. Even so, it seems that although Nehemiah completed the wall, the houses and structures still remained to be built after he had returned to Shushan. In fact, there were so few people living in the city that Nehemiah had to conscript more to live there.

*Neh 7:4 Now the city was large and great: but the people were few therein, and the houses were not builded.*

*Neh 11:1 And the rulers of the people dwelt at Jerusalem: the rest of the people also cast lots, to bring one of ten to dwell in Jerusalem the holy city, and nine parts to dwell in other cities.*

That was no doubt the major problem all along. There was ample housing outside the city, so nobody wanted to take on the task of cleaning up a lot and building a structure on it.

Having removed the perceived problem of the actual commandment to build the city from the choice of commandments, we find no difficulty in choosing a different commandment than the one given to Nehemiah in the 20th year of Artaxerxes. Using the commandment to Ezra in 458 BC gives us a very clean and elegant timetable for the 70 weeks to match secular history. Here is that commandment:

*Ezr 7:12 Artaxerxes, king of kings, unto Ezra the priest, a scribe of the law of the God of heaven, perfect peace, and at such a time.*

*13 I make a decree, that all they of the people of Israel, and of his priests and Levites, in my realm, which are minded of their own freewill to go up to Jerusalem, go with thee.*

Daniel 9:25 gave us the 49-year period to restore and build Jerusalem and followed that with a 62 week or 434-year period from then until Messiah the Prince. In essence, Daniel was told that his prayer in 539 BC to restore the kingdom to Israel would not be answered until Messiah came 483 years after the commandment to Ezra in 458 BC. 483 years from 458 BC takes us to the year 26 AD. When going from BC to AD one year must be subtracted because there is no zero year. (Thus, 458+26-1=483 years.) Many historians believe 26 AD is the year Jesus started His public ministry. It would be the year when He was baptized by John the Baptist and the Holy Ghost descended upon Him as a dove. He became the anointed one (Messiah) at that point.

Our calendar has been known to be in error regarding the birth year of Jesus Christ for a very long time. At one time the Roman world used the Julian calendar, ordered by Julius Caesar in the first century BC. This calendar still exists today and has helped us keep secular history fairly accurately, at least within a year or two for most events from its era and forward. However, the birth year of Jesus Christ was not recorded in Roman history and has been a source of contention. Most historians hold that Jesus was born somewhere in 4-6 BC. If He was born in 5 BC, as is most often accepted, then He would have turned 30 years old in 26 AD. According to Luke 3:23, Jesus began His public ministry when He was about 30 years old. This matches perfectly with the end of the first 69 weeks of Daniel's prophecy when using the commandment to Ezra in the 7th year of Artaxerxes. So, you can see that even if we moved all our dates up one year as some historians hold, or back one year the result still would have Jesus beginning His ministry 483 years after the commandment.

To this point, every detail of the prophecy given in Daniel 9:25 had been fulfilled perfectly on time. But this creates a problem for most prophecy teachers. They need to leap ahead in time to allow seven years starting with a covenant the Antichrist makes with the Jews. The crucifixion is the event that causes God to break the conditional Mosaic Covenant of the Law with Israel. Thus, they need the 483 years to end at that point so that a full seven years remain to the end of the prophecy. The commandment to Ezra only takes the 483 years to the beginning of Christ's 3.5 years of ministry with no reason to stop counting. In fact, the count does continue for another 3.5 years up until the crucifixion of our Lord. Thus, we will find 69 ½ weeks of years until the crucifixion of Christ.

*Dan 9:26 And after threescore and two weeks shall Messiah be cut off, but not for himself: and the people of the prince that shall come shall destroy the city and the sanctuary; and the end thereof shall be with a flood, and unto the end of the war desolations are determined.*

Messiah, according to Dan. 9:26, was to be cut off after the 62 weeks of years. Since the 62 weeks follow the first 7 weeks, we find Messiah being cut off after a total of 69 weeks or 483 years. On its surface, this phrase seems to support the majority of prophecy teachers. We've got 7 years remaining when Messiah is cut off or crucified. However, a careful reader would note that it does not say Messiah would be cut off concurrently with the end of the 69th week. It specifically says after 69 weeks. This would allow Messiah to be cut off one second after, or 100 years after, the 69 weeks with equal accuracy. In fact, He was cut off 3.5 years after the 69 weeks concluded. The 69 weeks are the marker for the start of His ministry as Messiah.

So, we have the answer to Daniel's prayer in stages. The commandment went out to restore and build Jerusalem in 458 BC. The city and the walls were completed 7 weeks later by 409 BC and then Messiah began His ministry 62 weeks after that in 26 AD. Finally, we find Messiah Jesus cut off (but not for Himself) 3.5 years after that in 30 AD. All these occurred consecutively and right on time as required in Daniel's vision. It was this point that the prophecy was paused for reasons I will develop within this chapter.

Messiah was cut off, but not for Himself. Messiah, Jesus, had to become the Lamb of God that taketh away the sins of the world. If Jesus had not been crucified, God's plan of redemption would have ended in failure. God had predetermined that without shedding of blood there could be no remission of sins (Heb. 9:22). Man's problem was that he had to shed his own blood for each sin he committed. However, with only one life, he could only atone for his first sin and would be remanded to hell for each, and every sin committed thereafter. As you can see this makes paying for our own sins impossible. Only the sinless and perfect blood of the God/Man has the power to atone for all the sins of mankind for all time, past present and future. By substituting His shed blood for ours we can find atonement for all our sins. The path to eternal life goes through Jesus Christ and Him alone. If we are willing to repent, that is turn from living to please ourselves to living to please our Savior, Jesus Christ, He will accept us into His kingdom and become our King of kings. The only alternative for us is eternity in hell.

### The Current Christian myth of The Antichrist

The second clause in this verse states:

*"and the people of the prince that shall come shall destroy the city and the sanctuary;"*

This prince that shall come has been commonly mis-identified as a character called Antichrist. The entire Antichrist character, as portrayed by most prophecy teachers, can be viewed as pure Christian mythology. He is a figment of John Nelson Darby's prolific imagination.

Christians have long known the truth about antichrists, but 'The Antichrist' as he is taught today is an invention popularized by John Nelson Darby (1800-1892).

This iteration of Antichrist was occasionally taught in the past, but it was normally acknowledged that there were many antichrists and further it was frequently taught that the Antichrist was whoever happened to be the pope at the time. Also, Christian scholars who embraced the Septuagint (see explanation below) tended to accept the pre-trib antichrist without the understanding of the rapture. But the Darby version so caught the imagination of the Church that he became for many 'the one and only'.

Darby began teaching the hitherto almost unknown doctrines of dispensationalism and the pre-tribulation rapture in the 1800's. Although he got the basic doctrines right, he failed on many others. Darby abandoned the true scriptures found in the KJV and translated his own version of the bible. His version allowed him, as we shall soon see, to produce The Antichrist as well as the fatally flawed doctrine of imminence that we discussed in chapter 2. I must stress most forcefully here; THESE LAST TWO DOCTRINES ARE NOT FOUND IN THE KING JAMES VERSION OF 1611. It is a mystery to me how good churchmen of that era were able to accept doctrines mostly found only in Darby's scriptures. Later, of course, they were incorporated into the modern versions spawned by the two heretics (or Satanists), Westcott and Hort.

By definition, Darby's Antichrist is a man who appears at the beginning of the seven-year tribulation. He is a worldwide hero who has the political authority and clout to make a firm seven-year peace treaty or covenant with Israel. He then breaks that covenant 3.5 years later at mid-trib and pronounces himself equal to or greater than JEHOVAH God. Thus, the Jews and all the world must abandon JEHOVAH and worship him or die. Then, at mid-trib he becomes the beast of Revelation chapter 13.

The term antichrist is mentioned five times in the first two of the Apostle John's three short epistles, and nowhere else in the Bible. In none of these cases is he identified as a single individual who will come at the start of the tribulation and make a seven-year covenant with the nation of Israel. Here are the verses in question:

*1Jn 2:18 Little children, it is the last time: and as ye have heard that antichrist shall come, even now are there many antichrists; whereby we know that it is the last time.*

*1Jn 2:22 Who is a liar but he that denieth that Jesus is the Christ? He is antichrist, that denieth the Father and the Son.*

*1Jn 4:3 And every spirit that confesseth not that Jesus Christ is come in the flesh is not of God: and this is that spirit of antichrist, whereof ye have heard that it should come; and even now already is it in the world.*

*2Jn 1:7 For many deceivers are entered into the world, who confess not that Jesus Christ is come in the flesh. This is a deceiver and an antichrist.*

That's it, folks. These are the only times the term is mentioned in scripture. Let's look at several things we can determine from these verses.

- First, please note that the term is never capitalized as it would be if it were a proper name of an individual.
- Second, in 1 Jn 4:3 he is a spirit who can be positively identified if he won't confess that Jesus Christ is come in the flesh. In fact, we see that multiple spirits can be called the spirit of antichrist if they will not make this confession.
- Third, according to verses 2:18 and 4:3 of 1 John, the spirit was already in the world when John penned these letters.
- Fourth, the "last time" had already started by the time John penned these letters around 100 AD.
- Fifth, from verse 2:18 we see antichrist had been prophesied and the prophecy had already come to

pass by the time John wrote his first epistle within the first century AD.
- Sixth, according to 2Jn 1:7, many deceivers were already in the world that were antichrists.
- Seventh, nowhere in these verses can antichrist be confined to a single individual who appears at the beginning of the seven-year tribulation.

We will see in a later chapter that these antichrists all seem to be obsessed with destroying the plan of God, especially in regard to His people. Thus, many Caesars, and many popes, and men like Grand Inquisitor Tomas de Torquemada, and Mao Zedong, and Hitler, and Stalin, and Lenin, and the last king of the north, the last king of the south, and Gog from Magog, are all antichrists. They may not deny that Jesus Christ is come in the flesh in so many words, but their disregard for His followers indicates they don't confess His blood-bought authority over the affairs of this world. Those last three will all be present when the day of the LORD starts, but one antichrist that won't be there is "The Antichrist" of most premillennialists. There will not be an antichrist that makes a seven-year covenant with Israel at the start of the tribulation which he will break at mid-trib. Incredibly, of all the antichrists that will be present, the only one the rapturists, that is premillennialists, want to talk about is one that is pure Christian mythology.

It seems that all the understanding of antichrists down through the ages was abandoned by many modern churchmen when they were introduced to "The Antichrist". In my opinion, Darby's lone, phony Antichrist has been preached about and written about and talked about more than any being, other than the deity Himself.

Such is the current fascination with this Antichrist, that this point of doctrine is more likely to make the reader fling this book down in disgust than any other doctrinal point mentioned in this tome.

Many scriptures are pointed to that they claim speak of this Antichrist. In fact, almost every one of those scriptures points to the most important actual antichrist in the Bible, also known as the Beast of Revelation chapter 13. This antichrist does not come on the scene until the end of the 1260-day ministry of the two witnesses of Revelation chapter 11. As pointed out in an earlier chapter, I believe that the final king of the north will die about 7 months into the tribulation and rise from the bottomless pit to become the final Beast at mid-trib, but he will not make any 7-year treaty with Israel, and he is not the character so many scriptures point to until he becomes the Beast. By applying those passages to a pre-trib antichrist much confusion is created for an otherwise much more straightforward eschatology.

**Titus, prince of Rome**

Returning to our clause under discussion:

*"and the people of the prince that shall come shall destroy the city and the sanctuary;"*

Prior to Darby, some very prominent commentators taught that this "prince that shall come" was "Messiah the Prince". However, it should be noted that the term "prince" is not capitalized here as opposed to the term "Messiah the Prince" in Dan. 9:25. To be consistent, if the term is capitalized when it refers to Messiah in one verse, then it should be capitalized for each usage in the passage. This may be insignificant for those who don't believe that God preserved His words perfectly in the KJV, but it should be quite meaningful to those who know this to be true. Also, Messiah never committed the acts ascribed to this prince so we can safely assume that the prince is not a reference to Messiah.

So, if the prince is not Messiah and he is not Antichrist, then who is he? This is so simple it amazes me that anyone could miss it. It is only by a feat of mental gymnastics that prophecy teachers manage to not see the simple truth. Here is the answer.

In 70 AD Titus, the son of the emperor Vespasian and thus prince of Rome, sacked Jerusalem and burned down the temple. This is one of the most well-known events in the history of the Jews and Jerusalem since the crucifixion of Christ. When they finally breached the city walls, the armies of Rome poured into the city killing as many as 1.1 million people according to the historian Josephus who was there at that time. The temple was burned along with the city. The soldiers noticed as the temple was burning that the gold that lined the walls was running down and filling the gaps between the stones of the outer wall. So, they came back when it cooled down and removed every stone of the walls down to the ground to recover the gold. This was the fulfillment of a prophecy of Jesus:

*Mar 13:2 And Jesus answering said unto him, Seest thou these great buildings? there shall not be left one stone upon another, that shall not be thrown down.*

There is a story that Titus refused to accept a wreath of victory, claiming he had not won the victory on his own, but had been the vehicle through which the God of the Jews manifested His wrath against His people. This will be seen as very prescient or an outright understanding of the prophecy in the next verse.

It is manifestly obvious that the clause *"and the people of the prince that shall come shall destroy the city and the sanctuary;"* was completely fulfilled by Titus, and that he is the "prince" spoken of in this prophecy. There is no reason then, to proclaim this "prince" as the mythical Antichrist. Moving to the final clause of verse 26, we read:

*"and the end thereof shall be with a flood, and unto the end of the war desolations are determined."*

The word "thereof" refers back to the city and the sanctuary of the previous clause. It is said to end with a flood which is a reference to the armies of Rome flooding into the city. There is precedence for invading armies being referred to as a flood in the scriptures (see Isa 59:19 and Jer. 46:8 for examples) so it is not unusual to use this terminology.

The clause also states that "unto the end of the war desolations are determined". In the years both before and after Jerusalem was destroyed, militant Jews waged a constant guerilla warfare on Rome. Small bands would attack their armies, cause great damage, and then flee. By the year 135 AD, Rome had enough. She had crushed another revolt and was determined not to have any more. All Jews were forbidden to enter Jerusalem and the Jews in Israel were marched out and placed in many cities in Europe, Asia, and Africa. The desolation of Israel was determined at the end of the war just as Daniel prophesied in this verse.

**Punctuation has a purpose in scriptures**

To this point then, every prophecy of verses 25 and 26 in Daniel 9 had been completely fulfilled in detail. There was and is no need to assign these prophecies to events yet future, or those now occurring in our times. Continuing to the final verse of the prophecy, we read:

*Dan 9:27 And he shall confirm the covenant with many for one week: and in the midst of the week he shall cause the sacrifice and the oblation to cease, and for the overspreading of abominations he shall make it desolate, even until the consummation, and that determined shall be poured upon the desolate.*

We must also take this verse apart and comment on a phrase or clause at a time. So:

*"And he shall confirm the covenant with many for one week:"*

This is the crux of the whole misinterpretation of this prophecy. We are now discussing the 70th week of the prophecy of 70 weeks. For most rapture adherents, the pronoun "he" in this clause refers back to the "prince" of the previous verse. Thus, the prince will confirm the covenant with many for one week of years or 7 years. It is necessary then to have a full week remaining if the prince is to be Antichrist who appears at the beginning of the 7-year tribulation. And indeed, the rules of English grammar often seem to back them up in modern translations. In many modern versions of scriptures, this conclusion is almost unavoidable. However, in the King James Bible that is not the case. Since we are showing how precisely the prophecy has been fulfilled to this point, we must now present the reason that the KJB provides the correct answer for the antecedent of the pronoun "he".

There are two possibilities for the antecedent noun to which the pronoun "he" may be tied. They are Messiah and the "prince". To review, we already know the "prince" here refers to Titus, prince of Rome in 70 AD. We also know **Titus never confirmed a covenant with the many of Israel.** So, historically, the "prince" is out of the running as the correct antecedent for "he", leaving only Messiah. Interestingly, the grammar of the KJB backs this up. So, let's put this together:

*Dan 9:26 And after threescore and two weeks shall Messiah be cut off, but not for himself: and the people of the prince that shall come shall destroy the city and the sanctuary; and the end thereof shall be with a flood, and unto the end of the war desolations are determined.*

*27 And he shall confirm the covenant with many for one week:*

Notice that the clause "And after threescore and two weeks shall Messiah be cut off, but not for himself:" ends with a colon. Here is why that matters.

This verse is one sentence with three clauses. The first clause establishes that Messiah is the subject of the sentence. That clause is followed by a colon. According to Richard Hughes, in his book *"An English Grammar for the Study of Scripture"*:

"The colon (:) has one primary use in scriptures: it separates independent clauses where the second clause helps explain the first clause."

Verse 26 is a compound sentence. Rapture teachers have treated the second clause as if it were not related to the first clause whereas its whole purpose is to add information about the first clause. Here, Messiah was cut off (crucified) and **because of that sin**, the city and the sanctuary were destroyed by the people of the prince. Thus, we see that although the second clause has its own subject, "the people", the overarching subject of the sentence is still "Messiah". The only purpose of the prepositional phrase "of the prince that shall come" is so we will recognize the people when they come. No new doctrinal ground is meant to be opened with the mention of this prince.

Now a colon could be replaced by a phrase such as "Oh, and by the way…" It is extra information that goes strictly with the preceding clause. Everything after the colon and within that sentence could be removed without affecting the flow or the overall integrity of the narrative. A writer today might be more inclined to use parenthesis. We will see that punctuation determines the proper reading of a sentence.

Richard Hughes writes:

"The comma, the semicolon and colon are used within a sentence to separate various elements of the sentence. They help to identify clauses and phrases and **to avoid confusion within the sentence**."

In the case I have shown, the colon is used to clear up the confusion as to whether the correct antecedent for the pronoun, "he", in verse 27 is the prince or Messiah. The colon tells us the prince is incidental to the narrative and in the next sentence we are still speaking of Messiah and not the prince. Thus, it says Messiah will confirm the covenant with many for one week.

Now let's look at the punctuation of a couple other versions. These changes were made by men *"Who changed the truth of God into a lie, and worshipped and served the creature more than the Creator, who is blessed for ever. Amen."* (Rom. 1:25)

### *Daniel 9: 26-27 New American Standard Bible (NASB)*

*26 Then after the sixty-two weeks the Messiah will be cut off and have nothing, and the people of the prince who is to come will destroy the city and the sanctuary. And its end will come with a flood; even to the end there will be war; desolations are determined.*

*27 And he will make a firm covenant with the many for one week, but in the middle of the week he will put a stop to sacrifice and grain offering; and on the wing of abominations will come one who makes desolate, even until a complete destruction, one that is decreed, is poured out on the one who makes desolate."*

In the NASB, verse 26 has been broken down into two sentences. The first sentence has a comma where the KJV used the colon. So how does this change the meaning? Referring back to Richard Hughes, we read:

...The primary purposes of the comma within the sentence: to separate introductory and closing elements and to set off internal elements."

Although the comma has many uses in English grammar,

the above is the primary usage and it applies here. The comma makes the phrase "and the people of the prince who is to come..." an equal element in the sentence. Thus, the grammatical rule that generally requires a personal pronoun to use the nearest applicable noun as its antecedent, favors the prince as the noun referenced by the pronoun "he". In this sentence structure, there is no reason not to believe the prince is the one who will confirm the covenant with many for one week. But this does not make sense if you understand that, historically, the prince was Titus, and he made no such covenant. Moving to the next version, we see:

### Daniel 9:26-27 Darby Translation

*26 And after the sixty-two weeks shall Messiah be cut off, and shall have nothing; and the people of the prince that shall come shall destroy the city and the sanctuary; and the end thereof shall be with an overflow, and unto the end, war,—the desolations determined.*

*27 And he shall confirm a covenant with the many [for] one week; and in the midst of the week he shall cause the sacrifice and the oblation to cease, and because of the protection of abominations [there shall be] a desolator, even until that the consumption and what is determined shall be poured out upon the desolate.*

Hmm...Now who might that there desolator be? And pray tell, in what manuscript did you find justification for him, Mr. Darby?

This version is John Nelson Darby's translation of the scriptures. Darby is the father of the modern pre-trib rapture movement. It was his writing and teaching back in the 1800's that caught people's fancy and made them aware that there was such a thing as a pre-trib rapture. Many pre-trib adherents have challenged some of the things he taught and have tried to distance themselves from him, but most have accepted his assertion that the prince is the correct antecedent for the pronoun "he" and further, that the prince is indeed Darby's Antichrist.

Darby apparently had enough problems with the KJV that he felt compelled to produce his own personal translation of the Bible. As galling as it sounds, he must have considered himself intellectually and spiritually superior to the translators of the KJV who worked under the guidance of the Holy Ghost. In the case of these verses though, he **needed** a different translation to prove his point.

Darby inserted a semicolon where the KJV inserted a colon. Hughes gives four main usages for the semicolon in scriptures. He spends some time indicating that semicolons are commonly used to indicate a parallelism. In this case all three clauses start with the conjunction "and". By using a semicolon, they exhibit a parallelism which means they are equal in value or weightiness. Again, the correct antecedent would be the prince.

Now let's look at a final punctuation possibility.

### Daniel 9:26-27 New International Version (NIV)
*26 After the sixty-two 'sevens,' the Anointed One will be put to death and will have nothing. The people of the ruler who will come will destroy the city and the sanctuary. The end will come like a flood: War will continue until the end, and desolations have been decreed.*

*27He will confirm a covenant with many for one 'seven.' In the middle of the 'seven' he will put an end to sacrifice and offering. And at the temple he will set up an abomination that causes desolation, until the end that is decreed is poured out on him.'*

The NIV pulls out all the stops and simply places a period where the colon is found in the KJV. This really simplifies the problem. The "Anointed One" is now too far removed from the pronoun to be under any consideration as a possible antecedent for "he". At this point (in the NIV) it would be necessary to restate the noun Messiah in order to make Him the one who carries out the actions that follow.

Modern translations have done so much harm to the doctrines of the Church that it is no wonder our Lord mused rhetorically:

*Luk 18:8 ...Nevertheless when the Son of man cometh, shall he find faith on the earth?*

So, some of the most popular modern versions change the colon to either a semicolon or a comma or a period. In each case the prince becomes the choice for the subject of the following verse. This may be at least one reason that there isn't a general acknowledgement that the prince of this passage was clearly Titus, prince of Rome. Titus and his Roman army fulfilled every detail of that part of this prophecy and yet prophecy teachers rarely give proper consideration to him. They cherish the idea of Antichrist so dearly that even the KJV-only people allow the modern versions to rule the day on this passage. As we look at the next major point, consider this verse:

*1Co 14:33 For God is not the author of confusion, but of peace, as in all churches of the saints.*

**Comparing Darby to pre-Darby KJV commentators**

It is important to realize that much of what we understand today as 'modern premillennialists' comes directly from John Nelson Darby's teachings on Daniel 9:24-27. Darby taught:

1. the "prince that shall come" is 'The Antichrist'.

2. The antecedent for the pronoun "he" at the start of verse number 27 is the "prince", so The Antichrist is the subject of the clause and the verse.

3. The Antichrist will confirm a covenant with Israel for one week of seven years.

4. The Antichrist will break his covenant with Israel in the midst of the week, or after 3 ½ years.

5. The Antichrist will commit the 'Abomination of Desolation" at that time and persecute and murder Jews and saved people for the final 3 ½ years.


So, what about commentators before Darby's time?

We will look at four KJV commentators that are still widely read and quoted today. In general, these men had difficulty with the 70 weeks, and some believed they should be tied to the original decree of Cyrus. Some admitted that much of this prophecy was difficult to understand, although they conceded that it was an important prophecy.


**Matthew Henry (1662 – 1714)**

Wrote *"Exposition of the Old and New Testaments"* completed 1708 -1710. Non-Conformist minister outside of the Church of England.

1. Antichrist is the Papacy.

2. Christ is the "prince" but Titus and the Roman armies are His agents.

3. "he" is therefore Christ.

### John Gill (1697 – 1771)

Wrote *"Exposition of the Old Testament"* completed in 1763.

Calvinistic Baptist.

1. the prince is the Emperor Vespasian and his son Titus

2. The people are the Romans.

3. "he" in verse 27 refers to the Romans who caused the sacrifice and oblation to cease when they sacked Jerusalem and destroyed the temple in 70 AD.

### John Wesley (1703- 1791)

Wrote *"Explanatory Notes Upon the Old Testament"* completed in 1765. Founder of the Wesleyan movement.

1. The "prince" is Titus in 70 AD.

2. "he" in verse 27 is Christ.

3. The covenant He confirmed was the 'New Covenant' found in Jer. 31:31 and three verses in Hebrews.

### Adam Clarke (1760 – 1832)

Wrote *"The Adam Clarke Commentary"* over the course of 40 years. Six volumes of over 1000 pages each. Considered the most comprehensive commentary on the

Bible ever prepared by one man.

British Methodist theologian.

1. Antichrist is the Catholic Church.

2. The "prince" is Titus.

3. "The people" are the Romans.

4. No commentary on "he".

So, we see that not one of the five key points noted above in Darby's doctrine is verified or supported by the four earlier, and widely acclaimed, theologians we looked at here. Darby gave us two hitherto unrecognized doctrines in dispensationalism and the pre-trib rapture, but in his pride of life he botched much of the truths that those doctrines had to offer. Sadly, modern theologians were so influenced by Westcott and Hort's twisted scriptures that they couldn't see the errors in his overall theology.

Although our passage in Daniel provides rapture teachers with the most important information about their Antichrist, they find him abundantly referenced throughout the scriptures. That theology has commandeered many otherwise valuable passages and rendered them something different than what God intended. One of the most frequently referenced passages is:

*2Th 2:3 Let no man deceive you by any means: for that day shall not come, except there come a falling away first, and that man of sin be revealed, the son of perdition;*

*4 Who opposeth and exalteth himself above all that is called God, or that is worshipped; so that he as God sitteth in the temple of God, shewing himself that he is God.*

*5 Remember ye not, that, when I was yet with you, I told you these things?*

*6 And now ye know what withholdeth that he might be revealed in his time.*

*7 For the mystery of iniquity doth already work: only he who now letteth will let, until he be taken out of the way.*

*8 And then shall that Wicked be revealed, whom the Lord shall consume with the spirit of his mouth, and shall destroy with the brightness of his coming:*

*9 Even him, whose coming is after the working of Satan with all power and signs and lying wonders,*

*10 And with all deceivableness of unrighteousness in them that perish; because they received not the love of the truth, that they might be saved.*

We will deal with this passage more fully in later chapters but mention it here because the "man of sin" has become Darby's Antichrist for such a large portion of the Church.

Historically, "he who now letteth" was considered so obviously to be the Roman Empire that anybody who differed in opinion strained credulity. Likewise, the "man of sin" was obviously the Roman pope whose power became indisputable for more than a millennium thereafter.

In fact, even some expositors that wrote well before this time imagined or predicted just such a scenario. In this number were Tertullian (circa 200 AD), Cyril of Jerusalem (circa 300 AD), and Jerome (circa 400 AD).

Commentators who insisted on this interpretation after the advancement of papal powers included, The Treatise on Antichrist (by the Waldensians in 1120 AD), Eberhard II (Catholic 1240 AD), John Wycliffe (1320's- 1384), John Huss (1371- 1415), Martin Luther (1483- 1586), and John Calvin (1509- 1564). Also, it is found in the commentaries of the above-mentioned John Gill and Matthew Henry along with such luminaries as Matthew Poole (1624- 1679) and Jonathan Edwards (1703- 1758).

None of these great churchmen connected this passage to Daniel 9:26-27 in the form of Darby's Antichrist. Now, let's look at why this latter-day interpretation became so popular.

## Daniel 9:27 in modern versions heavily influenced by the Septuagint

If you have examined verse 27, going back to the modern versions I presented earlier, you will note how different they are from the KJV and how much support they lend to the argument for the prince being the correct antecedent for "he", and, indirectly, for the prince being Antichrist. To understand what is going on here, you need to know about the manuscripts available for translating the Old Testament. There are two manuscripts of note. One is called the Masoretic text and the other is called the Septuagint, or alternatively the LXX. The Masoretic text is a recreation of the original language Hebrew text whereas the Septuagint is a translation from Hebrew into Greek.

Although many scholars claim the Septuagint preceded Christ by hundreds of years and further that Christ quoted some passages from it, it is simply not true. It turns out that the extant Septuagint manuscripts that existed before Christ are comprised of a few verses or a few chapters here and there that were translated into Greek. There is nothing unusual about that other than the fact there are so pitifully few of them. You see, Greek was the most widely spoken language of the day and was considered the language of the intellectuals. It was also widely spoken in

Northern Africa where the great library at Alexandria, Egypt was the most prestigious learning center in the known world. This was the world of Christian scholar, Origen Adamantius.

The first known full copy of the Septuagint appeared in a manuscript called the Hexapla. It contained 6 different versions of the Old Testament listed side by side for study purposes. It was produced by one of the most respected Christian scholars of the day, the above-mentioned Origen Adamantius before 240 AD.

**The Letter of Aristaeus**

The Hexapla was preceded by a letter called "The Letter of Aristaeus". Copies of this letter were widely circulated and determined by the scholarship of the day to be a fraud. Scholars of our present day also consider it to be a fraud and yet, oddly, the story it tells is accepted as fact.

This letter contained a story about a Greek translation of the Hebrew Bible in which 6 scholars out of each of the twelve tribes of Israel were brought together and translated the scriptures into the Greek language in the 3rd and 2nd centuries BC. Somehow, for all the great scholarship, 6 times 12 turned out to be 70. Thus, the LXX.

Despite all the stories, there is no real evidence that the Hexapla did not contain the first copy ever of the Greek Septuagint. It could well be the work of Origen himself who then used the phony Letter of Aristaeus to lend credibility to his work. The Septuagint was careful to reproduce Old Testament quotes by Jesus precisely as Jesus stated them, whereas some of His quotes were merely close approximations of the Masoretic text. This was pointed to as proof of its authenticity as well as proof it was the text Christ preferred. Few people seemed concerned that it would be easy to make the quotes match the quotes of Jesus if the text were produced long after His death. So, there is plenty of reason to doubt the authenticity of the Septuagint and yet many liberal scholars embrace it wholeheartedly.

The Masoretic text, on the other hand, is the one that most closely matches the KJV Old Testament translation. It is the one believed to be the closest to the original Hebrew text. Now we will present the verses in question in the Masoretic text (that is the KJV text in English) and the Septuagint for your convenience. We will use the Brenton English translation of the Septuagint. If you want to study this further on your own bear these facts in mind.

Upon examination, verse 27 of our Daniel 9 prophecy is wildly different than the KJV in many or most modern versions and the Septuagint.

| Daniel 9:26-27 | Daniel 9:26-27 |
|---|---|
| Masoretic (Hebrew) text | Septuagint (Greek) Text |
| KJV English translation | Brenton English translation |
| *Dan 9:26 And after threescore and two weeks shall Messiah be cut off, but not for himself: and the people of the prince that shall come shall destroy the city and the sanctuary; and the end thereof shall be with a flood, and unto the end of the war desolations are determined.* | *Dan 9:26 And after the sixty-two weeks, the anointed one shall be destroyed, and there is no judgment in him: and he shall destroy the city and the sanctuary with the prince that is coming: they shall be cut off with a flood, and to the end of the war which is rapidly completed he shall* |

| | |
|---|---|
| *27 And he shall confirm the covenant with many for one week: and in the midst of the week he shall cause the sacrifice and the oblation to cease, and for the overspreading of abominations he shall make it desolate, even until the consummation, and that determined shall be poured upon the desolate.* | *appoint the city to desolations.*<br><br>*27 And one week shall establish the covenant with many: and in the midst of the week my sacrifice and drink-offering shall be taken away: and on the temple shall be the abomination of desolations; and at the end of time an end shall be put to the desolation.* |

Note in Brenton's verse 27 above that the overspreading of abominations is changed to the abomination of desolations. Now, since there is an abomination of desolation in the middle of the tribulation (Matt. 24:15 and 2 Thes.2:3-4), the entire 70th week of the prophecy in this version needs to be moved to include the entire tribulation and the reading here requires this. Now compare this back to the above versions and you can see that although parts of their translation contain readings from the Masoretic text, they tend to move to the Septuagint for this verse. This could be termed 'cafeteria translating'. Just pick the one that fits your doctrine best. These translators are fitting the scriptures to their doctrine rather than matching their doctrine to the scriptures.

So, to conclude this discussion, we find that **Darby's Antichrist argument requires the very questionable Septuagint reading to make it work.** It is not an argument that ever was in the past, nor indeed truly can be now, successfully proven using only the Masoretic text of the KJV.

**Clearing up a final point of Antichrist confusion**

Although we have seen that the KJV text of Daniel 9:26-27 allows no room for Darby's Antichrist interpretation, modern rapturists imagine they have rescued him by creating an amalgamated antichrist to give this Darby Antichrist more credibility. This amalgamated antichrist combines Darby's Antichrist with up to three separate, but related characters into one antichrist. These three are: the little horn of Daniel 7, the little horn of Daniel 8 who is also the king of the north found in Daniel 11:29-39, and the final king of the north in Daniel 11:40-45. Often thrown in with these three are any mentions of the 666 Beast of Revelation 13 as well as almost every other unsavory character mentioned in the Bible as being Antichrist in typology. Thus, confusion reigns when trying to establish any kind of credible timeline for character appearances and their separate and distinct activities.

Before, and for a while after Darby, many KJV expositors did not find Darby's Antichrist in our passage. But eventually many/most reverse-engineered him into the passage. They bought a ticket on this bandwagon by essentially downplaying Titus, prince of Rome, and calling the prince of the passage Antichrist. So enamored were they with this character, they just had to have him. It amazes me how readily and eagerly they turned the truth of God into a lie despite an obviously better alternative. Some present- day rapture preachers and teachers seem totally unaware of the better alternative.

## The real truths about translations

Now I will give you some important facts about translations. In the KJV we read:

*Psa 12:6 The words of the LORD are pure words: as silver tried in a furnace of earth, purified seven times.*

*7 Thou shalt keep them, O LORD, thou shalt preserve them from this generation for ever.*

The LORD has tasked Himself alone with the preservation of His very words. God cannot do anything that is less than perfect. So, somewhere out there is a perfect Bible that absolutely cannot be improved upon. God promoted the British Empire to one on which the sun never set. He then promoted the English language to the one most widely spoken of all time. Finally, God gave us the seventh and final iteration of His perfect and completed word just as the world population began its most explosive growth period starting in the early 1600's and continuing. That is the King James Bible of 1611, translated from Greek and Hebrew to the Gothic and then the Anglo-Saxon languages, followed by several iterations through the still developing English language until finally reaching its seventh and final form in Modern English in the Authorized Version of 1611. I believe the LORD God made English the most widely spoken language in the world for this express purpose. So...

- Biblical Hebrew became a dead language sometime after 135 AD.
- Biblical (Koine) Greek became a dead language sometime not long after the scriptures were

completed.
- Hebrew-English dictionaries are educated guesses taken from a reconstructed dead language, centuries after it ceased to be used. They are not perfect or always reliable.
- Greek-English dictionaries are educated guesses taken from a reconstructed dead language, centuries after it ceased to be used. They are not perfect or always reliable.
- THERE ARE NO ORIGINAL MANUSCRIPTS!!! If your preacher takes you back to the original Greek text for a better understanding, to be honest he would have to take you back to a pile of dust somewhere. Nobody alive has ever seen an original manuscript or a guaranteed exact copy of one and nobody alive has ever consulted with an original Koine Greek or an original Hebrew speaker to authenticate word or idiom meanings.
- All current Bible versions are translated from manuscripts that were copies of copies of copies, sometimes including editing by the copier as evidenced by some having thousands of discrepancies with others.
- Unless the translators or copiers were influenced by the Holy Ghost to get the wording right, the translation they produced was the work of fallen, fallible, unreliable mankind.
- If the Holy Ghost is involved, the words will be precisely what God intended them to be.
- If the Holy Ghost is not involved in any translation, our religion is vain. Our religion is then based on the works of men, or Satan.

- The King James Bible is the only translation without provable error within its passages. Note: many detractors have charged the KJV with contradictions, but they always turn out to demonstrate a lack of insight or even knowledge by the accuser. Sometimes they are outright frivolous.

Here is how the NIV people translated the Psalm 12:6-7 passage:

6 And the words of the LORD are flawless, like silver purified in a crucible, like gold refined seven times.
7 You, LORD, will keep the needy safe and will protect us forever from the wicked,

No preservation by God there! In fact, doctrinally, verse 7 contains two LIES!

Translators cannot preserve the words of God unless they are under the guidance of the Holy Ghost. Since all English translations are different and, as you can see above, can be wildly different, there can be only one translation that the LORD himself has preserved forever. Although, I am not dealing exhaustively with that issue in this work, I am writing this from the earnest belief that the translation that the LORD Himself has preserved for us in the English language is the King James Bible.

Going further in the above discussion is really outside the scope of this work, but readers should be aware of some of these facts in order to recognize that many (all) modern version translations are utterly unreliable. Consider the words of Christ Jesus on this subject:

*Mat 5:18 For verily I say unto you, Till heaven and earth pass, one jot or one tittle shall in no wise pass from the law, till all be fulfilled.*

A jot is often described as equal to the dotting of an i and a tittle to the crossing of a t!

### The Davidic Covenant *confirmed* by Messiah

Now, back to our final verse - in the King James Bible:

*Dan 9:27 And he shall confirm the covenant with many for one week: and in the midst of the week he shall cause the sacrifice and the oblation to cease, and for the overspreading of abominations he shall make it desolate, even until the consummation, and that determined shall be poured upon the desolate.*

*"And he shall confirm the covenant with many for one week:"*

The glory of the Lord in this passage has been utterly denied by most rapturists. It is a powerful confirmation of an important part of the coming of Messiah. He confirmed a covenant that was desperate for confirmation. So, let's look at this covenant more closely.

Daniel 9 opens with Daniel's prayer for the restoration of the sanctuary and the city (of Jerusalem) and for Judah and for all the people of Israel. He had read in the scriptures that the captivity was foretold by Moses because of the sins of the nation. Further, he realized from the book of Jeremiah that the captivity should soon be over. So, his prayer is for the restoration of the kingdom of Israel. This kingdom would necessarily include religious Israel with the temple and with the priestly orders, and civil Israel with a Davidic king on the throne in Jerusalem.

The angel Gabriel told Daniel that the city and the wall would be rebuilt within seven weeks of years from the going forth of the commandment (v.25), but that it would be an additional sixty-two weeks of years until Messiah the Prince. So, the kingdom would exist without a legitimate king for at least 483 years following the decree. Now Daniel and all Jews were well aware that God had promised to David:

*2Sa 7:16 And thine house and thy kingdom shall be established for ever before thee: thy throne shall be established for ever.*

This Davidic Covenant is powerfully stated in Psalm 89:19-37. Yet, it seemed as if God had broken this covenant with David because there was no king on his throne and would not be until Messiah the Prince. Thus, when Jesus came as Messiah, He *confirmed* that the covenant was still in force.

It was this Davidic Covenant that the scriptures have so forcefully and voluminously claimed to be fulfilled in the birth of the King. The very first verse of the New Testament assures us that Jesus was the son of David:

*Mat 1:1 The book of the generation of Jesus Christ, the son of David, the son of Abraham.*

His mother's line was traced back through David in Luke 3. His stepfather's line was traced back through David in Matthew 1. He said He was the King of the Jews. Pilate wrote over his cross "THIS IS JESUS THE KING OF THE JEWS". Most of our Christmas hymns refer to Him as the King at some point in their lyrics. There is no doubt that Jesus confirmed the Davidic Covenant.

The anecdotal proofs that this passage refers to the Davidic Covenant are wide ranging and compelling. However, Gabriel, the same angel that spoke to Daniel, appeared to Mary, the mother of Jesus, about 534 years later and specifically confirmed that this covenant would become effective in the life of her Son Jesus:

*Luk 1:31 And, behold, thou shalt conceive in thy womb, and bring forth a son, and shalt call his name JESUS. 32 He shall be great, and shall be called the Son of the Highest:* **and the Lord God shall give unto him the throne of his father David:**
**33 And he shall reign over the house of Jacob for ever; and of his kingdom there shall be no end.**

This very confirmation was powerfully and marvelously prophesied by Isaiah 700 years earlier in the passage below. In fact, this passage assures us that Jesus is also the mighty God and the everlasting Father. WOW! Huh?

*Isa 9:6 For unto us a child is born, unto us a son is given: and the government shall be upon his shoulder: and his name shall be called Wonderful, Counsellor, The mighty God, The everlasting Father, The Prince of Peace.*
*7 Of the increase of his government and peace there shall*

*be no end, **upon the throne of David**, and upon his kingdom, to order it, and to establish it with judgment and with justice **from henceforth even for ever**. The zeal of the LORD of hosts will perform this.*

The prophet Jeremiah also had this to say on the importance of this covenant to God Almighty:

*Jer 33:19 And the word of the LORD came unto Jeremiah, saying,*

*20 Thus saith the LORD; If ye can break my covenant of the day, and my covenant of the night, and that there should not be day and night in their season;*

*21 Then may also my covenant be broken with David my servant, that he should not have a son to reign upon his throne; and with the Levites the priests, my ministers.*

This prophecy was given when king Zedekiah, the final king of Judah, had about one year of reign left. Nebuchadnezzar's army was soon to break through and burn both Jerusalem and Solomon's Temple to the ground and carry away Zedekiah and many Jews to Babylon. There would not be another Davidic king until Messiah came according to Daniel 9:24-27.

And yet, we see here that this covenant will be in effect as long as there is day and night. Notwithstanding, there was no Davidic king on the throne in Israel for over 600 years of days and nights. So, there was desperate need for **confirmation** that it was still in effect.

But, above all, Jesus is proven in these passages to be the messianic fulfillment and **confirmation** of the Davidic covenant. The covenant of 2 Sam 7:16 was fully **confirmed** to be still in effect by the coming of the Lord Jesus Christ.

I have bolded references to a confirmed covenant in the last paragraph because, although Daniel 9:27 clearly states "he shall **confirm the** covenant", even KJV people immediately after reading the passage frequently state "so Antichrist will **make a** covenant with the Jews". Total disregard for the words of God is displayed on this one point. The term "confirm the covenant", using the definite article **the**, requires a previous and very specific covenant that was in doubt. The term "make a covenant" allows for a brand-new covenant with no previous justification. It also allows JEHOVAH'S covenant to be replaced with Antichrist's covenant! Scary thought here; judgment day will happen to all such bible translators!

In truth, as we saw above, the NASB version (among others) renders verse 27 thusly:

*27 And he will make a firm covenant with the many for one week, but in the middle of the week he will put a stop to sacrifice and grain offering; and on the wing of abominations will come one who makes desolate, even until a complete destruction, one that is decreed, is poured out on the one who makes desolate."*

No confirming anything here. This verse is so wildly different from the KJV that destruction is poured out on the one who makes desolate rather than all those who are made desolate. So, is this the justification for making a new covenant instead of confirming an existing covenant?

This is what makes multiple versions so useful for charlatan Christians and so dangerous for true Christians. Again, Darby's Antichrist is almost required by the wording here.

And finally, God's judgment on the Jews for murdering His Son is nullified by this wording. (That determined shall be poured upon the desolate.) That is an abominable injustice to God's version of the story.

On the other hand, some premillennial teachers do teach that the conditional Mosaic covenant will be reinstated. But that is a repudiated covenant that is no longer being honored by God. All Jews should be aware of this. Not only because God has left them without a temple for 2000 years in which to observe the Mosaic covenant, but because their scriptures tell them that conditional covenant is permanently broken.

*Zec 11:10 And I took my staff, even Beauty, and cut it asunder, that I might break my covenant which I had made with all the people.*

*11 And it was broken in that day: and so the poor of the flock that waited upon me knew that it was the word of the LORD.*

*12 And I said unto them, If ye think good, give me my price; and if not, forbear. So they weighed for my price thirty pieces of silver.*

*13 And the LORD said unto me, Cast it unto the potter: a goodly price that I was prised at of them. And I took the thirty pieces of silver, and cast them to the potter in the house of the LORD.*

Those last two verses should tell any knowledgeable Christian that the point at which the covenant was broken was the crucifixion of Christ. So, neither side should accept this argument.

The term "make a covenant" frees these commentators to make Antichrist instead of Jehovah the covenant maker. However, it does not change the fact that Jesus **confirmed the** covenant. This trick of semantics simply does not defeat the clear wording of the KJV.

Furthermore, any such serious Christian should question why God would put deceptive wording in His scriptures. If a commentator uses the proper "confirm the" wording and the allows it to reference Antichrist confirming the Mosaic covenant, he is effectively saying God spoke a half-truth in this passage. God would be speaking as if a broken and forever nullified covenant could still be effectual. God would certainly have placed a qualifier here. This is why deceived but honest premillennialists MUST say "confirm a" or "make a" covenant.

Jesus confirmed the Davidic Covenant with many Jews. His ministry was obviously supposed to fulfill the six points mentioned in verse 24 of the Daniel passage within seven years. The first three and a half years were spent in ministry directly to the Jews, offering a physical kingdom with Him on the throne forever. Although He came to the Jews in the flesh, His full message was a call to the entire world to follow Him in the spiritual kingdom. Even though many accepted and followed Him, the Jews as a nation flatly rejected His offer and crucified Him after 3 ½ years of ministry. **At that point then, sixty-nine and a half of the seventy weeks were completed.** As prophesied in verse 26 of our passage, Messiah was cut off but not for Himself. Through the shedding of His guiltless blood, atonement satisfactory to the Father as sufficient to cover all the sins of the entire world for all time was made. Redemption was complete, and salvation was made possible such that "whosoever will, may come."

We now know from history that there was to be an entire Church Age inserted into the middle of the final week of the seventy weeks prophesied to Daniel. The Church Age was obviously planned by the Father from the beginning, but was hidden from everybody, including His Son in His flesh, so that the kingdom offer to the Jews would be genuine. In First Corinthians chapter two Paul explained to the Corinthians that he was preaching Christ crucified to Gentiles, or in other words, the gospel to the Church. He wrote:

*1Co 2:7 But we speak the wisdom of God in a mystery, even the hidden wisdom, which God ordained before the world unto our glory:*
*8 Which none of the princes of this world knew: for had they known it, they would not have crucified the Lord of glory.*

This interruption occurred because the nation of Israel rejected Jesus. If the Jews had accepted the Kingdom offer, the Romans would still have crucified our Lord. However, the Jews would have been innocent of His blood.

He still had to be crucified to fulfill the prophecies and, more importantly, to become the Lamb of God Whose blood would make atonement possible for all sinners in all the world over all time. It is important to know that, **had the Jews accepted the kingdom offer, all remaining unfulfilled prophecy would have been fulfilled in the next three and a half years.** The seventy weeks would have been completed at that time and the millennial kingdom would have arrived. Jesus would then have returned in power and glory to set up the final kingdom. Perhaps happily for the Church (but extremely unhappily for the Jews) the seventieth week was interrupted by Israel's rejection of her King (see Heb. 3:14-4:9). **Thus, there are still three and a half years (not seven years!) of the prophecy of verse 24 yet to be fulfilled.**

Clearly and unambiguously, it is Messiah who will (and did) confirm the covenant with many for one week. Therefore, the final week of the seventy weeks started when Messiah began His ministry. This passage simply does not prophesy Antichrist making a seven-year peace treaty with Israel. **Darby stole this glorious prophecy of Messiah from almost all of us and attributed it to his phony Antichrist. It's disgusting!**

Perhaps the most important point for us to take away from this entire prophecy is this. **The Church Age does not end until the middle of the tribulation!** Finally, some good news for the mid-trib adherents out there. We will further prove this from other scriptures later in this work.

With that important point cleared up, let's get back to our verse.

*Dan 9:27 And he shall confirm the covenant with many for one week: and in the midst of the week he shall cause the sacrifice and the oblation to cease, and for the overspreading of abominations he shall make it desolate, even until the consummation, and that determined shall be poured upon the desolate.*

The next phrase we must look at is:

*"and in the midst of the week he shall cause the sacrifice and the oblation to cease,"*

Messiah confirmed the Davidic Covenant when He began His public ministry in 26 AD. He had a 7-year task ahead of Him in order to fulfill all the six prophecies of verse 24 in our passage. In the midst of the week, He had to fulfill the greatest promise ever made to mankind. He had to become the Lamb of God that taketh away the sins of the world. Although modern rapture teachers want to make Antichrist the one who causes the sacrifice and oblation to cease during the tribulation, it already happened 2000 years ago.

It was Jesus who caused the sacrifice and the oblation to cease when He shed His blood on the cross. From that point on, His would be the only blood acceptable as atonement for sins. The temple sacrifice and oblations would forevermore be useless for covering sin. Although the animal sacrifices continued until 70 AD, they provided zero atonement in the sight of God. Eventually, they just ceased altogether. Sorry, the rapturists' Antichrist is TOO LATE!

Continuing:

*and for the overspreading of abominations he shall make it desolate,*

The KJV terminology is CRITICAL here! Nowhere does the text say, 'abomination of desolation'. Don't try to make the leap over the chasm of illogic here to fit the term 'abomination of desolation' from the modern translations. You will certainly fall down the line of confusion into the stones of emptiness if you try (Isaiah 34:11). This is speaking of the abominations committed by the Jews against their Messiah and His followers, period.

In fact, for the overspreading of abominations God made the system of animal sacrifices desolate, empty and devoid of people. The Jews murdered their Messiah and then proceeded to persecute and kill His followers in an effort to stamp out His name and memory. These abominations overspread the nation until judgment was unavoidable. If you try to force this into the tribulation, then you do great damage to the text and to the historical cause of the suffering of the Jewish people.

Consider these facts. The city of Jerusalem was sacked and burned down in 70 AD. Up to a million people, mostly Jews, were slaughtered. The very epicenter of their lives, the temple, was taken apart stone by stone and utterly destroyed. Later, in about 135 AD, the Romans removed all the Jewish people from the entire land of Israel and forbade them entrance into Jerusalem under any circumstances. They were taken to cities all over the Roman Empire and placed in Ghettoes where they were left penniless and hopeless. They endured massacres under the Pogroms of Eastern Europe and Russia. They were murdered and pillaged during the Papal Inquisitions of the Middle Ages. They were slaughtered by the millions in the gas furnaces of death camps like Auschwitz during World War II. History records a long list of other atrocities they endured over the last 1900 years, specifically because they were Jews.

**The cup of trembling**

There is a cup of trembling, also called a cup of fury which the LORD forces those who wickedly oppose Him to drink of. Sometimes the wicked refers to other nations and often it includes Israel. This cup was poured out into Judah for sins of disobedience in 586 BC, in the destruction of Jerusalem and Solomon's temple. It continued with the captivity and later, subjection to foreign rulers. This is the way Isaiah states this punishment:

*Isa 51:17 Awake, awake, stand up, O Jerusalem, which hast drunk at the hand of the LORD the cup of his fury; thou hast drunken the dregs of the cup of trembling, and wrung them out.*

*Isa 51:19 These two things are come unto thee; who shall be sorry for thee? desolation, and destruction, and the famine, and the sword: by whom shall I comfort thee?*

*Isa 51:20 Thy sons have fainted, they lie at the head of all the streets, as a wild bull in a net: they are full of the fury of the LORD, the rebuke of thy God.*

How much more should this cup be poured into a people who murdered their redeemer and refused the Son of God. This prophecy in Daniel shows what happened when the cup was poured out a second time in 70 AD.

*even until the consummation,*

Continuing, they were kept out of their homeland until the time of "the consummation". This interesting terminology is an often-overlooked prophecy. All these things would continue until the consummation. The consummation is the end point of this prophecy. Since the Jews are now in their land and it is no longer desolate, we should understand that we are now at the latter end of this prophecy. If you have understood the timing portrayed in this chapter, you should understand the prophecy in these next verses regarding the time of the consummation:

*Isa 51:22 Thus saith thy Lord the LORD, and thy God that pleadeth the cause of his people, Behold, I have taken out of thine hand the cup of trembling, even the dregs of the cup of my fury; thou shalt no more drink it again:*

*Isa 51:23 But I will put it into the hand of them that afflict thee; which have said to thy soul, Bow down, that we may go over: and thou hast laid thy body as the ground, and as the street, to them that went over.*

So, all this was done to them because they killed their Messiah. God determined that punishment was necessary because their cup of trembling was full. This was brought on by their own arrogance and pride. Hear the words of this verse.

*Mat 27:25 Then answered all the people, and said, His blood be on us, and on our children.*

And finally:

*and that determined shall be poured upon the desolate.*

This phrase hearkens back to the final phrases of the previous verse: *"and the end thereof shall be with a flood, and unto the end of the war desolations are determined."* **There was a predetermined punishment for the Jewish people for murdering the Son of God**. Jesus, referring to this verse of prophecy, assures us that this destruction of the temple and the city is the vengeance of God Himself in these passages:

*Isa 43:28 Therefore I have profaned the princes of the sanctuary, and have given Jacob to the curse, and Israel to reproaches.*

And:

*Luk 21:20 And when ye shall see Jerusalem compassed with armies, then know that the desolation thereof is nigh.*

*21 Then let them which are in Judaea flee to the mountains; and let them which are in the midst of it depart out; and let not them that are in the countries enter thereinto.*

**22 For these be the days of vengeance, that all things which are written may be fulfilled.**

*23 But woe unto them that are with child, and to them that give suck, in those days! for there shall be great distress in the land, and wrath upon this people.*

*24 And they shall fall by the edge of the sword, and shall be led away captive into all nations: and Jerusalem shall be trodden down of the Gentiles,* **until the times of the Gentiles be fulfilled.**

Here, in verse 24, is another of the many hints scripture gives us regarding the end-times. The Jews are back in their land and Jerusalem is their capital. Ergo, the times of the Gentiles are pretty much fulfilled. This agrees with 'even until the consummation' of the previous phrase we examined. Even so, come Lord Jesus!

Again, the final phrase of Daniel 9:27 says, "that determined" (by God) shall be *poured* upon the desolate. If you will review the history of the Jews from then until now, you should fully understand the phrase "**poured** upon the desolate".

### Summary

I will close out this chapter by summarizing each important statement of the prophecy with bullet points. I believe this summary is the plainest and simplest reading of this prophecy. It just takes what the Lord freely gives us. Armed with all the arguments above, this will help us see how straightforward and easy to follow the prophecy really is.

- *Dan 9:24 Seventy weeks are determined upon thy people and upon thy holy city,*

The seventy weeks are weeks of years so a special period of 490 years for dealing with Daniel's people, the Jews, were determined.

- *to finish the transgression, and to make an end of sins, and to make reconciliation for iniquity, and*

> to bring in everlasting righteousness, and to seal up the vision and prophecy, and to anoint the most Holy.

The conditions listed here will all be brought to fruition by the time the seventy weeks are up.

- *Dan 9:25 Know therefore and understand, that from the going forth of the commandment to restore and to build Jerusalem unto the Messiah the Prince*

Messiah became "the Prince" when He began His public ministry in the person of Jesus of Nazareth. This occurred in 26 AD, exactly 483 years from the commandment Artaxerxes 1 made to Ezra in 458 BC to beautify the temple. Since this commandment was a continuation of the original commandment given by Cyrus the Great, just as the later commandment given to Nehemiah in the 20th year of Artaxerxes 1 was a continuation of the original commandment, there is no reason to disqualify it because the temple was the main thrust of the wording in scriptures. Although the temple was always of primary importance, it is clear from several statements made within the text of the books of Ezra and Isaiah that the rebuilding the wall and the city were always part of the original commandment.

- *shall be seven weeks,*

This is the time allotted to rebuilding the walls and the city itself. By the time Ezra was sent to Jerusalem, the temple had already been completed 58 years earlier.  However, it was set in the middle of a pile of rubble.  Beautifying the temple would necessarily include cleaning up the mess around it which detracted from its glory.  Several passages in Ezra indicate that rebuilding the wall and the city were already happening, but slowly, by the time Nehemiah arrived in the city.

- *and threescore and two weeks:*

After the seven weeks of years, there were to be 62 weeks of years living in the rebuilt city until Messiah appeared.  This total of 69 weeks of years, or 483 years, ended at the very time the Lord Jesus Christ began His ministry.  He was baptized by John the Baptist and then anointed by the Holy Ghost descending upon Him as a Dove (Mat. 3:16-17).  He was announced as the Son of God, Messiah, to the whole nation.

- *the street shall be built again, and the wall, even in troublous times.*

Finishing the prophecy about the city, we find the street and the wall being built again, even in troublous times.  This is recorded starting in Ezra chapters 4-6.  Here we find that the wall was being built even before the temple was begun and that the Jews had a commandment to build it.  The troublous times continued when Nehemiah arrived some 94 years later and began working feverishly on the wall.  This is recorded in Nehemiah chapter 4.  There is no good reason to accept the troublous times in Nehemiah and reject the troublous times in Ezra as the correct fulfillment of the prophecy. The troublous times extended from 537 BC until the city was completed in 409 BC. There were 49 years of that time to come when Artaxerxes 1 sent Ezra to Jerusalem.

- *Dan 9:26 And after threescore and two weeks shall Messiah be cut off, but not for himself:*

62 weeks, or 434 years after the city was rebuilt, Messiah showed up right on time in 26 AD. Three and a half years after the 62 weeks ended, possibly on April 3, 30 AD. At the age of 33 ½, Messiah was cut off, that is crucified, but not for Himself. He allowed Himself to be crucified, shedding His sinless blood as a substitute for the blood requirement for all our sins for all time. He completed the great plan of redemption instituted 4000 years earlier due to the sins of Adam and Eve.

- *and the people of the prince that shall come shall destroy the city and the sanctuary;*

Consider the following verse as you ponder this passage:

*1Co 2:12 Now we have received, not the spirit of the world, but the spirit which is of God; that we might know the things that are freely given to us of God.*

As a result of having murdered their Messiah, God brought the Roman armies (in 70 AD) under prince Titus, son of the Emperor Vespasian, to destroy Jerusalem along with the temple. This event is nowhere in scriptures tied to the end-times. It happened, it's over, it meets no requirements for double fulfillment, and there is no scriptural justification for calling this prince Antichrist. There is a verse describing the treatment of this prince by so many prophecy experts:

2Pe 3:16 *As also in all his epistles, speaking in them of these things; in which are some things hard to be understood, which they that are unlearned and unstable wrest, as they do also the other scriptures, unto their own destruction.*

- *and the end thereof shall be with a flood, and unto the end of the war desolations are determined.*

There is precedent in scriptures for calling the invasion of an enemy army a flood. The end of the city and the sanctuary occurred when the armies of Rome breached the third wall and flooded into the city in 70 AD. The historian Josephus, who was involved in the battle, speculated that as many as 1.1 million people were slaughtered by Titus and his army. This would be one of the great slaughters in the history of the world. Some might rightfully say it was a slaughter of biblical proportions.

The end of the Jewish/Roman wars came in 135 AD when the Jews were forcibly removed from their homeland and placed in cities all over the Roman Empire. This left the land of Israel desolate and it left the Jewish people desolate as many arrived in foreign cities with little or no resources to start over with. This is exactly what Luke 21:24 was testifying to. More and more Jews are returning to their land whereby we should recognize that the times of the Gentiles are almost fulfilled. Scriptures have many such prophecies so that if we are taken by surprise when the rapture occurs, we have only ourselves to blame.

- *Dan 9:27 And he shall confirm the covenant with many for one week:*

Knowing that Titus never confirmed any covenant with the many of Israel, we understand that "he" in this phrase can only refer to Messiah. Also, the colon punctuation in the King James Bible indicates that "the prince that shall come" is not a candidate to be the correct antecedent for this pronoun.

Messiah confirmed the binding and unconditional covenant that God had made with King David and all Israel that there would be a king from the line of David on the throne of Israel forever (2 Sam. 7:16). This Davidic Covenant was proven to be in effect in the life of Messiah in many New Testament scriptures, especially in Luke 1:30-33.

The fact that Messiah Jesus confirmed the covenant for one week proves that the 70$^{th}$ week started at the beginning of His ministry of 3.5 years. He was cut off in the midst of the week and the prophecy was temporarily halted at that time. This was because God broke His conditional Mosaic Covenant (Heb. 8:13) when the Jews murdered His Son by Roman proxy on the cross at Calvary.

Scriptures assure us that the prophecy will be completed starting in the second half of the seven-year tribulation. Had the Jews accepted Jesus as their King, He would have been crucified at the hands of the Romans and then all remaining unfulfilled prophecy up to the millennium would have been fulfilled in the next 3.5 years.

Incidentally, the 1000-year millennium would have occurred immediately after that. In that case, man would have been living on the New Earth and in the New Jerusalem for 1000 years by now and you and I may never have been born. Read Heb. 3:7-4:11 to see how all this works out. It will help you understand that the final 3.5 years has been postponed. It broadly implies that the millennium immediately follows the end of the 70 weeks of years.

Because there are only 3.5 years left that God will be dealing so specifically with Israel, **the Church Age necessarily does not end until the middle of the tribulation.** (Fully explained in chapter 6)

- *and in the midst of the week he shall cause the sacrifice and the oblation to cease,*

When Jesus shed His blood on the cross at Calvary, He became the final sacrifice. No animal sacrifice could ever provide temporary atonement again. He bade us from that moment on to come boldly to the throne of grace (Heb 4:16). Further, He assured us that whosoever shall call upon His name shall be saved (Rom 10:13). Redemption was completed. Victory over sin and the grave was achieved. We need no earthly temple or altar or priest to provide atonement. Jesus became the High Priest (Heb 6:20), rendering earthly priests obsolete.

Jesus put an end to the efficacy of the temple sacrifice and oblation. Although temple worship continued until 70 AD, it ceased to have any value or effect in the sight of God.

- *and for the overspreading of abominations he*

> *shall make it desolate,*

Crucifying the Savior God had sent to the Jews, was an abomination too great to go unpunished. The abominations continued as the Jews sought to wipe out His followers along with His name and memory. So, God brought desolation on the temple and on the land and on His people. (Luke 21:20-24 "For these be the days of vengeance, that all things which are written may be fulfilled ".) This prophecy has indeed been fulfilled in a most horrific manner. **There is no future 'abomination of desolations' spoken of here!** Prophecy completed! The Jews have returned to their land.

- *even until the consummation,*

The consummation spoken of here is the end of the prophecy of 70 weeks. It does not necessarily speak of the very last moment but more a time period when all the attendant events wrap up. The fact that the Jews are back in their land proves that we are in the period of the consummation of this prophecy. I hope to stress to my readers how very near we are to the end.

- *and that determined shall be poured upon the desolate.*

This phrase tells us that certain punishments were determined against the Jews. There would be no mercy until all was accomplished. When we look at the history of the Jews over the last 2000 years, we see a people who have suffered, probably more than any other people over such a long period of time. Truly the hand of God was heavy upon them.

But that period is coming to an end. The Jews are being regathered to their land and will never be driven out again. The tribulation will be very tough on them, but it will ultimately make them turn from their unbelief and call upon God. They will be ready to say:

*Mat 23:39 For I say unto you, Ye shall not see me henceforth, till ye shall say, Blessed is he that cometh in the name of the Lord.*


Very soon they will all turn to their Savior just in time to enter His millennium of rest.

### Finally

The prophecy in Daniel 9:24-27 has been mostly fulfilled. In fact, 69.5 of the 70 weeks have been fulfilled. The remaining 3.5 years will be fulfilled in the last half of the seven-year tribulation. The most important takeaway from this prophecy for Church Age saints is this: The Church Age continues through the first 3.5 years of the tribulation. **We will show in this work how those Christians alive at that time can escape those 3.5 years of the tribulation.** Here's a start:

*Luk 21:36 Watch ye therefore, and pray always, that ye may be accounted worthy to escape all these things that shall come to pass, and to stand before the Son of man.*

## Chapter 5.  Carpe Diem, or…

### (What We Can Learn from the Old Testament Prophets)

*You got to be careful*

*If you don't know where you're going*

*Because you might not get there*

-Yogi Berra

In chapter 4 we learned about the true boundaries of the Church Age.  We also learned that the prophecy of 70 weeks will be resumed at the midpoint of the 7-year tribulation.  So, we learned a lot of important facts about the end-times, but just a little about recognizing when we get there.

In this chapter we will learn things to watch for in order to recognize when we 'get there'.  We will be discussing a very special day which, if you fully understand it, will crack open the end-times conundrum regarding the timing of the judgments in the Revelation.  We will also look at a man who will come on the scene just in time to warn us when they are about start.  And thankfully, that man will NOT be Yogi Berra.

So, carpe diem, which is to say, seize the day in this chapter.  Learn it well.

Beside the amazing things the prophet Daniel has told us about the end-times, there are many more references to the last days throughout the Old Testament. One of the most important topics is the 'day of the LORD'. We will look at this day from four different perspectives to help us pin it down and understand all we will need to know as it relates to the rapture.

It would be nice to think we could be exhaustive in this chapter, but the volume of material on the last days found in the books of the Old Testament prophets would fill many books this size. So, we will hit the most important points and dwell heavily on the passages relating to the day of the LORD up front.

### 1. The day of the LORD

Prophecies regarding the day of the LORD are the primary candidates for double fulfillment. That is because the day of the LORD had two possible fulfillment periods. As we saw in the last chapter, if the Jews had accepted Christ as their King, all unfulfilled prophecy would have occurred in the next 3.5 years and the millennium of rest would have begun immediately. The final fulfillment of all prophecy and the millennium are part of the day of the LORD, so when they were postponed, the day of the LORD was necessarily postponed.

Many day of the LORD prophecies are said to occur when the day of the LORD is at hand, or near, or similar terminology. The day of the LORD was near when Christ was ministering to the Jews, so all such prophecies had to be fulfilled in advance of that time. There are initial fulfillments of these prophecies found within the scriptures, but they are left open for further or differing fulfillments. Now the day of the LORD is near again, so all such prophecies must have a fulfillment in our time as well. This is the reason for double fulfillment prophecies. Harking back to the previous chapter, nothing is tied to the day of the LORD in the Daniel 9:24-27 prophecy so there is no call for two princes as some might claim.

There was no rapture associated with the start of Daniel's 70$^{th}$ week when the day of the LORD first was near. This can be determined historically because there is simply no record of such an event. We will see later, however, that the rapture is indelibly tied to the final time the day of the LORD is near. The introduction of the Church Age brought an additional set of prophecies found throughout the New Testament. Much of prophetic scripture in both testaments is tied to this day and it is critical to have this understanding before almost every end-times prophecy can be placed in its proper context and timeframe.

The phrase, "the day of the LORD" is found 26 times in 24 different verses and in ten different books in the Old Testament (OT). All these books are found in the section of the OT dedicated to prophecy ranging from Isaiah to Malachi. These mentions are often the topic of sermons or messages that range over several chapters, and in 2 cases are the main subject of the entire book. Seven of these mentions are part of a somewhat longer phrase such as: the day of the LORD'S vengeance (once); the day of the LORD'S anger (thrice); the day of the LORD'S wrath (once); the day of the LORD'S sacrifice (once); and the day of the Lord GOD (once). All of these occurrences are initially descriptions of terrible punishments and judgments on the world when that day arrives. However, in most cases the sermon ends with the nation of Israel at rest in her own land and peace on Earth. It is important to note that, in every use of this phrase in the OT, the word LORD (or in one case, Lord GOD) appears in all caps. When terms of deity such as GOD or LORD are in all caps in the King James Bible, they specifically refer to JEHOVAH God.

JEHOVAH is the name of God specifically given to Moses when God called him to lead His people out of Egypt. It was to be the most sacred name of God for Israel. God the Father is the Church Age equivalent of JEHOVAH. JEHOVAH is referenced only ten times in the New Testament (NT). Six times capitalization is used to introduce JESUS in the gospels so we can instantly recognize His Godhood, and in four cases the word is used as 'LORD' in a quote from the OT where king David wrote in Psalm 110:

*Psa 110:1* ***A Psalm of David.*** *The LORD said unto my Lord, Sit thou at my right hand, until I make thine enemies thy footstool.*

Here, you can see, it was important to distinguish between the LORD JEHOVAH and the Lord Messiah, or in the Church Age, Jesus Christ. The point is, there is no usage of JEHOVAH in the NT because that is God's special name given for Israel to use. The NT consistently uses a more generic "Lord" or "God" to refer to the deity. That is because it distinguishes between the Father and the Son by directly using their NT names frequently and allows context to determine which part of the Godhead is meant in the rest of the passages. If you find the term for deity capitalized in Darby's New Testament or other modern versions, just consider the sources.

In the New Testament, we find the phrases: "the day of the Lord" three times, and "the day of the Lord Jesus" twice. Additionally, we find "the day of Jesus Christ" once and "the day of God" once and "the day of Christ" three times. So, we see that there is a bit of a tangle here. We will deal with the phrase in the NT in a later chapter.

One more important point must be made about the various mentions of the day of the LORD in the OT. Although they speak of the same time period, they are in reference to various peoples. All of them include their relationship to Israel, but many also refer to specific nations around Israel such as Egypt, Ethiopia, Libya, modern Jordan (Ammon, Moab, and Edom are combined to form present day Jordan), and many times the entire world. We will look first at those mentions aimed more at the entire world.

**The day of the LORD includes both the tribulation and the millennium**

The day of the LORD in the OT can be best illustrated by using a specific example.

*Joe 3:14 Multitudes, multitudes in the valley of decision: for the day of the LORD is near in the valley of decision.*

*15 The sun and the moon shall be darkened, and the stars shall withdraw their shining.*

*16 The LORD also shall roar out of Zion, and utter his voice from Jerusalem; and the heavens and the earth shall shake: but the LORD will be the hope of his people, and the strength of the children of Israel.*

This passage starts when the day of the LORD is near. It says there will be multitudes of people that shall come against Jerusalem. At the same time, there will be tremendous environmental catastrophes occurring. God will save His people and then purify them (v.21). Once the tribulation is completed, only good things will come on Israel forever. So, the end of the sermon:

*17 So shall ye know that I am the LORD your God dwelling in Zion, my holy mountain: then shall Jerusalem be holy, and there shall no strangers pass through her any more.*

*18 And it shall come to pass in that day, that the mountains shall drop down new wine, and the hills shall flow with milk, and all the rivers of Judah shall flow with waters, and a fountain shall come forth of the house of the LORD, and shall water the valley of Shittim.*

*19 Egypt shall be a desolation, and Edom shall be a desolate wilderness, for the violence against the children of Judah, because they have shed innocent blood in their land.*

*20 But Judah shall dwell for ever, and Jerusalem from generation to generation.*

*21 For I will cleanse their blood that I have not cleansed: for the LORD dwelleth in Zion.*

## Finding the starting point for the day of the LORD as described in the Revelation

In the next several passages we will begin to enumerate points that will help us place the start of the day of the LORD as it is found in the book of the Revelation. I will number the points so you can put them in proper order for the event in the Revelation. See if you can figure out what event these points are aiming at before we finish.

Passage 1:

*Isa 2:10 Enter into the rock, and hide thee in the dust, for fear of the LORD, and for the glory of his majesty.*

*11 The lofty looks of man shall be humbled, and the haughtiness of men shall be bowed down, and the LORD alone shall be exalted in that day.*

*12 For the day of the LORD of hosts shall be upon every one that is proud and lofty, and upon every one that is lifted up; and he shall be brought low:*

*Isa 2:17 And the loftiness of man shall be bowed down, and the haughtiness of men shall be made low: and the LORD alone shall be exalted in that day.*

*18 And the idols he shall utterly abolish.*

*19 And they shall go into the holes of the rocks, and into the caves of the earth, for fear of the LORD, and for the glory of his majesty, when he ariseth to shake terribly the earth.*

*20 In that day a man shall cast his idols of silver, and his idols of gold, which they made each one for himself to worship, to the moles and to the bats;*

*21 To go into the clefts of the rocks, and into the tops of the ragged rocks, for fear of the LORD, and for the glory of his majesty, when he ariseth to shake terribly the earth.*

The important points for our quest from this passage are found in that last verse. First note that (1) the LORD will shake terribly the Earth. This speaks of a worldwide earthquake or series of earthquakes.

The second point here is that (7) men will go into the holes of the rocks and into the caves of the Earth [v.19] as well as the clefts of the rocks [v.21]. Men will be entering caves and safer places than manmade buildings or climbing to high places out of fear of the LORD. Also see verse 10 above which stresses (8) hiding in the rocks for fear of the LORD.

Passage 2:

*Isa 13:6 Howl ye; for the day of the LORD is at hand; it shall come as a destruction from the Almighty.*

*7 Therefore shall all hands be faint, and every man's heart shall melt:*

*8 And they shall be afraid: pangs and sorrows shall take hold of them; they shall be in pain as a woman that travaileth: they shall be amazed one at another; their faces shall be as flames.*

*9 Behold, the day of the LORD cometh, cruel both with wrath and fierce anger, to lay the land desolate: and he shall destroy the sinners thereof out of it.*

*10 For the stars of heaven and the constellations thereof shall not give their light: the sun shall be darkened in his going forth, and the moon shall not cause her light to shine.*

*11 And I will punish the world for their evil, and the wicked for their iniquity; and I will cause the arrogancy of the proud to cease, and will lay low the haughtiness of the terrible.*

*12 I will make a man more precious than fine gold; even a man than the golden wedge of Ophir.*

*13 Therefore I will shake the heavens, and the earth shall remove out of her place, in the wrath of the LORD of hosts, and in the day of his fierce anger.*

This passage occurs when the day of the LORD is at hand. It comes as a destruction from the Almighty. Let's take special note here, the stars, (2) the sun, and the moon will be darkened. Also, the (1) worldwide earthquake is mentioned again in verse 13, even to the point that the Earth's orbit will change somewhat. This includes the (3) shaking of the very heavens. Finally, notice that it is (9) a time of the LORD'S wrath and fierce anger.

Passage 3:

*Isa 34:1 Come near, ye nations, to hear; and hearken, ye people: let the earth hear, and all that is therein; the world, and all things that come forth of it.*

*2 For the indignation of the LORD is upon all nations, and his fury upon all their armies: he hath utterly destroyed them, he hath delivered them to the slaughter.*

*3 Their slain also shall be cast out, and their stink shall come up out of their carcases, and the mountains shall be melted with their blood.*

*4 And all the host of heaven shall be dissolved, and the heavens shall be rolled together as a scroll: and all their host shall fall down, as the leaf falleth off from the vine, and as a falling fig from the fig tree.*

*5 For my sword shall be bathed in heaven: behold, it shall come down upon Idumea, and upon the people of my curse, to judgment.*

*6 The sword of the LORD is filled with blood, it is made fat with fatness, and with the blood of lambs and goats, with the fat of the kidneys of rams: for the LORD hath a sacrifice in Bozrah, and a great slaughter in the land of Idumea.*

*7 And the unicorns shall come down with them, and the bullocks with the bulls; and their land shall be soaked with blood, and their dust made fat with fatness.*

*8 For it is the day of the LORD'S vengeance, and the year of recompences for the controversy of Zion.*

This passage describes a series of events and then informs us that the day of the LORD'S vengeance is what we are looking at per verse 8. There are several important points here. Verse 4 says (3) the host of heaven shall be dissolved. This is a reference to angels which are often called stars in the scriptures. Specifically, these are fallen angels who are servants of Satan. Satan is currently the god of this world (2Cor 4:4) and his angels have free access to the universe. There is a very real possibility here that these angels will leave heaven or the heavens and reveal themselves as extraterrestrials in order to confuse the people on Earth.

The next couple things to observe are:

a. that (5) the heavens shall be rolled together as a scroll and

b. it is (4) as a falling fig from the fig tree.


Passage 4:

*Joe 2:1 Blow ye the trumpet in Zion, and sound an alarm*

*in my holy mountain: let all the inhabitants of the land tremble: for the day of the LORD cometh, for it is nigh at hand;*

*2 A day of darkness and of gloominess, a day of clouds and of thick darkness, as the morning spread upon the mountains: a great people and a strong; there hath not been ever the like, neither shall be any more after it, even to the years of many generations.*

*3 A fire devoureth before them; and behind them a flame burneth: the land is as the garden of Eden before them, and behind them a desolate wilderness; yea, and nothing shall escape them.*

*4 The appearance of them is as the appearance of horses; and as horsemen, so shall they run.*

*5 Like the noise of chariots on the tops of mountains shall they leap, like the noise of a flame of fire that devoureth the stubble, as a strong people set in battle array.*

*6 Before their face the people shall be much pained: all faces shall gather blackness.*

*7 They shall run like mighty men; they shall climb the wall like men of war; and they shall march every one on his ways, and they shall not break their ranks:*

*8 Neither shall one thrust another; they shall walk every one in his path: and when they fall upon the sword, they shall not be wounded.*

*9 They shall run to and fro in the city; they shall run upon the wall, they shall climb up upon the houses; they shall enter in at the windows like a thief.*

*10 The earth shall quake before them; the heavens shall tremble: the sun and the moon shall be dark, and the stars shall withdraw their shining:*

*11 And the LORD shall utter his voice before his army: for his camp is very great: for he is strong that executeth his word: for the day of the LORD is great and very terrible; and who can abide it?*

In this passage the day of the LORD is nigh (or near) at hand. Again, it mentions an attack on Israel (by Gog of Magog as we soon shall see) is ongoing when the day arrives. Of note, we see (1) the Earth quaking, (2) the sun and moon are dark, and (10) the question of who can abide it.

Passage 5:

*Joe 2:30 And I will shew wonders in the heavens and in the earth, blood, and fire, and pillars of smoke.*

*31 The sun shall be turned into darkness, and the moon into blood, before the great and the terrible day of the LORD come.*

*32 And it shall come to pass, that whosoever shall call on the name of the LORD shall be delivered: for in mount Zion and in Jerusalem shall be deliverance, as the LORD hath said, and in the remnant whom the LORD shall call.*

This passage occurs before the day of the LORD and is notable primarily for its definitive statement that (2) the sun shall be darkened, and the moon turned to blood. Other passages speak of the moon darkened or not giving her light. They are the same. A blood moon, for instance, gives greatly reduced light because it reflects no direct sunlight. When we see other events occurring simultaneously, we will see that volcanos and other events are likely putting massive volcanic ash clouds into the air column. Ash in the air can be thick enough to block the sun and especially the moon almost entirely. This may or may not be important to the timing of the pre-trib rapture. If the moon is turned to blood color the way a total lunar eclipse makes it red, then the rapture date may be tied to such an event. The next total lunar eclipse from this writing is May 26, 2021.

Passage 6:

*Joe 3:14 Multitudes, multitudes in the valley of decision: for the day of the LORD is near in the valley of decision.*

*15 The sun and the moon shall be darkened, and the stars shall withdraw their shining.*

*16 The LORD also shall roar out of Zion, and utter his voice from Jerusalem; and the heavens and the earth shall shake: but the LORD will be the hope of his people, and the strength of the children of Israel.*

This passage occurs when the day of the LORD is near. Again, it starts with (2) the sun and moon darkened and the stars withdrawing their shining. In verse 16, (1) there is an earthquake and (6) the heavens are shaken.

Passage 7:

*Zep 1:14 The great day of the LORD is near, it is near, and hasteth greatly, even the voice of the day of the LORD: the mighty man shall cry there bitterly.*

*15 That day is a day of wrath, a day of trouble and distress, a day of wasteness and desolation, a day of darkness and gloominess, a day of clouds and thick darkness,*

This passage again occurs when the day of the LORD is near. It is (9) a day of wrath.

Passage 8:

*Zep 2:1 Gather yourselves together, yea, gather together, O nation not desired;*

*2 Before the decree bring forth, before the day pass as the chaff, before the fierce anger of the LORD come upon you, before the day of the LORD'S anger come upon you.*

*3 Seek ye the LORD, all ye meek of the earth, which have wrought his judgment; seek righteousness, seek meekness: it may be ye shall be hid in the day of the LORD'S anger.*

*4 For Gaza shall be forsaken, and Ashkelon a desolation: they shall drive out Ashdod at the noon day, and Ekron shall be rooted up.*

*5 Woe unto the inhabitants of the sea coast, the nation of the Cherethites! the word of the LORD is against you; O Canaan, the land of the Philistines, I will even destroy thee, that there shall be no inhabitant.*

This passage really belongs with the passages regarding the nations around Israel. Its main purpose here is to point out that it is here called (9) the day of the LORD'S anger or wrath.

Take special note of verse 3 here. It is addressed to all the meek of the Earth and it indicates that it is possible to be hid in the day of the LORD'S anger. This would seem to be a hint of a conditional rapture at that time! **The conditions here are seeking righteousness and meekness.**

Passage 9:

*Eze 38:16 And thou shalt come up against my people of Israel, as a cloud to cover the land; it shall be in the latter days, and I will bring thee against my land, that the heathen may know me, when I shall be sanctified in thee, O Gog, before their eyes.*

*17 Thus saith the Lord GOD; Art thou he of whom I have spoken in old time by my servants the prophets of Israel, which prophesied in those days many years that I would bring thee against them?*

*18 And it shall come to pass at the same time when Gog shall come against the land of Israel, saith the Lord GOD, that my fury shall come up in my face.*

*19 For in my jealousy and in the fire of my wrath have I spoken, Surely in that day there shall be a great shaking in the land of Israel;*

*20 So that the fishes of the sea, and the fowls of the heaven, and the beasts of the field, and all creeping things that creep upon the earth, and all the men that are upon the face of the earth, shall shake at my presence, and the mountains shall be thrown down, and the steep places shall fall, and every wall shall fall to the ground.*

OK, I'm asking for clemency in using this passage. It does not use the specific phrase, 'the day of the LORD', but we will demonstrate later that it speaks of the same time period. This passage is part of the Gog war on Israel. This war ends when God intervenes and destroys Gog and his nation of Magog, or Russia. This intervention occurs when God's fury comes up in His face (verse 18) and it is concurrent with Isa. 2:19 and the start of the day of the LORD. In this passage we also see in verse 19, (1) the great shaking or earthquake throughout Israel. Then, in verse 20 we see (6) the mountains thrown down and the whole world shaking.

In the passage we see only that it is in the latter days. However, there are several internal indicators that this occurs when the day of the LORD is near. According to the whole two-chapter passage, even the heathen will know exactly who JEHOVAH God is after this war. A couple more indicators are:

*Eze 38:8 After many days thou shalt be visited: in the latter years thou shalt come into the land that is brought back from the sword, and is gathered out of many people, against the mountains of Israel, which have been always waste: but it is brought forth out of the nations, and they shall dwell safely all of them.*

This describes Israel since 1948. And:

*Eze 39:8 Behold, it is come, and it is done, saith the Lord GOD; this is the day whereof I have spoken.*

Whenever you see 'the day' or 'that day' or similar terminology in prophetic scriptures you should check context. Often, you will be able to determine that the day spoken of is another mention of the day of the LORD. That is the case here, where we should understand *"the day whereof I have spoken"* is the day that so much of prophetic scripture is devoted to, that is, the day of the LORD.

### List of events referenced

Have you figured out what event we are talking about yet? Here are the events we have indicated numerically in these 'day of the LORD' passages:

*1. lo, there was a great earthquake;*

    Passages 1,2,4 and 6

*2. and the sun became black as sackcloth of hair, and the moon became as blood;*

    Passages 2,4,5 and 6

*3. And the stars of heaven fell unto the earth,*

    Passages 2 and 3

*4. even as a fig tree casteth her untimely figs, when she is shaken of a mighty wind.*

    Passage 3

*5. And the heaven departed as a scroll when it is rolled together;*

    Passages 3 and 6

*6. and every mountain and island were moved out of their places.*

    Passage 9

*7. And the kings of the earth, and the great men, and the rich men, and the chief captains, and the mighty men, and every bondman, and every free man, hid themselves in the dens and in the rocks of the mountains;*

    Passage 1

*8. And said to the mountains and rocks, Fall on us, and hide us from the face of him that sitteth on the throne, and from the wrath of the Lamb:*

    Passage 1

*9. For the great day of his wrath is come;*

    Passages 2,7 and 8

*10. and who shall be able to stand?*

    Passage 4


So, there you have it. We have just quoted Rev. 6:12-17 in the list above. The events associated with the sixth seal match the events listed when the day of the LORD is at hand, or near. This is an extremely important point for end-times prophecy. We will now see why.

## The opening of the sixth seal marks the starting point of the day of the LORD

Six of the above passages indicate that the day of the

LORD is near or at hand or similar terminology. The others imply that it is in progress when thy occur. Since they all speak of the same event, that is the opening of the sixth seal, it is only natural to conclude that, taken together, they all describe the start of the day of the LORD.

We have demonstrated that the start of the day of the LORD matches the events associated with the sixth seal. Now we need to place the sixth seal in its context with the seven-year tribulation. Revelation chapter 6 ends with the events of the sixth seal and is followed by this verse:

*Rev 6:17 For the great day of his wrath is come; and who shall be able to stand?*

This indicates the start of something new, the seven-year tribulation. Here is the reasoning.

The seventh seal is opened in chapter 8 where we find that the seal opens to seven trumpet judgments. Each of these judgments occur over a period of time. So how long does it take to complete all seven? Here is the very short form explanation.

In chapter 11 of The Revelation, two witnesses of God are introduced. These witnesses are given special power from God and will prophesy for 1260 days. That is 42 thirty-day months or 3.5 years. At the end of the 1260 days, the Beast will rise from the bottomless pit and kill them. In the chapter, we find that immediately after their death, the 7th and last trumpet of the trumpet judgments is sounded. After their death, the Beast continues for 42 months before he is cast into the Lake of Fire by King Jesus. Here are the proof verses:

*Rev 11:3 And I will give power unto my two witnesses, and they shall prophesy a thousand two hundred and threescore days, clothed in sackcloth.*

*4 These are the two olive trees, and the two candlesticks standing before the God of the earth.*

*5 And if any man will hurt them, fire proceedeth out of their mouth, and devoureth their enemies: and if any man will hurt them, he must in this manner be killed.*

*6 These have power to shut heaven, that it rain not in the days of their prophecy: and have power over waters to turn them to blood, and to smite the earth with all plagues, as often as they will.*

*7 And when they shall have finished their testimony, the beast that ascendeth out of the bottomless pit shall make war against them, and shall overcome them, and kill them.*

So, the witnesses have power over everybody for 1260 days. They also have power to call down plagues. Quite possibly, they call down the plagues of the first six trumpet judgments. When their testimony is finished, the Beast is given power over them, so he kills them.

*Rev 11:14 The second woe is past; and, behold, the third woe cometh quickly.*

*15 And the seventh angel sounded; and there were great voices in heaven, saying, The kingdoms of this world are become the kingdoms of our Lord, and of his Christ; and he shall reign for ever and ever.*

Immediately after the death of the two witnesses, the seventh angel sounds his trumpet, and the kingdoms of this world are given to Christ. Then, moving to chapter 13, we find the rise of the Beast.

*Rev 13:5 And there was given unto him a mouth speaking*

*great things and blasphemies; and power was given unto him to continue forty and two months.*

*6 And he opened his mouth in blasphemy against God, to blaspheme his name, and his tabernacle, and them that dwell in heaven.*

*7 And it was given unto him to make war with the saints, and to overcome them: and power was given him over all kindreds, and tongues, and nations.*

*Rev 13:16 And he causeth all, both small and great, rich and poor, free and bond, to receive a mark in their right hand, or in their foreheads:*

The Beast is given power over all the saints, including the two witnesses, for 42 months. He will force them to swear loyalty to him through taking his mark or die. Taking the mark will preclude all who accept it from eternal life (Rev. 14:9-10).

*Rev 19:11 And I saw heaven opened, and behold a white horse; and he that sat upon him was called Faithful and True, and in righteousness he doth judge and make war.*

*Rev 19:19 And I saw the beast, and the kings of the earth, and their armies, gathered together to make war against him that sat on the horse, and against his army.*

*20 And the beast was taken, and with him the false prophet that wrought miracles before him, with which he deceived them that had received the mark of the beast, and them that worshipped his image. These both were cast alive into a lake of fire burning with brimstone.*

*21 And the remnant were slain with the sword of him that sat upon the horse, which sword proceeded out of his mouth: and all the fowls were filled with their flesh.*

This is the great and final battle of Armageddon which is followed by the millennial reign of Christ. The Beast is cast into the Lake of Fire and his 42-month reign of terror is over.

So, working backwards, we had 42 months or 3.5 years of the power of the Beast. Before that we had 1260 days or 3.5 years of the power of the two witnesses. Right at the midpoint of these two periods we had the 7th trumpet sounding. That is a period of seven years in total. All these events occurred scripturally and chronologically after the sixth seal was opened.

How, you may ask, can we say this is all after the sixth seal is opened? The answer is in the fifth seal. The first four seals involve dire judgments on the Earth, and we have seen the direst of all in the sixth seal. But the fifth seal is very, very benign. It is remarkably different from the other seals, and so much so that it really grabs your attention. Here it is:

*Rev 6:9 And when he had opened the fifth seal, I saw under the altar the souls of them that were slain for the word of God, and for the testimony which they held:*

*Rev 6:10 And they cried with a loud voice, saying, How long, O Lord, holy and true, dost thou not judge and avenge our blood on them that dwell on the earth?*

*Rev 6:11 And white robes were given unto every one of them; and it was said unto them, that they should rest yet for a little season, until their fellowservants also and their brethren, that should be killed as they were, should be fulfilled.*

What these souls are saying in verse ten is that some of them have been there for a long time and they haven't seen any judgments that avenge their blood on the world as yet. Some commentators may have a problem with their attitude, but some commentators are so stuck on the love of God that they find His judgments on the world to be only allegorical, no matter how harshly they are described in scriptures.  **This seal is here to help Christians who respect the whole counsel of God understand that, chronologically, the tribulation has not started yet.**  The tribulation clearly starts with the opening of the sixth seal because we find all seven years accounted for after that point.  The first four seals then are opened somewhere across the previous 2000 years.  We will see this more clearly in a later chapter.

To this point, we have discussed only Old Testament scriptures regarding the day of the LORD.  There are similar scriptures in the New Testament that we will address in a later chapter.  Those passages will help place the start of the day of the LORD concurrent with the starting point for the seven-year tribulation.  In fact, we will see that the day of the LORD is comprised of the tribulation and the millennium.

It would be convenient if the Old Testament scriptures themselves would clearly state that the tribulation starts when the sixth seal is opened, but it is not so simply stated.  However, there is an important scriptural axiom in play here.  Remember the prayer of Jesus when He said:

*Luk 10:21  In that hour Jesus rejoiced in spirit, and said, I thank thee, O Father, Lord of heaven and earth, that thou hast hid these things from the wise and prudent, and hast revealed them unto babes: even so, Father; for so it seemed good in thy sight.*

To fully understand this principle, see 1 Cor. 1:19, 25-29 and 2:11-14.  God's word is intentionally cryptic in places in order to provide His deepest truths only to those who are serious about His Person and His word.  However, what He is saying in these passages is obvious enough to those who care enough to put it all together.

The day of the LORD clearly starts at the opening of the sixth seal. That 'day' clearly includes both a time of troubles and tribulation followed by a long period of peace (See Zech. 14 for a better and lengthier proof). The Revelation clearly shows seven years of tribulation after the opening of the sixth seal followed by 1000 years of peace described in chapter 20. Taken together, we call this period of tribulation and millennial rest the end-times. The real stretch of imagination would be to not believe the day of the LORD and the tribulation both start at the opening of the sixth seal.

## 2. The Gog war also marks the start of the end-times

Because Gog, of the land of Magog, is mentioned as the leader of the revolt against Christ the King at the end of the millennium in Rev 20: 7-10, some prophecy experts place the war of Ezekiel 38 and 39 at the end of the millennium. However, there is just too much internal evidence in the passage, placing it just prior to the tribulation, to allow for that interpretation.

Here is the passage with some commentary included.

*Eze 38:1 And the word of the LORD came unto me, saying, 2 Son of man, set thy face against Gog, the land of Magog, the chief prince of Meshech and Tubal, and prophesy against him, 3 And say, Thus saith the Lord GOD; Behold, I am against thee, O Gog, the chief prince of Meshech and Tubal:*

Some prophecy writers identify Magog, Meshech, and Tubal as ancient names for Russia, Moscow, and Tubolsk and Gog as a Russian leader. Thus, this war is often called the Russian Invasion. There is good reason for this as we shall show.

*Eze 38:4 And I will turn thee back, and put hooks into thy jaws, and I will bring thee forth, and all thine army, horses and horsemen, all of them clothed with all sorts of armour, even a great company with bucklers and shields, all of them handling swords:*

God Himself will compel Gog to attack Israel. He will put hooks in Gog's jaw and turn him from his original intentions. From the terminology "turn thee back" it would seem there may be an initial skirmish from which Gog decides to withdraw. This is very similar to God's dealings later with Pharaoh, the King of the South (Ezek. 29:4) and shows us an important facet of God's end-times program. God will proactively drive the events leading up to the return of His Son in power and great glory. God will not just wait for these things to occur; He will cause them to occur on His timetable. We need not be concerned whether the political or sociological climate of Bible prophecies matches the alliances and political powers of a given time. In this case we will see how precisely these events are lining up, or being lined up, right at this point in history.

*Eze 38:5 Persia, Ethiopia, and Libya with them; all of them with shield and helmet:*
*6 Gomer, and all his bands; the house of Togarmah of the north quarters, and all his bands: and many people with thee.*
*7 Be thou prepared, and prepare for thyself, thou, and all thy company that are assembled unto thee, and be thou a guard unto them.*
*8 After many days thou shalt be visited: in the latter years thou shalt come into the land that is brought back from the sword, and is gathered out of many people, against the mountains of Israel,*

*which have been always waste: but it is brought forth out of the nations, and they shall dwell safely all of them.*

Verse 8 adequately describes present day Israel. They dwell safely only in that they are not ruled by any other nation and currently are not officially at war, but prophetically it never gets any better for Israel until the tribulation has ended.

Verses 5 and 6 are of great help for identifying Gog and the land of Magog in that they eliminate a number of nations. We can eliminate Persia from consideration for Magog since Persia is listed as an ally of Magog. The Persian Empire at its zenith included most of the middle east (excluding the Arabian Peninsula) and approached the border of present-day Russia in the area around present-day Georgia. Also included in this empire would be most of present-day Turkey, Syria and Lebanon.

The text also eliminates Ethiopia and Libya which were eliminated anyway by virtue of being south of Israel. In verse 15, we will see that Gog is brought from the north parts. It is not surely known what nations Gomer and Togarmah represent but the popular consensus is that they refer to the peoples from present-day Georgia, Armenia, and possibly Turkey and could also include Germany and other nations with any Celtic influence. Whatever the truth may be in this regard, it seems almost certain that every nation between Russia and Israel will be an ally of Gog who, according to verse 15 in this passage came from his place out of the north parts. Turkey has only recently, and very suddenly, allied herself with Russia and Iran in the fight against the remnant of ISIS and Arabic rebels in Syria. She would, in any case, be considered part of the alliance by virtue of being part of ancient Persia. It would seem then that Russia is the only place left to identify as Magog within the confines of the text.

*Eze 38:9 Thou shalt ascend and come like a storm, thou shalt be like a cloud to cover the land, thou, and all thy bands, and many people with thee.*
*10 Thus saith the Lord GOD; It shall also come to pass, that at the same time shall things come into thy mind, and thou shalt think an evil thought:*
*11 And thou shalt say, I will go up to the land of unwalled villages; I will go to them that are at rest, that dwell safely, all of them dwelling without walls, and having neither bars nor gates,*
*12 To take a spoil, and to take a prey; to turn thine hand upon the desolate places that are now inhabited, and upon the people that are gathered out of the nations, which have gotten cattle and goods, that dwell in the midst of the land.*
*13 Sheba, and Dedan, and the merchants of Tarshish, with all the young lions thereof, shall say unto thee, Art thou come to take a spoil? hast thou gathered thy company to take a prey? to carry away silver and gold, to take away cattle and goods, to take a great spoil?*
*14 Therefore, son of man, prophesy and say unto Gog, Thus saith the Lord GOD; In that day when my people of Israel dwelleth safely, shalt thou not know it?*
*15 And thou shalt come from thy place out of the north parts, thou, and many people with thee, all of them riding upon horses, a great company, and a mighty army:*
*16 And thou shalt come up against my people of Israel, as a cloud to cover the land; it shall be in the latter days, and I will bring thee against my land, that the heathen may know me, when I shall be sanctified in thee, O Gog, before their eyes.*

Sheba and Dedan have been compellingly identified as peoples from the Arabian Peninsula. They will not be involved in this attack. In fact, they may still be aligned with the west meaning Europe and the western hemisphere. Tarshish has been identified with a few cities but never satisfactorily. It identifies better with some generalized faraway place reached by ship or a system of trade by ship. In essence, it probably refers here to the entire western civilization or the oil trading partners of Saudi Arabia.

Verse 13 here twice mentions that Gog is suspected of coming into Israel to take a spoil. Historically there probably hasn't been enough spoil in Israel to warrant such a great effort. However, it has recently been determined that a shale oil field in the Shfela basin, and the Leviathan oil and gas field in the Mediterranean Sea, as well as oil and gas fields near Gaza, and the most recently discovered giant field on the Golan Heights may soon make Israel one of the highest volume energy producers in the world. Israel now has the potential to become a very wealthy nation within the next ten years. Lebanon, Cyprus and Turkey are also claiming ownership of some of the offshore oil and are warning Israel to stay away. The Muslim nations of the Middle East, driven by hatred and jealousy, will almost certainly be looking to pick a fight with Israel over all this. Russia too, has built her miraculous recovery on her oil resources. Don't believe for a moment that her current intentions in Syria are about anything other than oil and gas.

Verse 16 says that one reason that **God will bring Gog against Israel is so that the heathen will come to know him.** Further verses in the passage will greatly amplify that theme. It is impossible that the heathen would not already know God at the end of the millennial reign of

Christ based on biblical descriptions of the duties of the nations at that time.  **For that reason alone, this event must occur long before the final Gog war of Revelation 20:8**

*Eze 38:17  Thus saith the Lord GOD; Art thou he of whom I have spoken in old time by my servants the prophets of Israel, which prophesied in those days many years that I would bring thee against them?*

God said that He had prophesied in old time that He would bring Gog against Israel in this manner.  There is no record that Gog was prophesied by name but there is a character called the Assyrian mentioned by both Isaiah and Micah some 150 years before Ezekiel's time.   Interestingly, the terminology used by Isaiah is very reminiscent of verses 10-13 above:

*Isa 10:5  O Assyrian, the rod of mine anger, and the staff in their hand is mine indignation.
6  I will send him against an hypocritical nation, and against the people of my wrath will I give him a charge, to take the spoil, and to take the prey, and to tread them down like the mire of the streets.
7  Howbeit he meaneth not so, neither doth his heart think so; but it is in his heart to destroy and cut off nations not a few.*

This passage is primarily speaking of the captivity of the ten northern tribes and Samaria and the subsequent attack on Jerusalem in Isaiah's day.  However, as with many such passages, there is also a definite end-times context here as seen in verses 20-23 of that chapter (i.e., 'that day'):

*Isa 10:20 And it shall come to pass in that day, that the remnant of Israel, and such as are escaped of the house of Jacob, shall no more again stay upon him that smote them; but shall stay upon the LORD, the Holy One of Israel, in truth.*
*21 The remnant shall return, even the remnant of Jacob, unto the mighty God.*
*22 For though thy people Israel be as the sand of the sea, yet a remnant of them shall return: the consumption decreed shall overflow with righteousness.*
*23 For the Lord GOD of hosts shall make a consumption, even determined, in the midst of all the land.*

It is important to note here that Gog is not out of ancient Assyria. Assyria was later swallowed up in subsequent empires including the Persian Empire. We have already established that Gog is not from any part of the Persian Empire. His attack will occur because he will be sent by God in a manner similar to the way the Assyrian was sent. He is the modern-day equivalent of the Assyrian in methodology and ruthlessness. Israel faces two invaders around the start of the tribulation:

*Jer 50:17 Israel is a scattered sheep; the lions have driven him away: first the king of Assyria hath devoured him; and last this Nebuchadrezzar king of Babylon hath broken his bones.*

The context of this passage is the last days and specifically says the king of Assyria will attack first. Thus, there is good evidence that Gog is the last days equivalent of the Assyrian.

*Eze 38:18 And it shall come to pass at the same time when Gog shall come against the land of Israel, saith the Lord GOD, that my fury shall come up in my face.*

*19 For in my jealousy and in the fire of my wrath have I spoken, Surely in that day there shall be a great shaking in the land of Israel;*
*20 So that the fishes of the sea, and the fowls of the heaven, and the beasts of the field, and all creeping things that creep upon the earth, and all the men that are upon the face of the earth, shall shake at my presence, and the mountains shall be thrown down, and the steep places shall fall, and every wall shall fall to the ground.*

This passage has several companion passages that lock in its time frame. Note the common themes of (1.) God's fury and jealousy and the fire of His wrath, (2.) An immense earthquake, (3.) the presence and fear of God which causes all men, worldwide, to shake and (4.) The tumbling down of mountains. By this point we know exactly what this is all about. Here are a couple of reminder verses.

*Isa 2:12 For the day of the LORD of hosts shall be upon every one that is proud and lofty, and upon every one that is lifted up; and he shall be brought low:*
*Isa 2:19 And they shall go into the holes of the rocks, and into the caves of the earth, for fear of the LORD, and for the glory of his majesty, when he ariseth to shake terribly the earth.*

And:

*Isa 13:13 Therefore I will shake the heavens, and the earth shall remove out of her place, in the wrath of the LORD of hosts, and in the day of his fierce anger.*

And:

*Rev 6:15 And the kings of the earth, and the great men, and the rich men, and the chief captains, and the mighty*

*men, and every bondman, and every free man, hid themselves in the dens and in the rocks of the mountains;*
*16 And said to the mountains and rocks, Fall on us, and hide us from the face of him that sitteth on the throne, and from the wrath of the Lamb:*
*17 For the great day of his wrath is come; and who shall be able to stand?*

Verse 17 in this companion passage tells us that this is the point at which the great day of God's wrath is come. **The day of the LORD has begun!** It is a wonder to me that there is ever any discussion about when the day of the LORD begins. These passages couldn't be clearer.

The sixth seal context for this passage in Ezekiel is very strong but it will get even better when we demonstrate later that the pre-tribulation rapture occurs when the sixth seal is opened. This rapture is strongly supported in this passage, so we must continue revealing some of the truths regarding it.

### The first trumpet judgment in the tribulation – Ezekiel 38:21-22.

We have now arrived at the day of the LORD as well as the seven-year tribulation. The next tribulation event that applies to the whole Earth is the first trumpet judgment, right at the beginning of the seven-year tribulation and right after the sixth seal events. This is brought on by the opening of the seventh seal. Compare the first trumpet judgment with verses 21 and 22 below.

*Rev 8:6 And the seven angels which had the seven trumpets prepared themselves to sound.*

*7 The first angel sounded, and there followed **hail and fire mingled with blood**, and they were cast upon the earth: and the third part of trees was burnt up, and all green grass was burnt up.*

Now back to our Ezekiel text:

*Eze 38:21 And I will call for a sword against him throughout all my mountains, saith the Lord GOD: every man's sword shall be against his brother.*
*22 And I will plead against him **with pestilence and with blood**; and I will rain upon him, and upon his bands, and upon the many people that are with him, an overflowing rain, and **great hailstones, fire, and brimstone.***

It is fascinating to discover where that blood comes from. Jesus lived as a flesh and blood man, yet when He rose from the grave, He referred to Himself as flesh and bones (Luke 24:39). This was because He had shed His blood on the cross. Additionally, Paul tells us in 1 Cor. 15:50 that flesh and blood cannot inherit the kingdom of God. He goes on in that passage to explain that our flesh must be changed to an incorruptible body. Finally, we are told:

*1Jn 3:2 Beloved, now are we the sons of God, and it doth not yet appear what we shall be: but we know that, when he shall appear, **we shall be like him**; for we shall see him as he is.*

The upshot of all this is that we will not have blood in our heavenly or celestial bodies. Therefore, if the pre-tribulation rapture has just occurred, it is entirely likely that, as the saints are rising into the heavens, they will shed their blood in the atmosphere which would then fall back down to the ground.

This explains why we will never have hunger or thirst again in our resurrected bodies. The whole purpose of blood is to bring nutrients to our cells so they can live and function. None of this is necessary when the Holy Ghost indwells every cell and is providing all the energy we need. John noted this when describing the Christians taken in the pre-tribulation rapture:

*Rev 7:16 They shall hunger no more, neither thirst any more; neither shall the sun light on them, nor any heat.*

This is also what Jesus was preaching when so many turned back from Him. They could not understand this concept. All who partook of Him would also partake of the Holy Ghost and thus eventually would receive a bloodless, glorified body.

*Joh 6:35 And Jesus said unto them, I am the bread of life: he that cometh to me shall never hunger; and he that believeth on me shall never thirst.*

We have established that the tribulation starts at the opening of the sixth seal and will later establish that the pre-tribulation rapture occurs at the same time. Therefore, we can see that there is no imminence in the timing of the pre-trib rapture. It will occur during the Gog war against Israel. This means that the real trick to knowing when the rapture is about to occur is in properly identifying Gog.

*Eze 38:23 Thus will I magnify myself, and sanctify myself; and I will be known in the eyes of many nations, and they shall know that I am the LORD.*

This passage is another one of several similar internal proofs that this war starts prior to the millennial reign of

Christ. It would be impossible for the nations to deny the existence of JEHOVAH God when Christ has reigned on the Earth for 1000 years. Therefore, the events of this verse must occur before the second coming of Christ.

*Eze 39:1 Therefore, thou son of man, prophesy against Gog, and say, Thus saith the Lord GOD; Behold, I am against thee, O Gog, the chief prince of Meshech and Tubal:*
*2 And I will turn thee back, and leave but the sixth part of thee, and will cause thee to come up from the north parts, and will bring thee upon the mountains of Israel:*
*3 And I will smite thy bow out of thy left hand, and will cause thine arrows to fall out of thy right hand.*
*4 Thou shalt fall upon the mountains of Israel, thou, and all thy bands, and the people that is with thee: I will give thee unto the ravenous birds of every sort, and to the beasts of the field to be devoured.*
*5 Thou shalt fall upon the open field: for I have spoken it, saith the Lord GOD.*
*6 And I will send a fire on Magog, and among them that dwell carelessly in the isles: and they shall know that I am the LORD.*

Returning to the passage on the Assyrian, we find an interesting companion theme:

*Isa 10:5 O Assyrian, the rod of mine anger, and the staff in their hand is mine indignation.*
*Isa 10:12 Wherefore it shall come to pass,* **that when the Lord hath performed his whole work upon mount Zion and on Jerusalem**, *I will punish the fruit of the stout heart of the king of Assyria, and the glory of his high looks.*
*Isa 10:16 Therefore shall the Lord, the Lord of hosts, send among his fat ones leanness; and under his glory he shall kindle a burning like the burning of a fire.*
**17 And the light of Israel shall be for a fire, and his Holy One for a flame:** *and it shall burn and devour his thorns and his briers in one day;*

*18 **And shall consume the glory of his forest, and of his fruitful field, both soul and body**: and they shall be as when a standardbearer fainteth.
19 And the rest of **the trees of his forest shall be few, that a child may write them.***

Here again we see destruction by fire in the land of the aggressor. Just as in the case of the first trumpet judgment the trees are specifically targeted. The land of the Assyrian and the land of Magog are both closely tied to the first trumpet judgment.

Remember, we saw in Revelation 8:6 that the third part of the trees on the Earth are burned up in the first trumpet judgment at the same time it was raining blood. Now, the pre-trib raptured saints will all rise to meet the Lord in the air and travel with Him into space just as Jesus rose through the clouds in Acts 1:9. Let's then, take a look at where heaven is located relative to our Earth. Isaiah quoted Satan as saying at his fall:

*Isa 14:13 For thou hast said in thine heart, I will ascend into heaven, I will exalt my throne above the stars of God: I will sit also upon the mount of the congregation, **in the sides of the north**:
14 I will ascend **above the heights of the clouds**; I will be like the most High.*

Notice that heaven is above the clouds and the stars, and in the north. This is verified in Psalm 48:2. Now let's look at another curious passage:

*Job 26:7 He stretcheth out the north over the empty place, and hangeth the earth upon nothing.*

*8 He bindeth up the waters in his thick clouds; and the cloud is not rent under them.
9 He holdeth back the face of his throne, and spreadeth his cloud upon it.*

Now watch how this all comes together. The saints rise over the northern hemisphere. God has kept the area over the north pole relatively free of stars, possibly for this reason. Here, it is called the empty place. As we pointed out, the saints shed their blood as they rise. This blood then falls over the upper portion of the northern hemisphere. Now from about 50 degrees of latitude north to 70 degrees north, all around the globe, are the great boreal forests. They represent the world's largest land-based biome and contain 29% of the Earth's Forest cover. So, when 33% of the Earth's trees are burned up by hail and fire mingled with blood in the first trumpet judgment, that almost assuredly includes the majority of the boreal forests. Do you know where the majority of the world's boreal forests are? That's right, Russia. The land of Magog! And not only Magog! Let's look again at verse 6 of our passage:

*6 And I will send a fire on Magog,* **and among them that dwell carelessly in the isles**: *and they shall know that I am the LORD.*

The second greatest boreal forest in the world is in North America, primarily Canada and Alaska. All of the western hemisphere is part of the biblical "isles of the sea" from the standpoint of Israel being on the mainland. So, the first trumpet judgment occurs primarily in the boreal forests that circle the Earth above 50 degrees north in latitude.

In addition to the rain of blood and hailstones, we see fire and brimstone raining down as well. This is not just figurative language either. There are several verses that tell us the mountains will melt or become molten just like a volcano. Here are a few: Psa. 104:32, Psa. 144:5, Nah. 1:5 and Isa. 64:1-3. Our comparative verses stressed that the hills would melt and run down. So, what is going on here is that volcanos are erupting at the same time. The fire and brimstone are molten lava blowing high into the atmosphere and then falling back to Earth. Brimstone in the Bible is the molten rock under the surface of the Earth. Bozrah is a place where brimstone breaks through the surface. The rising saints will see quite a spectacle below them!

Once you begin to understand the order of prophetic events and can place them in their proper chronological order, many more statements in the Bible become understandable. The most important point this exercise should drive home is that every word in the Book is important and nothing is superfluous. On the other hand, much of the Book will always be fuzzy unless you believe every word is exactly the word God intended to put there. (This only works in the KJV.)

Finally, in this passage we see that Gog will fall upon the mountains of Israel. Since this is quite different from the death of the Beast who was cast alive into the Lake of Fire according to Revelation 19:20, Gog cannot be the Beast, as some have speculated, who is the final antichrist prior to the millennium. Additionally, since his campaign is entirely against Israel, he cannot be confused with the king of the north. We must conclude that Gog is a separate end-times character who is primarily used by God to reveal Himself as the JEHOVAH God of Israel to His people and the whole world. From this point on, it will not take any faith to believe in the existence of the God of Israel.

## The announcement of the start of the day of the Lord - Ezekiel 39:8.

*Eze 39:7 So will I make my holy name known in the midst of my people Israel; and I will not let them pollute my holy name any more: and the heathen shall know that I am the LORD, the Holy One in Israel.*
*8 Behold, it is come, and it is done, saith the Lord GOD; this is the day whereof I have spoken.*

The day whereof the Lord has spoken is almost assuredly the day of the LORD. This type of language is frequently used, and the reader is always expected to understand what day is under discussion. This is additional evidence that this passage cannot be applied to the end of the millennium. It is plainly saying the day of the LORD has just started.

*Eze 39:9 And they that dwell in the cities of Israel shall go forth, and shall set on fire and burn the weapons, both the shields and the bucklers, the bows and the arrows, and the handstaves, and the spears, and they shall burn them with fire seven years:*

Here is yet more evidence that this war is not the Gog war of Revelation 20. Immediately after that war, we see the Great White Throne judgment and final destruction of this present universe. There is no time or need for burying the dead. All the dead are raised at that point. On the other hand, seven years is a very significant time frame if this war occurs just prior to the seven-year tribulation.

*Eze 39:10 So that they shall take no wood out of the field, neither cut down any out of the forests; for they shall burn the weapons with fire: and they shall spoil those that spoiled them, and rob those that robbed them, saith the Lord GOD.*
*11 And it shall come to pass in that day, that I will give unto Gog a place there of graves in Israel, the valley of the passengers on the east of the sea: and it shall stop the noses of the passengers: and there shall they bury Gog and all his multitude: and they shall call it The valley of Hamongog.*

In Joel chapter 2 we find a companion passage to this verse that again helps to establish the timeframe. Joel 2:30-31 establishes an end-times context for this passage.

*Joe 2:20 But I will remove far off from you the northern army, and will drive him into a land barren and desolate, with his face toward the east sea, and his hinder part toward the utmost sea, and his stink shall come up, and his ill savour shall come up, because he hath done great things.*

Back to Ezekiel:

*Eze 39:12 And seven months shall the house of Israel be burying of them, that they may cleanse the land.*
*13 Yea, all the people of the land shall bury them; and it shall be to them a renown the day that I shall be glorified, saith the Lord GOD.*
*14 And they shall sever out men of continual employment, passing through the land to bury with the passengers those that remain upon the face of the earth, to cleanse it: after the end of seven months shall they search.*
*15 And the passengers that pass through the land, when any seeth a man's bone, then shall he set up a sign by it, till the buriers have buried it in the valley of Hamongog.*
*16 And also the name of the city shall be Hamonah. Thus shall they cleanse the land.*
*17 And, thou son of man, thus saith the Lord GOD; Speak unto every feathered fowl, and to every beast of the field, Assemble yourselves, and come; gather yourselves on every side to my*

*sacrifice that I do sacrifice for you, even a great sacrifice upon the mountains of Israel, that ye may eat flesh, and drink blood.
18 Ye shall eat the flesh of the mighty, and drink the blood of the princes of the earth, of rams, of lambs, and of goats, of bullocks, all of them fatlings of Bashan.
19 And ye shall eat fat till ye be full, and drink blood till ye be drunken, of my sacrifice which I have sacrificed for you.
20 Thus ye shall be filled at my table with horses and chariots, with mighty men, and with all men of war, saith the Lord GOD.
21 And I will set my glory among the heathen, and all the heathen shall see my judgment that I have executed, and my hand that I have laid upon them.
22 So the house of Israel shall know that I am the LORD their God from that day and forward.
23 And the heathen shall know that the house of Israel went into captivity for their iniquity: because they trespassed against me, therefore hid I my face from them, and gave them into the hand of their enemies: so fell they all by the sword.*

This is a continuous theme through these two chapters. God stresses several times that from this point on all the world will know who He is and what His program with Israel has been. That is entirely consistent with the narrative of the tribulation. Once it starts there is a complete record of how it will progress. There is no longer room for any doubt about the existence of JEHOVAH God. There will be no unbelievers although there obviously will be many that doubt His omnipotence. This is when the world is first introduced to JEHOVAH God in such a way that His existence can no longer be denied. It completely precludes the war of these chapters from occurring at the end of the millennium when JEHOVAH will have already been known for a thousand years.

*Eze 39:24 According to their uncleanness and according to their transgressions have I done unto them, and hid my face from them.*

*25 Therefore thus saith the Lord GOD; Now will I bring again the captivity of Jacob, and have mercy upon the whole house of Israel, and will be jealous for my holy name;*
*26 After that they have borne their shame, and all their trespasses whereby they have trespassed against me, when they dwelt safely in their land, and none made them afraid.*
*27 When I have brought them again from the people, and gathered them out of their enemies' lands, and am sanctified in them in the sight of many nations;*
*28 Then shall they know that I am the LORD their God, which caused them to be led into captivity among the heathen: but I have gathered them unto their own land, and have left none of them any more there.*
*29 Neither will I hide my face any more from them: for I have poured out my spirit upon the house of Israel, saith the Lord GOD.*

These last 6 verses explain that God will bring all Jews back to Israel and bring them through the tribulation until they will fully understand and acknowledge who He is to them.

This passage definitively applies to Old Testament Israel and the Jews as an ethnic people. Many in the Church today try to deny that God's promises to the Jews are to be applied to an ethnic group. They claim that the Church Age Christians are now the spiritual Jews and heirs to all His promises to the Jews. They believe the Jews are no longer a chosen people, having been replaced by the Church. The language of these two chapters so specifically references the physical world that a Bible literalist has no choice but to affirm that Israel is still a special nation in the sight of God.

In conclusion, Gog is a last-days Russian leader who forms an alliance with many other nations and attacks Israel just before the tribulation begins. The attack is quite brutal, so much so that God's fury comes up in His face. God will then miraculously cause Gog's defeat and send a rain of fire and brimstone and great hail and blood on his armies and his homeland. The war begins just prior to the start of the seven-year tribulation and ends shortly after the pre-tribulation rapture occurs and the tribulation has begun, probably at the time of the first trumpet judgment. This is our best indicator yet for the timing of the pre-trib rapture. When Gog enters Israel, we are probably hours, days, weeks, or at most months from the tribulation!

### 3. Elijah the Prophet

*Mal 4:5 Behold, I will send you Elijah the prophet before the coming of the great and dreadful day of the LORD:*

*6 And he shall turn the heart of the fathers to the children, and the heart of the children to their fathers, lest I come and smite the earth with a curse.*

These are the final two verses in the Old Testament. It is very important to note that Elijah will come before the day of the LORD begins. Thus, there will be a mighty prophet of God to prepare us for what is coming and to prepare the way of the Lord. This is a critically important point to realize because there is a very high probability that he will be totally rejected by much of the leadership of the Church.

Have you ever heard the phrase: "We mustn't be date setters!!!"? This has become a rallying cry for the vast majority of the pre-trib believers. It is highly probable that this prophet will be a date setter. That, of course, would destroy the Darby doctrine of imminence. It would mean that these teachers had been wrong all along. They will therefore likely just write him off as another false prophet. Don't you get caught in this trap!

Verse 6 of the passage above kind of drops the hint on this reaction. Looking at it from a slightly different angle, we can say that if Elijah fails to *"turn the heart of the fathers to the children, and the heart of the children to their fathers"*, then God will come and smite the Earth with a curse. Since we see many curses on the Earth once the day of the LORD starts (and some before), we can safely conclude that part of his ministry will fail and that may be justification for the religious leadership to reject him as a prophet.

## Jesus identified Elijah when He walked the Earth 2000 years ago

Remember that we stressed that the day of the LORD was at hand when Jesus appeared as Messiah? When the Jews rejected Messiah, their King, the day of the LORD was postponed for 2000 years until the times of the Gentiles were fulfilled. However, before that postponement Elijah had to appear and in fact Jesus was careful to identify him. Here is what he said:

*Mat 17:10 And his disciples asked him, saying, Why then say the scribes that Elias must first come?*

*11 And Jesus answered and said unto them, Elias truly shall first come, and restore all things.*

*12 But I say unto you, That Elias is come already, and they knew him not, but have done unto him whatsoever they listed. Likewise shall also the Son of man suffer of them.*

*13 Then the disciples understood that he spake unto them of John the Baptist.*

In the New Testament, Elijah is called Elias. In verse 10 above, the disciples were remembering Mal. 4:5-6. It seems likely that they believed the day of the LORD was at hand but wondered where Elijah was. They were aware that many Jews questioned whether Jesus was actually Elijah Himself.

In verse 11 Jesus assured them that they were correct in their belief about Elijah. He then gave them an important part of Elijah's ministry or responsibility by saying he would "restore all things".

In verse 12, He drops the bombshell on them. He tells them Elijah had already come and that they had done unto him whatever they listed or pleased. At this point the disciples realized that He spoke of John the Baptist whom Herod had beheaded. And, not only had he already come, but he would come again a third time indicating that the day of the LORD would again be at hand at some later point in time. Now since he came as a different man with a different name the second time, it would seem prudent to expect an entirely different man the third time. Thus, we would expect that he won't be immediately recognizable when he comes back. We will have to recognize him by the accomplishment of his ministries.

So, Elijah came as a man named John the Baptist. He had a different name and returned as a baby born to different parents. And yet, he was truly Elijah. That is explained in the following verses.

*Luk 1:11 And there appeared unto him an angel of the Lord standing on the right side of the altar of incense.*

*12 And when Zacharias saw him, he was troubled, and fear fell upon him.*

*13 But the angel said unto him, Fear not, Zacharias: for thy prayer is heard; and thy wife Elisabeth shall bear thee a son, and thou shalt call his name John.*

*14 And thou shalt have joy and gladness; and many shall rejoice at his birth.*

*15 For he shall be great in the sight of the Lord, and shall drink neither wine nor strong drink; and he shall be filled with the Holy Ghost, even from his mother's womb.*

*16 And many of the children of Israel shall he turn to the Lord their God.*

*17 And he shall go before him in the spirit and power of Elias, to turn the hearts of the fathers to the children, and the disobedient to the wisdom of the just; to make ready a people prepared for the Lord.*

We see that Elijah was filled with the Holy Ghost even from his mother's womb. In Christian theology, only saved people are filled with the Holy Ghost. So, Elijah was born with his salvation intact. There was no double jeopardy for him in this reappearance.

In this prophecy we are told that he would turn many of the children of Israel to the Lord their God. And he did this in his baptizing ministry. Hopefully, this prophecy will be fulfilled again when he comes for the third time when the day of the LORD is at hand for the second time.

In verse 17, we see that he will go before Christ in the spirit and power of Elijah. So, although he was living in a different body in a different time era, he still had all the spiritual power of Elijah. His ministry was still to turn the hearts of the fathers to the children as Malachi had prophesied, but also to turn the disobedient to the wisdom of the just. His ministry then, was to make ready a people prepared for the Lord Jesus.

This is reinforced in the Apostle John's Gospel when, referring to John the Baptist, he wrote:

*Joh 1:6 There was a man sent from God, whose name*

*was John.*

*7 The same came for a witness, to bear witness of the Light, that all men through him might believe.*

John the Baptist was specifically sent from God. John was not raised up by God or mightily used of God, he was sent **from** God which means he was with God and then sent to Earth. This was not just another man. He was a man sent from heaven to Earth for the express purpose of bearing witness to the Light of the world, Jesus Christ. The man that God sent here from heaven was, in fact, the very soul of Elijah in the body of another man. He had been prophesied and now here he was. It is amazing to me that many people seem to reject such a straightforward prophecy-then-fulfillment record in the scriptures.

John the Baptist lived on Earth just long enough to deliver his message and then was removed through the death of a tribulation martyr (Rev. 20:4). His purpose and mission had been completed and he was allowed to return to glory rather than having to spend any more time in a vile and ungodly environment.

Luke quoted Jesus this way:

*Luk 7:26 But what went ye out for to see? A prophet? Yea, I say unto you, and much more than a prophet.*

*27 This is he, of whom it is written, Behold, I send my messenger before thy face, which shall prepare thy way before thee.*

*28 For I say unto you, Among those that are born of women there is not a greater prophet than John the Baptist: but he that is least in the kingdom of God is greater than he.*

John the Baptist was among the greatest of prophets! In

fact, he was much more than a prophet. He was a special messenger whose primary mission was to prepare the way of the Savior Messiah. Even with this glowing confirmation from the Lord Himself, John the Baptist did little or no actual prophesying of future events. Thus, the Lord must have been referring to his former ministry as Elijah.

The question we must ask is whether his ministry remains the same for his third appearance. It is very important to note that, although John the Baptist did not realize that he was Elijah, he did realize that he was meant to fulfill certain OT prophecies. It is recorded thusly:

*Joh 1:19 And this is the record of John, when the Jews sent priests and Levites from Jerusalem to ask him, Who art thou?*

*20 And he confessed, and denied not; but confessed, I am not the Christ.*

*21 And they asked him, What then? Art thou Elias? And he saith, I am not. Art thou that prophet? And he answered, No.*

*22 Then said they unto him, Who art thou? that we may give an answer to them that sent us. What sayest thou of thyself?*

*23 He said, I am the voice of one crying in the wilderness, Make straight the way of the Lord, as said the prophet Esaias.*

This prophecy in verse 23 is found in Isaiah chapter 40:

*Isa 40:3 The voice of him that crieth in the wilderness, Prepare ye the way of the LORD, make straight in the desert a highway for our God.*

*4 Every valley shall be exalted, and every mountain and hill shall be made low: and the crooked shall be made straight, and the rough places plain:*

*5 And the glory of the LORD shall be revealed, and all flesh shall see it together: for the mouth of the LORD hath spoken it.*

You should take note that John did not recite the full prophecy here. He left out the parts about the mountains falling down and the glory of the LORD being revealed. And in fact, they did not happen at that time, so he **must** come again and complete the original prophecy.

Verses 4 and 5 here tie this passage to the day of the LORD. Consider again this passage as a comparison here:

*Rev 6:14 And the heaven departed as a scroll when it is rolled together; and every mountain and island were moved out of their places.*

*15 And the kings of the earth, and the great men, and the rich men, and the chief captains, and the mighty men, and every bondman, and every free man, hid themselves in the dens and in the rocks of the mountains;*

*16 And said to the mountains and rocks, Fall on us, and hide us from the face of him that sitteth on the throne, and from the wrath of the Lamb:*

And:

*Isa 13:13 Therefore I will shake the heavens, and the earth shall remove out of her place, in the wrath of the LORD of hosts, and in the day of his fierce anger.*

This all happens at the same time that God "Ariseth to shake terribly the Earth" and "then shall my fury come up in my face". The following is speculation, but it fits precisely with the results we should expect from these events.

There will be a massive, worldwide earthquake so

powerful that Earth's overlapping tectonic plates will separate allowing the mountains to collapse and fill the valleys. This is what Rev 6:14 seems to be describing. The very Earth itself will undergo an alteration in its orbital position, likely altering the length of a solar year, and likely back to 360 days.

I am of the opinion that before the flood a solar year was 360 days, meaning the Earth moved exactly one degree per day around the sun. When the fountains of the great deep were broken up (Gen. 7:11), it is likely the explosion drove the Earth out of its orbit. You can see exactly where these fountains came from by examining a world map or globe that shows the topography of the ocean floor. There are great trenches almost circling the Earth where these fountains came from below the Earth's crust. There was likely a cushion of water below the crust of the Earth that hydraulically stabilized the crust. Some scientists say there is still water under the crust. It has been calculated that a cushion of water 2 miles thick would have been enough water to cover the entire Earth above the mountains.

You should also note that the dry land was split apart by this explosion, creating the continental drift that left the continents in their present position. This can be seen by comparing continental coastlines between the two hemispheres along with the mid-Atlantic Ocean trenches and seeing how they could all be fit back together in a single land mass.

Perhaps the Earth will return to that former position in time for the millennium when Christ reigns on Earth in His bodily form. Major changes will be necessary for the Earth to support the massive population that will exist by the end of that thousand years. It is likely that God is creating much more habitable and tillable land through the changes that occur in the tribulation.

So, Elijah will prophesy the words of Isaiah 40:3-5. Talk about a purveyor of gloom and doom! Scriptures make such matter-of-fact statements about major, catastrophic events that we tend to minimize them when we read about them. That is why we need to meditate on the words and consider what they are saying as they apply to individuals who experience them.

We should note that according to Luke 1, John the Baptist preceded Jesus by about six months and was murdered shortly after he had baptized the Lord. We might reasonably expect the duration of Elijah's ministry to be quite short again this time. He will come just in time to warn the world of what is coming and will become unnecessary once the two witnesses of Rev. 11 come on the scene.

Jesus also gave some information regarding this time in the following passage. When the times of the Gentiles are fulfilled, He says much the same things regarding the heavens but adds information about the sea and the waves. Along with such great shaking will come horrific tsunamis described in verse 25 below.

The upshot of this will no doubt be the utter decimation of the western hemisphere where both shores have mountain ranges that will collapse. There is no mention of the United States or any western hemisphere nations in prophecy, a fact which lends credence to this speculation. That is probably because those nations cease to exist when the day of the LORD starts.

*Luk 21:24 And they shall fall by the edge of the sword, and shall be led away captive into all nations: and Jerusalem shall be trodden down of the Gentiles, until the times of the Gentiles be fulfilled.*

*25 And there shall be signs in the sun, and in the moon, and in the stars; and upon the earth distress of nations, with perplexity;* **the sea and the waves roaring;**

*26 Men's hearts failing them for fear, and for looking after those things which are coming on the earth: for the powers of heaven shall be shaken.*

*27 And then shall they see the Son of man coming in a cloud with power and great glory.*

*28 And when these things begin to come to pass, then look up, and lift up your heads; for your redemption draweth nigh.*

The prophet Habakkuk foresaw this same time and summed it up very succinctly in this passage:

*Hab 3:6 He stood, and measured the earth: he beheld, and drove asunder the nations; and the everlasting mountains were scattered, the perpetual hills did bow: his ways are everlasting.*

*Hab 3:10 The mountains saw thee, and they trembled: the overflowing of the water passed by: the deep uttered his voice, and lifted up his hands on high.*

Verse 27 of the passage in Luke has its counterpart in sixth seal/start of the day of the LORD passage in Rev. 6:12-18 as follows:

*Rev 6:16 And said to the mountains and rocks, Fall on us, and hide us from the face of him that sitteth on the throne, and from the wrath of the Lamb:*

The Lord is "coming in a cloud" here and apparently sitting on His mobile throne. This throne, with its accompanying clouds, was painstakingly described by the prophet Ezekiel in Ezekiel chapter 1. If you compare these passages, you will find that clouds seem to accompany Jesus when He appears in His power and glory. Also see Acts 1:9-11, Rev. 1:7, and Job 26:9. Because it is mentioned first, it appears the face of the Lamb is more terrifying than His wrath.

The final important thing of note in this passage is found in verse 28. When these things **begin** to come to pass, our redemption draweth nigh. If this coming of the Lord were speaking of the second coming of Christ, we would have been looking up for seven years already and suffered many more terrible plagues. This is meant as a message of hope of redemption before all these things come to pass. In fact, this message from Jesus in Luke 21 ends with this statement:

*Luk 21:36 Watch ye therefore, and pray always, that ye may be accounted worthy to escape all these things that shall come to pass, and to stand before the Son of man.*

So, we find that conditioned on our worthiness, we can escape all these things and stand before the Son of man. Commit this to memory as it will be more fully developed in a later chapter. **The day of the LORD is also the day of redemption.** See also Eph. 4:30.

Continuing with verse 36, we see that we can watch for these things and avoid them. This is but one more nail in the coffin for the doctrine of imminence. Imminence tells us there are no signs or events we can count on occurring before the pre-trib rapture and yet the Lord here claims that there are.

There is one more passage we should look at. Not because it adds lots of new information but because it, just as Habakkuk did, so neatly puts all this together. This passage was written by King David hundreds of years before the prophets we are looking at came on the scene.

Here it is:

*Psa 46 To the chief Musician for the sons of Korah, A Song upon Alamoth.*

*1 God is our refuge and strength, a very present help in trouble.*

*2 Therefore will not we fear, though the earth be removed, and though the mountains be carried into the midst of the sea;*

*3 Though the waters thereof roar and be troubled, though the mountains shake with the swelling thereof. Selah.*

*Psa 46:6 The heathen raged, the kingdoms were moved: he uttered his voice, the earth melted.*

*Psa 46:8 Come, behold the works of the LORD, what desolations he hath made in the earth.*

Now that we know what the day of the LORD looks like, it is not difficult to understand what is spoken of here. Passages like this assure us that there is truly only one Author of the King James Bible.

**The final ministry of Elijah**

Elijah carried out many specifics of his ministry in the person of John the Baptist. But some fulfillments were not complete. We can't be sure if he will repeat the ministries specifically ascribed to John the Baptist in Luke 1, but we can fully expect him to fulfill all the prophecies before and after this time period. So, lets enumerate and then consider those prophecies.

A. *Mal 4:6 And he shall turn the heart of the fathers to the children, and the heart of the children to their fathers, lest I come and smite the earth with a curse.*

B. Isa 40:3 *The voice of him that crieth in the wilderness, Prepare ye the way of the LORD, make straight in the desert a highway for our God.*

*4 Every valley shall be exalted, and every mountain and hill shall be made low: and the crooked shall be made straight, and the rough places plain:*

*5 And the glory of the LORD shall be revealed, and all flesh shall see it together: for the mouth of the LORD hath spoken it.*

C. Mat 17:11 *And Jesus answered and said unto them, Elias truly shall first come, and restore all things.*

Here are the vital points of Elijah's prophesied ministry:

1. To restore the hearts of the fathers and their children to each other.

2. To cry in the wilderness:

    a. To prepare the way of the Lord.

    b. To call for a highway in the desert to be made for our God.

3. To prophesy the start of the day of the LORD and the opening of the sixth seal as described in so many prophecies we have already considered.

4. To prophesy the revelation of the glory of the LORD through the revealing of His Son Jesus.

5. To warn us that all flesh will see this glory together or at the same time.

6. To assure us that this has all been previously prophesied by the LORD

7. To restore all things.

**Putting it all together**

In this chapter we have seen that the start of the day of the LORD occurs at the opening of the sixth seal and that Elijah will come just prior to that time to preach and confirm the prophecies. This ministry is going to be quite sensational. It will likely be decried by the religious leadership but eagerly accepted by many among the laity. This is exactly what happened to John the Baptist (see Luke 7:28-30) and when it comes to 'day of the LORD' prophecies we see that history always repeats itself albeit with slight differences to fit the times.

The similarities to John the Baptist are required by the passage in Isaiah. John the Baptist came out of the wilderness to prepare the way of the Lord in his time (see Luke 3:2, Mark 1:4, John 16:1-8, and Matt. 11:10). This must happen again in some form. We have no record of John calling for a highway in the desert for our God, but surely Elijah will do that in this final appearance.

The last days Elijah will also cry or warn us about the great shaking that will cause the mountains to tumble down and fill the valleys along with all the attendant events. To accomplish this, he will necessarily have to tie many of the prophecies we have discussed in this chapter together. He will have to explain the first five seals of Rev. chapter 6 and put them in their proper context. We will discuss these in detail in a later chapter. There is a high probability that he will tell us the exact date of these events because there is no longer any reason to withhold that information (see Acts 1:6-7). He will, no doubt, point to Jesus' prophecy of great tsunamis and the massive loss of life that will accompany all of this.

Next, we see that he will prophesy the coming of the Lord Jesus to glorify the LORD JEHOVAH. Malachi, the very prophet who tells us Elijah will return, explains all this very succinctly in this verse:

*Mal 3:1 Behold, I will send my messenger, and he shall prepare the way before me: and the Lord, whom ye seek, shall suddenly come to his temple, even the messenger of the covenant, whom ye delight in: behold, he shall come, saith the LORD of hosts.*

Notice that Malachi makes the distinction very carefully here between the Lord (Messiah/Jesus) who comes to His temple and the LORD (JEHOVAH) who orchestrates the entire set of events. The messenger in this verse is Elijah. So, again and again we find scriptures that tell us the Lord is coming to Earth at the same point in time that we have been studying in this chapter.

The temple He comes to is arguable. We believe from several passages in Revelation that there will be a tribulation temple. We also know that the body of every Christian is a temple of God (1 Cor. 3:16-17). It would seem that there is room for both interpretations to be true in some sense in this one phrase.

This coming of the Lord, according to Rev. 6:12-18, occurs concurrently with the tumbling of the mountains and with the great tsunamis according to Luke 21:25-28 and with all the day of the LORD prophecies we discussed earlier. As you can see, these scriptures are making it progressively harder for me to hold back on fully revealing the rapture event that also occurs concurrently with this time. We will deal very specifically with that in a later chapter. In some manner, all the world will be able to see the Lord coming at that time.

Isaiah 40:5 ends with the phrase "for the mouth of the LORD hath spoken it". This is the justification that Elijah will give for his message. He will plainly say that he is the messenger of God just as Malachi prophesied.

Finally, Elijah will "restore all things". This is very cryptic, and I have found very little in scriptures to expand on this idea. Still there are a few things that must be found out before certain prophecies can be fulfilled. For instance, the tribes of Israel are sealed separately in Rev. 7:3-8, including 12,000 from each of twelve tribes. As of right now, we have no way of determining which Jews are from what tribe. In fact, we have trouble determining if some people are even Jews at all. So that knowledge definitely needs to be restored.

Another major problem is in the exact placement of the temple on the temple mount. There needs to be a tribulation temple according to Rev. 11:1-2 and 2 Thes. 2:4. There is an organization in Israel called the Temple Institute that has been faithfully gathering and making all the accoutrements for the third temple, but there are some obstacles they face due to incomplete information. They also are seeking a way to determine if someone is of the priestly line in order to dedicate the things they have made. Perhaps Elijah will help them to restore the temple to its proper specifications.

There is one more way in which Elijah might be a restorer. In Luke 1:17 we find:

*Luk 1:17 And he shall go before him in the spirit and power of Elias, to turn the hearts of the fathers to the children, and the disobedient to the wisdom of the just; to make ready a people prepared for the Lord.*

This passage could just as easily refer to Gentiles as to Jews. When we study the pre-trib rapture in its proper context, we will find that the Church has become lukewarm and smug and rebellious regarding the words of God by the time that rapture occurs. It is possible that Elijah will be successful in bringing revival to a certain segment of the Church. He may be able to turn some of the disobedient to the wisdom of the just. We will see how important that will be in a later chapter. Suffice it to say for now, that those taken in the pre-trib rapture must be "a people prepared for the Lord".

### 4. The Olive tree, the Vine, and the Fig tree

Israel is likened to the Olive tree, the Vine, and the Fig tree in scriptures. This is illustrated well in the following passage in which the trees mentioned are all candidates to rule over Israel. In this story, the men of the city of Schechem foolishly chose the bramble.

*Jdg 9:8 The trees went forth on a time to anoint a king over them; and they said unto the olive tree, Reign thou over us.*
*9 But the olive tree said unto them, Should I leave my fatness, wherewith by me they honour God and man, and go to be promoted over the trees?*
*10 And the trees said to the fig tree, Come thou, and reign over us.*
*11 But the fig tree said unto them, Should I forsake my sweetness, and my good fruit, and go to be promoted over the trees?*
*12 Then said the trees unto the vine, Come thou, and reign over us.*
*13 And the vine said unto them, Should I leave my wine, which cheereth God and man, and go to be promoted over the trees?*
*14 Then said all the trees unto the bramble, Come thou, and reign over us.*

*15 And the bramble said unto the trees, If in truth ye anoint me king over you, then come and put your trust in my shadow: and if not, let fire come out of the bramble, and devour the cedars of Lebanon.*

Here you should note that the olive tree and the vine are valued by both God and man. The fig, on the other hand, is not mentioned in connection with God. We will now demonstrate why that is the case and what each of these trees represents in relation to Israel. Israel is governed under God through the ministries of the prophet, the priest, and the king as can be seen in the following passages.

*1Ki 1:34 And let Zadok the priest and Nathan the prophet anoint him there king over Israel: and blow ye with the trumpet, and say, God save king Solomon.*

*Jer 37:3 And Zedekiah the king sent Jehucal the son of Shelemiah and Zephaniah the son of Maaseiah the priest to the prophet Jeremiah, saying, Pray now unto the LORD our God for us.*

Note that the prophet does the praying rather than the priest. That is because the prophet was the one who was responsible to exhort the people to come to a personal and loving relationship with their God. The priest was responsible for overseeing obedience to the ceremonial law. That is, the set of rules that the people covenanted with God that they would follow. The priest was not as concerned with a man's personal, emotional relationship with God as the prophet was, but rather with the precise, judicial observance of the details of the law. Finally, the king was responsible for enforcing the civil laws of the land. So, the priest and the prophet were concerned with the religious and spiritual side of the government while the king was the overseer of the secular side of the state. This difference will be seen in the representations of the three types of trees.

The olive tree represents the Holy Spirit of God to Israel. This is the arena of the prophets. The prophets were the great traveling preachers in the land. They spoke for God through the ministering of the Holy Ghost.

*Zec 4:1 And the angel that talked with me came again, and waked me, as a man that is wakened out of his sleep, 2 And said unto me, What seest thou? And I said, I have looked, and behold a candlestick all of gold, with a bowl upon the top of it, and his seven lamps thereon, and seven pipes to the seven lamps, which are upon the top thereof: 3* **And two olive trees by it, one upon the right side of the bowl, and the other upon the left side thereof.**
*4 So I answered and spake to the angel that talked with me, saying, What are these, my lord?*
*5 Then the angel that talked with me answered and said unto me, Knowest thou not what these be? And I said, No, my lord.*
*6 Then he answered and spake unto me, saying, This is the word of the LORD unto Zerubbabel, saying, Not by might, nor by power,* **but by my spirit***, saith the LORD of hosts.*


*Rev 11:3 And I will give power unto my two witnesses, and* **they shall prophesy** *a thousand two hundred and threescore days, clothed in sackcloth.*
*4 These are* **the two olive trees***, and the two candlesticks standing before the God of the earth.*

The Vine represents the soul of Israel. It is within the domain of the priests. The priests were overseers of the religious and legalistic aspects rather than the spiritual aspects of the Jewish people. They were responsible for strict observance of the legal covenant between Israel and JEHOVAH God. The vine was necessary to provide the drink offerings required by the laws of the sacrifice.

*Lev 23:13 And the meat offering thereof shall be two tenth deals of fine flour mingled with oil, an offering made by fire unto the LORD for a sweet savour: and* **the drink offering thereof shall be of wine**, *the fourth part of an hin.*

Melchizedek was priest of the Most High God in Abraham's day and thus responsible for enforcing the covenants of His time. In Abraham's case, he brought forth wine and received Abraham's tithes to God on all his spoils of war.

*Gen 14:18 And Melchizedek king of Salem brought forth bread* **and wine:** *and* **he was the priest of the most high God.**
*19 And he blessed him, and said, Blessed be Abram of the most* **high God, possessor of heaven and earth:**
*20 And blessed be the most high God, which hath delivered thine enemies into thy hand. And he gave him tithes of all.*


The observance of the ceremonial law brought temporary justification to the soul of the OT Jew. It is the soul of the Church Age Christian that the Father declares justified when a modern man receives salvation. Thus, we conclude that the vine represents the ministry of the priests on behalf of the Father.

Finally, the fig tree represents the physical body of Israel under the king. It is civil and currently secular Israel. It is the ultimate realm of Messiah in His role as the King of kings when He finally and completely fulfils the prophecy of the Davidic Covenant.

*Jer 24:1 The LORD shewed me, and, behold, two baskets of figs were set before the temple of the LORD, after that Nebuchadrezzar king of Babylon had carried away captive* **Jeconiah the son of Jehoiakim king of Judah**, *and the princes of Judah, with the carpenters and smiths, from Jerusalem, and had brought them to Babylon.*
*2 One basket had very good figs, even like the figs that are first ripe: and the other basket had very naughty figs, which could not be eaten, they were so bad.*
*3 Then said the LORD unto me, What seest thou, Jeremiah? And I said, Figs; the good figs, very good; and the evil, very evil, that cannot be eaten, they are so evil.*
*4 Again the word of the LORD came unto me, saying,*
*5 Thus saith the LORD, the God of Israel;* **Like these good figs**, *so will I acknowledge them that are carried away captive of Judah, whom I have sent out of this place into the land of the Chaldeans for their good.*
*6 For I will set mine eyes upon them for good, and I will bring them again to this land: and I will build them, and not pull them down; and I will plant them, and not pluck them up.*
*7 And I will give them an heart to know me, that I am the LORD: and they shall be my people, and I will be their God: for they shall return unto me with their whole heart.*
*8 And as* **the evil figs**, *which cannot be eaten, they are so evil; surely thus saith the LORD, So will I give* **Zedekiah the king of Judah**, *and his princes, and the*

*residue of Jerusalem, that remain in this land, and them that dwell in the land of Egypt:*
*9 And I will deliver them to be removed into all the kingdoms of the earth for their hurt, to be a reproach and a proverb, a taunt and a curse, in all places whither I shall drive them.*
*10 And I will send the sword, the famine, and the pestilence, among them, till they be consumed from off the land that I gave unto them and to their fathers.*

Judah, under king Jeconiah was likened to good figs. Judah under king Zedekiah was likened to evil figs. Judah was committed to captivity due to her accumulation of sins. It just happened to occur under Jeconiah who reigned for only three months in 597 BC. He was carried away by Nebuchadnezzar's army because of the sins of his fathers. Zedekiah, on the other hand, was told to yield to Nebuchadnezzar by Jeremiah the prophet of God, but he refused. Thus, he personally brought further judgment on the people of Judah. In both cases, Israel under the king is likened to the fruit of the fig tree.

Understanding that the olive tree refers to Israel under the prophets, the vine refers to Israel under the priesthood and the fig tree refers to Israel under the king, we can have a greater understanding of many prophecies. For example, we see that this passage speaks of Israel in idolatry, a fruitless vine:

*Hos 10:1 Israel is an empty vine, he bringeth forth fruit unto himself: according to the multitude of his fruit he hath increased the altars; according to the goodness of his land they have made goodly images.*

*2 Their heart is divided; now shall they be found faulty: he shall break down their altars, he shall spoil their images.*

You may remember that we referenced the next passage when discussing the opening of the sixth seal at the start of the tribulation. Only the fig tree is used because Israel is currently a very secular state with very little official room for God in her political deliberations.

*Rev 6:12 And I beheld when he had opened the sixth seal, and, lo, there was a great earthquake; and the sun became black as sackcloth of hair, and the moon became as blood;*
*13 And the stars of heaven fell unto the earth, even as a fig tree casteth her untimely figs, when she is shaken of a mighty wind.*

We saw how secular Israel was shaken of a mighty wind in the Russian (Gog) invasion. That is why she cast her untimely figs. Her secular leadership will be destroyed, and she will later be raised up anew under the leadership of the King of kings.

Knowing about these trees will be very helpful for understanding passages such as:

*Hab 3:17 Although the fig tree shall not blossom, neither shall fruit be in the vines; the labour of the olive shall fail, and the fields shall yield no meat; the flock shall be cut off from the fold, and there shall be no herd in the stalls:*
*18 Yet I will rejoice in the LORD, I will joy in the God of my salvation.*

In this passage the prophet is stating that, even when the nation of Israel is cut off, and is no more in their land, he will rejoice in his God. This is a prophecy of encouragement to the people of Israel during the diasporas from 586 BC to 539 BC and 135 AD to 1948 AD although it is primarily aimed at the Russian invasion and into the tribulation.

You can check out the following verses with your new understanding of the significance of these trees in scriptures. Check out 1 Kings 4:25, Isaiah 34:4, Isaiah 36:16, Jeremiah 8:13, Joel 1:7,12, Micah 4:4, Haggai 2:19, and Zechariah 3:10.

**Summary of chapter 5**

Here is a quick summary of what we learned in chapter 5.

- The start of the day of the LORD is concurrent with the start of the seven-year tribulation.
- The start of the day of the LORD and the start of the tribulation are concurrent with the opening of the sixth seal.
- The start of the day of the LORD and the start of the tribulation and the opening of the sixth seal are concurrent with Jesus' prophecy in Luke 21:25-28.
- The start of the day of the LORD and the start of the tribulation and the opening of the sixth seal and Jesus' prophecy in Luke 21:25-28 are concurrent with the Gog attack on Jerusalem.
- The start of the day of the LORD and the start of the tribulation and the opening of the sixth seal and Jesus' prophecy in Luke 21:25-28 and the Gog attack on Jerusalem are concurrent with the coming of the Lord in glory for the redemption of

His obedient saints (Luke 21:28).
- Elijah will come as a prophet to reinforce the concurrent prophecies of the start of the day of the LORD and the start of the tribulation and the opening of the sixth seal and the fulfillment of Jesus' prophecy in Luke 21:25-28 and the Gog attack on Jerusalem and the coming of the Lord of glory for the redemption of His obedient saints (Luke 21:28).

Finally, we noted that the fig tree mentioned in Rev. 6:13 is a reference to secular Israel under attack from Gog and his allies. It is the only tree that governs all of Israel at the start of the day of the LORD.

# Chapter 6. A House Divided, or...

## (What We Can Learn from the Gospels)

*The Church is always trying to get other people to reform;*

*It might not be a bad idea to reform itself a little,*

*By way of example*

*-Mark Twain*

Jesus, while on Earth, gave us some of the most important prophecies in scriptures and, more importantly, He put many otherwise ambiguous prophecies in their proper order. The Age of Law was coming to an end and the Age of Grace was becoming more likely almost by the day when He gave four of His disciples a progress report for the state of prophecy at that point in time. The most comprehensive account of this discourse is found in the gospel of Matthew chapter 24. Another appears in the gospel of Mark chapter 13, and another is spread around a little in the gospel of Luke. This discourse naturally took place on the Mount of Olives. I say naturally because, if you recall, we established that the Olive tree represents the ministry of the prophets in Israel as led by the Holy Ghost. It is worth looking again at how the Apostle Peter wrote of this special relationship:

*2Pe 1:19 We have also a more sure word of prophecy; whereunto ye do well that ye take heed, as unto a light that shineth in a dark place, until the day dawn, and the day star arise in your hearts:*

*20 Knowing this first, that no prophecy of the scripture is of any private interpretation.*

*21 For the prophecy came not in old time by the will of man: but holy men of God spake as they were moved by the Holy Ghost.*

We will first deal with the discourse as recorded in Matthew and bring in the other passages as needed. Because it occurred on the Mount of Olives, it is commonly called the Olivet Discourse.

**The Olivet Discourse**

> *Mat 24:3 And as he sat upon the mount of Olives, the disciples came unto him privately, saying, Tell us, when shall these things be? and what shall be the sign of thy coming, and of the end of the world?*

This discourse occurred shortly after Christ's triumphal entry into Jerusalem and just days before His crucifixion. Jesus had just finished excoriating the religious leadership in Jerusalem while prophesying they would overspread the abominations on themselves that we saw in our study of Daniel 9:24-27. He then foretold the same result Daniel had prophesied.

*Mat 23:38 Behold, your house is left unto you desolate.*

*39 For I say unto you, Ye shall not see me henceforth, till ye shall say, Blessed is he that cometh in the name of the Lord.*

Having just witnessed that sermon, some of His disciples were beginning to catch on that Jesus would be leaving them soon. That naturally brought on the questions that they asked about when it would happen and when He would return and about the end of the world.

It is interesting to note another reason they were on the Mount of Olives. That is almost assuredly where they slept overnights during that week (Luke 21:37). It was the time of the Passover Feast when all the males of Israel were supposed to show up in Jerusalem. It is believed there was not nearly enough lodging for the great influx of people, so many travelers slept under the stars on the Mount of Olives. Jesus and His disciples were travelers from the province of Galilee and probably hadn't arranged lodging prior to coming south.

**The Beginning of Sorrows**

> ➤ *Mat24:4 And Jesus answered and said unto them, Take heed that no man deceive you.*

Jesus warned His disciples (and us) that deception was going to be a problem. The warning to "take heed" is still in effect. Deception in our age often comes in the form of flawed scriptures that produce bad doctrine such as Darby's Antichrist and imminence.

> ➤ *Mat 24:5 For many shall come in my name, saying, I am Christ; and shall deceive many.*
> ➤ *6 And ye shall hear of wars and rumours of wars: see that ye be not troubled: for all these things must come to pass, but the end is not yet.*

The first two signs are false Christs and wars and rumors of wars. Then we see an important statement: "but the end is not yet." This has caused some to ask where all these "many" are, that claim to be Christ. If we are near the end and this occurs before the end, they should be everywhere by now.

So, we must look at this from the viewpoint of a true

deception per verse 4 above.  If someone came up to you and said, "I am Christ", would you believe him?  Neither would I!  No, such openness would not deceive most of us.  But we have seen this warning.  What about those who haven't seen this warning or have seen it but forgotten it?  We have seen this happen occasionally where a man such as Jim Jones gains a following.  But have we seen him deceive many?  It is rarely more than a few thousand and I know of no one making this claim that I would categorize as deceiving many, especially when compared to the whole world, or even the Christian population.

This brings us to the importance of the little word "many".  Many frequently refers to a majority of some population.  In fact, it is often used to denote a large majority.  It is to be contrasted with "few" which indicates a small minority of some population.  Without knowing the population spoken of, neither word would have any meaning.  The population here is those that **come in Christ's name**.  They are to be recognized because they say, "I am Christ".  But who says that?

Well, does someone have to say it in so many words?  What if someone, by his actions or his words, could replace Christ in a man's heart?  We come to love our pastors and when they say something that doesn't quite ring true, we give them a pass.  If that pastor continues to promote bad doctrine, we tend to doubt our personal discernment and move like sheep in the direction our shepherd leads us.  On the other hand, if you have ever tried it, you understand that pastors, good or bad, are very difficult to challenge.  If you speak up, you might be quickly encouraged to shut up or move on so as not to cause division within the fellowship.

So, when the pastor takes his doctrine from a flawed bible

and leads us away from the true Jesus to another Jesus, we hardly ever complain and often don't even notice. Too often, that new Jesus takes the image and likeness of our pastor. It turns out that Jesus shares our pastor's beliefs. At this point, our beloved pastor has essentially, although likely unwittingly, moved from saying "I come in Christ's name" to, "I am Christ". He is saying, "I am the final word on how to read the scriptures and understand the message from God in this congregation". I believe this is going on in enough churches to constitute "many".

The Apostle Paul warned:

*2Co 11:2 For I am jealous over you with godly jealousy: for I have espoused you to one husband, that I may present you as a chaste virgin to Christ.*

*3 But I fear, lest by any means, as the serpent beguiled Eve through his subtilty, so your minds should be corrupted from the simplicity that is in Christ.*

*4 For if he that cometh preacheth another Jesus, whom we have not preached, or if ye receive another spirit, which ye have not received, or another gospel, which ye have not accepted, ye might well bear with him.*

(Also see: Gal. 1:6 and 1 Tim. 6:3-5)

Some pastors cast doubt on the virgin birth of Christ, some on the deity of Christ and some on the efficacy of the blood of Christ. Some teach salvation by works in every age or by water baptism or by learning the Church catechism. All of these doctrines and many more like them are likely defensible in one or more of the modern versions, but none are found in the King James version.

This goes right along with what we learned about the spirit

of antichrist in the first and second epistles of John. False christs are, by definition, antichrists. John told us that antichrists deny that the Jesus of the scriptures is the Christ (1 Jn 2:22). Sometimes this is carried even further, by presenting another Jesus than the one even the modern versions present. This happens in pulpits all around the world Sunday after Sunday when preachers use cleverly altered or 'interpreted' scriptures to produce a Jesus that agrees with their personal rebellions. Thus, if they want to promote the homosexual lifestyle, so does their Jesus. If the pastor believes abortion is a good thing, so does his Jesus. These preachers are presenting scriptures of their own authorship and, as the passage says, "deceive many".

All of these are indeed false christs and therefore antichrists. John stated in 1 Jn. 2:18, that already in his time there were many antichrists. The problem has only gotten worse as Christianity has gained a wider reach over time.

The term "many" then indicates that the majority of Christian leadership could be false christs, or as John states it, antichrists! Christian, beware! They are deceivers. Anti-Christian doctrine from flawed bibles abounds. Ask the Lord Jesus for discernment regarding your church and your pastor. Forget about Darby's false, smokescreen Antichrist and worry about the antichrist who may be standing in the pulpit of your church. He is much more dangerous to you. Paul warned us:

*Act 20:29 For I know this, that after my departing shall grievous wolves enter in among you, not sparing the flock.*
*30 Also of your own selves shall men arise, speaking*

*perverse things, to draw away disciples after them.*

*31 Therefore watch, and remember, that **by the space of three years I ceased not to warn every one night and day with tears.***

Continuing with Matthew 24:
> *7 For nation shall rise against nation, and kingdom against kingdom: and there shall be famines, and pestilences, and earthquakes, in divers places.*
> *8 All these are the beginning of sorrows.*

Verse 7 is a continuation of the prophecy of verse 6, so we know at this point the end is still not yet. This concludes a series of five signs "of thy coming" which collectively are called "the Beginning of Sorrows". They all occur before the end, that is to say, within the Church Age. In fact, they occur across the entire span of the Church Age. We will study these signs in greater detail when we look at the Revelation. For now, it is important that you recognize that these signs are within the Church Age and more importantly prior to the tribulation.

### The pre-tribulation state of the Church

We have just discussed the state of the Church prior to the tribulation as we can understand it from Matthew 24. But there are a number of other important passages that tell us things will get even worse in the last days. We need to look at a few of them to reinforce the importance of understanding the times.

*2Ti 3:1 This know also, that in the last days perilous times shall come.*

*2 For men shall be lovers of their own selves, covetous, boasters, proud, blasphemers, disobedient to parents, unthankful, unholy,*

*3 Without natural affection, trucebreakers, false accusers, incontinent, fierce, despisers of those that are good,*

*4 Traitors, heady, highminded, lovers of pleasures more than lovers of God;*

*5 Having a form of godliness, but denying the power thereof: from such turn away.*

*6 For of this sort are they which creep into houses, and lead captive silly women laden with sins, led away with divers lusts,*

*7 Ever learning, and never able to come to the knowledge of the truth.*

*8 Now as Jannes and Jambres withstood Moses, so do these also resist the truth: men of corrupt minds, reprobate concerning the faith.*

*9 But they shall proceed no further: for their folly shall be manifest unto all men, as theirs also was.*

If we are in the last days then, according to this passage, we are in perilous times. The passage lists 19 evils that will be prevalent. But importantly, notice that none of these are murderers, or adulterers, or kidnappers, or bank robbers or other hardcore, depraved sinners. These are everyday Church members. Take a close look. Haven't all these evils been present among the unsaved at all times since the creation? So, why even bring this up if it is a prophecy about the unsaved? No! This is the state of the Church in the last days. What exactly makes the days so perilous that we need a special warning? Keep this question in your mind as we move toward the end of this chapter.

Just to reinforce that the Church is in view in this prophecy we should point out that the world is always unholy and lovers of pleasures more than lovers of God and de-facto denying the power of godliness. These attributes are only worth stressing if they, shockingly, apply to the Church. The times would be no more perilous than any other time if the prophecy spoke of the lost world. They would be quite normal.

A few verses later, we find these statements:

*2Ti 3:12 Yea, and all that will live godly in Christ Jesus shall suffer persecution.*
*13 But evil men and seducers shall wax worse and worse, deceiving, and being deceived.*


Remember the false christs and grievous wolves and different jesus's and antichrists we just looked at? This is a second warning from Paul that this problem would continue to grow. These seducers lure away God's people, making them believe things that are not true.

Here are a couple more to ponder:

*2Ti 4:3 For the time will come when they will not endure sound doctrine; but after their own lusts shall they heap to themselves teachers, having itching ears;*
*4 And they shall turn away their ears from the truth, and shall be turned unto fables.*

And:

*2Pe 2:1 But there were false prophets also among the*

*people, even as there shall be false teachers among you, who privily shall bring in damnable heresies, even denying the Lord that bought them, and bring upon themselves swift destruction.*

*2 And **many** shall follow their pernicious ways; by reason of whom the way of truth shall be evil spoken of.*

*3 And through covetousness shall they with feigned words make merchandise of you: whose judgment now of a long time lingereth not, and their damnation slumbereth not.*

Are you getting this ugly picture of the Church which seems to us so benign and safe and loving and caring and accepting in our day? We have seen a Church of which portions are disappointing and even repulsive to the Bridegroom. But there is an element to the Church that goes far beyond that. Here's a really bad one.

*Rom 1:18 For the wrath of God is revealed from heaven against all ungodliness and unrighteousness of men, who hold the truth in unrighteousness;*

*19 Because that which may be known of God is manifest in them; for God hath shewed it unto them.*

*20 For the invisible things of him from the creation of the world are clearly seen, being understood by the things that are made, even his eternal power and Godhead; so that they are without excuse:*

*21 Because that, when they knew God, they glorified him not as God, neither were thankful; but became vain in their imaginations, and their foolish heart was darkened.*

*22 Professing themselves to be wise, they became fools,*

*23 And changed the glory of the uncorruptible God into an image made like to corruptible man, and to birds, and fourfooted beasts, and creeping things.*

*24 Wherefore God also gave them up to uncleanness*

*through the lusts of their own hearts, to dishonour their own bodies between themselves:*

*25 Who changed the truth of God into a lie, and worshipped and served the creature more than the Creator, who is blessed for ever. Amen.*

*26 For this cause God gave them up unto vile affections: for even their women did change the natural use into that which is against nature:*

*27 And likewise also the men, leaving the natural use of the woman, burned in their lust one toward another; men with men working that which is unseemly, and receiving in themselves that recompence of their error which was meet.*

*28 And even as they did not like to retain God in their knowledge, God gave them over to a reprobate mind, to do those things which are not convenient;*

*29 Being filled with all unrighteousness, fornication, wickedness, covetousness, maliciousness; full of envy, murder, debate, deceit, malignity; whisperers,*

*30 Backbiters, haters of God, despiteful, proud, boasters, inventors of evil things, disobedient to parents,*

*31 Without understanding, covenantbreakers, without natural affection, implacable, unmerciful:*

*32 Who knowing the judgment of God, that they which commit such things are worthy of death, not only do the same, but have pleasure in them that do them.*


By now I hope you are thinking, "I don't know any Church people that are so evil". Hopefully, that is because your church and pastor and congregation aren't part of this mess. Obviously, these are people who hold the truth – but in unrighteousness. God has shown them what may be known of Him and even manifested it in them. Yet, they willfully turned the truth of God into a lie. These are people who look like average Christians, but in their heart and in their life away from the Church, they are evil hypocrites. They reinforce each other to justify their sins while maintaining a normal and respectable outward appearance. But let me show you one final passage on this subject to give you pause for reflection.

*Rev 3:14 And unto the angel of the church of the Laodiceans write; These things saith the Amen, the faithful and true witness, the beginning of the creation of God;*
*15 I know thy works, that thou art neither cold nor hot: I would thou wert cold or hot.*
*16 So then because thou art lukewarm, and neither cold nor hot, I will spue thee out of my mouth.*
*17 Because thou sayest, I am rich, and increased with goods, and have need of nothing; and knowest not that thou art wretched, and miserable, and poor, and blind, and naked:*

This is a message to the final Church in the book of the Revelation. This Church of Laodicea is taught by many to represent the state of the Church just before the pre-trib rapture. Notice carefully how this Church sees itself. It says I am rich and increased with goods and have need of nothing. That is the outward appearance, and the Church sincerely believes that about itself. This Church has arrived. Never has the Church been so prosperous and had everything it could want. It thinks it has arrived at the ultimate state of spirituality and God must be very proud and happy because of it.

But just look at what the Lord sees here. It is wretched and miserable and poor and blind and naked. This Church is so wrapped up in its goodness and worthiness and personal righteousness that it has no idea how ugly it has become in the sight of God. So, what does the Lord do when He comes for this Church? He spues it out of His mouth. It is so distasteful; He throws it back to Earth. Doesn't sound like a rapture to me. How about to you?

According to the next passage, this Church will be sharply rebuked by her Lord. The act of spueing her out of His mouth is that sharp rebuke. After that will come a special chastening. The chastening will consist of having to endure to the end of the first half of the tribulation, the ultimate end of the Church Age.

*Rev 3:19 As many as I love, I rebuke and chasten: be zealous therefore, and repent.*


A Church that thinks highly of itself is more likely to be smug and rebellious than to be godly and obedient. In fact, let's move on in this passage to see something even more surprising.

*20 Behold, I stand at the door, and knock: if any man hear my voice, and open the door, I will come in to him, and will sup with him, and he with me.*


This Church that has it so 'all together' is missing one major component. Jesus is out on the front porch knocking to get in. Great music, great preaching, great fellowship, great good works projects, great growth, but Jesus is almost an afterthought. It's all about, "look at what great things we are doing, truly we are the people"! Yet, Jesus is still willing to draw close to any individual within that Church that will allow Him. What a forgiving Lord we have!

But clearly not every Church will be this way, and not all the people in such a Church will be this way. We will prove this later in this chapter and again when we prove a pre-trib rapture. Understanding this, we are ready to move deeper into Matthew chapter 24.

**The first half of the tribulation**

Before discussing verse 9, I want to point out a very curious thing. Jesus makes no mention of a rapture anywhere in this discussion of the last days. That is almost assuredly because it was still unknown to all but the Father whether His second coming would be in 3.5 years or closer to 2000 years. That information couldn't be known until after the crucifixion. However, it provides a strong argument for the post-trib adherents.

> *Mat 24:9 Then shall they deliver you up to be afflicted, and shall kill you: and ye shall be hated of all nations for my name's sake.*

Commentators sometimes complain that Matthew 24 is one of the more difficult passages in the Bible to exegete. So, it behooves us to be very careful with the wording here because precision matters in this passage.

This verse starts with the word "then". We have just completed a passage that stated, "all these are the

Beginning of Sorrows". That is obviously meant to create an endpoint for that part of the message. "Then" indicates a new portion of the message with a change of direction or emphasis. So, after the Beginning of Sorrows period, Jesus starts listing events that will occur in the next time period.

Although, according to Mark 13:3, Jesus is speaking directly to Peter and John and James and Andrew, the tone of the following commentary indicates that He is speaking to a large number of people. In fact, He is speaking to all those like the disciples. He is speaking here to all that are loyal to Him. As we shall see, He is speaking to both Jews and Christians who accept His blood atonement as payment for their sins.

Examining the verse closely, we see that it must be for a yet future time because not all nations were aware that there were followers of Christ at that time. In fact, at that time very few nations were aware that there was a Christ. So, we are looking for a time when all nations will not only be aware of Jesus but will also hate His followers enough to afflict and kill them. Although Christians and Jews are universally despised by the nations at this time, it has not yet come to the point where their governments routinely afflict and kill them, at least not in most western nations.

It will become clear that, timewise, we have entered the tribulation in this section of the discourse. Remember, from Daniel 9, we determined that the Church Age is still ongoing when the tribulation starts.

We have entered a new era where killing the servants of Jesus will be considered doing a good thing.

> *Mat 24:10 And then shall many be offended, and shall betray one another, and shall hate one another.*

Here's that little word "many" again. This will be a time when the majority of people will be willing to betray one another, and hatred will rule the day. Notice Darby's Antichrist is nowhere mentioned as a cause of all this chaos. The comparable verse in Mark's gospel spells it out a little closer to home.

*Mar 13:12 Now the brother shall betray the brother to death, and the father the son; and children shall rise up against their parents, and shall cause them to be put to death.*

This will be a very unpleasant time, but we will find out that every one of us can avoid that time. It is a time when the people you love the most will betray you **to death** for being a follower of Christ.

If you are wondering why this drastic change in social order will occur, you should review chapter 5 of this work again. Remember, catastrophic changes have just happened to the topography of the planet with immense loss of life. JEHOVAH God has revealed Himself in such a way that nobody can deny His existence. (Review the section on Gog's attack on Israel.) He has willfully caused all the catastrophes we have discussed and now commands complete obedience from His followers.

From the point of view of the unsaved, he is a terrifying figure, likely from outer space. He seems to represent pure evil and those who serve Him, by extension, must be pure evil too. People may reason that if His followers are expunged from the Earth, He will go away. We will see that fake 'aliens' from space will likely play a role in these events.

> *Mat 24:11 And many false prophets shall rise, and shall deceive many.*

We saw that many of the false prophets of the Church Age were found among Church leadership. Remember, some of them are still on Earth at this time. These are men who thrive on the admiration of others and certainly won't want to give up just because others in the Church have disappeared. They will continue on because they are, no doubt, still convinced that they have the truth.

But this seems to go beyond that. Circumstances will have changed at this point in time. In a few verses, we will see that this time will be just as in the days of Noah in several respects. By far the most notable pre-flood events in the days of Noah had to do with the arrival of the "sons of God" on the Earth. We first see these guys in Genesis chapter 6. Now note what was remarkable about them:

*Gen 6:1 And it came to pass, when men began to multiply on the face of the earth, and daughters were born unto them,*

*2 That the sons of God saw the daughters of men that they were fair; and they took them wives of all which they chose.*

*3 And the LORD said, My spirit shall not always strive with man, for that he also is flesh: yet his days shall be an hundred and twenty years.*

*4 There were giants in the earth in those days; and also after that, when the sons of God came in unto the daughters of men, and they bare children to them, the same became mighty men which were of old, men of renown.*

*5 And GOD saw that the wickedness of man was great in the earth, and that every imagination of the thoughts of his heart was only evil continually.*

*6 And it repented the LORD that he had made man on the earth, and it grieved him at his heart.*

*7 And the LORD said, I will destroy man whom I have created from the face of the earth; both man, and beast, and the creeping thing, and the fowls of the air; for it repenteth me that I have made them.*

*8 But Noah found grace in the eyes of the LORD.*

*9 These are the generations of Noah: Noah was a just man and perfect in his generations, and Noah walked with God.*

*10 And Noah begat three sons, Shem, Ham, and Japheth.*

*11 The earth also was corrupt before God, and the earth was filled with violence.*

*12 And God looked upon the earth, and, behold, it was corrupt; for all flesh had corrupted his way upon the earth.*

*13 And God said unto Noah, The end of all flesh is come before me; for the earth is filled with violence through them; and, behold, I will destroy them with the earth.*

Many theologians have portrayed these "sons of God" as the godly line of Seth whereas the daughters of men are portrayed as the sinful daughters of Cain. I won't go into the whole argument here, but just ask you to consider why the daughters of Seth couldn't have been just as attractive as the daughters of Cain and why the sons of Cain must be considered ungodly. Why did the offspring of such mingling become giants?

Some teach that Cain was fathered by Satan and thus a half-human. But this goes against the teaching of scriptures which clearly say that Adam fathered Cain. Also, Eve stated of him, "I have gotten a man from the Lord". If Satan were the father, Cain clearly could not be said to have come from the Lord. There is no getting around the fact that Cain was fully a man and thus redeemable to God. There are no other good earthly explanations as to why all of one line should be evil and more importantly, given the fallen nature of man, all of the other line should be godly. Theologians are supposed to know better!

The only explanation that has merit theologically and logically and scripturally all together is that these are the same "sons of God" found in the book of Job (38:4-7) who witnessed the current creation as it occurred. They were angels who had already been created. At some point one third of them aligned themselves with Satan when he rebelled against God. They fell from God's favor forever and became soldiers in Satan's war against God.

Just as in the days of Noah (Matt. 24:37-39), it seems these fallen angels called the "sons of God" will arrive on Earth with the whole 'truth' about what has just happened. They will assure the population that they are the good guys and JEHOVAH is the intergalactic bad guy they have been battling for millennia. It is likely that information on extraterrestrials will be coming out for this purpose more and more frequently and will provide more and more amazing technologies over the next two years. Be ready for it, because its purpose will be to confuse you and convince you that Christianity and Judaism are just ancient JEHOVAH myths. The new US Space Force may have much to do with this program. We are being conditioned to believe in extraterrestrial life for a good reason. This is a program of Satan. He has known for a long time what is about to happen and has timed all this out to deceive the whole world. Governments are already allowing formerly classified files on extraterrestrials to get out. By now, few would be completely surprised if space aliens were announced by our governments.

These sons of God took wives of all whom they chose. This indicates that earthly men were no match for them. If they wanted a woman, they took her. Their offspring were giants and mighty men. Apparently, they polluted the entire gene pool because the scriptures make a point to note that Noah was perfect in his generations. That is, his DNA was fully and purely human. That was unusual enough to make a point of it. I believe that mankind was so thoroughly mixed with angel DNA that most of these offspring were no longer God's creation of man. It seems likely they did not have savable souls and thus had no more value to God than the animals.

The result of all this was *"the wickedness of man was great in the earth, and that every imagination of the thoughts of his heart was only evil continually."* And *"The earth also was* **corrupt** *before God, and the earth was filled with violence."*

Compare this Genesis passage to the tone of the verses in Matthew 24:9-13, and you can get an idea why men's hearts turned so cold.

These 'sons of God' were devils from off-Earth. In fact, they were in heaven when God created the current Earth.

*Job 38:4 Where wast thou when I laid the foundations of the earth? declare, if thou hast understanding.*

*Job 38:7 When the morning stars sang together, and all the sons of God shouted for joy?*

The sons of God were in heaven when Satan was oppressing Job (Job 1:6, 2:1). So, we find them in heaven and on Earth at various times. The only created beings we find in heaven at that time were angels. These angels came to Earth and did evil.  Thus, we must assume that they were Satan's angels.  Now consider:

*Rev 12:7 And there was war in heaven: Michael and his angels fought against the dragon; and the dragon fought and his angels,*

*8 And prevailed not; neither was their place found any more in heaven.*

*9 And the great dragon was cast out, that old serpent, called the Devil, and Satan, which deceiveth the whole world: he was cast out **into the earth,** and his angels were cast out with him.*

If these angels are cast into the Earth, they need earthly bodies to be effective in the workings of Satan.  So, it seems they can come to us in the body of a man or a space alien.  There are many instances in scriptures where angels are called men.  Here is a very telling instance:

*Heb 13:2 Be not forgetful to entertain strangers: for thereby some have entertained angels unawares.*

When Noah was 480 years old, God determined to bring a worldwide flood and kill everything that breathed because the situation had become so dire.  He gave Noah 120 years to build an ark to save himself and his family and pairs of animals to rebuild a post-flood world.  Notice in Gen. 6:4 there were giants in the land and also after that.  That is because, after all those sons of God were killed in the flood, more showed up later in the promised land prior to the time the Israelites came in.  On the other hand, those who had taken on flesh and were killed at this time lost their position in Satan's army.

*Jud 1:6 And the angels which kept not their first estate, but left their own habitation, he hath reserved in everlasting chains under darkness unto the judgment of the great day.*

There are still lots of these fallen angels available for the war Satan is constantly waging with God. Read Daniel chapter ten to get important insight into the nature of this warfare in both the physical and spiritual realms. These guys showed up again in Canaan after God promised the land to Abraham and his descendants. It was Satan's intention to present an obstacle to God's purpose in giving a homeland to his people. In fact, it was the peoples' discouragement over having to defeat giants that caused God to punish Israel with forty years wandering in the wilderness. But God's plan eventually prevailed. Again, they were a problem when David became king of Israel. It was through the line of David that the Savior was to come, so Satan made another attempt, this time to kill David and defeat God's plan using Goliath and his brothers. So, we should expect to see them again in one final attempt to foil God's purposes on Earth as a last stand in the last days. In fact, we are warned of them in these New Testament passages:

*Eph 6:11 Put on the whole armour of God, that ye may be able to stand against the wiles of the devil.*

*12 For we wrestle not against flesh and blood, but against principalities, against powers, against the rulers of the darkness of this world, against spiritual wickedness in high places.*

And

*Jud 1:10 But these speak evil of those things which they know not: but what they know naturally, as brute beasts, in those things they corrupt themselves.*

*11 Woe unto them! for they have gone in the way of Cain, and ran greedily after the error of Balaam for reward, and perished in the gainsaying of Core.*

*12 These are spots in your feasts of charity, when they feast with you, feeding themselves without fear: clouds they are without water, carried about of winds; trees whose fruit withereth, without fruit, twice dead, plucked up by the roots;*

*13 Raging waves of the sea, foaming out their own shame; wandering stars, to whom is reserved the blackness of darkness for ever.*

*14 And Enoch also, the seventh from Adam, prophesied of these, saying, Behold, the Lord cometh with ten thousands of his saints,*

The latest false prophets we mentioned may be men who propagate the story that alien visitors have come to rescue humanity from JEHOVAH. This may be the inspiration behind this passage:

*2Th 2:11 And for this cause God shall send them strong delusion, that they should believe a lie:*

*12 That they all might be damned who believed not the truth, but had pleasure in unrighteousness.*

Back to Matthew 24:
> *Mat 24:12 And because iniquity shall abound, the love of many shall wax cold.*

There is an interesting passage of scripture that ties into this verse. It is interesting because it is quite cryptic. Many early commentators have taught that the following passage was speaking of Rome in a negative way. Thus, it would have been banned by the government and Paul possibly would have been guilty of a crime if he didn't word it carefully. Whether that is true or not, the passage has been interpreted in many different ways. Hopefully, the things we have discussed thus far will help us get this right.

*2Th 2:7 For the mystery of iniquity doth already work: only he who now letteth will let, until he be taken out of the way.*
*8 And then shall that Wicked be revealed, whom the Lord shall consume with the spirit of his mouth, and shall destroy with the brightness of his coming:*
*9 Even him, whose coming is after the working of Satan with all power and signs and lying wonders,*
*10 And with all deceivableness of unrighteousness in them that perish; because they received not the love of the truth, that they might be saved.*

The crux of the problem at this point is the solution to "he who now letteth". "Letteth" here is widely understood to mean "restraineth" so to let is to restrain (as used in Rom. 1:13). So, who is he that restrains? If it was the civil Roman government as some say, then 'he' was taken out of the way by the 7th century AD and that Wicked might be expected to have been revealed by now. It is more likely that the restrainer has not yet been taken out of the way. We will therefore be looking for someone or something that is yet going to be taken out of the way.

It is patently obvious who that Wicked is. We know he has a specific identity because his identifier "Wicked" is capitalized as a proper noun should be. Most modern clergymen claim he is Darby's Antichrist, but we have already demonstrated in chapter 4 why that Antichrist is a myth. As is the case with almost all these references, it is actually a reference to the Beast of Rev. 11, 13ff, (1 Thes. 2:3-8). You can quickly determine this by comparing verse 9 above with Revelation chapter 13, specifically verses 11-15. Also, he is destroyed at the Lord's coming which occurs at the war of Armageddon.

We are left with the problem of determining who the restrainer is. We know from Matt. 24:12 above that the mystery of iniquity begins to work much more freely at some point. We also are beginning to understand that we are in a new dispensational economy based on what we have learned from Matt. 24:9-12. So, the removal of the restrainer must be the difference or start point of the new dispensation. We looked at this point in time extensively in chapter five. It is the start point of the tribulation and many other events.

Now I am going to have to reveal more fully another event that occurs at the same time and beg for your clemency one more time. For the sake of the overall flow of this narrative, I will save the full proof of this statement for a later chapter. So, bear with me for a little longer and consider this a hypothetical for now if you must. I have already pointed at this several times, but it must be reinforced in the minds of some readers. Here it is. There is a pre-tribulation rapture! (Notice I used the indefinite article to allow for another, similar situation.) AND, not all the Church will be raptured at that time! The Church Age continues after the pre-trib rapture. (Yes, more repetition but please be patient. It will help in the long run.)

What we are about to see is that, once the tribulation starts, the rules for salvation change. If this offends you, I am sorry, but the scriptures are very clear on this doctrine. The first point we must realize is that current Christians are sealed by the Holy Ghost only until the day of redemption:

*Eph 1:13 In whom ye also trusted, after that ye heard the word of truth, the gospel of your salvation: in whom also after that ye believed,* **ye were sealed with that holy Spirit of promise***,*

*14 Which is the earnest of our inheritance until the redemption of the purchased possession, unto the praise of his glory.*

*Eph 4:30 And grieve not the holy Spirit of God, whereby* **ye are sealed unto the day of redemption**

So, when is the day of redemption? If you've been following carefully, you might have an idea by now. But in case you haven't got it yet, Luke spelled it out for us.

*Luk 21:28 And when these things begin to come to pass, then look up, and lift up your heads; for your redemption draweth nigh.*

This chapter in Luke spends verses 7-24 telling us about the time up to the destruction of the temple by prince Titus in 70 AD. Then in verse 25, it turns to the coming of the Lord. It gives some signs regarding the start of the day of the LORD. Then it follows this with the verse above. So, it is telling us that the day of redemption is concurrent with the day of the LORD.

Another passage that speaks to this day is:

*Isa 63:1 Who is this that cometh from Edom, with dyed garments from Bozrah? this that is glorious in his apparel, travelling in the greatness of his strength? I that speak in righteousness, mighty to save.*

*2 Wherefore art thou red in thine apparel, and thy garments like him that treadeth in the winefat?*

*3 I have trodden the winepress alone; and of the people there was none with me: for I will tread them in mine anger, and trample them in my fury; and their blood shall be sprinkled upon my garments, and I will stain all my raiment.*

*4 For the day of vengeance is in mine heart, and the year of my redeemed is come.*

In this passage we find the Lord asking and answering His own questions. It appears that He will personally come to Bozrah and turn that area into perpetual wastes. This will happen when *"the year of my redeemed is come"*. It seems reasonable to equate these two passages to the same future prophecy since neither one has yet come to pass. The *"day of vengeance"* mentioned here is surely a reference to the day of the LORD as we studied in the previous chapter. (See, for instance, Jer. 46:10.)

The conclusion here is that we are sealed with the Holy Spirit of God within us until the day of the LORD. If we enter the day of the LORD, we lose that sealing and thus have no protection from sin staining our soul.

It works like this:

*2Co 1:21 Now he which stablisheth us with you in Christ, and hath anointed us, is God;*

*22 Who hath also sealed us, and given the earnest of the Spirit in our hearts.*

God seals us and gives us the earnest of the spirit in our hearts. This is the key. Prior to the Church Age, the Holy Spirit was not sealed in men's hearts. He was free to come and go based on their spiritual state (Psalm 51:11). The sealing only applies to those saved from the time of the cross to the pre-tribulation rapture.

Returning now to our quest, we can look at who or what restrainer is taken out of the way. Here, we see that a special ministry of the Holy Ghost is removed or taken away. While sealed Christians were on Earth, iniquity was in a mystery state. There is a drag on the power of evil due to the protective presence of the Holy Spirit of God within His people. When these people are removed, sin becomes unrestrained. Now read Matt. 24:9-12 again understanding that unrestrained iniquity is operational.

**Dispensational aspects of salvation**
> *Mat 24:13 But he that shall endure unto the end, the same shall be saved.*

We are about to see the reason for the conflict between the Arminians and the Calvinists on the issue of losing one's salvation. It all depends on where you are in time as to which theology is correct. Within the tribulation the Arminians, who allow that salvation can be lost, are clearly correct, with one caveat.

Arminians generally teach that it is possible to lose one's salvation and then regain it. To respond to this teaching, we must consult Hebrews, the source book for the differences between the ages of the Law, Grace, and Tribulation. At the risk of alienating even more readers, I will refer to these ages using the Bible term, dispensations. It doesn't really matter what you call them, it is clear that there are different economies of theology within the scriptures with different rules for believers. Hebrews tells us:

*Heb 6:4 For it is impossible for those who were once enlightened, and have tasted of the heavenly gift, and were made partakers of the Holy Ghost,*

*5 And have tasted the good word of God, and the powers of the world to come,*

*6 If they shall fall away, to renew them again unto repentance; seeing they crucify to themselves the Son of God afresh, and put him to an open shame.*

Clearly, if we lose our salvation post-crucifixion, it is impossible to get it back! Christ died once for sinners and became the propitiation for our sins. He will not die again for a new set of sins for anyone. He has shed His blood and no longer has blood to shed for a second round of salvations.

In the Old Testament Age of Law, a man could lose and regain his salvation any number of times because the final sacrifice had not yet been made. Animal sacrifices were substituted to demonstrate a repentance and an acknowledgement of a man's need for redemption. Ezekiel stated this situation like this:

*Eze 18:20 The **soul** that sinneth, it shall die. The son shall not bear the iniquity of the father, neither shall the father bear the iniquity of the son: the righteousness of the righteous shall be upon him, and the wickedness of the wicked shall be upon him.*

*21 But if the wicked will turn from all his sins that he hath committed, and keep all my statutes, and do that which is lawful and right, he shall surely live, he shall not die.*

*22 All his transgressions that he hath committed, they shall not be mentioned unto him: in his righteousness that he hath done he shall live.*

*23 Have I any pleasure at all that the wicked should die? saith the Lord GOD: and not that he should return from his ways, and live?*

*24 But when the righteous turneth away from his righteousness, and committeth iniquity, and doeth according to all the abominations that the wicked man doeth, shall he live? All his righteousness that he hath done shall not be mentioned: in his trespass that he hath trespassed, and in his sin that he hath sinned, in them shall he die.*

*25 Yet ye say, The way of the Lord is not equal. Hear now, O house of Israel; Is not my way equal? are not your ways unequal?*

*26 When a righteous man turneth away from his righteousness, and committeth iniquity, and dieth in them; for his iniquity that he hath done shall he die.*

*27 Again, when the wicked man turneth away from his wickedness that he hath committed, and doeth that which is lawful and right, he shall save his **soul** alive.*

*28 Because he considereth, and turneth away from all his transgressions that he hath committed, he shall surely live, he shall not die.*

*29 Yet saith the house of Israel, The way of the Lord is not equal. O house of Israel, are not my ways equal? are not your ways unequal?*

*30 Therefore I will judge you, O house of Israel, every one according to his ways, saith the Lord GOD. Repent, and turn yourselves from all your transgressions; so iniquity shall not be your ruin.*

*31 Cast away from you all your transgressions, whereby ye have transgressed; and make you a new heart and a new spirit: for why will ye die, O house of Israel?*

You can see from these verses that an Old Testament man could be righteous and saved all his life and then turn to iniquity in his old age and die a sinner. Clearly in verse 20, the state of the soul is what is spoken of in this passage. There is an open, unconditional invitation to all in verses 30-31 to turn from their transgressions regardless of where they have been up to that present point. The way was always open to salvation for these people regardless of whether they had gone from righteousness to unrighteousness and back any number of times.

The Holy Spirit of God was never sealed within them and could come to them when they were in righteousness and leave them when they were in iniquity. That is why David cried out to God after the affair with Bathsheba:

*Psa 51:9 Hide thy face from my sins, and blot out all mine iniquities.*

*10 Create in me a clean heart, O God; and* **renew a right spirit within me.**

*11 Cast me not away from thy presence; and* **take not thy holy spirit from me.**

*12 Restore unto me the joy of thy salvation; and* **uphold me with thy free spirit.**

Turning now to tribulation salvation, we find some significant changes. There is once again an element of works involved. Consider this passage:

*Rev 12:7 And there was war in heaven: Michael and his angels fought against the dragon; and the dragon fought and his angels,*

*8 And prevailed not; neither was their place found any more in heaven.*

*9 And the great dragon was cast out, that old serpent, called the Devil, and Satan, which deceiveth the whole world: he was cast out into the earth, and his angels were cast out with him.*

*10 And I heard a loud voice saying in heaven, Now is come salvation, and strength, and the kingdom of our God, and the power of his Christ: for the accuser of our brethren is cast down, which accused them before our God day and night.*

*11* **And they overcame him by the blood of the Lamb, and by the word of their testimony; and**

***they loved not their lives unto the death.***

At this point, a new condition has been added to overcoming Satan. Not only are these people saved by the blood of the Lamb, now they must also be saved by the word of their testimony. That is, they cannot deny JEHOVAH is their God and Christ is their Lord. Remember from our discussion of the Gog attack we learned that by the time the tribulation starts, the entire lost world will know about and hate JEHOVAH God. Also, the verses from Matthew 24 we have just been discussing tell us how dangerous it will be to confess to being a Christian. Faith in God's existence will no longer be a problem or factor in salvation. The requirement for faith will only be in Christ's saving blood and will be accompanied by the requirement for loyalty.

Loyalty, at this point is crucial to maintaining salvation. The soul is no longer sealed from the stain of sin and disloyalty is a stain that will not be cleansed. Disloyalty will drive the Holy Ghost away forever. This is the point at which the following scripture applies. Consider it carefully.

*Mat 10:32 Whosoever therefore shall confess me before men, him will I confess also before my Father which is in heaven.*

*33 But whosoever shall deny me before men, him will I also deny before my Father which is in heaven.*


It is interesting to read of the terrible deaths that Christians died as reported in *Foxe's Book of Martyrs* and consider that these people could have denied Christ, without losing their salvation, and avoided their torture. Might some of them have chosen death because of a lack of understanding the dispensational aspects of salvation?

Verses such as Matt. 24:13 might have terrified them if they didn't fully understand salvation in their age.

So, the dispensational aspects of salvation are these:
- Age of Law – Salvation could be lost and regained any number of times. Works plus faith-based salvation, looking forward to the cross for grace.
- Age of Grace – Salvation cannot be lost until the day of redemption. Salvation by grace through faith plus nothing
- Tribulation – Salvation can be lost and NEVER regained. Salvation by grace plus work of unwavering loyalty, even unto death.

**This book is written specifically to tell the reader how to avoid entering the tribulation and facing the possibility of losing salvation forever.**

Returning to our text:
> *Mat 24:14 And this gospel of the kingdom shall be preached in all the world for a witness unto all nations; and then shall the end come.*

The gospel of the kingdom was initially offered to the Jews in a physical kingdom, but they rejected their King. So, the gospel of God or in other words, of Christ, was offered to the entire world in a spiritual kingdom. Within the tribulation, when the Holy Spirit of God is no longer sealed within the believer, we are back to the physical kingdom. Works matter again. This rendition of the gospel is also known as the everlasting gospel because the Church Age gospel was just an interlude in the overall plan of God.

Our text verse, Matt 24:14, matches with Rev. 14:6 in which we find the gospel being preached to all the world in the most efficient manner. It has often been preached that the rapture could not happen until every person in the world had been reached. What these preachers thought would take man centuries, God will accomplish in a one-time event. They should have read Rev. 14:6 and put their hearts at ease. We are just about at mid-trib when the rapture of the remaining of the Church occurs. The hour of judgment spoken of here (v.7 below) is not the Great White Throne judgment at the end of the millennium, so it speaks of the judgment seat of Christ for raptured and resurrected saved people.

*Rev 14:6 And I saw another angel fly in the midst of heaven, having the everlasting gospel to preach unto them that dwell on the earth, and to every nation, and kindred, and tongue, and people,*

*7 Saying with a loud voice, Fear God, and give glory to him; for the hour of his judgment is come: and worship him that made heaven, and earth, and the sea, and the fountains of waters.*

*Rev 14:12 Here is the patience of the saints: here are they that keep the commandments of God, and the faith of Jesus.*

*13 And I heard a voice from heaven saying unto me, Write, Blessed are the dead which die in the Lord from henceforth: Yea, saith the Spirit, that they may rest from their labours; and their works do follow them.*

In verse 12, we see tribulation salvation becoming more exhaustive. These saints must have patience and they must keep the commandments of God as well as have faith in Jesus. When they die, their works follow them. In other words, their works are considered when their salvation is judged. This is not a good place to be. See to it that you never face it!

We see at the end of Matt. 24:14 above, the statement "then shall the end come". This does not deal with the end of the world because we still have the rest of the tribulation and the 1000-year millennium. So, it would seem to be a little cryptic. What end could we be talking about here, then? The most important clue is found in the following verse where we will see the "abomination of desolation, spoken of by Daniel the prophet". When we study that verse, we will see this happens right about mid-trib. We know from our study that the last half of Daniel's 70th week begins at mid-trib. That is a return to the terminal stage of God's original plan for the ages. So, it is definitely an end in that sense.

But there is another end in view here. That is the end of the Church Age. When we come to the rapture chapter, we will see better what is going on here.

Reread the first half of the tribulation portion of Matthew 24 with the next verse for discussion. See if it begins to be more understandable now.

> *Mat 24:9 Then shall they deliver you up to be afflicted, and shall kill you: and ye shall be hated of all nations for my name's sake.*
> *10 And then shall many be offended, and shall betray one another, and shall hate one another.*
> *11 And many false prophets shall rise, and shall deceive many.*
> *12 And because iniquity shall abound, the love of*

> *many shall wax cold.*
> ➢ *13 But he that shall endure unto the end, the same shall be saved.*
> ➢ *14 And this gospel of the kingdom shall be preached in all the world for a witness unto all nations; and then shall the end come.*

> ➢ *Mat 24:15 When ye therefore shall see the abomination of desolation, spoken of by Daniel the prophet, stand in the holy place, (whoso readeth, let him understand:)*

That punctuation is DEFINITELY NOT a smiley face at the end of this passage. This is a time of extreme danger for the religious faction among the Jews. The Beast will be given a special power over them and all the people of God. He will slaughter all who he and his armies can find. We must see from the scriptures why this is at mid-trib.

*2Th 2:1 Now we beseech you, brethren, by the coming of our Lord Jesus Christ, and by our gathering together unto him,*
*2 That ye be not soon shaken in mind, or be troubled, neither by spirit, nor by word, nor by letter as from us, as that the day of Christ is at hand.*
*3 Let no man deceive you by any means: for that day shall not come, except there come a falling away first, and that man of sin be revealed, the son of perdition;*
*4 Who opposeth and exalteth himself above all that is called God, or that is worshipped; so that he as God sitteth in the temple of God, shewing himself that he is God.*

Here we go again. We are not yet to the point where we can fully deal with the day of Christ (verse 2). We will hold that until the next chapter.  Let me just point out that verse 1 here speaks of a coming of our Lord Jesus Christ to gather His people.  That should give you a hint now that you know there is a mid-trib rapture.

This is such a critical passage though, that we must give a little more away here.  The day of Christ will be preceded by a falling away and that "man of sin be revealed".  Understanding the timing of Daniel's 70$^{th}$ week makes this pretty straightforward.  So, there comes a falling away first.  That is the pre-trib rapture.  Then, the man of sin is revealed just before mid-trib:

*Rev 11:3  And I will give power unto my two witnesses, and they shall prophesy a thousand two hundred and threescore days, clothed in sackcloth.*

*Rev 11:7  And when they shall have finished their testimony,* **the beast** *that ascendeth out of the bottomless pit shall make war against them, and shall overcome them, and kill them.*

We will see that this beast, who is also called the man of sin and the son of perdition, will kill the two witnesses just before the mid-trib rapture.  After this, the day of Christ will arrive when He raptures the remaining of His Church.  Finally, the beast will commit the abomination of desolation spoken of by Daniel the prophet in Daniel 12 just after the remaining of the Church is removed.

*Dan 12:11  And from the time that the daily sacrifice shall be taken away, and the abomination that maketh desolate set up, there shall be a thousand two hundred and ninety days.*

Recapping, 2 Thes. 2:1 tells of the pre-trib rapture. Verses 2 and 3 of that passage tell us that the day of Christ occurs after that 'falling away' rapture and after the man of sin is revealed. Then verse 4 of the passage tells us that the man of sin commits the abomination of desolation. This positively identifies the man of sin as the beast. The man of sin is revealed when he murders the two witnesses which occurs just prior to the seventh trump sounding at mid-trib. So, Paul explains that no pre-trib rapture has occurred and therefore the day of Christ is not at hand.

We have just looked at why these Thessalonians would be "shaken in mind". They would be in peril of losing their salvation under extreme persecution if they had entered the tribulation.

**The second half of the tribulation – the Great Tribulation**

This gives a good understanding of the layout of Matthew chapter 24. Since the thrust of this tome is the rapture of the Church and since that is in the past at this point of the passage, we will just comment on a few verses referring to the second half of the tribulation and move on to more on-target passages. Here is Matthew's description of the last 3.5 years of the tribulation.

> - *Mat 24:15 When ye therefore shall see the abomination of desolation, spoken of by Daniel the prophet, stand in the holy place, (whoso readeth, let him understand:)*
> - *16 Then let them which be in Judaea flee into the mountains:*
> - *17 Let him which is on the housetop not come down to take any thing out of his house:*

- 18 Neither let him which is in the field return back to take his clothes.
- 19 And woe unto them that are with child, and to them that give suck in those days!
- 20 But pray ye that your flight be not in the winter, neither on the sabbath day:
- 21 For then shall be **great tribulation**, such as was not since the beginning of the world to this time, no, nor ever shall be.
- 22 And except those days should be shortened, there should no flesh be saved: but for the elect's sake those days shall be shortened.
- 23 Then if any man shall say unto you, Lo, here is Christ, or there; believe it not.
- 24 For there shall arise false Christs, and false prophets, and shall shew great signs and wonders; insomuch that, if it were possible, they shall deceive the very elect.
- 25 Behold, I have told you before.
- 26 Wherefore if they shall say unto you, Behold, he is in the desert; go not forth: behold, he is in the secret chambers; believe it not.
- 27 For as the lightning cometh out of the east, and shineth even unto the west; so shall also the coming of the Son of man be.
- 28 For wheresoever the carcase is, there will the eagles be gathered together.
- 29 Immediately after the tribulation of those days shall the sun be darkened, and the moon shall not give her light, and the stars shall fall from heaven, and the powers of the heavens shall be shaken:
- 30 And then shall appear the sign of the Son of man in heaven: and then shall all the tribes of the earth mourn, and they shall see the Son of man coming in the clouds of heaven with power and great glory.
- 31 And he shall send his angels with a great sound of a trumpet, and they shall gather together his elect from the four winds, from one end of heaven to the other.

There are lots of fascinating points to be made on this section, but it takes away from the subject at hand. So, I would just like to point out a few things. One is that in every time period false christs and false prophets and antichrists abound. More is made of it in this last section than the first two sections of this passage.

Another fascinating point here is that the (number of) days have to be shortened or there should no flesh be saved. This seems to indicate that the second coming of Christ has been timed to the last second. God, in His foreknowledge, has looked ahead to the last moment before man would completely destroy himself and the planet. That is the point at which He intervenes with all the events attendant to the second coming. That is called longsuffering. To put up with the mess that is sinful mankind as long as that is proof that He loved this creation (John 3:16).

You should notice the prominent mentions of the "elect" in this Great Tribulation passage. The Church is a subset of the elect of God. Thus, when the Church is gone, those saved afterward are called the "elect" as opposed to the "bride of Christ" or other Church-only nomenclature. People of God in all ages are called "saints" and "elect".

Finally, verses 29-31 above sound very much like the events of the sixth seal. For this reason, many prophecy teachers put the two events together. They have the sixth seal opening just before the second coming of Christ.

Revelation 16:17-21 describes this very event here in Matthew, but there are several reasons why these cannot be the same event as the sixth seal. For one, it just doesn't work chronologically. The entire series of trumpet judgments comes as a result of opening the seventh seal. And we have seen that the bulk of the reign of terror by the Beast occurs after the seventh trumpet when he continues for 42 months. This Matthew passage is said to occur after the great tribulation (v. 21 above). So, we must recognize there are two such events with slight differences. They bookend the tribulation. By examining the difference between the two, we can see they don't fit together.

One difference is found with the mountains falling down at the sixth seal. Describing the similar event at the end of the tribulation in Revelation chapter 16, we find confirmation of the difference in this verse:

*Rev 16:20 And every island fled away, and the mountains were not found.*

The mountains are not found here because they collapsed seven years earlier (Ezek. 38:20). The Islands of the Sea, primarily the western hemisphere, have now joined the mainland. A couple more differences are that the Rev. 16 event is called a vial judgment and it is number seven in the series. The final battle of Armageddon follows very soon thereafter, whereas seven years can be easily accounted for after the sixth seal in the seal series.

In chapter five we learned that the continental plates will probably spring apart allowing the mountains to collapse and fill the valleys. From that point the plates will drift back to their original pre-flood position. It is like stretching a rubber band and letting it go. When these plates arrive back at their original positions, there is another great earthquake when they collide. This quake is greater than the original one because it involves a collision rather than just slippage.

*Rev 16:18 And there were voices, and thunders, and lightnings; and there was a great earthquake, such as was not since men were upon the earth, so mighty an earthquake, and so great.*

These verses allow us to understand that the continents are restored to their original position as a single land mass with no mountains. Part of the tribulation story is the reforming or terraforming of the Earth to its preflood state. And here we are, after seven years of steady continental drift and nearly at the end of the tribulation in Revelation 16, and the Earth has been made ready for the millennium.

### The parable of the fig tree

There is a break in the continuous narrative at this point. We have seen the progression of the Church Age and the first and second halves of the tribulation. This was the answer to the question, "when shall these things be?" (Matt. 24:3). Moving on, the Lord answers the next question in Matt. 24:3 by giving the greatest sign of His coming.

> - *Mat 24:32 Now learn a parable of the fig tree; When his branch is yet tender, and putteth forth leaves, ye know that summer is nigh:*
> - *33 So likewise ye, when ye shall see all these*

> *things, know that it is near, even at the doors.*
> * 34 *Verily I say unto you, This generation shall not pass, till all these things be fulfilled.*
> * 35 *Heaven and earth shall pass away, but my words shall not pass away.*

This is one of the most fascinating prophecies for the time we are living in. It should be terrifying for those who have not accepted Jesus as their personal savior and scary for those who have but are not living like it. But for those who are living a life that meets the Savior's expectations and approval, it should be the most exhilarating.

Remember that we discussed the prophetic meaning of the trees back in chapter 5 of this book. We saw that the fig tree represents Israel under civil government. It makes no difference what the spiritual state of the people is, the king rules the righteous and the unrighteous under the same social rules. The fig tree represents secular government over the people just as we see in Israel today. Religion and the state are completely separate, and the state is currently in ascendancy.

For many centuries there was no state of Israel and in fact very few Jewish people in the land. Then in the 19th century Jews began drifting back to the land and buying houses and farms. The land was slowly brought back from desert to verdant farmland and thriving industries.

*Isa 35:1 The wilderness and the solitary place shall be glad for them; and the desert shall rejoice, and blossom as the rose.*

In 1947, the land of Palestine was divided by the United Nations and a portion was given to the Jews and a portion was given to the Palestinians. They were each given a mandate to form a government and begin self-rule within one year.

One year later, on May 14, 1948 (5 Lyyar, 5708 at midnight on the Jewish calendar) the Jews submitted their declaration of statehood. The Palestinians refused because they did not want to share the land with Jews. Even so, they had sold much of their property to the Jews. Now, they want the land back and that has caused the great conflicts between the two groups.

Remember God's cup of trembling from chapter 4? We will see it in a different and glorious light here.

**Jerusalem, A Cup of Trembling and a Burdensome Stone**

*Zec 12:2 Behold, I will make Jerusalem a **cup of trembling** unto all the people round about, when they shall be in the siege both against Judah and against Jerusalem.*
*3 And in that day will I make Jerusalem a **burdensome stone** for all people: all that burden themselves with it shall be cut in pieces, though all the people of the earth be gathered together against it.*

The neighboring nations who have warred with Israel since 1948 have learned what the cup of trembling is all about. They have all been quickly and soundly defeated with hugely disproportionate losses of soldiers and resources. This prophecy has been, and is still being, spectacularly and precisely fulfilled in the generation that has seen Israel move from a fast-growing group of settlers to a new nation.

There is a second part to this prophecy as seen in verse 3 of this passage. There has been a continuing effort by many other nations, including the USA and the EU, to force peace on the region through diplomacy and political machinations. For these interfering nations, Israel has truly become a burdensome stone. She has been as hard as flint in refusing to be dictated to or led into dangerous compromises.

The motives of some of these nations seem dubious at best. Most have refused to even accept Jerusalem as the capital of Israel. Israel named Jerusalem its capital in 1950 and yet these nations have the gall to tell Israel that Tel Aviv is her capital. This, of course, is done to appease the Palestinians who presumptuously claim Jerusalem as the future capital of their non-existent state. Fortunately, the US under President Donald Trump has finally acknowledged the truth and recognized Jerusalem as the capital of Israel. A handful of other nations have followed or are following suit.

In late 2016, the United Nations Security Council (UNSC) began working toward **imposing** a two-state solution, composed of Israel and Palestine, on the tiny nation of Israel. They planned to divide the land according to their own perception of who deserves what portions regardless of Israel's wishes. This would make Israel seem to be a child among the nations and the UN the parents who know what's best for her. This insufferable and demeaning attitude will, no doubt, lead to the fulfillment of the rest of the prophecy in our verse.  The Lord has decreed that ALL who burden themselves with Jerusalem will be cut in pieces, even if it includes all the people of the Earth!

This prophecy, seemingly, is being fulfilled right now, in our time and before our eyes.  If the UNSC continues to pursue this course of action, we will see this entire world cut in pieces to biblical proportions by the God of Israel.  God does not do things halfway.  This 'cutting in pieces' may well be a reference to the judgments of the tribulation.  Although this push has slowed with Donald Trump as US president, make no mistake.  It is still the goal of much of the UN membership.

To better understand why the UNSC feels justified in imposing this solution on Israel, a brief history of modern Israel is necessary.  We will start with the Balfour Declaration of 1917.  The United Kingdom's foreign secretary wrote in a letter to Jewish leaders among the recently arrived settlers in the land, the following:

*"His Majesty's government view with favour the establishment in Palestine of a national home for the Jewish people, and will use their best endeavours to facilitate the achievement of this object, it being clearly understood that nothing shall be done which may prejudice the civil and religious rights of existing non-Jewish communities in Palestine, or the rights and political status enjoyed by Jews in any other country."*

World War 1 was just ending, and the world was being re-divided and pieced back together.  Many mistakes with serious repercussions were made in this effort.  It resulted in nations such as Iraq and Jordan, composed of ethnic groups who had been enemies from ancient times. The Middle East has been a total mess ever since.

The Balfour Declaration was included in other documents and became part of the British Mandate for Palestine. This mandate was an act of the League of Nations giving Great Britain temporary rule over Palestine, ending at midnight on May 14, 1948. The League of Nations subsequently failed when World War 2 started and was replaced by the United Nations in 1946. The United Nations inherited many of the agencies and organizations of the League of Nations and many of its mandates and agreements were honored. The British Mandate was one such agreement.

Following the horrific holocaust perpetrated on world Jewry by Nazi Germany during WW2, there was a short period of worldwide sympathy for the plight of the Jews. It was in this period that the British Mandate was, providentially, set to expire. In 1947 the United Nations General Assembly adopted a partition plan for Mandatory Palestine specifying the borders for the two potential new states of Israel and Palestine. Both groups were given until midnight, May 14, 1948, the expiration date of the British Mandate, to form a new nation. Israel complied while the Palestinians did not.

The Palestinians refused to form a state because, in their view, all the land given to Israel belonged to their Muslim god Allah. Thus, it was an abomination to agree to anything that legitimized the worship of any other God. Palestinian sympathizers do whatever they can to hide this issue because it casts the Palestinians in a bad light. This one issue makes peace impossible in the region.  Good Muslims are obligated to remove the infidel and infidel systems from Allah's land.  Israel must be driven into the sea.  See Psalm 83.

The dream of all good Muslims is to return to the form of government that the prophet Mohammed instituted.  That government is called a Caliphate and is stewarded by a Caliph.  A Caliph is a Muslim leader who rules over both the civil and religious lives of all Muslims.  Any land where Muslims form 50% of the population is automatically part of the Caliphate and the non-Muslim infidels must either convert, pay a significant fine, or be executed.  In any case, non-Muslims may not practice any other religion while in Muslim land.

**The birth of modern Israel foretold in Bible prophecy.**

No nation is mentioned in the Bible more frequently and profusely with regards to the last days than Israel.  Much detail is given and in fact Israel is the key to understanding the role and position of the rest of the nations just prior to, and within, the tribulation.  In light of this, it is very surprising that some theologians believe that Israel has no special significance in the last days.  A Bible literalist, however, can entertain no such fancies.  The prophetic statements are not obtuse and allow little latitude for allegorical interpretation.  The very fact that Israel now resides in the land given to her by God, just as prophesied, proves beyond doubt that the literal interpretation is the correct one.  Consider the following verses for one example that the literal interpretation best fits the biblical narrative:

*Isa 11:10 And in that day there shall be a root of Jesse, which shall stand for an ensign of the people; to it shall the Gentiles seek: and his rest shall be glorious.*
*11 And it shall come to pass in that day, that the Lord shall set his hand again the second time to recover the remnant of his people, which shall be left, from Assyria, and from Egypt, and from Pathros, and from Cush, and from Elam, and from Shinar, and from Hamath, and from the islands of the sea.*
*12 And he shall set up an ensign for the nations, and shall assemble the outcasts of Israel, and gather together the dispersed of Judah from the four corners of the earth.*

This passage quite clearly states that in the time when the Gentiles seek the root of Jesse (Jesus Christ), Israel will be gathered together for a second time. The first time Israel was gathered back together as a nation was after the Babylonian captivity. Now consider that this prophecy was made many years before Israel was regathered after the first diaspora. Yet, it is very specific that this prophecy deals with only the second and most recent regathering.

Although always under the thumb of foreign rulers, after returning from Babylonia and Persia, Israel remained a viable and recognized state in her own land until the second great diaspora of the Jews. This dispersion, ordered and executed by Rome, was due to revolts that ended in 70 AD and 135 AD. From 135 AD until 1948 AD the Jews had no state to call their own and rarely comprised more than a small minority of the population in Israel.

On May 14, 1948, the Jewish People's Council made a proclamation declaring the Establishment of the State of

Israel. This was under the auspices of the United Nations mandate called Mandatory Palestine directing Israel to form a nation by that date.  On that very night of the 14th, the United States, Iran, Guatemala, Iceland, Nicaragua, Romania, and Uruguay recognized the new state, precisely fulfilling another specific prophecy.  Here is that prophecy:

*Isa 66:8  Who hath heard such a thing? who hath seen such things? Shall the earth be made to bring forth in one day? or shall a nation be born at once? for as soon as Zion travailed, she brought forth her children.*
*9  Shall I bring to the birth, and not cause to bring forth? saith the LORD: shall I cause to bring forth, and shut the womb? saith thy God.*
*10  Rejoice ye with Jerusalem, and be glad with her, all ye that love her: rejoice for joy with her, all ye that mourn for her:*

It is hard to imagine that someone who loves the Lord could read this and not be thrilled at this literal validation of His prophetic Word to Israel. **Zion** (Israel) travailed in the meeting of the Jewish People's Council and **the Earth** (United Nations) brought forth the nation of Israel in the evening of that very day just as verse 8 above prophesied. When May 14, 1948 (again, 5 Lyyar, 5708 on the Jewish calendar) began, Israel was not a nation.  When May 15, 1948 began, Israel was recognized as a nation by the entire world through the auspices of the United Nations as an organization as well as by 7 specific nations of the world. Joseph Stalin of Russia also immediately recognized the new nation and Russia and most other nations followed with formal recognition shortly thereafter.  Another way to look at this is that Israel travailed in the furnaces of Auschwitz and other such venues which directly led the

United Nations to decide that the Jews needed a homeland.

Since modern Israel became a nation, the world has been privileged to watch another prophecy play out time after time with regard to Israel's status among the nations. Consider once again this passage:

*Zec 12:1 The burden of the word of the LORD for Israel, saith the LORD, which stretcheth forth the heavens, and layeth the foundation of the earth, and formeth the spirit of man within him.*
*2 Behold, I will make Jerusalem a cup of trembling unto all the people round about, when they shall be in the siege both against Judah and against Jerusalem.*
*3 And in that day will I make Jerusalem a burdensome stone for all people: all that burden themselves with it shall be cut in pieces, though all the people of the earth be gathered together against it.*

This prophecy was made shortly after the Jews had returned from the Babylonian captivity. From that time until 1948 AD, the Jews were always the subjects of each succeeding world empire. They were never a feared military power. Since 1948, all of Israel's neighbors have (as prophesied in Psalm 83 and other places) hated her and vowed to destroy her. Though always outmanned, Israel has soundly defeated every nation or alliance of nations that has come to destroy her. It seems obvious that we are now in "that day" mentioned in verse 3 of the above passage.

**Timing the start of the tribulation and the pre-trib rapture**

It should not seem like a stretch at all to consider May 14, 1948 as the day the fig tree put forth leaves. The nation had been like a dormant tree up to that point. Since then, it has grown and flourished. To refresh our memory:

> ➢ *Mat 24:32 Now learn a parable of the fig tree; When his branch is yet tender, and putteth forth leaves, ye know that summer is nigh:*
> ➢ *33 So likewise ye, when ye shall see all these things, know that it is near, even at the doors.*
> ➢ *34 Verily I say unto you, This generation shall not pass, till all these things be fulfilled.*
> ➢ *35 Heaven and earth shall pass away, but my words shall not pass away.*

The parable tells us that when we see the fig tree put forth leaves that 'it' is near, even at the doors. So, what is "it"? It is what Jesus had just told His disciples in answer to their questions:

"Tell us, when shall these things be? and what *shall be* the sign of thy coming, and of the end of the world?"

"It" as a singular pronoun, answers most closely to the question: "what shall be the sign of thy coming"? When Israel comes out of her dormancy period, the coming of Jesus is at the door. When Jesus comes as a Thief, the day of the LORD begins which is the 'last day' of this world's history. Recapping for clarity then we see that Israel's return to statehood is the sign of the coming of Christ, and the end of the generation that starts at the same time is the latest possible time for His coming.

So, how close is that? This close!

> 34 *Verily I say unto you, This generation shall not pass, till all these things be fulfilled.*

This is a very important statement. If we know how long a generation is, we can time the end-times events we have just seen. Before we deal with a generation, I need to point out that Christ's coming is going to turn out to be a multiple event coming, so we are interested here in the first time that happens. The next two (though really three) times are clearly delineated in the book of Revelation. If you can find the first one, there is no more need for the special revelation we are receiving in this parable.

Many generation time lengths have been offered as solutions, but it really seems quite simple as to what is intended here. If we believe, as I am convinced, that we are living in the generation that will see this event, then we just need to see if the Bible mentions a suitable generation time span for verification. And happily, it does.

*Psa 90:10 The days of our years are threescore years and ten; and if by reason of strength they be fourscore years, yet is their strength labour and sorrow; for it is soon cut off, and we fly away.*

This wonderful verse is part of the song of Moses found in Psalm 90. At the time Moses penned this, he was probably close to 120 years old and had seen many of his aunts and uncles and parents and recent ancestors die at well over a hundred years old. This short lifespan was probably an odd concept to him unless he knew it was a prophecy for a future time. The verse adequately describes the lifespan of a person in the early 21st century, however. You must wonder whether he really understood the concept of flying away which likely describes rising to meet the Lord on our way to glory.

**DISCLAIMER:**

**\*\*So, *if* we are reading this parable correctly\*\***,

(OK, as of this December 2021 editing, the dates listed below were obviously not the date of the pre-trib rapture. However, they were never intended to be taken that way. I am leaving this section here because there is still great value in being aware of this prophecy.)

Let's see where we are.  The passage gives us a lifespan of 70-80 years for a generation.  Applying this to our parable, we see that a man born in 1948 as national Israel was, could on average expect to live comfortably until 2018.  After that, if he is strong, he can expect on average to live with labor and sorrow, possibly until 2028.  So, why the terms "labour" and "sorrow"?  I'm glad you asked.

The sorrow part of this likely refers to the sorrows of the tribulation.  The passage tells us that all the things just prophesied must come to pass within the 80 years (*This generation shall not pass, till* **all these things** *be fulfilled.)* and we have seen that the Lord's Matthew 24 prophecy takes us to the end of the seven-year tribulation.  So, those seven years must be subtracted from the 80 if the rapture is to be pre-trib.  (I sometimes wonder about the wisdom of hiding the full pre-trib rapture proof for so long.)  Therefore, from where we are now, the pre-trib rapture must occur before the end of year 2021.  Some might carry it a step further and choose the 73-year anniversary of Israel's independence at midnight Jerusalem time on May 14, 2021 on the Gentile calendar. Remember, Israel's statehood took effect at midnight.

Some might also choose the Jewish calendar celebration date for their independence as the rapture day. Each day starts at sundown on the Jewish calendar. So, their Independence Day celebration would start Wednesday, 3 Lyyar, 5781 at sundown, Jerusalem time which would be Wednesday, April 14, 2021 Gentile time, and look for the rapture to occur at midnight, Jerusalem time on that date.

Another candidate date might be May 26. That is the date of the next total lunar eclipse which was discussed in the previous chapter.

WOW, Huh? There is much that must still occur between now and then that we will discuss, so you must begin watching for the signs of the Lord's return very carefully now.

So, what of the labor part of the last ten years? I believe this is a cryptic confirmation that works will once again become a part of salvation when the tribulation starts. Review what we just discussed about that thus far in this chapter of the book.

Here is an awesome takeaway from this parable. Remember how we discussed in chapter 4 that we had a problem of precision in our calendar? Well, in this parable our great God gives us a 1948 reset point to get us back on track as far as the years go. Think about how amazingly simple and clever that was.

If we are reading this parable correctly, we can now tie prophecies to specific years so we only need be looking for the day and hour of a particular year to pin down the pre-trib rapture. On the other hand, if we are reading this parable incorrectly, all the events we have discussed **will still occur,** but probably at a later rather than the earlier dates.

Just one more point before we move on. The Lord assures us that although heaven and Earth will surely pass away (2 Pet. 3:10-13), His very words will not pass away. His very words are here to consult about the times we are living in. As we noted earlier, you need to be very sure you find those words. Hint: Look in your King James Bible, Authorized Version of 1611.

### Understanding the 'day and hour' statements in scripture

- ❖ *Mat 24:36 But of that day and hour knoweth no man, no, not the angels of heaven, but my Father only.*

If the passage we just discussed is the most fascinating for our time, this verse is the most grossly quoted out of context for our time. We discussed this early in the book, but I will expand on it here. You should notice that there are four instances of such language in the following verses to tie each of the situations to the same thought. In the last three cases watch for a division in the body of Christ. I am going to place this verse in the middle of the verses before it and the verse after it. See if you can tell what is different about this one.

- ➢ *Mat 24:34 Verily I say unto you, This generation **shall** not pass, till all these things be fulfilled.*
- ➢ *35 Heaven and earth **shall** pass away, but my words shall not pass away.*
- ❖ *36 But of that day and hour **knoweth** no man, no, not the angels of heaven, but my Father only.*
- ➢ *37 But as the days of Noe were, so **shall** also the*

*coming of the Son of man be.*

Do you see that? The Lord is speaking in the future tense in most of this passage, but when He comes to statements regarding the **timing** of His second coming, He changes to present tense. He is saying that as of right then (2000 years ago) nobody knows when He will return, but **the Father does know.** In the sister passage in the gospel of Mark, Jesus stressed that even He did not know. Understanding this is very important to recognize there is a specific, set time for His return which the Father knew. People who tend to say "if the Lord tarries…" haven't read this verse closely. The end-times are set in stone and always have been set in stone. (See Hab.2:3 and Heb.10:37.)

The reason Jesus didn't know (in His flesh) is that He was not permitted to know whether His death would be caused by the Jews or the Romans. This was to ensure the legitimacy of His kingdom offer to the Jews. There were two possible dates for His return as we have discussed in chapter four of this work. One date was 3.5 years after His crucifixion and the other was about 2000 years later.

So, now that He has been crucified at the fault of the Jews, there is no reason for Him not to know anymore and in His Godhood, He absolutely must know. There is also no reason that we cannot know now either. We will discuss this in more detail in a later chapter.

> *Mat 24:37 But as the days of Noe were, so shall also the coming of the Son of man be.*
> *38 For as in the days that were before the flood they were eating and drinking, marrying and giving in marriage, until the day that Noe entered*

> *into the ark,*
> ➢ *39 And knew not until the flood came, and took them all away; so shall also the coming of the Son of man be.*

Earlier in this chapter we discussed the reappearance of fallen angels, this time in the guise of space aliens. There is more to the passage, though. Although Noah, as a preacher of righteousness, surely must have warned everybody who would listen, it appears his preaching fell on deaf ears. When the flood came the people were busy about their normal personal and social lives and completely unaware that catastrophe was coming.

The coming of the Son of man will be exactly the same this time around. Only this time it will be worse. Most of those remaining in Noah's day were probably only part human and thus not savable. This time not only will most be human, but many will be saved people. We will begin to see now that there will be a division, a breaking up of the Church into two groups. One group will be raptured at that time and the other will enter the tribulation.

A statement like that is anathema and fightin' words to many or most in the Church. They will protest loudly that Christ would never allow His Body to be broken up or divided. But we are choosing to believe the scriptures here over their protests. The Church is broken up every time one Christian dies and the rest remain alive. There are many divisions within the body of Christ. Some live in countries where their lives are in doubt every moment while some live in the United States with no sense of physical danger for their faith whatsoever. Furthermore, there is an elaborate system of rewards and losses of rewards for individual Christians. Some Christians get crowns, some get jewels for their crowns, some see their rewards burned up, others don't. Some Christians, as we shall soon see, appear before Christ naked and ashamed. Some shine as the brightness of the firmament. Some get spued out of His mouth, others get cities to rule over. Some of those get five cities and some ten. You can look it all up. It's in the book. There are divisions and levels of rewards all through the scriptures for the saved and levels of hell for the lost.

Many self-righteous individuals say it is an insult to God to do His work for any reason other than to please Him. That sounds pretty good to me as well. So, why does God point out the rewards to us for service so often? Could it be He wants us to strive for those rewards? Could it be we were designed to be rewards-based workers? I don't know, I just go by the book.

### Three parables regarding Christ separating the spiritual from the carnal in the Church

> ➤ *Mat 24:40 Then shall two be in the field; the one shall be taken, and the other left.*
> ➤ *41 Two women shall be grinding at the mill; the one shall be taken, and the other left.*
> ❖ *42 Watch therefore: for ye know not what hour **your Lord** doth come.*

Now we come to a section where the Lord stresses three times the pain that will come from not knowing the very hour of His return. Notice again the change in tense in these three verses. These people are in the same grouping but are separated with one taken and the other left. Many try to argue here that the difference is between the saved and the lost. But as we read on down through the chapter, context will not permit that. We will see that this is between the saved and the saved. There are two more examples of this to come where each one becomes more obviously a division between saved and saved people.

Those that are advised to watch here have this important point in common. They are told to watch for YOUR Lord. The division here is between the watchers and the not-watchers for THEIR Lord. These, by context, are all Christians.

Also note that the time frame is the very hour. It is not the year or the month or even the day, but the very hour. The command to watch is very strong. The term watch implies that we can be prepared for it before it happens. Yet, someone was not prepared, and someone was prepared in each case. Let's stop here and look at the next passage for more help.

> *Mat 24:43 But know this, that if the goodman of the house had known in what watch the thief would come, he would have watched, and would not have suffered his house to be broken up.*
>
> ❖ *44 Therefore be ye also ready: for in such an hour as ye think not the Son of man cometh.*

Now we are getting somewhere. Again, notice the change in tense. The first of these three passages we are looking at, occurred at the time of the rapture. The next two are in the sense of looking back after the rapture has occurred. So, verse 43 is from the viewpoint of the event already having happened while verse 44 brings us back to the time at which Christ was speaking. Also, the very hour is stressed again.

The solution for the goodman to keep his house together is to be watching for the Thief. In this verse, if he had only known the "watch" the Thief would come in, he would have been able to keep his household together. A watch in Jewish time reckoning is three hours, still less than a day. The significance of a watch of time is this. When the Son of man does come, it is sudden and there is no time to warn anybody. So, a watch allows the goodman a small space of time, but enough to warn his household before the final hour.

Again, we are seeing a separation of people. The goodman here is any person in charge of a household, or a congregation, or a denomination. He is a goodman, so-called because he is a saved man with responsibility for others' spiritual welfare. Thus, if his house is broken up, he has failed some of them. This is where things get scary for such people.

So, are the people taken safe or are the people left behind the safe ones? Based on our reckoning of a thief, we would naturally assume that the people left behind were kept safe. But we will find this Thief to be a different kind of thief. Let's use our KJV super sleuth method of solving this problem. Can we find a thief whose primary interest is in the household of God? How about this one?

*Rev 16:15 Behold, I come as a thief. Blessed is he that watcheth, and keepeth his garments, lest he walk naked, and they see his shame.*

These words are the words of Christ. He is characterizing Himself as a Thief, but for Him to be a Thief, it must be in a righteous sense. So, those who are taken by this Thief are the ones kept safe. This is a rapture event then in which only some of the household of God are removed. In addition, this Thief is preoccupied with the very hour of His coming to steal away part of His Church. Consider these words of Jesus:

*Rev 3:3 Remember therefore how thou hast received and*

*heard, and hold fast, and repent. If therefore thou shalt not watch, I will come on thee as a thief, and thou shalt not know what hour I will come upon thee.*

Really awesome verse, right? So, what elements repeat again here? Well, I see watching and Christ as a Thief and the very hour of His coming! I see something else that is just thrilling. To see it in its most understandable form, let's reverse the polarity of the elements of the sentence. It then says:

"If therefore thou shalt watch, I will NOT come on thee as a Thief, and thou shalt KNOW what hour I will come upon thee."

So, Christ comes as a Thief ONLY to those in the Church who are not watching. They are the only ones who will not know the very hour of His coming. We will see the sad fate of those who did not know the hour.

Remember, we have many signs to watch for and an assurance that Elijah will come and prophesy the coming of Christ. Many well-meaning pastors today are vigilant to put down and denigrate date-setters. Let's pray they don't continue in this attitude when the truthful date-setter arrives.

> ➢ *Mat 24:45 Who then is a faithful and wise servant, whom his lord hath made ruler over his household, to give them meat in due season?*
> ➢ *46 Blessed is that servant, whom his lord when he cometh shall find so doing.*
> ➢ *47 Verily I say unto you, That he shall make him ruler over all his goods.*

We are continuing the theme of the goodman of the house here. The first case we find is the servant who actually did what his Lord commanded. He gave his people meat in due season. That is, he nourished them until they were ready for meat. The Lord is very serious about seeing Christians mature from milk drinkers to meat eaters. Meat is what this author is attempting to provide. But meat causes long-time, immature milk drinkers to lash out with accusations of heresy or even apostasy. That is why I put so many verses from so many sources into the text. It must be demonstrated that this is entirely scriptural wherever it is needed.

So, let's look at what the Lord thinks of milk toast Christians.

*Heb 5:12 For when for the time ye ought to be teachers, ye have need that one teach you again which be the first principles of the oracles of God; and are become such as have need of milk, and not of strong meat.*

*13 For every one that useth milk is unskilful in the word of righteousness: for he is a babe.*

*14 But strong meat belongeth to them that are of full age, even those who by reason of use have their senses exercised to discern both good and evil.*

Baby Christians are unskillful in the word of righteousness and are poor at discernment of good and evil. That is why they complain when they see or hear strong meat.

*1Co 3:1 And I, brethren, could not speak unto you as unto spiritual, but as unto carnal, even as unto babes in Christ.*

*2 I have fed you with milk, and not with meat: for hitherto ye were not able to bear it, neither yet now are ye able.*

Baby Christians are not truly spiritual. But the faithful and wise servant weans his household from milk and feeds them strong meat to make them strong and discerning

Christians. They can read the things in this book without wincing and squirming. This servant is going to be promoted to ruler over all the master's goods. He is completely trustworthy. Just one more familiar anti-milk drinker passage here.

*Isa 28:9 Whom shall he teach knowledge? and whom shall he make to understand doctrine? them that are weaned from the milk, and drawn from the breasts.*

*10 For precept must be upon precept, precept upon precept; line upon line, line upon line; here a little, and there a little:*

Now, let's look at the case of the servant who will not feed his people the strong meat knowledge necessary to be taken in the pre-trib rapture. He preaches that God loves everybody and wouldn't hurt a flea. Thus, he would never preach on hell, or punishment, or chastisement, or division of the body of Christ. Here is what the Lord has to say about that guy:

- *Mat 24:48 But and if that evil servant shall say in his heart, My lord delayeth his coming;*
- *49 And shall begin to smite his fellowservants, and to eat and drink with the drunken;*
- *50 The lord of that servant shall come in a day when he looketh not for him, and in an hour that he is not aware of,*
- *51 And shall cut him asunder, and appoint him his portion with the hypocrites: there shall be weeping and gnashing of teeth.*

That is scary, isn't it? This man is a servant of God but is not doing God's will at the last day. He doesn't believe the coming of the Lord draweth nigh because he hasn't studied the meat of the word. Smiting his fellowservants is a reference to the harm he does to his fellows by not teaching them about the impending coming of the Lord. He is said to eat and drink with the drunken. I don't believe this is a physical drunkenness, but rather a drunkenness on the milk toast principles of initial salvation. He does not obey this instruction:

*Heb 6:1 Therefore leaving the principles of the doctrine of Christ, let us go on unto perfection; not laying again the foundation of repentance from dead works, and of faith toward God,*

*2 Of the doctrine of baptisms, and of laying on of hands, and of resurrection of the dead, and of eternal judgment.*

At some point, a Christian needs to graduate from nursery school. This leader or pastor might get away with it in another age. But he will not get away with it if he is preaching these things at the time his Lord returns. Look at what happens.

The Lord comes at a day and an hour that he should have been aware of. Because of that he is cut asunder! He is cut off from the Christians who were worthy, along with all his baby Christian followers. He is appointed his portion with the hypocrites. Hypocrites don't get raptured; they end up in hell if they don't repent. Further, it seems they must repent before the rapture occurs or they may be subjected to strong delusion.

The final end of this evil servant seems to be loss of salvation. He will not survive the temptations in a works-based environment and ends up in a place where there will be weeping and gnashing of teeth. Do a search on that phrase and prepare to shudder.

Chapter 25 of Matthew shows us one more case of separation of God's people. This is even more forcefully presented as a separation of the Church.

> ➤ *Mat 25:1 Then shall the kingdom of heaven be likened unto ten virgins, which took their lamps, and went forth to meet the bridegroom.*
> ➤ *2 And five of them were wise, and five were foolish.*
> ➤ *3 They that were foolish took their lamps, and took no oil with them:*
> ➤ *4 But the wise took oil in their vessels with their lamps.*
> ➤ *5 While the bridegroom tarried, they all slumbered and slept.*
> ➤ *6 And at midnight there was a cry made, Behold, the bridegroom cometh; go ye out to meet him.*
> ➤ *7 Then all those virgins arose, and trimmed their lamps.*
> ➤ *8 And the foolish said unto the wise, Give us of your oil; for our lamps are gone out.*
> ➤ *9 But the wise answered, saying, Not so; lest there be not enough for us and you: but go ye rather to them that sell, and buy for yourselves.*
> ➤ *10 And while they went to buy, the bridegroom came; and they that were ready went in with him to the marriage: and the door was shut.*
> ➤ *11 Afterward came also the other virgins, saying, Lord, Lord, open to us.*
> ➤ *12 But he answered and said, Verily I say unto you, I know you not.*
> ❖ *13 Watch therefore, for ye know neither the day nor the hour wherein the Son of man cometh.*

As a parable, this story is not a point-by-point accounting of doctrine. Rather it is an illustration to show us that oil is necessary to enter into the wedding feast of the saved. Oil is an often-used picture of the Holy Ghost in scriptures. (Remember the Olive tree.) These were all virgins indicating that all were equally members of the Church. Here we must note that for the sake of the parable they were called virgins in order to avoid ascribing many brides to Christ. Taken together, they are the bride of Christ, but individually they are virgins. Those without oil had let their fulness of the Spirit wane to the point they were no longer in a state of watchfulness.

By now you should be able to surmise who is making that midnight call. That's right, our old friend Elijah.

Notice that the parable ends with the same language we saw in the earlier examples. Verse 13 is back to present tense in Christ's time. Before the crucifixion this knowledge was carefully guarded by the Father. But now, there is a great need to know the day and hour. Most of these virgins could have avoided the situation they find themselves in here simply by living righteously and watching for the Thief rapture.

This is a final example of the goodman's house being broken up. The tense changes then, are there to get our attention. So, let's give them our attention.

Remember the verses we pointed to earlier about this:

*1Co 2:12 Now we have received, not the spirit of the world, but the spirit which is of God; that we might know the things that are freely given to us of God.*
*13 Which things also we speak, not in the words which man's wisdom teacheth, but which the Holy Ghost teacheth; comparing spiritual things with spiritual.*
*14 But the natural man receiveth not the things of the*

*Spirit of God: for they are foolishness unto him: neither can he know them, because they are spiritually discerned.*

*15 But he that is spiritual judgeth all things, yet he himself is judged of no man.*

This understanding is for the people of God, and further for those who have been weaned from milk to strong meat.

**The prophecy of Luke chapter 21**

Before we end this chapter, we must take a brief look at Luke chapter 21. This prophecy contains wording very similar to the wording in the Olivet Discourse of Matthew 24, but we need to understand it starts earlier and ends earlier from a chronological viewpoint. Whereas Matthew took us from that time through the tribulation, Luke only takes us up to the tribulation. But Luke also provides prophecy from the time of Jesus to the destruction of the temple in 70 AD. Here we go.

*Luk 21:7 And they asked him, saying, Master, but when shall these things be? and what sign will there be when these things shall come to pass?*

*8 And he said, Take heed that ye be not deceived: for many shall come in my name, saying, I am Christ; and the time draweth near: go ye not therefore after them.*

*9 But when ye shall hear of wars and commotions, be not terrified: for these things must first come to pass; but the end is not by and by.*

*10 Then said he unto them, Nation shall rise against nation, and kingdom against kingdom:*

*11 And great earthquakes shall be in divers places, and*

*famines, and pestilences; and fearful sights and great signs shall there be from heaven.*

These signs are easily recognized as Matthews' Beginning of Sorrows signs. Again, we see the caution to not be deceived by antichrists. And again, we see the cautioning that the end is not yet. It is important to note that the disciples asked the same questions regarding when these things would be and what would be the proof sign. Continuing:

*Luk 21:12 But before all these, they shall lay their hands on you, and persecute you, delivering you up to the synagogues, and into prisons, being brought before kings and rulers for my name's sake.*

In Matthew the word 'then' followed the Beginning of Sorrows. Here in Luke we see that the next events all occur **before** any of the Beginning of Sorrows events occur.

*Luk 21:13 And it shall turn to you for a testimony.*

*14 Settle it therefore in your hearts, not to meditate before what ye shall answer:*

*15 For I will give you a mouth and wisdom, which all your adversaries shall not be able to gainsay nor resist.*

*16 And ye shall be betrayed both by parents, and brethren, and kinsfolks, and friends; and some of you shall they cause to be put to death.*

*17 And ye shall be hated of all men for my name's sake.*

*18 But there shall not an hair of your head perish.*

*19 In your patience possess ye your souls.*

Here again we see the betrayal by family members for

following Christ, but this time His followers do not die because of it. The meaning that must be inferred here is that they do not die spiritually. That's because what is about to come is for the Jews who rejected Christ.

We saw these next events prophesied in our study of Daniel 9:24-27. Remember he told us: *"for the overspreading of abominations he shall make it desolate, even until the consummation, and **that determined** shall be poured upon the desolate."* Here we see what was determined or pre-determined for the Jews if they rejected their Messiah.

*Luk 21:20 And when ye shall see Jerusalem compassed with armies, then know that the desolation thereof is nigh.*

*21 Then let them which are in Judaea flee to the mountains; and let them which are in the midst of it depart out; and let not them that are in the countries enter thereinto.*

*22 For these be the days of vengeance, that all things which are written may be fulfilled.*

*23 But woe unto them that are with child and to them that give suck, in those days! for there shall be **great distress in the land, and wrath upon this people**.*

*24 And they shall fall by the edge of the sword, and shall be led away captive into all nations: and Jerusalem shall be trodden down of the Gentiles, until the times of the Gentiles be fulfilled.*

To refresh your memory, the Jews were led away captive into many nations by the Romans in 135 AD.

Verse 24 contains a powerful prophecy. As we saw earlier, in chapter 4, when the Jews are brought back from all nations, the times of the Gentiles would be over or fulfilled. Look where we are right now. If you doubt we are close to the start of the day of the LORD, you are overlooking a lot of prophetic scriptures.

*Luk 21:25 And there shall be signs in the sun, and in the moon, and in the stars; and upon the earth distress of nations, with perplexity; the sea and the waves roaring;*

*26 Men's hearts failing them for fear, and for looking after those things which are coming on the earth: for the powers of heaven shall be shaken.*

*27 And then shall they see the Son of man coming in a cloud with power and great glory.*

*28 And when these things begin to come to pass, then look up, and lift up your heads; for your redemption draweth nigh.*

This portion of Luke 21 takes us right up to the start of the day of the LORD. We find the signs we have looked at repeatedly along with the Son of man coming on His mobile throne with power and great glory. Compare this to Rev. 6:17 where He is called the Lamb. So, we are right at the time of redemption and the start of the day of the LORD.

Next, Luke gives us the parable of the fig tree which, as in Matthew, signals the end of the question "when shall these things be?" and turns to the sign of His coming.

*Luk 21:29 And he spake to them a parable; Behold the fig tree, and all the trees;*

*30 When they now shoot forth, ye see and know of your own selves that summer is now nigh at hand.*

*31 So likewise ye, when ye see these things come to pass, know ye that the kingdom of God is nigh at hand.*

*32 Verily I say unto you, This generation shall not pass away, till all be fulfilled.*

*33 Heaven and earth shall pass away: but my words shall not pass away.*

Following the parable of the fig tree, Jesus gives us one more warning. Verse 36 is a verse we have quoted often in this work because it has some very important messages in it. If we WATCH and PRAY, we can be accounted worthy to escape all these things. All what things, you ask? All the things mentioned with respect to the day of the LORD recounted in verses 25 and 26 above.

*Luk 21:34 And take heed to yourselves, lest at any time your hearts be overcharged with surfeiting, and drunkenness, and cares of this life, and so that day come upon you unawares.*

*35 For as a snare shall it come on all them that dwell on the face of the whole earth.*

*36 Watch ye therefore, and pray always, that ye may be accounted worthy to escape all these things that shall come to pass, and to stand before the Son of man.*

*37 And in the day time he was teaching in the temple; and at night he went out, and abode in the mount that is called the mount of Olives.*

I will close this chapter with a familiar passage we should again consider very soberly.

*Luk 18:8 ...Nevertheless when the Son of man cometh, shall he find faith on the earth?*

# Chapter 7. The Day of Reckoning for the Church, or…

## (What We Can Learn from the New Testament Epistles)

There was this day, a few years ago, that I learned a brand-new word. That word was feckless. On that single day, I think I heard the word forty or fifty times. Maybe you remember that day. It was a talking point seemingly used by every talking head in the liberal media news outlets and a goodly percentage of the conservatives as well. It kind of proved that most all the day's news comes from a single source that puts it out early in the morning of every day. It seems the news we are provided by the mainstream sources is mostly preplanned, canned, and programmed into our minds. This way, everybody stays on the same page and the truth is often buried.

Something similar happens with many prophecy writers as well. They read each other's work and throw back the same stuff with maybe a little wrinkle here or there to make it their own. So, it is not surprising that so many agree certain things are true that can easily be disproven with just a little deeper bible study. We will look at one such example in this chapter when we deal with the day of Jesus Christ. Too many have equated it with the start of the day of the Lord, but it is clearly a different day. Knowing the truth about this day will clear up one of the more wrestled with and wrested scriptures in their works. So, let's take this thing apart.

There is much we can learn about the raptures from the Epistles of Paul and Peter and James and John and Jude and the writer of Hebrews.  There is also much we have already learned from these Epistles throughout this book.  But there are just a few more critical studies we need to see before the big reveal on the raptures.

**The day of the Lord versus the day of the LORD**

We spent quite a bit of time on the day of the LORD in chapter 5 and now we need to look at the corresponding scriptures in the New Testament.  In the NT the day is called the day of the Lord.  It is nowhere found in all caps.  You should remember that LORD in all caps speaks always of JEHOVAH, a particularly Jewish name for the soulish part of the Godhead.  The NT is written to all people, whether Jew or Gentile, so we now call this part of the Godhead 'The Father'.  When the general terms like Lord and God are mentioned in the NT, context must be used to distinguish between Jesus the Son, and the Father.  With that in mind, let's look at the three passages using the phrase 'day of the Lord' where the determination is by context only.

*Act 2:16 But this is that which was spoken by the prophet Joel;*
*17 And it shall come to pass in the last days, saith God, I will pour out of my Spirit upon all flesh: and your sons and your daughters shall prophesy, and your young men shall see visions, and your old men shall dream dreams:*
*18 And on my servants and on my handmaidens I will pour out in those days of my Spirit; and they shall prophesy:*

*19 And I will shew wonders in heaven above, and signs in the earth beneath; blood, and fire, and vapour of smoke:*

*20 The sun shall be turned into darkness, and the moon into blood, before that great and notable day of the Lord come:*

*21 And it shall come to pass, that whosoever shall call on the name of the Lord shall be saved.*

As a preamble to this discussion, we must more precisely define the 'last-days'. In some contexts, the term refers to the days when the tribulation is near and beyond. This is an imprecise time period that allows much flexibility of definition. In other cases, as here, it refers to all the days after the 'first days' and generally is looked at as 1000-year days. We will delve into these days more deeply later on.

In Acts 2:17, Peter, the speaker here, referenced the last days. This is a term, along with 'last time' or 'last times', for the time from the appearance of Messiah, Christ until the end of the Millennium. Also see Heb. 1:2 and 1 John 2:18 and 1 Peter 1:5 and 1 Peter 1:20. The days before that were the first days. From this understanding, we can begin to get a concept of how long this creation can continue. There had been 4000 years to the coming of Messiah and thus would be no more than 4000 years remaining before the Great White Throne judgment of Rev. 20:11-15. In fact, we will find 3000 years remaining.

So, what Peter is saying in this passage is that the last days has begun. The reference here is tied to the day of the LORD in Joel 2:31. Thus, the day of the Lord here is the same as the day of the LORD in the Old Testament. This is important because we are establishing a difference between the day of the Lord (JEHOVAH or the Father) and the day of Christ Jesus.  The fact that some of these specific events do not occur until the day of the LORD starts is often overlooked.  Some try to force all of this prophecy into Peter's lifetime which, not surprisingly, does not work out well doctrinally.  They occur within the last days which allows them the full 2000 years until the day of the Lord begins.  The important part of the quote for that era was that the times had come when "whosoever shall call upon the name of the Lord shall be saved". Sometimes it is necessary to apply good old common sense to the scriptures and allow the facts of history to guide you into a correct understanding of a passage.

*1Th 5:1 But of the times and the seasons, brethren, ye have no need that I write unto you.*
*2 For yourselves know perfectly that the day of the Lord so cometh as a thief in the night.*
*3 For when they shall say, Peace and safety; then sudden destruction cometh upon them, as travail upon a woman with child; and they shall not escape.*

This passage gives us more information on the day of the Lord/LORD.  It will come as a thief, at a time when man will believe he is establishing peace and safety.  Also, it will come suddenly and there is no escaping it.  I would argue that we are in such a time right now.  Regardless of wars that are currently making the news, these are minor skirmishes in the grand scheme and organizations such as the United Nations have brought temporary order to the most developed nations.  In fact, there is an even greater US-policy-driven lull now, in late 2019-early 2020, compared to the last 50 years or so. But this order could break in an instant of time. And when it does, most believe it will be World War III.

The most important new thing we learn from this passage, however, is that it comes as a thief in the night. This is a major New Testament reveal. Where have we seen this concept of coming as a Thief before? That's right. Jesus comes as a Thief. This terminology in the KJV is no accident. The Author purposely gave this nugget to those willing to accept divine Authorship of this passage. Folks, we must accept what the scriptures **freely** give us. Read 1 Cor. 2:6-16 one more time. It is sooo important.

*2Pe 3:10 But the day of the Lord will come as a thief in the night; in the which the heavens shall pass away with a great noise, and the elements shall melt with fervent heat, the earth also and the works that are therein shall be burned up.*

*11 Seeing then that all these things shall be dissolved, what manner of persons ought ye to be in all holy conversation and godliness,*

*12 Looking for and hasting unto the coming of the day of God, wherein the heavens being on fire shall be dissolved, and the elements shall melt with fervent heat?*

*13 Nevertheless we, according to his promise, look for new heavens and a new earth, wherein dwelleth righteousness.*

*14 Wherefore, beloved, seeing that ye look for such things, be diligent that ye may be found of him in peace, without spot, and blameless.*

The New Testament just keeps on giving here.  There is so much more to learn about the day of the Lord.  First of all, there is reinforcement that it comes or starts as a thief in the night.  Then we see that at some point within the day all the elements in the universe will explode and then melt and burn up.  Verse 11 uses the term dissolved to give another description of the event.  In terms of physics, we can say that all matter is converted to energy.  This is further explained when we arrive at the Great White Throne final judgment at the end of the millennium here:

*Rev 20:11  And I saw a great white throne, and him that sat on it, from whose face the earth and the heaven fled away; and there was found no place for them.*


There was no place found for heaven and Earth because there was no physical universe to put them in.  The only thing in existence at this point is pure energy, possibly in the form of light.  What is left is in the realm of the soul and this is where the souls of the unrighteous dead are judged.  This is the end of the day of the Lord.

After the final judgment, the Lord creates a brand-new heaven and Earth and remakes the bodies of all men.  In terms of physics, He converts some of the energy back to matter.

*Rev 21:1  And I saw a new heaven and a new earth: for the first heaven and the first earth were passed away; and there was no more sea.*
*2  And I John saw the holy city, new Jerusalem, coming down from God out of heaven, prepared as a bride adorned for her husband.*

A final point of interest to note here, which is often overlooked, is that the Lake of Fire will be clearly visible on the surface of the **new Earth** along with the unrighteous dead and Satan and his angels who will populate it.

*Isa 66:22 For as the new heavens and the new earth, which I will make, shall remain before me, saith the LORD, so shall your seed and your name remain.*
*23 And it shall come to pass, that from one new moon to another, and from one sabbath to another, shall all flesh come to worship before me, saith the LORD.*
*24 And they shall go forth, and look upon the carcases of the men that have transgressed against me: for their worm shall not die, neither shall their fire be quenched; and they shall be an abhorring unto all flesh.*

So, our passage in Peter gives us the boundaries of the day of the Lord. It starts when the Thief comes and ends 1000+ years later at the final judgment. We saw in chapter 5 many other events that mark the start of the day of the LORD.

### The judgment seat of Christ

Before we look at the day of Christ, we need to look at the judgment seat of Christ. This will help us locate where we are in time on that day. First thing to note is that this is not the same judgment as the Great White Throne judgment. This one deals only with rewards and loss of rewards for the saints. We will see that it occurs after the resurrection of the dead in Christ along with all the righteous saved from Adam to the day of this resurrection. Here are two passages that elucidate the event.

*Rom 14:10 But why dost thou judge thy brother? or why*

*dost thou set at nought thy brother? for we shall all stand before the judgment seat of Christ.*

*11 For it is written, As I live, saith the Lord, every knee shall bow to me, and every tongue shall confess to God.*

*12 So then every one of us shall give account of himself to God.*

And:

*2Co 5:10 For we must all appear before the judgment seat of Christ; that every one may receive the things done in his body, according to that he hath done, whether it be good or bad.*

The judgment seat of Christ is a judgment on the works we have done in our earthly bodies up to the time of our death or rapture. Some of us have done good works and some of us have done evil works even though we were saved. Our works will be tried by fire to see if they will bring reward or loss. Here are a couple proof passages for this point.

*1Co 3:12 Now if any man build upon this foundation gold, silver, precious stones, wood, hay, stubble;*

*13 Every man's work shall be made manifest: for the day shall declare it, because it shall be revealed by fire; and the fire shall try every man's work of what sort it is.*

*14 If any man's work abide which he hath built thereupon, he shall receive a reward.*

*15 If any man's work shall be burned, he shall suffer loss: but he himself shall be saved; yet so as by fire.*

*Rev 22:12 And, behold, I come quickly; and my reward is with me, to give every man according as his work shall be.*

We touched on this earlier. There is an elaborate system of crowns and jewels and cities to reign over and other possibilities. Some will get lots of these things and others few.

*1Th 2:19 For what is our hope, or joy, or crown of rejoicing? Are not even ye in the presence of our Lord Jesus Christ at his coming?*
*20 For ye are our glory and joy.*

On the other hand, some will get nothing. In fact, they will lose everything!

*Rev 16:15 Behold, I come as a thief. Blessed is he that watcheth, and keepeth his garments, lest he walk naked, and they see his shame.*

This passage in Revelation is curiously placed. It is inserted just before the seventh vial of wrath is poured out upon the Earth. This vial ushers in the battle of Armageddon which is the final battle at the end of the tribulation. It is not in chronological order for a very good reason. Here, the Lord is saying in effect, 'If you don't want to be part of all this, you can avoid it by not entering the tribulation to begin with'. Keeping one's garments is a reference to the robe of the righteousness of Christ (Rev. 7:9-14). If we are living righteously and watching carefully for the Lord, we can be raptured out before the tribulation.

But our point to be made for the judgment seat of Christ is that you can end up losing everything and being naked and ashamed before Him. Of course, you can easily avoid that situation by getting any unrighteousness out of your life right now and learning to watch eagerly for His coming.

Then you will never see any of these tribulation judgments from Earth.

*1Jn 2:28 And now, little children, abide in him; that, when he shall appear, we may have confidence, and not be ashamed before him at his coming.*

We now know what the judgment seat of Christ is all about, but when will it occur?

*Rev 11:14 The second woe is past; and, behold, the third woe cometh quickly.*

*15 And the seventh angel sounded; and there were great voices in heaven, saying, The kingdoms of this world are become the kingdoms of our Lord, and of his Christ; and he shall reign for ever and ever.*

*16 And the four and twenty elders, which sat before God on their seats, fell upon their faces, and worshipped God,*

*17 Saying, We give thee thanks, O Lord God Almighty, which art, and wast, and art to come; because thou hast taken to thee thy great power, and hast reigned.*

*18 And the nations were angry, and thy wrath is come, and* **the time of the dead, that they should be judged, and that thou shouldest give reward unto thy servants the prophets, and to the saints, and them that fear thy name, small and great***; and shouldest destroy them which destroy the earth.*

As you can see from verse 1 of this passage, *"**the time of the dead, that they should be judged, and that thou shouldest give reward unto thy servants the prophets, and to the saints, and them that fear thy name, small and great**"* occurs immediately after the 7th angel sounds the seventh and **last** trumpet of the trumpet judgments. It is critically important to get this. This is the judgment seat of Christ when rewards are passed out. It is also the time of the dead. That is a reference to the resurrection of the dead in Christ.

We have already seen that the 7th trumpet sounds right at mid-trib. The two witnesses have just been killed by the Beast before the trumpet and then the Beast continues for 42 months until he is defeated at Armageddon and cast into the Lake of Fire. There is no other logical way to read this. The 7th trumpet sounds at mid-trib, and the resurrection and judgment seat of Christ occur at mid-trib. Now, we are prepared to look at the day of Christ.

**The day of Christ Jesus**

The day of the Lord/LORD is specifically the day of JEHOVAH or the Father. There is another day, however, that is specifically the day of the Son, Jesus, or Messiah the Christ. We have spent some time looking at the following passage and so we do not need to dwell on it at length. However, we can now better understand what it has to say about the day of Christ. Read it again, paying special attention to the bolded words.

*2Th 2:1 Now we beseech you, brethren, by the coming of our Lord Jesus Christ, and by our gathering together unto him,*
*2 That ye be not soon shaken in mind, or be troubled, neither by spirit, nor by word, nor by letter as from us, as that **the day of Christ** is at hand.*
*3 Let no man deceive you by any means: for **that day***

***shall not come, except*** *there come a falling away first, and that man of sin be revealed, the son of perdition;*

*4 Who opposeth and exalteth himself above all that is called God, or that is worshipped; so that he as God sitteth in the temple of God, shewing himself that he is God.*

*5 Remember ye not, that, when I was yet with you, I told you these things?*

*6 And now ye know what withholdeth that he might be revealed in his time.*

*7 For the mystery of iniquity doth already work: only he who now letteth will let, until he be taken out of the way.*

*8 And then shall that Wicked be revealed, whom the Lord shall consume with the spirit of his mouth, and shall destroy with the brightness of his coming:*

*9 Even him, whose coming is after the working of Satan with all power and signs and lying wonders,*

*10 And with all deceivableness of unrighteousness in them that perish; because they received not the love of the truth, that they might be saved.*

*11 And for this cause God shall send them strong delusion, that they should believe a lie:*

*12 That they all might be damned who believed not the truth, but had pleasure in unrighteousness.*

The first thing to watch for here is that this passage provides a strong proof for a pre-trib rapture. We will not use it in our formal proof in chapter 9, but just keep it in mind.

Some of the Thessalonians were concerned that they had missed the pre-trib rapture. Apparently, this was because a letter had come from someone credible making this claim. So, they wrote to the apostle Paul asking for an explanation of what was going on. In their letter to Paul, they asked specifically if the day of Christ was at hand.

Paul's answer fills in a lot of the blanks about this special day.

Paul gave two conditions that had to be met **before** the day of Christ could come. The first was a falling away. Some take this to mean a falling away of Christians from the faith, and that is a very valid and factual meaning. We went over that falling away in the previous chapter and saw that is gets quite ugly. But I believe there is another meaning here. The falling away of the part of the Church that is raptured out by the Thief is also in view here. That can be determined by the wording of the passage. We see that after the falling away, the man of sin, otherwise known as the son of perdition and that Wicked, will be revealed. Verse 4 above clearly identifies this person as the Beast because he is the one who commits the abomination of desolation described in that verse. Remember, we discussed this earlier.

And that is the second condition that must be met before the day of Christ. The man of sin must be revealed before the day of Christ, which leaves mid-trib and the last trumpet as the earliest possibility for the day of Christ. As pointed out before, the Beast appears just prior to the 7th trumpet sounding and kills the two witnesses. That event is broadcast worldwide, so it would be very difficult to miss it (Rev.11:9-10, read it!) That is 3.5 years past the coming of the Thief at the start of the tribulation, and the start of the day of the Lord.

Paul had very carefully and clearly explained the sequence of events to this Church (verse 5 above), but their source was believable enough to confuse them. Many who teach on these scriptures today presume that these people could have expected to live to see the day of Christ. Thus, they think it is a proof for imminence. But that is because they proceed from a false assumption about when that day is. It is true that there are a number of scriptures that speak of the day of Christ in the New Testament that seem somewhat ambiguous as to exactly what day they are speaking of. But, if studied carefully, it is clear they contain the hope of future rewards. And that doesn't happen until the day of the resurrection.

In the following passages, Paul was giving assurance that he and these saints would all find reason to **rejoice in their rewards** on that **far future** day of Christ at the resurrection of the just. Looking at this as a day of rewards at their resurrection in the far future when reading these passages brings the solution to light.

*1Co 1:7 So that ye come behind in no gift; waiting for the coming of our Lord Jesus Christ:*

*8 Who shall also confirm you unto the end, that ye may be blameless in the day of our Lord Jesus Christ.*


*2Co 1:14 As also ye have acknowledged us in part, that we are your rejoicing, even as ye also are ours in the day of the Lord Jesus.*


*Php 1:6 Being confident of this very thing, that he which hath begun a good work in you will perform it until the day of Jesus Christ:*

*7 Even as it is meet for me to think this of you all, because I have you in my heart; inasmuch as both in my bonds, and in the defence and confirmation of the gospel, ye all are partakers of my grace.*

*8 For God is my record, how greatly I long after you all in the bowels of Jesus Christ.*

*9 And this I pray, that your love may abound yet more and more in knowledge and in all judgment;*

*10 That ye may approve things that are excellent; that ye may be sincere and without offence till the day of Christ;*

Rom 2:16 *In the day when God shall judge the secrets of men by Jesus Christ according to my gospel.*

Php 2:14 *Do all things without murmurings and disputings:*
*15 That ye may be blameless and harmless, the sons of God, without rebuke, in the midst of a crooked and perverse nation, among whom ye shine as lights in the world;*
*16 Holding forth the word of life; that I may rejoice in the day of Christ, that I have not run in vain, neither laboured in vain.*

All of these passages speak of hope of rewards at a future day. Paul fully expected to be a part of the day of Christ. That is, he would be resurrected and receive his rewards for service at that time.

So, we see that what these Thessalonians were worried about is that they had missed the pre-trib, Thief rapture and were inside the tribulation. Paul assured them that there were signs and events that they would not be able to miss if that were the case. This verse has consistently been misrepresented by commentators who did not realize that the day of Christ is a single point in time or thought it was at the start of the day of the LORD. It occurs at the middle of the tribulation when He will resurrect all the righteous dead not in heaven already and rapture the living saints and then judge them all based on their works on Earth.

There is one passage that is a notable example. In his first letter to the Corinthians, Paul directed the Church to put out a man that had married his father's wife. He assured them that, even though he was put out of the Church, his spirit would be saved in the day of the Lord Jesus. This is an obvious reference to the resurrection and is actually as strong an indication of when and what this day is all about, as we might find. Remember those who appear before Him naked and ashamed? Here is that passage:

*1Co 5:4 In the name of our Lord Jesus Christ, when ye are gathered together, and my spirit, with the power of our Lord Jesus Christ,*
*5 To deliver such an one unto Satan for the destruction of the flesh, that the spirit may be saved in the day of the Lord Jesus.*


The clear conclusion we are left with then, is that the day of the Lord Jesus aka the day of Christ is the day of the resurrection and the judgment seat of Christ. It was necessary to go through this whole exercise in order to correct the assumption of very many premillennialists that the day of the Lord and the day of Christ are, or occur on, the same day. That creates lots of the confusion in their writings. Many prophecy writers have created far more confusion than they have cleared up. It causes discouragement among those they had hoped to edify.

**The mystery of God**

In order to lock down the timing of the mid-trib rapture, we need to establish what is meant when the Bible talks about the mystery of God. This will provide powerful proof regarding the end of the Church Age in the final reveal. The mystery is also known as the mystery of his will and the mystery of Christ and the mystery of the kingdom of God and sometimes just the mystery. In each case, the context proves them all the same mystery. So, let's take a quick look at a few scriptures. The first one is just to assure you that they all are in the same basket.

*Col 2:2 That their hearts might be comforted, being knit together in love, and unto all riches of the full assurance of understanding, to* **the acknowledgement of the mystery of God, and of the Father, and of Christ;**
*3 In whom are hid all the treasures of wisdom and knowledge.*

Ephesians has some of the most definitive passages in the scriptures for this subject, so let's look there.

*Eph 3:1 For this cause I Paul, the prisoner of Jesus Christ for you Gentiles,*
*2 If ye have heard of the* **dispensation of the grace of God** *which is given me to you-ward:*
*3 How that by revelation he made known unto me the mystery; (as I wrote afore in few words,*
*4 Whereby, when ye read, ye may understand* **my knowledge in the mystery of Christ)**
*5 Which in other ages was not made known unto the sons of men, as it is now revealed unto his holy apostles and prophets by the Spirit;*
*6* **That the Gentiles should be fellowheirs, and of the same body, and partakers of his promise in**

***Christ by the gospel:***

*7 Whereof I was made a minister, according to the gift of the grace of God given unto me by the effectual working of his power.*

*8 Unto me, who am less than the least of all saints, is this grace given, that I should preach among the Gentiles the unsearchable riches of Christ;*

*9 **And to make all men see what is the fellowship of the mystery, which from the beginning of the world hath been hid in God, who created all things by Jesus Christ:***

*10 To the intent that now unto the principalities and powers in heavenly places might be known by the church the manifold wisdom of God,*

*11 According to the eternal purpose which he purposed in Christ Jesus our Lord:*

*12 In whom we have boldness and access with confidence by the faith of him.*

As we showed earlier, Paul was caught up to the third heaven (2 Cor. 12:1-7) where he was carefully and exhaustively instructed by the Lord Jesus Christ Himself in the mystery of God. He was given all the details necessary and then sent back to Earth to usher in the new dispensation of the grace of God which we often call the Age of Grace.

*Col 1:25 Whereof I am made a minister, according to the dispensation of God which is given to me for you, to fulfil the word of God;*

*26 **Even the mystery which hath been hid from ages and from generations, but now is made manifest to his saints:***

*27 To whom God would make known what is the riches of **the glory of this mystery among the Gentiles;***

> ***which is Christ in you, the hope of glory:***
> *28 Whom we preach, warning every man, and teaching every man in all wisdom; that we may present every man perfect in Christ Jesus:*

There are other passages with various aspects of the mystery of God, but from these few we have looked at the mystery is solved. The mystery is the Church Age pure and simple. This had to be kept a mystery until the Jews made their choice whether to accept or decline the kingdom offer that Messiah brought to them. Had it been known before then that there would be a Church Age, then it would have been known in advance what the Jews would do. The whole kingdom offer by Christ would then have been a sham.

Until the crucifixion by the Jews, God's offer to man was always in the physical realm. The promises were long life, good health, wealth accumulation, victory over enemies, and after the resurrection, eternal life on Earth. In the new dispensation the offer is all within the spiritual realm. They include love, joy, peace with God, victory over sin, and eternal life with the Lord Jesus Christ.

But the dispensation of grace is only an interlude in the original plan. There is still ½ week of Daniel's 70 weeks prophecy remaining. The Church Age will pass from the scene and the physical kingdom will return in time for the remaining 3.5 years of the 70 weeks and then the millennium of rest, just after the tribulation.

The term mystery is used rather than secret because, in retrospect, we can see many passages in the Old

Testament that alluded to the Church Age. They may have caused a few raised eyebrows to ancient scholars, but the solution was unguessable to them. In the New Testament we can trace a period in the book of Matthew where the only kingdom being offered was the physical kingdom to Israel.

*Mat 15:24 But he answered and said, I am not sent but unto the lost sheep of the house of Israel.*

But as time went on and rejection began to appear more likely, Jesus resorted to preaching and teaching in parables that could be applied to either the physical kingdom or the spiritual kingdom of the Church Age.

*Mat 13:34 All these things spake Jesus unto the multitude in parables; and without a parable spake he not unto them:*

*35 That it might be fulfilled which was spoken by the prophet, saying, I will open my mouth in parables; I will utter things which have been kept secret from the foundation of the world.*

In this manner, the mystery was still completely safe even though there was a shift in emphasis in the message. The last clause of verse 35 here tells us that the mystery was being proclaimed without people, and more importantly Satan, being any the wiser. If Satan had caught on to what was planned, he would never have permitted the crucifixion of the Lord of Glory (1 Cor. 2:8).

### Summary of chapter 7

There is much more to deal with in the New Testament Epistles, but they are things that work better with the final solution, so we will hold them until that chapter. There are, however, several very important things that we have established here.

- The day of the Lord in the New Testament matches to the day of the LORD in the Old Testament.
- The judgment seat of Christ occurs after the general rapture of the Church and the resurrection of the just immediately following the sounding of the seventh and last trumpet of the trumpet judgments.
- The day of Christ Jesus is the day of the mid-trib rapture of the Church and the resurrection of the just and the judgment seat of Christ immediately following the sounding of the seventh and last trumpet of the trumpet judgments.
- The mystery of God is clearly the Church Age which had to be kept a secret or in mystery form until the Jews rejected their Messiah. Once rejection was complete and the mystery revealed, the Church Age was fully implemented. Even so, the New Testament is full of mentions of the mystery to remind us of how special and unique this age is in the grand plan of God.

## Chapter 8.  The Hockey Sticks of the Revelation

An ornately painted porcelain vase was recently found in an old shoebox in the attic of a house in France. The owners who discovered the vase had enough sense to wonder about its value. So, they asked Sotheby's in Paris to appraise it. To their shock and amazement, the vase turned out to be from the Qing dynasty and dating from the 18th century. It appraised at $590,000 to $825,000 and sold at auction for about $19 million! So, somebody apparently thought the vase was just an ordinary piece and had no problem keeping it in a shoebox.

The scriptures we are about to examine have been kept in a literary shoebox since the 19th century by prophecy writers who have followed John Darby's lead.  It's about time we took them to the Expert and allowed Him to exhibit their true value.  Folks, it's just comparing scripture with scripture, precept upon precept, and line upon line, here a little and there a little.

The Revelation of Jesus Christ is a book packed with information about the end-times.  Its story starts back at the beginning of the Church Age and carries us through history to the New Heaven and the New Earth and the New Jerusalem.  But our primary interest is finding the passages relating to the Church Age and the raptures.  So, we are just scratching the surface in this book.

Chapter one of the Revelation opens with the Apostle John in exile on the Isle of Patmos for his faith. Jesus appears to him in His glorified body in the midst of seven golden candlesticks with seven stars in His right hand. He tells John to write in a book the things He is about to be shown.

Chapters 2 and 3 contain seven messages, one for each of seven Churches in Asia. Several possibilities are raised for the significance of these messages. First, they could simply be messages that John was instructed to deliver when the vision was over. Second, they could be messages for the entire Church describing church types concurrently in existence throughout the Church Age. Third, they could each represent the prevailing strengths and weaknesses of the Church for a series of seven eras in time.

This last idea has been by far the most popular viewpoint for most premillennialists in our time. Many eras have been laid out and explanations given for why each one fits the particular Church described in these two chapters of the Revelation. This viewpoint gives much greater relevance to the study of these chapters and some of the time divisions are quite insightful and very convincing. Personally, I believe all three of these positions are possible at the same time without any contradiction. So, that is the way I lean here.

Interestingly, many pre-trib adherents hold this position while espousing a belief in imminence at the same time. That, of course, is an irreconcilable contradiction. If the Laodicean Age is prophesied, then the Church Age must exist until that age has ended. The rapture could never have occurred in the Age of Sardis or Philadelphia. Otherwise, the scriptures would have been in error.

We have touched on some important parts of two of these messages for our study and will touch on them again. But it is outside the scope of this book to develop these churches more fully. There are many good books out there that have done a better job than this author could do on that subject.

Moving to chapter 4, we run into the second biggest mistake that many pre-trib adherents make. They are very anxious to force the rapture into verse one of this chapter and we will see how it utterly destroys the coherency of the next several chapters. It just isn't there, no matter how exquisite and sophisticated their line of reasoning is. When we finally find the point of the pre-trib rapture, you will see how the entire book of the Revelation flows so much more logically and straightforwardly.

To refresh our memory from chapter 2 of this book, chapter four of the Revelation opens with this statement:

*Rev 4:1 After this I looked, and, behold, a door was opened in heaven: and the first voice which I heard was as it were of a trumpet talking with me; which said, Come up hither, and I will shew thee things which must be hereafter.*

We will again point out the obvious failures of the pre-trib adherents here. If you need a refresher, go back and check out what we studied in chapter 2. Remember, we pointed out that there is no last trump here, there is a voice that is as (like) a trumpet. Also, there are no first-person plural pronouns here. John never writes that 'we' looked, and 'we' heard and talking to 'us'. It was I looked, and I heard, and talking with me.

This pattern continues throughout both chapters 4 and 5. Never does John give any hint that anybody else went up with him. Chapter 4 describes the throne room of God and chapter 5 deals with the opening of the book with seven seals. When John arrives, there is no one there worthy to open the book and it caused him to weep much. But just then he is told:

*Rev 5:5 And one of the elders saith unto me, Weep not: behold, the Lion of the tribe of Juda, the Root of David, hath prevailed to open the book, and to loose the seven seals thereof.*
*6 And I beheld, and, lo, in the midst of the throne and of the four beasts, and in the midst of the elders, stood a Lamb as it had been slain, having seven horns and seven eyes, which are the seven Spirits of God sent forth into all the earth.*

While John was weeping, the Lion of the tribe of Juda, Jesus Christ appeared as a Lamb as it had been slain. While many pre-trib adherents teach that John went ahead in time, we can see that clearly, he went back in time to a point just after the crucifixion. The Lamb had earned the right to open the book through His sacrificial death, burial, and resurrection. In Revelation chapter 1, this Lamb assured us He had the keys of death and hell. He now has all power and in fact has earned the right to be king of creation.

It is a little long to explain, but it comes down to this. When God created Adam, He made him king of the physical creation. Satan had held this position in the past but lost it when he tried to defeat God and become king of the spiritual realm as well as the physical realm. When Satan caused Adam and Eve to fall in the Garden of Eden, he regained his kingdom of the physical realm. So, in defeating death and hell, Jesus won back the physical kingdom.

At this point we must deal with a verse that pre-trib adherents believe gives them the goods on their argument. That is:

*Rev 5:8 And when he had taken the book, the four beasts and four and twenty elders fell down before the Lamb, having every one of them harps, and golden vials full of odours, which are the prayers of saints.*
*9 And they sung a new song, saying, Thou art worthy to take the book, and to open the seals thereof: for thou wast slain, and hast redeemed us to God by thy blood out of every kindred, and tongue, and people, and nation;*

Since we will be using a similar argument later, it would be very wrong not to deal with this passage now. The argument is that there are people here redeemed out of every kindred and tongue and people and nation. That would indicate a rapture of Gentile people has occurred. But there are really only 24 humans saying this. So, there are 24 very special people that are in heaven at this time that have come from various nations and peoples. The explanation is not simple because there is no other indication who they might be other than they were redeemed by the blood of the Lamb. But all people in heaven will have that claim. Old Testament saints were not fully redeemed until Jesus shed His blood on the cross. After that, He descended into Abraham's bosom and led captivity captive when He ascended to heaven (Eph 4:8-10, Luke 16:22-26). So, there are people in heaven 2000 years before the rapture. There is really no good evidence that these are raptured saints. Beyond that we find many accounts of saved people that are Gentiles in the Old Testament. Some examples would be Job and his three friends, Moses' father-in-law, Balaam, Noah and his sons, Lot, and of course the many pre-flood saints. So no, these don't qualify as raptured, Church Age saints.

Many have demonstrated that the book with seven seals is, in essence, the title deed to the physical realm. In chapter 6, Jesus begins opening the seals to the book He has won. For each of the first four seals, a judgment is sent to strike men on Earth. This is reminiscent of the ten plagues of Egypt. God sent the plagues as judgments and to demonstrate His power and authority over the affairs on Earth. Here Satan is allowed by the permissive will of God to bring four sore judgments upon mankind.

Jesus started opening the seals shortly after He rose from the grave and ascended to heaven. John is watching the Church Age begin to unfold as Jesus opens these seals one by one. This is a view across the Church Age that will culminate in the prophesied end-times events later in the Revelation.

## The first four seal judgments – the four horsemen of the Church age.

Moving on to Revelation chapter 6, our Lord begins opening the seals. For each seal He opens in heaven, something very important happens on Earth. The first four seals produce four riders on horses of different colors. In this chapter we will show why these must necessarily happen during the Church Age. By comparing scripture with scripture, we will find who these horsemen are.

Most of the prophecies in the Bible apply either to Israel or the Church and revolve around their relationship with Jesus the Messiah. There is another set of prophecies, however, that apply to all mankind, including the secular world. Notable examples are Daniel, chapters 2 and 7, Zephaniah 2:3, and Revelation chapter 6. Pre-trib adherents insist on trying to place Revelation chapter 6 within the seven-year tribulation. It cannot be done and those who try end up with a nearly incoherent book that leaves you feeling like either you or the author needs psychiatric help. It is always totally confusing.

Understanding who the four horsemen of Revelation chapter 6 are will prove necessary to an understanding of the timeline of eschatological events. There is important evidence in the scriptures on this subject that has been largely overlooked, even by some of the most ardent students of end-times theology.

The key verse that will begin to unlock the solution to their identity is found in:

*Ezek 14:21 For thus saith the Lord GOD; How much more when I send my four sore judgments upon Jerusalem, the sword, and the famine, and the noisome beast, and the pestilence, to cut off from it man and beast?*

Here we find that God has four particular punishments called 'sore judgments'. A quick word study reveals that the sword, famine, and pestilence judgments are found in various combinations frequently enough for us to understand that the ancient Israelites and other ancient people were keenly aware that these were God's specific judgments.

For instance, the words sword and famine are found together in 40 verses. As well, the phrases 'the sword' and 'the famine' are found in the same verse 28 times. Continuing just for emphasis, sword and pestilence are found together 29 times; famine and pestilence 26 times; and sword and famine and pestilence are all found together in the same verse 24 times. You can see from this study that these three are frequently used all together and only occasionally is one left out. Interestingly, all four judgments, the sword, the famine, the pestilence, and the beast are used with that specific terminology in a single verse only twice, both times in Ezekiel. That is because the beast judgment was only used in circumstances of extreme punishment.

These are not the only scriptures where these judgments are mentioned. Sometimes they are spread throughout a passage. In fact, they are mentioned in the book of Job, thought to be the most ancient book in the Bible. In Job 5:20-22 they occur as famine, sword, destruction (for pestilence) and beasts of the Earth. Another instance would be in Solomon's prayer of dedication of the temple. In that prayer, each judgment is at least alluded to over several verses. I should also note here that these judgments are not reserved just to Israel. Other nations are specifically included in Jer. 27:8. In addition, the sword was brought against the Amorites by the hand of Joshua only when their iniquity was full. Scriptures are quite clear that this was a judgment of God upon those peoples.

Another interesting passage using these judgments is found in 2 Sam. 24:13-25. Here David has sinned in numbering the people and is offered his choice of famine for 7 years or the sword for 3 months or pestilence for three days as punishment.

David chose pestilence which consisted of the angel of the Lord smiting the people. This is an important point to note because pestilence takes a variety of forms in the scriptures. In Exodus 9:14 the plague of hail and fire is called pestilence and one could readily infer the meaning that all the following plagues on Egypt were pestilences. Psalm 78:49-51 confirms that the last plague, the plague of death was a pestilence. One thing that seems certain is that pestilence and death are closely connected. It would seem the pestilence could be a sort of catch all for any form of judgment not involving the other three which could explain such a general, non-definitive term as a death judgment. Also of note, when death is used for pestilence, it is death meted out at the hands of angels or the Angel of the Lord.

Armed with that knowledge we should now note the following verse:

*Jer 15:2 And it shall come to pass, if they say unto thee, Whither shall we go forth? then thou shalt tell them, Thus saith the LORD; Such as are for death, to death; and such as are for the sword, to the sword; and such as are for the famine, to the famine; and such as are for the captivity, to the captivity.*

Here we see four judgments again. The sword and the famine are quite self-explanatory and should need no further discussion. It would appear that death is used here for pestilence and captivity is used for the noisome beast judgment. The captivity here is obviously due to military conquest. This verse is very helpful in fully identifying the forms these judgments may take.

The exact nature of the rarely used beast judgment is a little more difficult to pin down at this point but hopefully it will become clearer as we move to the Revelation. Regarding the identification of the beast judgment with captivity, it is very significant that Nebuchadnezzar, who carried Judah into captivity, actually became a literal beast for seven years per Dan 4:24-34. Daniel mentioned many beasts in his prophecies and identified them with kings and kingdoms who would rule over Israel. Also, we should note that sin began when Adam and Eve encountered a beast in the form of a serpent and sin will not end until that same beast is cast into the Lake of Fire where the 666 Beast and the false prophet will be waiting for him. All of these beasts are given power and rule over at least some of the people of God! So, we should begin to realize that the beasts of these judgments are a special class of men.

Prepared with the knowledge of the four sore judgments of God, we may view Revelation 6:1-8 in a new light and finally understand the beast judgment. For convenience, I will copy that passage here:

*Rev 6:1 And I saw when the Lamb opened one of the seals, and I heard, as it were the noise of thunder, one of the four beasts saying, Come and see.*

*2 And I saw, and behold a white horse: and he that sat on him had a bow; and a crown was given unto him: and he went forth conquering, and to conquer.*

*3 And when he had opened the second seal, I heard the second beast say, Come and see.*

*4 And there went out another horse that was red: and power was given to him that sat thereon to take peace from the earth, and that they should kill one another: and there was given unto him a great sword.*

*5 And when he had opened the third seal, I heard the third beast say, Come and see. And I beheld, and lo a black horse; and he that sat on him had a pair of balances in his hand.*

*6 And I heard a voice in the midst of the four beasts say, A measure of wheat for a penny, and three measures of barley for a penny; and see thou hurt not the oil and the wine.*

*7 And when he had opened the fourth seal, I heard the voice of the fourth beast say, Come and see.*

*8 And I looked, and behold a pale horse: and his name that sat on him was Death, and Hell followed with him. And power was given unto them over the fourth part of the earth, to kill with sword, and with hunger, and with death, and with the beasts of the earth.*

The white horse rider has almost universally been identified as either Christ or the Darby version of

Antichrist. However, both of those identities cause problems with correct exegesis of the passage. If the white horse rider is a specific person, then who is the black horse rider? This rider is widely understood to represent famine and what significant person could be, or represent, famine, or for that matter war or death in the case of the red and pale horse riders? The passages don't really lend themselves to identifying a specific person as the rider. If these three are not specific persons, then it would be illogical to designate the white horse rider as a specific person.

Most premillennialists really go off the rails at this point of the Revelation. They reason that this rider must be The Antichrist and thus the tribulation must start right here. However, starting the tribulation here and forcing all the seals into the tribulation wreaks havoc with the rest of the timetable for the whole book of Revelation. They can never decide which of the seal, trumpet and vial judgments belongs where within the tribulation.

But see how simple the chronology is when these judgments are placed in their correct time frame. The first six seals are Church Age judgments. The seventh seal is the seven trumpet judgments. When it is opened, the result is the seven trumpet judgments start. The seven trumpet judgments occur in the first half of the tribulation and end immediately after the Beast rises from the bottomless pit to murder the two witnesses. Finally, the seven vial judgments occur in the second half of the tribulation and culminate in the final battle of Armageddon. It is so simple. Three sets of judgments are meted out, and each with a very specific and exclusive time era.

The whole key to our eight-verse passage is the word 'them' in verse 8. A casual reading would leave the reader with the impression that 'them' refers to death and hell. A more thoughtful reading would lead to an understanding that 'them' cannot refer to both death and hell because one is a rider and the other is a place. A place cannot purposefully kill one fourth of the Earth and hell has never been capable of killing in any other passage of scripture. Hell is there to receive those who die at the hand of the rider.

The problem that has confounded so many teachers and expositors is found in the way the verses are set out in the chapter. Remember, the chapter and verse markings were never used by the Holy Ghost in writing the scriptures. They were a much later addition, designed by men to help other men quickly find any particular part of the scriptures. But we have a tendency to memorize scriptures by verses whether they are a complete sentence or a fragment of a sentence or a sentence and a half and so on. We have come to look at verses as a complete unit which they most often are not. Thus, we miss nuances like this because our brain tells us that everything in that verse refers to other things within that verse. But verse 8 has two sentences which are not dependent on each other in any way. It always should have been two verses. So, let's look at the passage the way it was initially given by the Holy Ghost (but with bolding by me).

*And I saw when the Lamb opened one of the seals, and I*

*heard, as it were the noise of thunder, one of the four beasts saying, Come and see. And I saw, and behold a white horse: and* **he that sat on him had a bow**; *and a crown was given unto him: and he went forth conquering, and to conquer. And when he had opened the second seal, I heard the second beast say, Come and see. And there went out another horse that was red: and* **power was given to him that sat thereon to take peace from the earth**, *and that they should kill one another: and there was given unto him a great sword. And when he had opened the third seal, I heard the third beast say, Come and see. And I beheld, and lo a black horse; and* **he that sat on him had a pair of balances in his hand**. *And I heard a voice in the midst of the four beasts say, A measure of wheat for a penny, and three measures of barley for a penny; and see thou hurt not the oil and the wine. And when he had opened the fourth seal, I heard the voice of the fourth beast say, Come and see. And I looked, and behold a pale horse: and* **his name that sat on him was Death**, *and Hell followed with him.* **And power was given unto them** *over the fourth part of the earth, to kill with sword, and with hunger, and with death, and with the beasts of the earth.*

Here it is much easier to see that there were four horsemen and the power to kill was given unto all of them.

Logically, 'them' must refer to the four riders! The rest of the verse then further identifies the four horsemen by their specific killing methods. Understanding this, we can now see that these riders carry out the four sore judgments of God as noted back in Ezekiel 14:21. Please note how the four sore judgments are listed here in verse 8b from above.

*And power was given unto them over the fourth part of the earth, to kill (1) with sword, and (2) with hunger, and (3) with death, and (4) with the beasts of the earth.*

The red horse rider kills with the sword, and the black horse rider with hunger or famine. The pale horse rider kills with death and here is where it is necessary to realize that death and pestilence can be interchangeable. So, we have the judgments of the sword, the famine, the pestilence and finally the beast. Here the white horse rider is referred to as the beasts (plural) of the Earth. It becomes a problem to assign a single specific rider to be beasts.

The solution is found in one of our pestilence passages:

*Psa 78:49 He cast upon them the fierceness of his anger, wrath, and indignation, and trouble, by sending evil angels among them.*
*50 He made a way to his anger; he spared not their soul from death, but gave their life over to* **the pestilence**;
*51 And smote all the firstborn in Egypt; the chief of their strength in the tabernacles of Ham:*

Here we see pestilence brought by evil angels. If that is the manner in which one judgment is delivered, then logically it could be the manner in which all are delivered. That would seem to solve our problem of keeping all the riders consistent. We could then say that the white horse rider is the angel of beasts or as we noted before he could be called the angel of captivity. Additionally, since angels are also referred to as spirits, it would be correct to call him the spirit of beasts or the spirit of captivity. Likewise, we could say that the red horse rider is the spirit of war, the black horse rider is the spirit of famine and the pale horse rider is the spirit of pestilence.

Returning to the white horse rider, we see that he has a crown and he went forth conquering (as he rode out) and to conquer (in the future). I submit that identifying him as antichrist is almost correct. He is actually the spirit of antichrist. He is the spirit that empowers THE Beast of Revelation 13 as well as the beasts (plural) of the Earth and makes them conquerors

Now it is important to note that there is nothing tribulational about the four sore judgments of God. They are the normal everyday judgments by which He has judged the nations from the very beginning. In fact, the scriptures tell us the spirit of antichrist had already ridden out by the time the apostle John wrote his first epistle. He wrote:

*1 John 2:18 Little children, it is the last time: and as ye have heard that antichrist shall come, even now are there many antichrists; whereby we know that it is the last time.*

*1 John 4:3 And every spirit that confesseth not that Jesus Christ is come in the flesh is not of God: and* **this is that spirit of antichrist, whereof ye have heard that it should come; and even now already is it in the world.**

Remember he rode forth conquering and TO CONQUER. He kills with beasts in the present and he will kill with THE Beast in the future. He kills with antichrists right now because his job or ministry is to influence men to conquer, slaughter, and sometimes take captive other men, specifically the people of God. Many Caesars and popes were influenced by this spirit. No doubt Hitler and Stalin were under his influence, and we can be sure he is influencing men right now to carry on the work. All of these men may then be referred to as beasts of the Earth.

I should add here that many well-meaning but duped modern-day pastors take the souls of men captive with 'another' Jesus and another gospel other than what Paul preached. They often do this unwittingly by preaching from flawed bibles filled with false doctrine. The two heretics Westcott and Hort served their master well in influencing most modern translations of the Bible.

Understanding that these four spirits started riding out over 1900 years ago and they are not tribulational, we must conclude that, if the book of Revelation is chronological, then the tribulation starts sometime after Rev. 6:8. We will show that it starts at Rev. 6:12 when the sixth seal is opened.

**The Beginning of Sorrows**

We studied the Beginning of Sorrows events in Matthew 24 and now we need to review them again with our new knowledge regarding the four sore judgments of God and the four horsemen of Revelation 6. This time we will look at Luke's account.

*Luk 21:8 And he said, Take heed that ye be not deceived: for many shall come in my name, saying, I am Christ; and the time draweth near: go ye not therefore after them.*
*9 But when ye shall hear of wars and commotions, be not terrified: for these things must first come to pass; but the end is not by and by.*

*10 Then said he unto them, Nation shall rise against nation, and kingdom against kingdom:*

*11 And great earthquakes shall be in divers places, and famines, and pestilences; and fearful sights and great signs shall there be from heaven.*

*12 But before all these, they shall lay their hands on you, and persecute you, delivering you up to the synagogues, and into prisons, being brought before kings and rulers for my name's sake.*

With our new understanding of the four sore judgments and the four horsemen, we can now see what Christ is warning us about. First, He warns us of the false christs. These are the antichrists that we discussed in assessing Matthew 24. This is a reference to the white horse rider who, as the spirit of antichrist, has been tasked by Satan with creating many false christs in the Earth.

We will interrupt the narrative on these events for a moment to make a very important point here. After all these Beginning of Sorrows events Jesus says something very interesting in Luke's account. In verse 12, He says:

*12 But before all these, they shall lay their hands on you, and persecute you, delivering you up to the synagogues, and into prisons, being brought before kings and rulers for my name's sake.*

He goes on from here to describe events leading up to the destruction of Jerusalem by Titus the prince of Rome in 70 AD. So, we see that before the white horse rider rode out, Jerusalem was sacked and destroyed by Rome. Now, John wrote his three epistles about 20 years later, somewhere around 90 AD or later. John wrote:

*1Jn 2:18 Little children, it is the last time: and as ye have heard that antichrist shall come, even now are there many antichrists; whereby we know that it is the last time.*

Do you see that? Jesus said that Jerusalem would be destroyed before any of the four horsemen rode out. By around 90 AD, John said that the spirit of antichrist had already recruited many antichrists. So, the white horse rider rode out somewhere between 70 AD and 90 AD!

**The hockey sticks of the Revelation**

Could it be possible to determine when the other three riders rode out? I can't say for sure, but I can show you some interesting possibilities. I will be attempting to represent this in some graphs. However, for the record I must tell you that many of the early century plot points are just educated guesses by historians and others of that ilk. Records are very poor up until about 1500 AD or so. But let's take a look. We will start with a graph of overall population growth on the entire planet by century. This is just for reference, but we can note several important facts.

I have called these hockey stick graphs after the famous global warming graphs intended to reduce the world to a mass of sobered and repentant humanity, terrified at the prospect of global warming killing all of us by 2030. Although it might be very real at this moment, it could not be less important whether man-made global warming is real or contrived. We are seeing what the world really needs to be concerned about and furthermore we are seeing that the coming of the Lord will alter any global warming scenario. The world will survive and thrive all through the 1000-year reign of Christ on Earth.

The significance of the hockey stick shape of the plotted line is this. When a graph ceases to keep the ratio between the x and y axis consistent, then the situation being graphed is no longer in stasis. Something has changed dramatically. This is a warning to find out if the change has a negative or positive effect for you or the world.

There is a law of the universe that is known to physicists as 'the Second Law of Thermodynamics'. It is also known to others as the Law of Entropy. Entropy simply means randomness and we understand that randomness is the opposite of order. Randomness brings chaos. While I am not a physicist, I can briefly state this law of the universe like this. All systems run down and collapse without additional outside input. This law is the reason we say things like, "in this world, nothing lasts forever". So, when we see a graph like this, we are often looking at the end result of entropy working on a system. The end result is that entropy moves from increasing geometrically to increasing exponentially. Shortly after that, the system collapses. It should be noted that this law applies to all systems whether physical or social or whatever you may imagine. I leave it to the reader to decide if that is what's going on here.

So, if God, being outside our system, puts input into our system, He can fix the cause of, or change the rate of, increasing randomness. If He does not, the system will run down. The Bible term for this law of entropy is **The Curse**. So, let's look at a few results of the curse here.

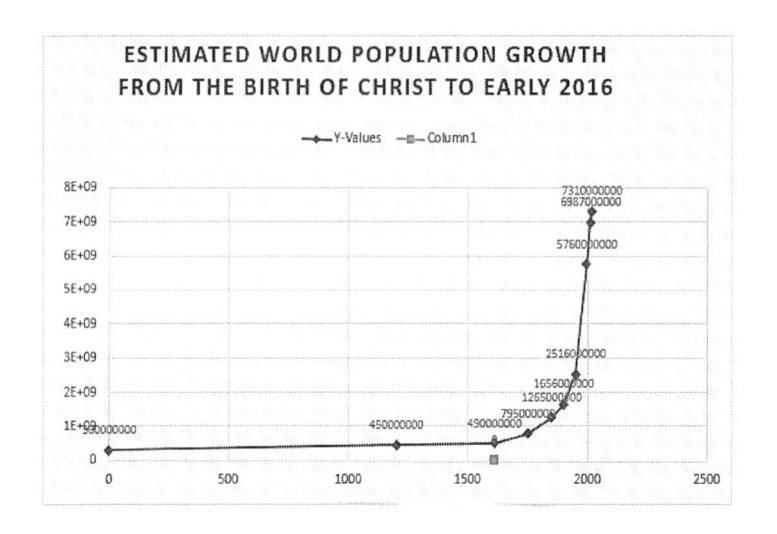

**ESTIMATED WORLD POPULATION GROWTH FROM THE BIRTH OF CHRIST TO EARLY 2016**

| Year | Population |
|---|---|
| 0 | 990000000 |
| 1000 | 450000000 |
| 1500 | 490000000 |
| ~1600 | 795000000 |
| ~1700 | 1265000000 |
| ~1800 | 1656000000 |
| ~1900 | 2516000000 |
| ~1950 | 5760000000 |
| ~2000 | 6987000000 |
| 2016 | 7310000000 |

The change in world population growth really started to become significant around 1600 AD. That is right about the same time that the King James Bible translation was completed in 1611. It is very significant for these reasons.

As the King James Bible was being completed in 1611, the British Empire was beginning to grow. Eventually, it came to be known as the empire on which the sun never set. The King's new Bible was chained to a platform on the bridge of every British ship. It was soon made available around the world.

At the same time, English became the most important and dominant language in the world. In time, the British

Empire was supplanted in importance by the United States, another English-speaking country. From the 17th century until the present, English has become the language of the world. It is the official language of some 60 nations. English is the most widely learned second language worldwide. It is an official language of the United Nations and the European Union. English is the leading language of international discourse, especially in professional contexts such as navigation, as well as the sciences and international legal matters.

In her excellent work *"In Awe of Thy Word"*, Gail Riplinger has traced the King James Bible of 1611 back through history. She has compared the following iterations of the Bible, verse by verse and word by word, to demonstrate a clear, unbroken line from the early Church to our KJV: From the initial works to the Gothic Bible, then to the Anglo-Saxon Bible, the Wycliffe Bible, the Tyndale Bible, the Geneva Bible, the Bishop's Bible, and finally the King James Bible. Thus, if Gail Riplinger is correct, we see a most important prophecy of scriptures fulfilled in our KJV:

*Psa 12:6 The words of the LORD are pure words: as silver tried in a furnace of earth,* **purified seven times.** *7 Thou shalt keep them, O LORD, thou shalt* **preserve** *them from this generation for ever.*

You should note from these verses, that God promised His very precise, exact, perfect, unalterable, unchanging words would be **preserved,** generation by generation, at every point in time. This does not mean it was to be made available to every individual. But for those who care to look for it, it can be found. In fact, the time will come (and is here already) when many people won't even be able to figure out where to look. That is because our present-day Church leaders have unintentionally duped their congregations about the translations issue. Consider this prophecy:

*Amo 8:11 Behold, the days come, saith the Lord GOD, that I will send a famine in the land, not a famine of bread, nor a thirst for water, but of hearing the* **words** *of the LORD: 12 And they shall wander from sea to sea, and from the north even to the east, they shall run to and fro to seek the word of the LORD, and shall not find it.*

As we can see, it behooved our God to perfect His Word in the English language. Or viewed another way, God saw to it that the English language would become the most important language to know in the entire world so that His final iteration would be available to the greatest number of people.

In that vein, there has been another fascinating phenomenon of world history within the same timeframe. By the early 1600's, the entire world population has been estimated at still under ½ billion people. From that point in time, the world population has exploded. It has been estimated that about 22 billion people have been born since then to arrive at an early 2020 world population of about 7.62 billion people. This means that over one third of the people born since 1611 are alive today!

Now, some evolutionists teach that from their first man in about 50,000 BC, it took almost 42,000 years for the first 1 billion births. As Bible believers though, we have only about 6000 years since Adam and only about 4360 years since the population was reduced to 8 by the flood in

Noah's day. The point here is that populations grew slowly at first and only later began expanding rapidly. For instance, from 1200 AD to 1600 AD, only about 12 billion were born over the entire 400-year period. Today, over half that many have been born in less than 100 years.

The preceding graph, including mostly Population Reference Bureau estimates, illustrates this fact clearly. Look at what happened immediately after 1611 when the King James Bible was completed! Now ask yourself: "Was this mere coincidence or proof of the mighty hand of God in choosing the precise, perfect moment in history to give us His seventh purification and thus final translation of His Word?"

All of this means that the Word of God has been available to a huge percentage of all the people that have ever been born since it was completed in about 100 AD. The greatest percentage of those people have been born since 1611 when the KJV was completed. The KJV itself has been available to the greatest percentage of those people because of the importance of the English language worldwide. English translations that were done since 1881 have reached significantly less than that partly because they were met with rejection from portions of the Church for many years. It took many years for Satan to train his grievous wolves in the art of intimidating and ridiculing the rank and file of the Church into submission. It had to be done while still maintaining their aura of godliness and humility. Remember how Paul warned us:

*Act 20:29 For I know this, that after my departing shall grievous wolves enter in among you, not sparing the flock.
30 Also of your own selves shall men arise, speaking perverse things, to draw away disciples after them.
31 Therefore watch, and remember, that by the space of three years I ceased not to warn every one night and day* **with tears.**

After the white horse rider rode out between 70-90 AD, we see the red horse rider riding out to take peace from the Earth. He brings the sword of Ezekiel 14:21 and causes wars and commotions. He is especially adept at causing nation to rise against nation. Again, after pointing to this spirit of war, Jesus points out that the end is not yet. He is very careful to tell us we are still within the Church Age. Can you see a point at which he might have ridden out? Remember, we are primarily interested in the death toll from these riders.

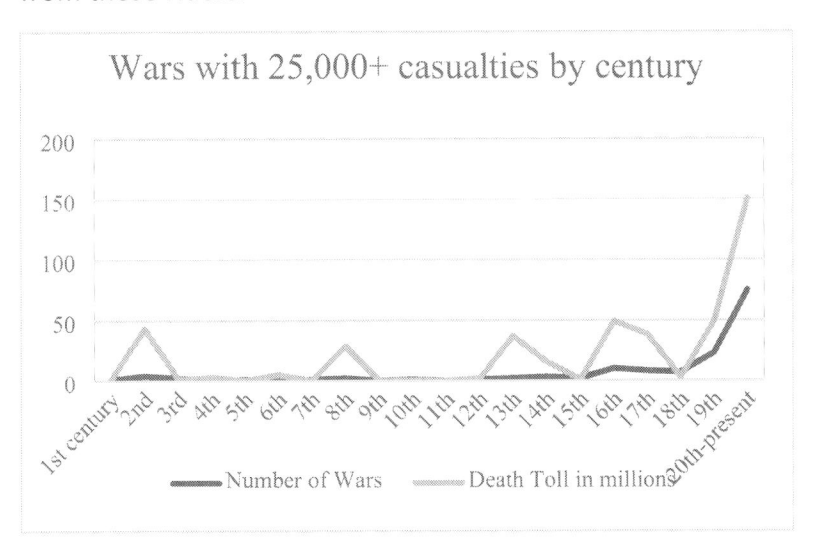

*Wars with 25,000+ casualties by century — Number of Wars, Death Toll in millions (1st century through 20th-present)*

Following this, Jesus mentions earthquakes. There is not a horseman associated with earthquakes, but on the other hand, we have seen a dramatic rise in both the number and power of earthquakes since early in the twentieth century. And they are continuing to increase decade over decade. It is truly an amazing phenomenon. We have seen that it will culminate in a worldwide earthquake event when the day of the LORD starts. Earthquakes may not get their own horseman, but they are a clear sign of the end-times.

Famines are next in the list that Jesus gives us here and we see that the order has remained true to the one in Revelation 6. Famines are definitely a function of population density. Before the population explosion, there was plenty of tillable acreage per person. But with more and more people and a finite amount of tillable land, the problem of producing adequate food supplies grows more intense. Again, we see a sharp uptick in famines at a certain point here.

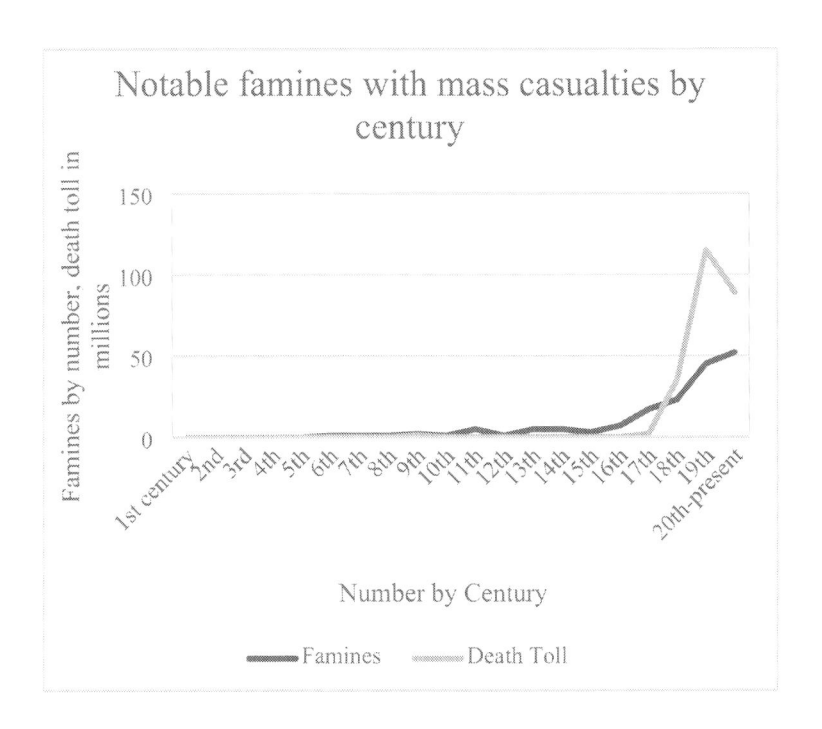

*Notable famines with mass casualties by century*

The pale horse rider can be called the spirit of pestilence or alternately the spirit of death. This horseman has the power to kill by fatal epidemic diseases, or by any manner of mass deaths, or by simply outright killing masses of people without a known cause. He is a particularly nasty horseman. He may be responsible for all those deaths caused by the upheaval of the Earth at the start of the day of the Lord. The only one of these possibilities we can quantify is that of epidemics. So, this is how they graph out.

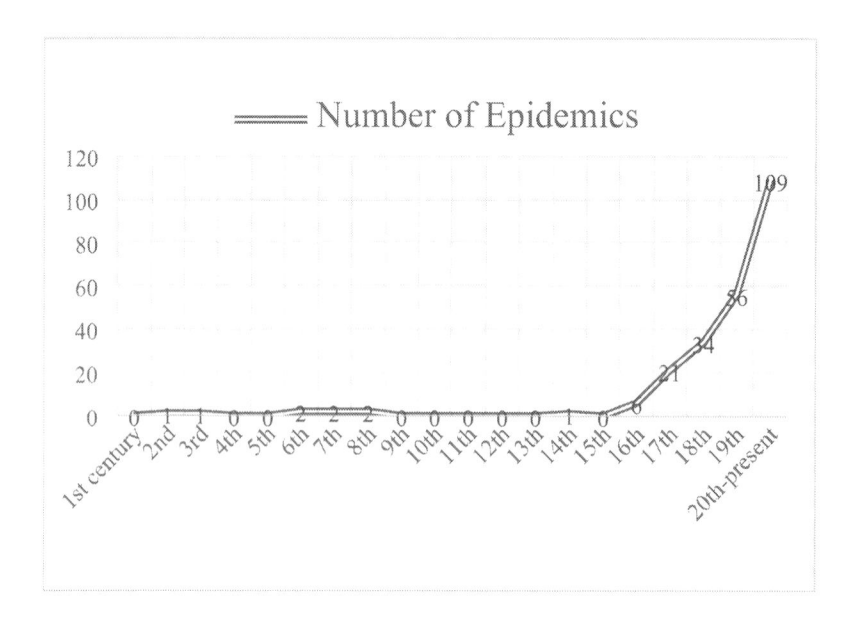

**Number of Epidemics**

| Century | Number |
|---|---|
| 1st century | 0 |
| 2nd | 1 |
| 3rd | 1 |
| 4th | 0 |
| 5th | 0 |
| 6th | 2 |
| 7th | 2 |
| 8th | 2 |
| 9th | 2 |
| 10th | 0 |
| 11th | 0 |
| 12th | 0 |
| 13th | 0 |
| 14th | 0 |
| 15th | 1 |
| 16th | 0 |
| 17th | 8 |
| 18th | 21 |
| 19th | 34 |
| 20th-present | 86 → 109 |

Update: These numbers do not include the Covid-19 Coronavirus of 2020 and beyond.

None of these riders are by any means finished with their work. In fact, by examining the recent rate of increase, we can determine that **the worst is probably yet to come**. Buckle up! Because the ride only gets rougher over the coming months or years! Look around and understand what (or who) the real source of all the mayhem is.

**The dawn of Modern Civilization**

As you can see by examining all these graphs, everything changed dramatically in about the 16th century. That would be the century of the 1500's. The 16th century was known as the starting point of the rise of Western Civilization. At the same time, it saw the rise of the Islamic Gunpowder Empires. Gunpowder was invented at the very beginning of the century and that led to the development of weapons from small firearms to cannons. These weapons were used to rapidly expand Islam throughout the middle east from Eastern Europe to current Bangladesh.

In the spiritual realm, the Shi'ite branch of Islam began to take hold and spread, especially in Persia, while Sunni Islam ruled in the more southern nations. This created a new 'king of the north/king of the south' division which I believe will ultimately produce the last-days kings of the north and south that we saw in chapter 3 of this book. These factions began warring with each other, with each side anxious to promote their preferred theology. That war continues to this day but in a less outright confrontational manner. From scriptures we can determine that the king of the north will finally defeat the king of the south militarily just after the day of the LORD begins.

In the western world, this period saw the rise of what is today known as Western Civilization. The 16th century was a time of great men who did great things. Many of the greatest artists and explorers and writers and inventors in history lived in this century. Consider just a few of the many great men from this century: da Vinci, Michelangelo, Balboa, Cartier, Coronado, Drake, da Gama, Ponce de Leon, de Soto, Magellan, Shakespeare, Erasmus, Machiavelli, Galileo Galilei, and Copernicus.

In the spiritual realm, in 1517 Martin Luther posted his 95 Theses on the door of a Church in Saxony that started the Protestant Reformation. This caused political uproar in the western nations that led to the nearly constant series of assassinations and deposing of many kings and queens, especially in England which was wrenched back and forth between Protestantism and Catholicism for over a century.

As Protestantism became more established, it produced religious thinkers like John Calvin (1509-1564) whose theology to this day holds sway over a large faction of protestant Christianity. Jacobus Arminius (1560-1609), a Dutch Protestant rejected the Calvinistic doctrine of predestination and had a great influence on Methodism.

A great, empire-wide study was done on the scriptures by Erasmus of Rotterdam who ultimately produced the Textus Receptus, much to the chagrin of the Roman Catholic Church which had funded his research hoping for a different result. Textus Receptus is a compilation of many full and partial manuscripts from all over Europe into a complete Greek New Testament. It was meant to produce the purest scriptures possible. The English translation of this text is an almost perfect match for the protestant King James Bible of 1611.

Seemingly everything changed in the 1500's. The world had remained essentially the same for almost 4000 years. But, combined with the recent development of the printing press, and with the discovery of new worlds and the ability to sail around the world, established trade routes brought new knowledge and methods to the whole world. No longer would the world be an agrarian-only society. The world was coming of age and men began to realize that they were capable of more than they had thought. This was the beginning of the end-times in many ways.

The explosion of knowledge since the 16th century has brought us to the point where we are capable of destroying all life on our planet through nuclear annihilation. There are many other ways we could destroy our civilization through germ or chemical warfare or even through such seemingly innocuous realms as scientific research. We could now think up many doomsday scenarios that would not have been possible before. If ever there was a time when intervention by an almighty God might be necessary, we are in that time now. In fact, the Bible indicates that we will come to that point just before the end of the tribulation. Consider this scripture again:

*Mark 13:19 For in those days shall be affliction, such as was not from the beginning of the creation which God created unto this time, neither shall be.*
*20 And except that the Lord had shortened those days, no flesh should be saved: but for the elect's sake, whom he*

*hath chosen, he hath shortened the days.*

If ever there was a time to start sending out the last three horsemen, it would have been around 1500 AD and following. You can interpret our hockey stick graphs however you like, but the evidence that the seals on Christ's book are opened during the Church Age is strong. The scriptures prove that the seals are opened during the Church Age and from my viewpoint secular history supports that view very strongly.

**The fifth seal**

Following the opening of the four horsemen seals, another and very different seal was opened. Much mayhem followed the opening of the first four seals, and we will see even greater mayhem when the sixth seal is opened. But seal number five is utterly benign. There is almost no action at all here. So, what is its purpose? Let's take a look at the scriptures:

*Rev 6:9 And when he had opened the fifth seal, I saw under the altar the souls of them that were slain for the word of God, and for the testimony which they held:*

*10 And they cried with a loud voice, saying, How long, O Lord, holy and true, dost thou not judge and avenge our blood on them that dwell on the earth?*

*11 And white robes were given unto every one of them; and it was said unto them, that they should rest yet for a little season, until their fellowservants also and their brethren, that should be killed as they were, should be fulfilled.*

Because many martyrs are created in the tribulation when the Beast appears on the scene, it is easy for rapturists to leap to the conclusion that these souls are tribulation martyrs. But there have been millions of martyrs within the Church Age already. Glance through *Foxe's Book of Martyrs* and you will see the grisly story in detail. Sadly, Christians in this late age know almost nothing of the history of Christianity. It is a history with a long trail of blood behind it.

If these souls are within the tribulation, then their lament in verse 10 is petty and self-centered. There are terrible judgments reigning down on mankind in rapid succession. In only seven years, 14 horrific judgments between the trumpets and the vials of Revelation 16, are meted out. Additionally, four horrific judgements have already been completed just among the seals.

However, if this occurs within the Church Age, then four judgments are spread out over as many as 2000 years. It is more understandable that they grow weary of waiting. **It should be abundantly clear that this seal is opened within the Church Age and before the tribulation!** That is probably the primary purpose for placing this passage right where it is. Yet, as we have seen time and again, it is overlooked by premillennialists because it doesn't fit with their revered doctrine of Antichrist

### The sixth seal

This is a major turning point in history. The tribulation will begin here, and life will be forever changed for every person who survives on Earth. It may never seem pleasant again until the millennium. We have been all through this in chapter 5, but we will take a fresh look before we move quickly along. If you recall, this describes the start of the day of the LORD. Unimaginable disasters will affect most of the planet. Also, remember that it occurs just about when the armies of Gog enter Jerusalem and begin to rape and plunder and murder God's chosen people. JEHOVAH God says of this time:

*Eze 38:18 And it shall come to pass at the same time when Gog shall come against the land of Israel, saith the Lord GOD, that **my fury shall come up in my face.***

*19 For in my jealousy and in the fire of my wrath have I spoken, Surely in that day there shall be a great shaking in the land of Israel;*

*20 So that the fishes of the sea, and the fowls of the heaven, and the beasts of the field, and all creeping things that creep upon the earth, and **all the men that are upon the face of the earth, shall shake at my presence, and the mountains shall be thrown down**, and the steep places shall fall, and every wall shall fall to the ground.*

*21 And I will call for a sword against him throughout all my mountains, saith the Lord GOD: every man's sword shall be against his brother.*

*22 And I will plead against him with pestilence and with blood; and I will rain upon him, and upon his bands, and upon the many people that are with him, an overflowing rain, and great hailstones, fire, and brimstone.*

*23 Thus will I magnify myself, and sanctify myself; and I will be known in the eyes of many nations, and they shall know that I am the LORD.*

There are several companion passages that we looked at when the day of the LORD is at hand. One more important one is:

*Isa 2:19 And they shall go into the holes of the rocks, and into the caves of the earth, for fear of the LORD, and for the glory of his majesty,* **when he ariseth to shake terribly the earth.**

So, now we come to that terrible time. Here is that passage:

*Rev 6:12 And I beheld when he had opened the sixth seal, and, lo, there was a great earthquake; and the sun became black as sackcloth of hair, and the moon became as blood;*

What we are seeing here is a worldwide earthquake event. All around the world, stresses built up in the tectonic plates in the Earth's crust will be released simultaneously. This will include the release of volcanic pressures as well. The result will be an atmosphere filled with volcanic ash in volume so great that the sun and moon will be barely visible for a time.

This will be the fulfillment of the prophecy in Isaiah 40:3-5 where we see every mountain and hill knocked down, filling in all the valleys. It will be much like a baker sifting flour and then shaking it level for measurement. We see in Isaiah 2:2 that the Temple Mount will rise to be the highest point on the Earth after this time. The Earth's orbit will be slightly altered at the same time.

All of this will be prophesied by the last days Elijah when he appears shortly before the opening of the sixth seal per

Malachi 4:5-6. He will be here in time to make one last, mostly futile, effort to exhort the people of God to ready themselves for the pre-tribulation rapture we will present in the next chapter. Naturally, this will leave the Earth a startlingly different planet and will be followed by a cascade of terrible events including meteor or comet strikes chronicled in the first four trumpet judgments.

All of this will be accompanied by the massive tsunamis that Luke spoke of in chapter 21 of his gospel. They will kill coastal dwellers for hundreds of miles inland in some places.

*Rev 6:13 And the stars of heaven fell unto the earth, even as a fig tree casteth her untimely figs, when she is shaken of a mighty wind.*

Rev. 6:13, on its face, is a curious verse. Stars falling from heaven are likened to a fig tree shaken by a mighty wind. It is patently obvious that even one physical star would obliterate the planet. So, something else must be in play here. In Rev. 1:20 we see seven stars which the Lord says specifically are the angels of the seven churches. In many other passages, angels are likened to stars or the host of heaven as in Isaiah 34:4 above. This is, no doubt, what is in play here. There is, and has been, constant war in heaven (see Rev. 12:7 and Daniel 10) between the angels of God and the angels of Satan and this war moves down to Earth. (Refer back to the fallen angels and fake aliens we discussed in chapter 6 of this book.)

The likening of this event to a fig tree also has an easy solution. We saw in chapter 5, that the vine and the fig tree are representations of Israel's governance. The vine represents religious Israel following the law with regard to temple worship. This side of Israel is currently laid waste and dried up according to Joel 1:7,12. The fig tree represents civil Israel under the king or secular government. So, when this verse tells us that the fig tree is shaken of a mighty wind, it indicates an event of tremendous importance is occurring in the secular State of Israel at this time. Indeed, we have seen that a brutal invasion chronicled in Ezekiel chapters 38-39 is occurring. For every event with spiritual implications that happens on Earth, a corresponding battle occurs in the spiritual kingdom of God. Daniel chapter 10 provides some insight into this principle. So, by comparing scripture with scripture we see that this verse cryptically speaks of the situation in Israel at that moment in time.

*Rev 6:14 And the heaven departed as a scroll when it is rolled together; and every mountain and island were moved out of their places.*

Rev. 6:14 essentially repeats what the previous 2 verses have stated but in reference to the mountains and islands. The picture of the scroll rolling together depicts a rapid event. If you ever unrolled a map or piece of stiff paper out of a tube container, you will remember you had to hold it to the table with both hands. When you raise your hands the map quickly rolls back up to its original shape. God's restraining hand is similarly lifted, and these events are the immediate result.

There are a number of curious mentions of islands in prophecy that seem to elevate them to a surprisingly prominent position.  The islands here are any land that is not part of the continental mainland on which Israel is found.  The Western Hemisphere drifted away from the mainland when, as implied in Genesis 7:11, the Earth cracked all the way around creating the great trenches in the oceans between continents.  There had initially been a thin layer of water under the crust that was released under great pressure due to the flood and thereby increasing the flood.  This is exhaustively explained in a fascinating book by Walt Brown, Ph.D. titled *"In the Beginning, Compelling Evidence for Creation and the Flood"* and published by Center for Scientific Creation.

The western hemisphere then became islands of the sea from the perspective of Israel.  Thus, as part of the islands, the United States is cryptically referenced in prophecy.  Even so, it plays no major role in end-times events.  It will be utterly destroyed by these events.

*Rev 6:15  And the kings of the earth, and the great men, and the rich men, and the chief captains, and the mighty men, and every bondman, and every free man, hid themselves in the dens and in the rocks of the mountains;*

*16  And said to the mountains and rocks, Fall on us, and hide us from the face of him that sitteth on the throne, and from the wrath of the Lamb:*

Rev. 6:15-16 assures us that even the greatest men on Earth, those that we all look to for strength and leadership, will run like cockroaches exposed to the light when they see the glory of God.  At this time everything around them is crumbling and their best hope is that something will land on them and kill them so that they won't be exposed to the terror of the wrath of the Lamb. Their understanding of the situation and their thoughts regarding it are eloquently expressed in verse 17 below. The passages we looked at in chapter 5 describing the day of the LORD greatly enhance our understanding of what is happening here. It seems this description is very matter-of-fact when describing the physical catastrophes that are occurring. Except for one issue.

**The Thief on the throne**
Verse 16 gives us a very important enhancement on this whole day. The wrath of JEHOVAH is clearly shared by the Lamb. Here we see the Lamb of God coming down to the Earth, sitting on His mobile (see Ezek. Chapter 1) throne of glory. Although the Lamb is terrifyingly visible to the whole world, He is at the same time coming as a Thief to His Church. So, how can we reconcile these seemingly contradictory descriptions?
Jesus has ordered His bride, the Church, to watch for His coming in many scriptures. And many evangelicals and fundamentalists did just that in the middle years of the 20$^{th}$ century. There was a rapture fever sweeping through those Churches that may well have gotten its legs from Hal Lindsey's popular book titled *"The Late, Great Planet Earth"*. Many more prophecy writers produced a plethora of books right through the 1980's. They were mostly predicting a pre-trib rapture before the end of the century. Sermons on the soon return of the Lord abounded. But the Lord did not come in that century and the fervor died down. Sadly, this included mostly the premillennialist part

of the Church, and these soon merged back into the smug and rebellious majority Church.

Since then, much of the Church that was watching in the last century has concluded that not only were they wrong, but His return could be far in the future. So here we are, so close that His return should be counted down in months rather than years, and the Church as a whole is totally unaware and refuses to be roused from her lethargy. How can this be in the face of what our Lord has commanded us? How can we afford to be found unworthy at this time?

*Luk 21:34 And take heed to yourselves, lest at any time your hearts be overcharged with surfeiting, and drunkenness, and cares of this life, and so that day come upon you unawares.*

*35 For as a snare shall it come on all them that dwell on the face of the whole earth.*

*36 Watch ye therefore, and pray always,* **that ye may be accounted worthy to escape all these things that shall come to pass, and to stand before the Son of man.**

What we find then is the Lamb is coming back for His Church and they have ignored and disobeyed Him. They will have no idea what is going on. When it is all quickly over, those few that survive the earthquakes and tsunamis will say, "how was I supposed to know that was the rapture"? Because of the chaos and confusion all over the world, many Christian survivors may not figure out what really happened for weeks or months. There is no space for repentance here. What will the Lamb do about the careless and disobedient portion of the Church? Take a look.

*Rev 3:14 And unto the angel of the church of the Laodiceans write; These things saith the Amen, the faithful and true witness, the beginning of the creation of God;*

*15 I know thy works, that thou art neither cold nor hot: I would thou wert cold or hot.*

*16 So then because thou art lukewarm, and neither cold nor hot,* **I will spue thee out of my mouth.**

Folks, this is the power of the word of God. A typical Independent Baptist preacher would take fifty minutes and thousands of words to tell the story that God tells in these three short verses. Don't mistake brevity for low importance. These people are Christians who the Lord finds so distasteful he spits them out. Many have been in this state throughout the age of this Laodicean Church. But something has abruptly changed here. What is that something? Well, consider that this is the final Church before the tribulation and that the tribulation starts with a partial rapture of the Church.

This is that breakup of the Church that we saw repeatedly in our study of Matthew 24 and 25. Is it any wonder that the Lamb is filled with wrath when He comes with such glory to a Church that doesn't recognize Him or realize He is even coming at that time? However, those of us who care will return with Him to glory.

When He opens that seventh seal and takes title to the physical universe, He will become King of the physical domain. He was rejected the first time He offered the kingdom, but He won't be denied this time. As King, Jesus plans to rule over a clean and sinless world. Over the next seven years He will be purging sin and sinners out of the world. Before He finally begins His physical reign on Earth, He will throw the Beast and the false prophet into the Lake of Fire and then bind Satan and throw him into the bottomless pit. He will also kill, in an instant, all the armies that come against Him at Armageddon. Then His reign can start in a cleaned up and terraformed planet capable of sustaining the large population that will exist by the end of His 1000-year reign on Earth.

*Rev 6:17 For the great day of his wrath is come; and who shall be able to stand?*

The pre-tribulation rapture and the start of the Day of the Lord are tied together in this sixth seal passage. We have seen what happens in the physical world at this time, but there is also an important occurrence in the spiritual realm. What has happened here is that the Lord has called for His watching Church. They are immediately caught up into the air. As they rise, their bodies are changed or glorified. Their blood is shed and replaced with the power of the Holy Ghost infused in each cell of their bodies. Heaven opens to receive them and the sin stained universe shudders violently at the exposure to the full holiness of JEHOVAH. JEHOVAH has arisen to shake terribly the Earth at this time and is pouring out his wrath when heaven opens to receive the Lamb and His raptured saints. This violent reaction of the universe always occurs when it is exposed to the holiness of God. At the end of the millennium, the exposure will be long enough to vaporize the entire universe. Prior to that, short exposures cause lesser damage. Some passages to bear this point out are: Nahum 1:5, 2 Peter 3:10-12, Ezekiel

38:20, Psalm 144:5, Isaiah 64:1-3, Micah 1:3-4 and Revelation 20:11.

So here we see that simply by taking the scriptures "here a little and there a little", the entire doctrine of the start of the day of the Lord falls right into our lap. It is only due to the fact that the pre-trib believers forced the rapture to occur at Rev. 4:1 so that Antichrist could appear in Rev. 6:1 that they never looked at the sixth seal as a possibility. Really, really dumb mistake there. Thus, they are lost regarding where many other events should be placed in time.

**The seventh seal**

Just to close out this section and this chapter in the book, we will look briefly at the seventh and final seal. It is important to understand what this seal is all about, because it is book-ended by raptures. The pre-trib rapture has just occurred and there are a couple scenes in chapter 7, one of which we will look at in the next chapter. For now, let's look at the opening passage in Revelation 8 which describes the seventh seal.

*Rev 8:1 And when he had opened the seventh seal, there was silence in heaven about the space of half an hour.*

*2 And I saw the seven angels which stood before God; and to them were given seven trumpets.*

*3 And another angel came and stood at the altar, having a golden censer; and there was given unto him much incense, that he should offer it with the prayers of all saints upon the golden altar which was before the throne.*

*4 And the smoke of the incense, which came with the prayers of the saints, ascended up before God out of the angel's hand.*

*5 And the angel took the censer, and filled it with fire of the altar, and cast it into the earth: and there were voices, and thunderings, and lightnings, and an earthquake.*

*6 And the seven angels which had the seven trumpets prepared themselves to sound.*

This is an extremely momentous occasion in heaven. Heaven is a place of constant verbal praises. Here is one place where this is mentioned:

*Rev 4:8 And the four beasts had each of them six wings about him; and they were full of eyes within: and they rest not day and night, saying, Holy, holy, holy, Lord God Almighty, which was, and is, and is to come.*

So, the sudden dead silence is shockingly out of the ordinary. There is another out of the ordinary event in this verse. That is the time of the silence. When have we ever seen anything in scriptures timed to half an hour? In the eternal plan, half an hour would seem to be insignificant. Based on the thunderings and lightnings and the earthquake in verse 5 here, it could be argued that the seventh seal is opened while the events of the sixth seal are ongoing. Otherwise, the earthquake might seem a little anticlimactic. I know of no scriptures that explain the half hour of silence, but could it be the amount of time that the saints traverse from Earth to heaven? Just speculation and nothing more.

But when the seventh seal is opened, the seven trumpet angels, each with a judgment on Earth, begin their operations. The seventh seal judgment is one and the same with the seven angels' trumpet judgments. We have seen that these judgments occur over 3.5 years and end right at mid-trib. As a point of interest then, we can see that the seven seals are all within the Church Age as it extends into the tribulation. There is another rapture of the Church immediately after the seventh angel sounds his trumpet. We have finally come to the point of fully revealing this rapture.

We are now ready to move to the next chapter and produce the proofs of the two raptures of the Church. If you have been reading carefully there should only be a few surprises left to learn.

## Chapter 9.  Obviously..., or...

### (Raptures in the Revelation)

Clearly, plainly, evidently, patently, visibly, discernably, manifestly, noticeably, unmistakably, undeniably, indubitably, incontrovertibly, demonstrably, unquestionably, without a doubt, of course, naturally, needless to say, it goes without saying, doubtless there are two raptures for the Church.  You have seen both of them again and again.  So now, all we need to do is formalize the arguments for each one.  It will be a relief to finally get this off my chest.  I have been hinting and outright proclaiming this for eight chapters.  You, on the other hand, have had to be gracious and pretend it wasn't a little annoying.  I only hope it is somewhat unnecessary by now.  Still, it is good to know that these arguments can be readily developed within the scriptures.

In this chapter we will see that the Day of the Lord starts with a rapture or removal of certain Christians from the Earth.  These Christians are taken to heaven while still alive.  Their bodies will be changed or glorified and made adequate for life in heaven or on Earth.  Immediately following this rapture, the seven-year tribulation will start. In the middle of the tribulation, there will be another rapture for the Church.  That is the general rapture of all the remaining of the Church.  The last half of the tribulation is often called the Great Tribulation because of extreme persecution by the Beast of Revelation 13 at that time (Matt. 24:21).  At the end of the seven-year tribulation Christ will return with power and great glory to defeat His enemies and establish His 1000-year physical reign as King of kings upon the Earth. The event we call the 'Second Coming' of Jesus Christ is actually a three-stage event. He will come **for His obedient saints** (1 Thes. 5:1-4 with Rev. 3:3) at the beginning of the tribulation. Then He will come **for His chastened saints** (1 Thes. 4:13-17) at the middle of the tribulation. Finally, He will come **with all His saints** (1 Thes. 3:12-13) at the end of the Great Tribulation to defeat His enemies and set up His 1000-year physical reign upon the Earth.

At the end of the 1000-year reign of Christ on Earth, there will be one last rebellion. The armies of the rebellious will be defeated and then will come the Great White Throne judgment. All sinners will be committed to the Lake of Fire and the righteous will enter eternity as servants of the true God. A new universe will be created along with a new Earth and the program that started with Adam and Eve will be restored. All this can be gleaned from Revelation chapters 21 and 22.

Before we go any further it is helpful to realize how important this knowledge of the pre-trib rapture is to every individual. This scripture is self-explanatory.

*1Jn 3:2 Beloved, now are we the sons of God, and it doth not yet appear what we shall be: but we know that, when he shall appear, we shall be like him; for we shall see him as he is.*
*3* **And every man that hath this hope in him purifieth himself**, *even as he is pure.*

We have seen the system of rewards for Christians at the Judgment Seat of Christ, so we know that Jesus rewards His servants according to their works or service to the kingdom. We have also seen that there is a special reward for those who are taken in the pre-trib rapture. It is called the crown of righteousness and it is awarded to all those who love His appearing (2 Tim 4:8). It is a special crown for those who are obediently watching and living in righteousness when He comes to rapture the Church. This is one side or portion of the Church. In chapter 6 of this work, we looked at the other side of the Church. We saw a rebellious, smug, and ugly Church that Jesus will find so repulsive and distasteful that He will spue it out of His mouth when He comes. In looking forward to such a time 2000 years ago, our Lord mused rhetorically:

*Luk 18:8 . . . Nevertheless when the Son of man cometh, shall he find faith on the earth?*

Do we even need to ask why there are two raptures by this point? But let's go through this anyway. The Church Age clearly extends from Calvary to the middle of the tribulation. Daniel 9 makes this abundantly evident. That means that there is a 3.5-year period when unworthy Christians can lose their salvation. These Christians are not accounted unworthy of Heaven because Jesus has ransomed them with His own blood, rather they are unworthy of the **reward** of the pre-tribulation rapture. Now, this time is necessary because much of the Church will be so sickeningly wicked by the start of the day of the Lord. Remember the perilous times and the seducing spirits and the doctrines of devils and the antichrist pastors and the reprobate minds and the wretched and the miserable and the poor and the blind and the naked state of much of the Church that we looked at in chapter 6?

The Church of the last days, generally, has so abandoned the true scriptures that they couldn't recognize God if He showed up in church. They have painted such a false image of God the Father and of His Christ that they are barely recognizable. They have so mutilated and compromised His Bible that truth is almost indiscernible in their bibles. Yet, they are so smug! They think they are rich and increased with goods and have need of nothing. So, the first half of the tribulation is a time of cleansing and chastening so that unworthy souls will not populate heaven. Those who are unworthy of the pre-trib rapture will either respond properly to the chastening and become worthy or face the possibility of losing their salvation.

*Eph 5:26 That he might sanctify and cleanse it with the washing of water by the word,*

*27 That he might present it to himself a glorious church, not having spot, or wrinkle, or any such thing; but that it should be holy and without blemish.*

### The big reveal

Here is the big reveal with doctrinal and logical justification. Such chastening is not necessary for the obedient saints. There is no need for them to face the tribulation. And they won't! This rapture is **part of the system of rewards** that the Lord will award to His children (Rev. 1:3). **Just as there was no good reason to drown Noah and his family in the flood, there is no good reason to send the obedient saints of this age through the trial of the tribulation.**

*Rev 3:10 Because thou hast kept the word of my patience,* ***I also will keep thee from the hour of temptation****, which shall come upon all the world, to try them that dwell upon the earth.*

We will be using many facts and concepts that have been developed throughout this work to bring us to this critical point of doctrine. Just review the chapters referenced within if you don't remember a particular detail.

In chapter six we learned that *in the last days perilous times shall come.* The peril here is peril for the Church. The passage goes on to tell us that among men (of the Church) *evil men and seducers shall wax worse and worse, deceiving, and being deceived.*

If we could graph the evil in the Church based on these statements, we would expect it to produce a 'hockey stick' graph with evil rising exponentially at the end. See Chapter 8 for review in this paragraph. The hockey stick graph is quite predictable because the Church is nowhere exempted from the Law of Entropy. **That curse** was placed on the whole creation, including the righteous and the unrighteous. This law is immutable so the Church, as a social system, must run down and collapse without additional outside input. This is not the gates of hell (chapter 2) prevailing against the Church, it is the universal law of God prevailing upon the Church. That is exactly what the scriptures just quoted are saying. But God will step in and provide additional, from outside the system, input in the form of a rapture.

We saw in chapter 6 that God will shorten the days of the tribulation (provide additional outside input) to avoid the loss of all mortal men on earth. It is not unreasonable to suspect that God has also planned the start of the day of the LORD to occur when the Church has become completely ineffective. He will pull out all the obedient saints but will leave for chastening those who are destroying His Church with their apathy, and smugness, and outright sin. This rapture will wake up those remaining saints to their horrible state. Remember, they mostly believe they are pleasing God with their great works and righteous living (Rev. 3:17).

*Heb 12:5 And ye have forgotten the exhortation which speaketh unto you as unto children, My son, despise not thou the chastening of the Lord, nor faint when thou art rebuked of him:*

*6 For whom the Lord loveth he chasteneth, and scourgeth every son whom he receiveth.*

*7 If ye endure chastening, God dealeth with you as with sons; for what son is he whom the father chasteneth not?*

Following the pre-trib rapture, as we saw in chapter 6, the rules for salvation change. The day of redemption has come and the sealing with the Holy Ghost has ceased. At this time, the passages that say *he that shall endure unto the end, the same shall be saved*, become the doctrinal standard for salvation.

This may be a doctrinal black hole for Calvinists, but scriptures do not lie. We are plainly told, in a verse we have quoted many times, that we must be accounted worthy to escape all these things. And that verse is not written to the lost world. It would be unreasonable to warn the lost world to watch and pray always that they may be accounted worthy. They have no idea what is going on here. Also, we are not told in this verse to be born again to be accounted worthy. This verse indicates that worthiness is required of Christians to escape all these things.

So, here is a list of passages that should open our eyes to the truth of this doctrine. Not everybody in these scriptures is saved, but all are part of the Church, dragging her down to their own low level. These scriptures all describe the last-days Church. By the time you get to the bottom of the list you may be gasping with horror. How do you think God feels about it? Are these people worthy?

- *in the last days perilous times shall come*

- *For men shall be lovers of their own selves, covetous, boasters, proud, blasphemers, disobedient to parents, unthankful, unholy, Without natural affection, trucebreakers, false accusers, incontinent, fierce, despisers of those that are good,
Traitors, heady, highminded, lovers of pleasures more than lovers of God;
Having a form of godliness, but denying the power thereof: from such turn away.*

- *evil men and seducers shall wax worse and worse, deceiving, and being deceived*

- *Now the Spirit speaketh expressly, that in the latter times some shall depart from the faith, giving heed to seducing spirits, and doctrines of devils;*

- *For the time will come when they will not endure sound doctrine; but after their own lusts shall they heap to themselves teachers, having itching ears; And they shall turn away their ears from the truth, and shall be turned unto fables.*

- *But there were false prophets also among the people, even as there shall be false teachers among you, who privily shall bring in damnable heresies, even denying the Lord that bought them, and bring upon themselves swift destruction. And many shall follow their pernicious ways; by reason of whom the way of truth shall be evil spoken of.*

- *For there are certain men crept in unawares, who were before of old ordained to this condemnation, ungodly men, turning the grace of our God into lasciviousness, and denying the only Lord God, and our Lord Jesus Christ.*

- *Likewise also these filthy dreamers defile the flesh, despise dominion, and speak evil of dignities.*

- *But these speak evil of those things which they know not: but what they know naturally, as brute beasts, in those things they corrupt themselves.*

- *These are spots in your feasts of charity, when they feast with you, feeding themselves without fear: clouds they are without water, carried about of winds; trees whose fruit withereth, without fruit, twice dead, plucked up by the roots; Raging waves of the sea, foaming out their own shame; wandering stars, to whom is reserved the blackness of darkness for ever.*

- *These are murmurers, complainers, walking after their own lusts; and their mouth speaketh great swelling words, having men's persons in admiration because of advantage.*

- *they told you there should be mockers in the last time, who should walk after their own ungodly lusts. These be they who separate themselves, sensual, having not the Spirit.*

- *Knowing this first, that there shall come in the last days scoffers, walking after their own lusts, And saying, Where is the promise of his coming? for since the fathers fell asleep, all things continue as they were from the beginning of the creation.*

- *I know thy works, that thou art neither cold nor hot: I would thou wert cold or hot. So then because thou art lukewarm, and neither cold nor hot, I will spue thee out of my mouth. Because thou sayest, I am rich, and increased with goods, and have need of nothing; and knowest not that thou art wretched, and miserable, and poor, and blind, and naked:*

- *For the wrath of God is revealed from heaven against all ungodliness and unrighteousness of men, who hold the truth in unrighteousness;*

*Because that which may be known of God is manifest in them; for God hath shewed it unto them. For the invisible things of him from the creation of the world are clearly seen, being understood by the things that are made, even his eternal power and Godhead; so that they are without excuse:*

*Because that, when they knew God, they glorified him not as God, neither were thankful; but became vain in their imaginations, and their foolish heart was darkened.*

*Professing themselves to be wise, they became fools, And changed the glory of the uncorruptible God into an image made like to corruptible man, and to birds, and fourfooted beasts, and creeping things.*

*Wherefore God also gave them up to uncleanness*

*through the lusts of their own hearts, to dishonour their own bodies between themselves:*

*Who changed the truth of God into a lie, and worshipped and served the creature more than the Creator, who is blessed for ever. Amen.*

*For this cause God gave them up unto vile affections: for even their women did change the natural use into that which is against nature:*

*And likewise also the men, leaving the natural use of the woman, burned in their lust one toward another; men with men working that which is unseemly, and receiving in themselves that recompence of their error which was meet.*

*And even as they did not like to retain God in their knowledge, God gave them over to a reprobate mind, to do those things which are not convenient;*

*Being filled with all unrighteousness, fornication, wickedness, covetousness, maliciousness; full of envy, murder, debate, deceit, malignity; whisperers, Backbiters, haters of God, despiteful, proud, boasters, inventors of evil things, disobedient to parents, Without understanding, covenantbreakers, without natural affection, implacable, unmerciful:*

*Who knowing the judgment of God, that they which commit such things are worthy of death, not only do the same, but have pleasure in them that do them.*

- *For I know this, that after my departing shall grievous wolves enter in among you, not sparing the flock.*
  *Also of your own selves shall men arise, speaking perverse things, to draw away disciples after*

*them.*

Now let's separate the apples from the oranges.

**The coming of the Thief**

There is little new ground in the following study, but please bear with me. Much of this is review but we now need to put it together in such a way that the pre-trib rapture becomes readily apparent. Hopefully, many readers will have already reached that point.

*2Pe 3:10 But the day of the Lord will come as a thief in the night; in the which the heavens shall pass away with a great noise, and the elements shall melt with fervent heat, the earth also and the works that are therein shall be burned up.*

As we have discussed, the apostle Peter gave the boundaries of the Day of the Lord very succinctly in a single verse. The time when the elements melt with a fervent heat is described in Rev. 20:7 – 21:1. It is a time we call the Great White Throne judgment for obvious reasons if you read the passage. It is the judgment of the damned and it occurs immediately after the physical universe is converted to pure energy, leaving only the soulish state of man. We can see from the passage that it is immediately after the thousand year, or millennial, reign of Christ. This is pretty straightforward leaving only the question of when it starts.

I just want to interject a somewhat off-topic point here for greater understanding. Notice that I wrote pure energy.

We all tend to describe energy using the term pure. That is because, at some level, we recognize this truth. The curse was only placed on matter. So, when matter is converted back to energy, it is purified. It can then be converted back to matter with order restored and no curse. That is exactly what God does at the Great White Throne judgment to reverse the curse. Now, back to our narrative.

Peter wrote that the day of the Lord would start or come as a thief in the night. If we can determine from scriptures what that phrase refers to, we should be able to pinpoint the start of that day. The apostle Paul concurred with Peter regarding the start of the day of the Lord:

*1 Th 5:2 For yourselves know perfectly that the day of the Lord so cometh as a thief in the night.*

This is good confirmation, but it is not enough information to understand the meaning of the phrase. Revelation 3:3 helps us greatly:

*Rev 3:3 Remember therefore how thou hast received and heard, and hold fast, and repent. If therefore thou shalt not watch, I will come on thee as a thief, and thou shalt not know what hour I will come upon thee.*

This is written to a specific church, but we understand that it is representative of the type of issues that any church might face. That is one of the great benefits of the letters to the seven churches in Revelation chapters 2 and 3. They are admonishments to all churches throughout the Church Age and expose major weaknesses that the corporate Church must be watchful for. Although different groups of Christians will be treated differently, it won't be based on which church they attend.  It will be based on each individual's relationship with the savior.

This verse gives us some very critical information.  First, the Lord will come upon His Church unexpectedly **only if they are not watching**.  This admonition to watch for His coming is repeated quite forcefully and unambiguously in a number of other scriptures.  Second, His coming will be as a thief would come.  That is, He will come unexpectedly.  The thief will enter the house and take only the most precious things.  He has no interest, for instance, in stealing the dirty laundry.  Finally, the implication here is that the Church should know to the very hour when He will come as a Thief.

The Lord goes even further and reaffirms His Thief coming in this verse:

*Rev 16:15  Behold, I come as a thief. Blessed is he that watcheth, and keepeth his garments, lest he walk naked, and they see his shame.*

There will be much shame for those Christians who remain after the pre-tribulation rapture.  They will realize how ignorant and smug they were.  Both of these Revelation passages were spoken by Jesus and stated in the first person.  He says: "I come as a thief".  The verses we have looked at present Jesus as the Thief who comes for His Church.  Peter says the day of the Lord also comes as a thief.  Understanding that God uses matching wording to help us put doctrines together, it becomes obvious that the two are meant to be tied together.  The full proof of this is found in the definitive New Testament passage on the start of the day of the Lord. Review chapter 5, if necessary.

*Rev 6:15 And the kings of the earth, and the great men, and the rich men, and the chief captains, and the mighty men, and every bondman, and every free man, hid themselves in the dens and in the rocks of the mountains;*
*16 And said to the mountains and rocks, Fall on us, and* **hide us from the face of him that sitteth on the throne, and from the wrath of the Lamb:**
*17 For the great day of his wrath is come; and who shall be able to stand?*

So, Peter and Paul say the day of the Lord comes as a Thief. Jesus, the Lamb of God, says He comes as a Thief. And here the Lamb, who has bought the Church with His own shed blood, shows up on Earth at the start of the day of the Lord. The day of the Lord coming as a thief and the Lamb coming as a Thief are inseparably tied together in this passage.

In Rev. chapter 7 we find a powerful proof that a rapture has just occurred. This chapter is inserted between the sixth and seventh seals to bring us up to date on a couple other events from that time period. Here we actually see the raptured saints arriving in heaven.

*Rev 7:9 After this I beheld, and, lo, a great multitude, which no man could number, of all nations, and kindreds, and people, and tongues, stood before the throne, and before the Lamb, clothed with white robes, and palms in their hands;*
*10 And cried with a loud voice, saying, Salvation to our God which sitteth upon the throne, and unto the Lamb.*
*11 And all the angels stood round about the throne, and*

*about the elders and the four beasts, and fell before the throne on their faces, and worshipped God,*

*12 Saying, Amen: Blessing, and glory, and wisdom, and thanksgiving, and honour, and power, and might, be unto our God for ever and ever. Amen.*

*13 And one of the elders answered, saying unto me, What are these which are arrayed in white robes? and whence came they?*

*14 And I said unto him, Sir, thou knowest. And he said to me, These are they which came out of great tribulation, and have washed their robes, and made them white in the blood of the Lamb.*

*15 Therefore are they before the throne of God, and serve him day and night in his temple: and he that sitteth on the throne shall dwell among them.*

*16 They shall hunger no more, neither thirst any more; neither shall the sun light on them, nor any heat.*

*17 For the Lamb which is in the midst of the throne shall feed them, and shall lead them unto living fountains of waters: and God shall wipe away all tears from their eyes.*

Notice how prominently the Lamb is mentioned here among His Church. In the sixth chapter of the Revelation He was on Earth meting out His wrath on men and now here He is in heaven with His raptured saints. These saints have all cleaned themselves up by washing their robes in the blood of the Lamb. It is hard NOT to conclude that these folks have just been brought to heaven en-masse by the Lamb of God. If you plan to be taken in the pre-trib rapture, this is a description of your first event in heaven. Go ahead and read it again. Enjoy! It will likely happen a matter of months from now! One question. Is it possible John saw you in that crowd?

We have pointed out repeatedly why there are still seven years of tribulation between the sixth seal and the seventh vial judgment of Revelation 16. This is clearly at the very beginning of the tribulation. Nevertheless, some have pointed out that these saints came out of great tribulation and therefore this is an end of the tribulation event. However, it never says they came out of THE great tribulation. Our Lord told us we would always have tribulation in this world (John 16:33). Further we were told that in the last days perilous times would come. We looked at several passages describing a last days Church that would be so dangerous that our Lord rhetorically pondered whether He would even find faith on the Earth when He comes. In America and most of the western world, our tribulation is found in abundant access to ungodly entertainment and high stress lifestyles that take our eyes off the Savior for the majority of every day. I'm sure most readers will know exactly what I am talking about here. If you need more understanding, check out why the men of Sodom became so evil in Ezekiel 16:49-50.

The final conclusion we must understand regarding the Thief, or pre-tribulation rapture, is this. This rapture is conditioned on being found (1) watching and (2) living in righteousness. This is the **only** way to be raptured out pre-trib. This is that special reward (Rev. 1:3) for Christians living at that time. That crown of righteousness is just one of the rewards that will be given out on the day of Jesus Christ when He sits and judges the Church immediately after the resurrection of the just. Make sure you earn that crown.

So, there we have the pre-tribulation rapture. It is quite different from the rapture that the traditional rapturist teaches. It is conditional and only a percentage of the Church will be taken.

This has been a quick proof using all the most necessary passages. But there are other supporting scriptures, some of which we have seen. Let's go through a few more just to lock this doctrine up. We will start by restating an Old Testament passage that will establish an important principle:

*Zep 2:3 Seek ye the LORD, all ye meek of the earth, which have wrought his judgment; seek righteousness, seek meekness: it may be ye shall be hid in the day of the LORD'S anger.*

The context of this passage is the Day of the Lord as can be determined from the text in chapter 1 of Zephaniah which expressly says that the Day of the Lord is at hand and it is near, it is near. The passage tells us that people who **seek meekness and righteousness** have a **possibility** of being hid in the day of the Lord's fierce anger. Although the context of the book is the situation in Israel, this verse is spoken to all the meek of the Earth. The indication here is that there is, conditionally, a way to avoid the day of the Lord's anger for those who are alive at that time. This will happen when the Day of the Lord and therefore the tribulation is very, very near. Thus, we call this the pre-tribulation rapture. It is important to remember here **the conditions** of seeking righteousness and meekness in order to be hid in the day of the Lord's anger.

Now let's move to the New Testament and review what the One who comes as a Thief had to say about it when He was here the first time as the Christ. This is part of the Olivet Discourse. In it, Jesus explains to His disciples what will come to pass from that time until His second coming. The following verses occur prior to His second coming but very near that time. We can see from context that they apply to when He comes as a Thief, or right at the start of the Day of the Lord. Again, we see how important it is to **watch** for this event.

*Mat 24:37 But as the days of Noe were, so shall also the coming of the Son of man be.*
*38 For as in the days that were before the flood they were eating and drinking, marrying and giving in marriage, until the day that Noe entered into the ark,*
*39 And knew not until the flood came, and took them all away; so shall also the coming of the Son of man be.*

This coming of the Lord will be like the coming of the flood in Noah's day. It took the world by surprise, but Noah and his family were aware, prepared, and watching for it. Noah, as the goodman of his house, was a preacher of righteousness according to 2 Peter 2:5:

*2Pe 2:5 And spared not the old world, but saved Noah the eighth person, a preacher of righteousness, bringing in the flood upon the world of the ungodly;*

Up to this point we have seen that **watching for the coming of the Lord and living righteously are very important requirements for being taken in the Thief rapture.** So it was for Noah. Noah believed the Lord, even in the face of all the rest of the world who probably thought he was crazy. Noah knew the truth when no one else did. Noah was watching and preparing for the flood and preaching righteousness. The Thief rapture will not be quite so exclusive but the requirements to be hid in the day of the Lord's anger will be the same.

Continuing the passage in Matthew 24:

*Mat 24:40 Then shall two be in the field; the one shall be taken, and the other left.*
*41 Two women shall be grinding at the mill; the one shall be taken, and the other left.*
*42 **Watch therefore**: for ye know not what hour your Lord doth come.*

Many teach that those taken in this passage are Christians and those left are lost persons. I have read and heard some teachers who openly mock any who don't read it this way. That is about all the ammunition they have to fight the concept of Christians being separated at this rapture. However, we can see here that this is a strong admonition to be found watching and even more to watch for YOUR Lord. Jesus is only YOUR Lord to Christians. The rest of the passage bears out the fact that all these people are Christians. So again, we have a conditional rapture in which only part of the Church is removed.

*Mat 24:43 But know this, that if the goodman of the house had known in what watch **the thief** would come, he would have **watched**, and would not have suffered his house to be broken up.*
*44 Therefore be ye also ready: for in such an hour as ye think not the Son of man cometh.*

Here again, we see how important it is to **watch** for this event. Because the goodman of the house didn't watch for the **Thief** here, his house was broken up. That is, some of his household were taken and some were not. We see here yet another confirmation of the prophecy of Zephaniah when he said, "it **may** be ye shall be hid in the day of the Lord's anger". Some will be hid, and some will experience at least part of the Lord's anger.

Luke 17 deals with this subject as well. After comparing Christ's coming to the days of Noah, it goes on to compare it to the days of Lot.

*Luk 17:28 Likewise also as it was in the days of Lot; they did eat, they drank, they bought, they sold, they planted, they builded;*
*29 But the same day that Lot went out of Sodom it rained fire and brimstone from heaven, and destroyed them all.*
*30 Even thus shall it be in the day when the Son of man is revealed.*

*Luk 17:32 Remember Lot's wife.*

Lot, just as Noah above, is also the goodman of his household but his house is broken up. Lot had to run for the hills with his two unmarried daughters but lost his sons-in-law and their families as well as his wife. Lot was a righteous man but was an evil servant in that he became ensnared in the cares of this world.

*2Pe 2:6 And turning the cities of Sodom and Gomorrha into ashes condemned them with an overthrow, making them an ensample unto those that after should live ungodly;*
*7 And delivered just Lot, vexed with the filthy conversation of the wicked:*

*8 (For that righteous man dwelling among them, in seeing and hearing, vexed his righteous soul from day to day with their unlawful deeds;)*

Both Noah and Lot were specifically called **righteous** men in the Word of God but had different outcomes.  Noah was **watching** and preparing and therefore his entire family was hid in the day of the Lord's fierce anger.  On the other hand, **Lot was not found watching** for the coming tribulation, so his family entered into the time of tribulation.  He tried desperately to save his sons-in-law but just ran out of time to convince them of the truth.  He lost his sons-in-law and their wives to an immediate special judgment of God on sinners. (Recall the events at the start of the day of the LORD.)  He, himself had to run for the hills with his wife and two remaining daughters.  His household was broken up.  At that point his wife turned back to the world and she too lost the salvation the angels had come to protect.  Bear her in mind when you look at tribulation salvation.  Noah and Lot are examples of the importance of watching for the day of the Lord's fierce anger.

**Noah and Lot: Two examples of the goodman of the house.**

The goodman of the house below refers to anyone with spiritual authority over others.  Anybody familiar with the scriptures should understand that the goodman represents church leaders, local pastors and heads of households.  A few scriptures that present this order are 1 Cor. 11:3 and Heb. 13:17.  It is so important for the goodman to watch that there is a severe punishment for those who fail to do so and great reward for obedience. The passage continues:

*Mat 24:43 But know this, that if the goodman of the house had known in what watch the thief would come, he would have watched, and would not have suffered his house to be broken up.*
*44 Therefore be ye also ready: for in such an hour as ye think not the Son of man cometh.*
*45 Who then is a faithful and wise servant, whom his lord hath made ruler over his household, to give them meat in due season?*
*46 Blessed is that servant, whom his lord when he cometh shall find so doing.*
*47 Verily I say unto you, That he shall make him ruler over all his goods.*

Here we see what happens to the obedient servant of God whose whole house, like Noah's, is taken in the Thief rapture. This servant feeds his household meat because they are mature Christians rather than milk which is for baby Christians.

*Heb 5:12 For when for the time ye ought to be teachers, ye have need that one teach you again which be the first principles of the oracles of God; and are become such as have need of milk, and not of strong meat.*
*13 For every one that useth milk is unskilful in the word of righteousness: for he is a babe.*
*14 But strong meat belongeth to them that are of full age, even those who by reason of use have their senses exercised to discern both good and evil.*

It is more than coincidence that the milk user here is unskillful in the word of **righteousness**. Just as Noah was a preacher of righteousness, we must be righteous in order to discern what is good and what is evil. How many preachers and teachers teach the principles found in this work? Many of them are too busy teaching (inaccurately) the love of God or the positive scriptures in the Bible. They avoid all the negative passages and thus the vast majority of the scriptures. They pretend that God has a positive outlook for mankind and his future. Pure milk, yum!

The faithful and wise servant of verse 45 above will have an important role in the household of God in the eternal kingdom. By contrast, the evil servant who is not found teaching his household to watch and live righteously, is dealt with quite harshly.

*Mat 24:48 But and if that evil servant shall say in his heart, My lord delayeth his coming;*
*49 And shall begin to smite his fellowservants, and to eat and drink with the drunken;*
*50 The lord of that servant shall come in a day when he looketh not for him, and in an hour that he is not aware of,*
*51 And shall cut him asunder, and appoint him his portion with the hypocrites: there shall be weeping and gnashing of teeth.*

This is scary stuff. Verse 48 here assures us that this goodman is a servant of the Lord, but he is an evil servant because he wasn't watching for His Lord. He is quite sure that the Lord will not come in his time so, just as Lot did, he becomes very lax. He may even begin to ridicule those who are watching and begin to keep company with other disobedient goodmen. This seems to be the message of verse 49 here. Verse 50 implies that, because like Lot he was not watching, he will not be aware of the day and hour of the Lord's coming. Finally, verse 51 tells us that he will be cut asunder and grouped with the hypocrites.

Remember our study in the gospels included reference to the ten virgins in Matthew 25? That passage indicates that Christ came upon them suddenly in the middle of the night. That is when the Thief comes. While all of them were sleeping, some were prepared for His coming while others were not. It is a passage that really hits the nail on the head. Even those of us who are watching diligently for the return of Christ tend to get caught up in the affairs of this world and lose concentration at times. In fact, we lose concentration for most of the time. Yet, because our overall attitude is that we are hoping for the rapture and wanting to go with our Lord, we are safe. That is our preparation. That is our extra oil. Those who shrug off or even deny the Thief rapture are like the five foolish virgins. They are completely unprepared. They have not read their Bible and believed what the Lord has revealed to them throughout the scriptures. Because of the deception of this age, many of these may have only rarely seen or heard the true scriptures. This is the state in which Lot found himself. The hour is late for us. It is time to get right(eous) with God,

Lot's situation is dealt with more fully in the book of Luke and turning to that book we find:

*Luk 12:45 But and if that servant say in his heart, My lord delayeth his coming; and shall begin to beat the menservants and maidens, and to eat and drink, and to be drunken;*

*46 The lord of that servant will come in a day when he looketh not for him, and at an hour when he is not aware, and will cut him in sunder, and will appoint him his portion with the unbelievers.*

Unbelievers do not get taken in the pre-tribulation rapture! This servant of the Lord gets the same treatment as the unbelievers.

*47 And that servant, which knew his lord's will, and prepared not himself, neither did according to his will, shall be beaten with many stripes.*

Some knowledgeable Christians fall back into the world and just stop watching for their Lord and caring about His coming.

*48 But he that knew not, and did commit things worthy of stripes, shall be beaten with few stripes. For unto whomsoever much is given, of him shall be much required: and to whom men have committed much, of him they will ask the more.*

Lot was among those that 'knew not' in verse 48. He was living righteously but was so into the world that he didn't realize judgment was coming. He was saved from immediate judgment but still had to endure in a suddenly hostile world.

When the foolish virgins of our parable finally got prepared, it was too late. The door was shut. When they called upon the Lord, He gave a curious answer. He said: "I know you not." They were part of His Church, but they were disobedient at a very important time. Disobedience up to that point had been tolerated but suddenly it was no longer tolerated. The Day of the Lord had begun here and a new era of God's dealings with man had started.

The phrase "I know you not" is interesting when compared with another phrase:

*Mat 7:21 Not every one that saith unto me, Lord, Lord, shall enter into the kingdom of heaven; but he that doeth the will of my Father which is in heaven.*
*22 Many will say to me in that day, Lord, Lord, have we not prophesied in thy name? and in thy name have cast out devils? and in thy name done many wonderful works?*
*23 And then will I profess unto them, I never knew you: depart from me, ye that work iniquity.*

Here Christ is dealing with hypocrites. To them He says: "I never knew you." These were false prophets and exorcisers and faith healers, all pretenders who made merchandise of the people of God as described in 2 Peter 2:1-3. It would appear then, that Christ had known the foolish virgins as His own and then denied them. We must then ask how this is possible in light of the many scriptures that assure us of our security in Christ. The answer is quite obvious. These virgins had come to the day of redemption and were no longer sealed with the Holy Ghost.

In the face of the terrifying possibility of losing one's salvation forever, we must now point out that there is a special blessing for reading and keeping the prophecies of the Revelation. Christians must be able to understand what the prophecies in the Revelation really address in order to be prepared. The prophecies in that book have enough information to insure being caught up in the pre-tribulation rapture. Figuratively, they must keep an adequate supply of oil for their lamps. Just as it was for Noah, **they must understand the times and be watching and living righteously when He comes.**

*Rev 1:3 Blessed is he that readeth, and they that hear the words of this prophecy, and keep those things which are written therein: for the time is at hand.*

Finally, in addition to being hid in the day of the Lord's anger, there is a special reward for those Christians found watching and living righteously. There is a specific crown for all those who love His appearing and that crown is – what else? – **the crown of righteousness!**

*2Ti 4:8 Henceforth there is laid up for me a crown of righteousness, which the Lord, the righteous judge, shall give me at that day: and not to me only, but unto all them also that love his appearing.*

We are about to conclude the section on the pre-trib rapture and move to the much more strongly supported mid-trib rapture. But there are a couple more important points to be made regarding the pre-trib rapture.

**Final issues of concern regarding the pre-trib rapture of the obedient Church**

Before we conclude this section, I should deal with a couple issues of concern to many. One is the issue regarding the rapture of children under the age of accountability. This is really tough stuff, but it is necessary to understand it.

Most believe all children under the age of accountability will be raptured. This is sort of necessary because they believe the pre-trib rapture is unconditional. Now that we have made it conditional, we open the possibility for some children to be left behind.

So, we must search the scripture to see what it says on the subject. Paul addressed the issue thusly:

*1Co 7:13 And the woman which hath an husband that believeth not, and if he be pleased to dwell with her, let her not leave him.*
*14 For the unbelieving husband is sanctified by the wife, and the unbelieving wife is sanctified by the husband: else were your children unclean; but now are they holy.*

Here we see that if children are being raised by a saved person, they are considered clean and holy. Thus, we have a condition for the children as well. It would seem that if the parent is raptured in the Thief rapture, then any children living with them will be raptured as well. This should be a solemn warning for Christian parents at this time in history. The scriptures also give us the proper outlook for a parent in a difficult situation. Ponder this:

*2Co 4:16 For which cause we faint not; but though our outward man perish, yet the inward man is renewed day by day.*
*17 For our light affliction, which is but for a moment, worketh for us a far more exceeding and eternal weight of glory;*
*18 While we look not at the things which are seen, but at the things which are not seen: for the things which are seen are temporal; but the things which are not seen are eternal.*

Secondly, to the oft-mentioned issue of pilotless planes and driverless cars. As we saw in the sixth seal description, there will be a massive, world-wide earthquake. The damage will be so extensive that many millions of people will be buried in debris or otherwise lost. Virtually all cars on the road will become uncontrollable and airplanes will have few if any unbroken landing strips or air traffic control towers to help them land safely. Confusion will reign for quite some time. It will take a long time to realize that some Christians were raptured. So, it might take the remaining of the Church quite some time to realize they were left behind.

A third point to be made regards the western hemisphere. That would seem to be the place where much of the damage we discussed in chapter 5 and other places will be concentrated. So, many Christians living on those continents will be killed quickly or instantly by the upheaval. They will be the best off of all that remain from the rapture because they will not have much or any opportunity to lose their salvation. It should be a source of comfort for us if our loved ones won't accept a belief in the rapture.

Here is a final passage to ponder:

*Luk 18:8 . . . Nevertheless when the Son of man cometh, shall he find faith on the earth?*

We have come back to this verse a few times because it is deeply poignant.

Hopefully, by now, you have seen the power of just taking what the scriptures freely give us. By simply believing what we read and applying the principles that Isaiah laid out for building doctrine, we find powerful, readily attainable truths. It will be no different in the next section. We will see how easy it is to pinpoint the general rapture of the Church in the book of the Revelation.

By this point, you can clearly see that the pre-trib crowd blew it on this rapture. So, we won't bother to rail on most of them anymore, at least for now. The main reason we singled the pre-trib adherents out was because they were so close to the truth but just missed the mark. Many others in the Church, such as Amillennialists and Covenant Theologians and Moralists, never even got in the same ballpark. They believe much of the Bible does not need be taken literally so they are free to make it up as they go along. I sometimes envy them because La La Land can be such a beautiful and carefree place if you want to make it that way. For them, the scriptures say whatever it pleases them to believe they say. Ignorance is bliss. Until it isn't!

**The mid-tribulation rapture of the remaining of the Church.**

There are two scripture passages that address the mid-trib rapture. These are 1 Cor 15:51-54 and 1 Thes 4:13-18. Pinning down this rapture couldn't be easier when using the King James Bible.

Right in the middle of the tribulation a second rapture occurs. This is the general rapture of the Church. It occurs at the end of the Church Age and includes all the remaining of the Church. The scriptures that describe this rapture are often used to prove the pre-tribulation and post-tribulation raptures but as we shall see, they fit much better at mid-tribulation.

The clearly prophesied rapture of the Church occurs at the seventh trumpet judgment at the midpoint of the tribulation. Placing the seventh trumpet judgment at the midpoint of the tribulation is rather easily accomplished. It involves comparing the ministry of the two witnesses of Rev. 11 to the reign of the beast of Rev. 13. (We mentioned this earlier, but will provide a slightly different argument here.)

Rev. 19:20 – 20:2 gives the account of the defeat of the beast which brings the end of the tribulation and the start of the millennial reign of Christ. Working backwards from his death, the reign of the beast had lasted 42 months which is the final 3.5 years of the tribulation.

*Rev 13:1 And I stood upon the sand of the sea, and saw a beast rise up out of the sea, having seven heads and ten horns, and upon his horns ten crowns, and upon his heads the name of blasphemy.*

*5 And there was given unto him a mouth speaking great things and blasphemies; and* **power was given unto him to continue forty and two months.**

*7* **And it was given unto him to make war with the saints, and to overcome them: and power was given him over all kindreds, and tongues, and nations.**

Notice that the Beast **continues** forty-two months. Continues after what? When the beast arrived on the scene, there were two witnesses of God that could not previously be defeated.

*Rev 11:3 And I will give power unto my two witnesses, and they shall prophesy a thousand two hundred and threescore days, clothed in sackcloth.*

*5 And if any man will hurt them, fire proceedeth out of their mouth, and devoureth their enemies: and if any man will hurt them, he must in this manner be killed.*

*7 And when they shall have finished their testimony, the beast that ascendeth out of the bottomless pit shall make war against them, and shall overcome them, and kill them.*

*14 The second woe is past; and, behold, the third woe cometh quickly.*
*15 **And the seventh angel sounded**; and there were great voices in heaven, saying, The kingdoms of this world are become the kingdoms of our Lord, and of his Christ; and he shall reign for ever and ever.*

Here we see that the ministry of the two witnesses lasts for 1260 days and ends just prior to the sounding of the seventh trumpet. That is 42 thirty-day months or 3.5 years out of a seven-year tribulation. The two witnesses cannot be defeated until their ministry is completed. Then the beast of chapter 13 arises. He is able to slay the witnesses because he is given power to overcome the saints for 42 months (Dan. 12:7). Immediately following their death, the last trumpet sounds and then the beast continues for 42 months. So, we find two consecutive 42 month or 3.5-year time periods with the seventh trumpet sounding right around the midpoint of the seven-year tribulation.

With that in mind, we can return to the matter of the general rapture of the Church. One of the prominent mentions of the rapture of the Church is set forth in 1 Cor. 15:51-54 as follows:

*1Cor 15:51 Behold, I shew you a mystery; We shall not all sleep, but we shall all be changed,*
*52 In a moment, in the twinkling of an eye, at the last trump: for the trumpet shall sound, and the dead shall be raised incorruptible, and we shall be changed.*
*53 For this corruptible must put on incorruption, and this mortal must put on immortality.*
*54 So when this corruptible shall have put on incorruption, and this mortal shall have put on immortality, then shall be brought to pass the saying that is written, Death is swallowed up in victory.*

The apostle Paul, the writer here, is clearly revealing a mystery. At least part of that mystery is the revelation that we shall not all die (sleep) but we shall all be changed from corruptible to incorruptible bodies. This change is described in verses 53 and 54. The passage also asserts that this change will occur at the sound of a last trumpet. Finally, the resurrection of the dead in Christ will occur for those who are "raised incorruptible". So, there are three specific events here. These are the revelation of a mystery, a last trumpet, and the resurrection of the dead in Christ by which to recognize this rapture event if we find it again in scriptures.

A confirmation of this event is found in 1 Thes. 4:13-18 as follows:

*1Thes 4:13 But I would not have you to be ignorant, brethren, concerning them which are asleep, that ye sorrow not, even as others which have no hope.*

*14 For if we believe that Jesus died and rose again, even so them also which sleep in Jesus will God bring with him.*
*15 For this we say unto you by the word of the Lord, that we which are alive and remain unto the coming of the Lord shall not prevent them which are asleep.*
*16 For the Lord himself shall descend from heaven with a shout, with the voice of the archangel, and with the trump of God: and the dead in Christ shall rise first:*
*17 Then we which are alive and remain shall be caught up together with them in the clouds, to meet the Lord in the air: and so shall we ever be with the Lord.*
*18 Wherefore comfort one another with these words.*

Verses 13-15 here assure us that the resurrection of the dead in Christ is as sure as the resurrection of Jesus Himself. In verse 16, we find a list of events that will accompany that resurrection. They are the Lord descending with a shout, the voice of the archangel, a trumpet, and the resurrection of the dead in Christ.

From these two passages, we can determine that at some point in time, Christians will be changed from corruptible to incorruptible bodies and caught up to meet the Lord in the air and then ever to be with the Lord without experiencing death. This is the definition of a rapture event. I must note that there are absolutely no conditions associated with this rapture. It includes all the righteous dead and all the righteous living saints. (If we are saved, we are saints in the eyes of God!)

Summarizing, the given events that will accompany this rapture are:

1. The Lord descending from heaven with a shout.
2. The voice of the archangel.

3. The revelation of a mystery
4. A last trumpet
5. The resurrection of the dead in Christ

We can now go to the events surrounding the seventh, and LAST, trumpet judgment of Rev. chapters 10 and 11, where we find all of these events prominently mentioned. It begins with Rev. 10:1-7. At this point, the sixth trump has sounded, and the judgment associated with it has occurred.

*Rev 10:1 And I saw another mighty angel come down from heaven, clothed with a cloud: and a rainbow was upon his head, and his face was as it were the sun, and his feet as pillars of fire:*
*2 And he had in his hand a little book open: and he set his right foot upon the sea, and his left foot on the earth,*
*3 And cried with a loud voice, as when a lion roareth: and when he had cried, seven thunders uttered their voices.*

There is little dispute that this mighty angel is the Lord Jesus Himself. He is similarly described elsewhere in scriptures and the rainbow matches to Rev. 4:3 and Gen. 9:13-16. Additionally, the now open little book He holds brings to mind the one of Revelation chapter 5 which only the Lamb of God was worthy to open. In this passage, the Lord is crying out with a loud voice as when a lion roareth. This satisfies the point (1) above as we noted the Lord descending from heaven with a shout.

*Rev 10:4 And when the seven thunders had uttered their voices, I was about to write: and **I heard a voice from***

***heaven*** *saying unto me, Seal up those things which the seven thunders uttered, and write them not.*

On its face, the voice from heaven of Rev.10:4 may or may not satisfy point (2) with the voice of the archangel, but we can find more to go on than just this. According to Jude, the name of the archangel is Michael.

*Jude 1:9 Yet Michael the archangel, when contending with the devil he disputed about the body of Moses, durst not bring against him a railing accusation, but said, The Lord rebuke thee.*

Michael shows up in the same time frame (mid-tribulation) back in Daniel 12:1-7 as follows:

*Dan 12:1 And at that time shall Michael stand up, the great prince which standeth for the children of thy people: and there shall be a time of trouble, such as never was since there was a nation even to that same time: and at that time thy people shall be delivered, every one that shall be found written in the book.*
*2 And many of them that sleep in the dust of the earth shall awake, some to everlasting life, and some to shame and everlasting contempt.*
*3 And they that be wise shall shine as the brightness of the firmament; and they that turn many to righteousness as the stars for ever and ever.*
*4 But thou, O Daniel, shut up the words, and seal the book, even to the time of the end: many shall run to and fro, and knowledge shall be increased.*
*5 Then I Daniel looked, and, behold, there stood other two, the one on this side of the bank of the river, and the other on that side of the bank of the river.*
*6 And one said to the man clothed in linen, which was upon the waters of the river, How long shall it be to the end of these wonders?*

*7 And I heard the man clothed in linen, which was upon the waters of the river, when he held up his right hand and his left hand unto heaven, and sware by him that liveth for ever that it shall be for a time, times, and an half; and when he shall have accomplished to scatter the power of the holy people, all these things shall be finished.*

That this appearance of Michael the archangel occurs around the middle of the tribulation can be determined from verses 1 and 7. Verse 1 describes the greatest time of trouble in the history of the nation (of Israel). This ends in the deliverance of the people, much as will occur in the millennial reign of Christ. Comparing this time of trouble to the one described by Matthew when speaking of the final three and a half years of the tribulation, we see they are essentially the same.

*Mat 24:16 Then let them which be in Judaea flee into the mountains:*

*21 For then shall be great tribulation, such as was not since the beginning of the world to this time, no, nor ever shall be.*

*22 And except those days should be shortened, there should no flesh be saved: but for the elect's sake those days shall be shortened.*

Verse 7 describes the reign of the beast for 3 1/2 years (time, times, and a half = 1+2+1/2) when he has power over the holy people and implies it is just beginning. Verse 2 refers to a resurrection which includes the righteous dead and provides strong evidence for point 5 above.

So, here is Michael, the archangel, explicitly mentioned in this time frame. Then, in Daniel 12:4, we find the same message as the angel of Rev. 10:4. In both cases the writer is instructed to seal up what he has seen and heard. Our rapture scriptures require the voice of the archangel and here we find him prominently mentioned at the time of the event I am proposing for the rapture. Though it is somewhat anecdotal, the evidence is too strong here to deny the likelihood that, as required by point 2 above, the voice of the archangel is present.

Looking at all the mentions of Michael the Archangel in the KJV, we find an interesting association between Michael and Jesus Christ. In Daniel chapter 10, Jesus Christ as Messiah reveals to Daniel the final prophecy of his book. The description of the announcement angel in Daniel chapter 10 matches the description of Jesus in Revelation chapter 1 so closely as to leave little room for doubt as to His identity. In this chapter, Jesus, as Messiah, battles the spiritual prince of Persia for 21 days. Finally, He calls Michael the prince of Israel to help Him get through to Daniel. This prophecy covers the final three chapters of the book of Daniel and chronicles the history of the Jewish nation right up to the end of the tribulation. As we have seen, chapter 12 starts at the middle of the tribulation. At the end of chapter 10, Jesus the Messiah makes a curious statement:

*Dan 10:21 But I will shew thee that which is noted in the scripture of truth: and there is none that holdeth with me in these things, but Michael your prince.*

Michael is the spiritual prince of the Jewish people and Jesus is the Bridegroom of the Church and the King of creation. They have fought side by side in the spiritual kingdom. Both understand the future history of the Jewish nation to the exclusion of all others. Both are prominently mentioned at the mid-tribulation events. It is at the middle of the tribulation that Jesus assumes His power over the world and begins His Reign as King of kings:

*Rev 11:15 And the seventh angel sounded; and there were great voices in heaven, saying, The kingdoms of this world are become the kingdoms of our Lord, and of his Christ; and he shall reign for ever and ever.*

*17 Saying, We give thee thanks, O Lord God Almighty, which art, and wast, and art to come; because thou hast taken to thee thy great power, and hast reigned.*

So, we find the new King of kings to the world and the spiritual prince of Israel present at the rapture of the Church and the resurrection of the just. It is not a great stretch to imagine Michael, the spiritual prince of Israel, calling the righteous dead and the saved of Israel while Jesus calls the righteous dead and the saved of the rest of the world. Israel is always treated as being distinct from the rest of the world in prophetic scriptures.

Returning to the Revelation account, let's examine point (3), the revelation of a mystery.

*Rev 10:5 And the angel which I saw stand upon the sea and upon the earth lifted up his hand to heaven,*
*6 And sware by him that liveth for ever and ever, who created heaven, and the things that therein are, and the earth, and the things that therein are, and the sea, and the things which are therein, that there should be time no longer:*

*7 But in the days of the voice of the seventh angel, when he shall begin to sound, **the mystery of God** should be finished, as he hath declared to his servants the prophets.*

At this point comes the end of the Mystery of God. Remember, we saw that the mystery of God is, in fact, the Church Age. So, here we see it has just ended. This is the mystery Paul was referring to in 1 Cor. 15:51. A casual reading might leave the impression that the mystery of that verse is the rapture. However, that chapter begins with the death, burial, and resurrection of Christ and concludes with the general (mid-trib) rapture of the church. That includes the entire Church Age. It should be understood Paul is saying that he is showing us a mystery in this chapter, not just in the verse the phrase is found in. This is another example of the verse divisions messing with our brains. It is the mystery "hid from ages and generations, but now made manifest." Here Paul is referring to the entire Church Age which is, in fact, the very Mystery of God Paul was charged with revealing as we studied in chapter 7 of this work. The Church Age then, does not end until the seventh angel sounds his trumpet. To review, he verifies this definition of the mystery in Col. 1:25 - 2:2 cited below.

*Col 1:25 Whereof **I am made a minister, according to the dispensation of God which is given to me for you**, to fulfil the word of God;*
*26 **Even the mystery which hath been hid from ages and from generations, but now is made manifest to his saints:***
*27 To whom God would make known what is the riches of the glory of this mystery among the Gentiles; which is Christ in you, the hope of glory:*

*2:2 That their hearts might be comforted, being knit together in love, and unto all riches of the full assurance of understanding,* **to the acknowledgement of the mystery of God, and of the Father, and of Christ;**

So, at this point, we understand that point (3) the revelation of a mystery is satisfied

*Rev 11:15* **And the seventh angel sounded***; and there were great voices in heaven, saying, The kingdoms of this world are become the kingdoms of our Lord, and of his Christ; and he shall reign for ever and ever.*

This is clearly the last trumpet in a series of seven trumpet judgments and clearly satisfies point (4) above. It signals the end of the church age and the beginning of the physical reign of Christ over the kingdoms of this world. **The trumpet judgments incorporate a coronation ceremony!**

Turning now to point (5) the resurrection of the dead in Christ, we read further:

*Rev 11:16 And the four and twenty elders, which sat before God on their seats, fell upon their faces, and worshipped God,*
*17 Saying, We give thee thanks, O Lord God Almighty, which art, and wast, and art to come; because thou hast taken to thee thy great power, and hast reigned.*
*18 And the nations were angry, and thy wrath is come,* **and the time of the dead, that they should be judged, and that thou shouldest give reward unto thy servants the prophets, and to the saints, and them that fear thy name, small and great;** *and shouldest destroy them which destroy the earth.*

In verse 18 above, the time of the dead is come. This must refer to the resurrection of the dead in Christ because it is followed by judgment and then rewards. This is the judgment seat of Christ as described in 2 Cor. 5:10. Here verse 18 agrees with Daniel 12:2 above that the resurrection of the righteous dead occurs when Michael stands up at mid-tribulation. It goes further and verifies what Dan. 12:3 hints at. That is, the fact that rewards are given to the righteous dead. This is the day of Christ that we looked at in chapter 7.

So now we have found that all the events specifically associated with the general rapture of the Church clearly occur in conjunction with the sounding of the seventh trumpet of the trumpet judgments right at the middle of the tribulation. There is no attempt in scripture to hide this or make it difficult to find out. This rapture will not be a surprise to anyone who enters the tribulation. Scriptures are quite clear that from the start of the tribulation everyone will know who JEHOVAH God is and what He intends to do. He laid it all out for us thousands of years ago in the most widely owned and read book in the history of the world. Plus, the two witnesses will likely preach the truth of this quite plainly to the whole world for 1260 days. Unbelief will be virtually impossible. Unfortunately, the vast majority of the unsaved world will then view JEHOVAH God as a meddling, malevolent and malicious super being that can and must be defeated.

A couple more points regarding the timing of the mid-tribulation rapture should be made. The scripture almost belabored the point that this rapture was for those that remain:

*1Th 4:15 For this we say unto you by the word of the Lord, that* **we which are alive and remain** *unto the coming of the Lord shall not prevent them which are asleep.*
*16 For the Lord himself shall descend from heaven with a shout, with the voice of the archangel, and with the trump of God: and the dead in Christ shall rise first:*
*17 Then* **we which are alive and remain** *shall be caught up together with them in the clouds, to meet the Lord in the air: and so shall we ever be with the Lord.*

Note that including verses 15 and 17 above the phrase 'and remain' occurs twice. If you believe there is only one rapture and then remove that phrase, the meaning is exactly the same. The phrase is entirely superfluous. Those who do not believe God was serious when He promised to preserve His very words have no problem with that. It may be just another quirky result of error creep that occurred as the scriptures came down the pipeline. However, if you believe God kept His promises and preserved His very words generation by generation, then you need to ask what the phrase refers to.

If we remain, we must remain after something related that has happened prior to this time. If there were a previous rapture, that would be the most logical explanation for the phrase and, not surprisingly, that is the case here.

There is a very helpful related passage in First Thessalonians. Because of the way this passage is laid out it is not immediately clear, but all the information needed to properly place the raptures is found within this epistle.

The simple fact is that Paul is working backwards in the major end-times events as they relate to the Church.

### The three-event second coming of Christ is found in 1 Thessalonians.

In chapter three of this epistle we find the second coming of Christ at the end of the tribulation:

*1Th 3:12 And the Lord make you to increase and abound in love one toward another, and toward all men, even as we do toward you:*
*13 To the end he may stablish your hearts unblameable in holiness before God, even our Father, at the coming of our Lord Jesus Christ* **with** *all his saints.*

In chapter four, as just discussed above, we are dealing with the general rapture of the Church at the middle of the tribulation. Then, in chapter five, we see the pre-tribulation rapture of those saints who are not in darkness about that day:

*1Th 5:1 But of the times and the seasons, brethren, ye have no need that I write unto you.*
*2 For yourselves know perfectly that the day of the Lord so cometh as a thief in the night.*
*3 For when they shall say, Peace and safety; then sudden destruction cometh upon them, as travail upon a woman with child; and they shall not escape.*
*4 But ye, brethren, are not in darkness, that that day should overtake you as a thief.*

Now, putting this all together in chronological order rather than chapter order, we find a perfectly logical flow of the three events as follows:

*1Th 5:1 But of the times and the seasons, brethren, ye have no need that I write unto you.*
*2 For yourselves know perfectly that **the day of the Lord so cometh as a thief in the night**.*
*3 For when they shall say, Peace and safety; then sudden destruction cometh upon them, as travail upon a woman with child; and they shall not escape.*
*4 But ye, brethren, are not in darkness, that that day should overtake you as a thief.*
*5 Ye are all the children of light, and the children of the day: we are not of the night, nor of darkness.*
*6 Therefore let us not sleep, as do others; **but let us watch and be sober**.*

*9 For God hath not appointed us to wrath, but to obtain salvation by our Lord Jesus Christ,*
*10 Who died for us, that, **whether we wake or sleep**, we should live together with him.*

*1Th 4:13 But I would not have you to be ignorant, brethren**, concerning them which are asleep**, that ye sorrow not, even as others which have no hope.*
*14 For if we believe that Jesus died and rose again, even so them also which sleep in Jesus will God bring with him.*
*15 For this we say unto you by the word of the Lord, that **we which are alive and remain** unto the coming of the Lord shall not prevent them which are asleep.*
*16 For the Lord himself shall descend from heaven with a shout, with the voice of the archangel, and with the trump of God: and the dead in Christ shall rise first:*

*17 Then **we which are alive and remain** shall be caught up together with them in the clouds, to meet the Lord in the air: and so shall we ever be with the Lord. 18 Wherefore comfort one another with these words.*

*1Th 3:12 And the Lord make you to increase and abound in love one toward another, and toward all men, even as we do toward you:*
*13 To the end he may stablish your hearts unblameable in holiness before God, even our Father, at the coming of our Lord Jesus Christ **with** all his saints.*

When the passage is put together like this, we find three comings of the Lord Jesus Christ. In 5:2 above, He comes as a Thief (compare to 1 Peter 3:10) **for** His saints that are watching (not in darkness), then in verses 4:15-17 we see Him coming **for** His saints, both the dead and those which are alive **and remain**, and finally in 3:13 we find Him coming **with** His saints.

Finally, much is made of the fact that we will meet the Lord in the air according to 1 Thessalonians 4:17. Many prophecy experts contend that this means that the Lord never sets His feet on the ground and thus this passage cannot be tied to Revelation chapters 10-11. That is simply not deducible from this passage. Verse 16 tells us the Lord descended. From the description of this descent in Revelation 11:1-2, I see that He set His feet on the Earth and the sea. The simple explanation is that after calling His Church and the resurrected saints from the grave, the Lord will ascend and bring His saints with Him. He will lead, ascending first, and then the saints will be caught up to meet Him in the air.

# Chapter 10. Anticipation, or...

## (How to Watch for the Coming of the Lord)

So, now we come to the final chapter of the book. It's not the end of the world, but you can see it from here.

You may have noticed by now that we have seen a number of verses that instruct us to watch for the return of our Lord. Some are quite simply stated such as:

*Mar 13:37 And what I say unto you I say unto all, Watch.*

This is not advice or a suggestion. It is spoken in the imperative mood. It is a command. In fact, if you parse out the overall tone of the New Testament Epistles, you will find that we are expected to know the very day and hour of our Lord's return. I will quote again the two most instructive verses on the subject. You MUST get this.

The DAY:

*1Th 5:4 But ye, brethren, are not in darkness, that that day should overtake you as a thief.*

The HOUR:

*Rev 3:3 Remember therefore how thou hast received and heard, and hold fast, and repent. If therefore thou shalt not watch, I will come on thee as a thief, and thou shalt not know what hour I will come upon thee.*

Reverse the polarity (negative to positive and positive to negative) of that second verse to see more clearly what our Lord is saying. Remember these verses as we go through this chapter. These tell us that the most important way to watch for our Lord is to determine where we are in time.

**The date-setter dilemma**

There have been many dates proposed for the return of the Lord. Some for His return at the end of the tribulation and some for a pre-trib rapture. Some famous and historic names are on the list of prophets such as Hippolytus of Rome and Irenaeus who called out 500 AD for the second coming of Christ. Pope Sylvester II predicted 1/1/1000. Sir Isaac Newton supported the year 2000 AD and John Wesley said it would happen in 1836. There are many more recent additions to the list who gained wide followings because of their predictions. Some of these are:

William Miller said the Lord was coming October 22, 1844. He took Bible prophecies that talked about the sanctuary and misapplied them to the second coming.

The Jehovah's Witnesses chose 1914.

Herbert W. Armstrong chose 1935, 1943, 1972, and 1975, obviously failing each time.

Harold Camping prophesied 9/6/1994, and later, 3/21/2011 and 10/21/2011.

Jack Van Impe made too many predictions to enumerate.

Ronald Weinland just had a big miss in the last year. He predicted June 9, 2019.

There are still a number of predictions for the future including one of interest. The late Dr. F. Kenton Beshore has predicted 2021 based on the same reasoning we have presented in this book.

Hal Lindsey wrote several books on the subject and gave his opinion that Christ would return in the 1980's. Thousands got excited, but it didn't happen. Today, Lindsey still has a TV program where he explains prophecy. Edgar C. Whisenant came along and distributed (with the help of a wealthy benefactor) 4.5 million copies of his booklet "*88 Reasons Why the Lord Is Going to Come by 1988*". This was probably the peak of the rapture fever, although it continued well into the 1990's. I had recently become a Christian, so naturally I bought the book. I learned a lot of great scriptural truths from the book but ultimately, I could not accept his premise. Perhaps this was influential in my personal obsession with the subject ever since.

The upshot of all of this was that Christians who believed these modern-day prophets were badly disappointed. Even worse, they were mocked by other Christians and the world in general. With recent predictions becoming so plentiful, they started being reported on the national news in the USA. The news networks carefully and disdainfully pointed out each failure.

The result of all this was that Christian leadership of every stripe felt humiliated and belittled. The mantra became, "We mustn't be date-setters". No one in the Church is vilified and put down more forcefully than a date-setter. Many of these predictions for the second coming of Christ were made by Godly, well-intentioned men. But they were wrong. They made themselves into false prophets. You can only imagine the personal pain some felt when they realized that.

This is the environment that the prophet Elijah will face when he comes to prepare the way of the Lord. There was never a more urgent need for discernment of truth than the time we are in. Satan has used every wrong prediction to his advantage. He has now set the Church up for failure to accept the true prophet of God when he arrives. So, now we need to know what to watch for in order to discern the truth at the right time. Here it comes.

The Russian invasion of Israel, and especially their entry into Jerusalem, has to be the number one sign to watch for with regard to the rapture. We saw in chapter 5 of this book that the rapture occurs precisely at the time that God's fury comes up in His face. A second method we determined for watching purposes was to understand the parable of the fig tree in Matthew 24:32-35. Thirdly, we also determined that there is a high probability that Elijah will return and tell us the date. Unfortunately, because of the rapture fever of the mid to late 1900's date-setting has become anathema to much of the Church. Thus, he will likely be soundly rejected by even the most conservative pastors and churches.

There is one more way to watch and judge the nearness of Christ's return. That is to look at Israel's neighbors and the way they will interact. We will find this means we need to watch world news very closely. So, let's get into a rather fun and interesting final chapter. Beyond these excellent points to watch for, there are many more ways to determine where we are in time. We will run through several of these.

**The day = millennium method of counting time.**

Although succeeding dispensations have existed over various lengths of time given in the scriptures, there is another, somewhat cryptic method of counting time in the Bible. We will call this the day/millennium method. The important verses for this method are:

*2Pe 3:8 But, beloved, be not ignorant of this one thing, that one day is with the Lord as a thousand years, and a thousand years as one day.*

*Psa 90:4 For a thousand years in thy sight are but as yesterday when it is past, and as a watch in the night.*

The Bible gives plenty of information regarding time spans for various events. If you will do a count of these times you will find that it is possible to account for all the time up to the death of Jesus on the cross with the exception of the time between the end of the Babylonian captivity of Israel and the 7th year of Artaxerxes, king of Persia. Fortunately, secular history seems to be reasonably reliable for this period and gives us a probable time span of 81 years. Putting all the time spans together, we can find a likely birth time for Christ at about 4000 years from creation.

Adding the approximately 2000 years since the birth of Christ we arrive at a present time of about 6000 years from creation. We know from Revelation chapter 20 that there is still a 1000-year millennial reign of Christ remaining to the history of this present Earth. If we are very close to the start of the millennium, then we could postulate just about 7000 years or 7 millennia of total history for this creation.

The final millennium has been referred to in the scriptures as the day of the Lord and as a day of rest for the people of God (see Heb. 4:1-11). If that millennium is the seventh millennium, then we find that just as there were 7 days of creation ending with a day of rest sanctified by God, there are 7 millennia of history ending with a millennial day of rest sanctified and ruled over by God the Son. In this system, we apply 1000 years of history for each day of creation.

Takeaway? The pre-trib rapture is at the door!

Applying this 1000-year day to many scriptures using these postulations produces some very interesting prophetic possibilities. These scriptures seem to confirm that this system is intended by God to be used to understand the timing of the second coming of Christ. We will examine just a couple of these. You can watch for this application in other passages.

*Hos 5:15 I will go and return to my place, till they acknowledge their offence, and seek my face: in their affliction they will seek me early.*

*Hos 6:1 Come, and let us return unto the LORD: for he hath torn, and he will heal us; he hath smitten, and he will bind us up.*
*2 After two days will he revive us: in the third day he will raise us up, and we shall live in his sight.*

Using our thousand-year day scenario we see here a cryptic statement to the effect that Christ returned to heaven after being rejected by His people (verse 5:15). In 70 AD Jerusalem was sacked and Israel was eventually driven out of the land (verse 6:1), thus torn and smitten. If this is prophecy, then from verse 6:2 we can conclude that after 2000 years (2 days) God will heal and revive the nation of Israel. Indeed, we are now about 2000 years removed from that time and Israel is once again gathering together in the promised land. After that they will live in His sight under His physical, earthly 1000-year (third day) reign. This passage seems almost to require such a system in order to be meaningful.

*Mat 17:1 And after six days Jesus taketh Peter, James, and John his brother, and bringeth them up into an high mountain apart,*
*2 And was transfigured before them: and his face did shine as the sun, and his raiment was white as the light.*

This passage can be viewed as prophesying that Jesus will appear in His glory to reign on Earth after 6000 years of history. There are more of these little hints that imply events at thousand-year marks over 7 thousand total years of history. A few of these you can check out are Mark 14:58, Luke 2:46, Luke 13:32, John 2:1 (the marriage supper of the Lamb), John 2:19, and John 4:40.

Using this theory, we can understand a couple of scriptures that otherwise would seem to support the preterist storyline that almost all prophecies were fulfilled by the end of the first century AD. Consider this scripture:

*Heb 1:1 God, who at sundry times and in divers manners spake in time past unto the fathers by the prophets,*
*2 Hath in these last days spoken unto us by his Son, whom he hath appointed heir of all things, by whom also he made the worlds;*

This first century writing claims to be written in the last days. If Jesus arrived on Earth at 4000 years from creation and at the start of the fifth day of seven, then all the days after the fourth day can logically be called the last days. The implication here is that there were the first three days, the middle fourth day, and the three last days of the total of seven days. This also applies to the following scripture:

*1Pe 1:18 Forasmuch as ye know that ye were not redeemed with corruptible things, as silver and gold, from your vain conversation received by tradition from your fathers;*
*19 But with the precious blood of Christ, as of a lamb without blemish and without spot:*
*20 Who verily was foreordained before the foundation of the world, but was manifest in these last times for you,*

Peter called his era "these last times". Here again, if there are 7000 years of history, then all the times after the first four thousand years are the last times. Also see Acts 2:16-17.

Again, in Hebrews we see this pattern of the end of time holding:

*Heb 9:25 Nor yet that he should offer himself often, as the high priest entereth into the holy place every year with blood of others;*
*26 For then must he often have suffered since the foundation of the world:* **but now once in the end of the world hath he appeared** *to put away sin by the sacrifice of himself.*
*27 And as it is appointed unto men once to die, but after this the judgment:*
*28 So Christ was once offered to bear the sins of many; and unto them that look for him shall he appear the second time without sin unto salvation.*


Another biblical demonstration of this day/millennium method is found in the life of Adam. God told Adam that in the day he ate of the fruit of the tree of knowledge of good and evil he would surely die. Adam ate of the fruit and died when he was 930 years old. God took Adam before the 1000-year day had expired.

Finally, and perhaps the most compelling for Christians, we read in Hebrews:

*Heb 4:3 For we which have believed do enter into rest, as he said, As I have sworn in my wrath, if they shall enter into my rest: although the works were finished from the foundation of the world.*

*4 For he spake in a certain place of the seventh day on this wise, And God did rest the seventh day from all his works.*

*5 And in this place again, If they shall enter into my rest.*

*6 Seeing therefore it remaineth that some must enter therein, and they to whom it was first preached entered not in because of unbelief:*

*7 Again, he limiteth a certain day, saying in David, To day, after so long a time; as it is said, To day if ye will hear his voice, harden not your hearts.*

*8 For if Jesus had given them rest, then would he not afterward have spoken of another day.*

*9 There remaineth therefore a rest to the people of God.*

Clearly, we are not talking about a 24-hour seventh day here. This day had been available down through the earlier ages but could not be instituted because of the unbelief of God's chosen people. Remember, Hebrews was written after the first four thousand years, so the offer had moved to the seventh day by that point. So, now it is available to all people of God which includes the Gentiles. We find ourselves now, after 6000 years of history, on the verge of entering the seventh millennium as a day of rest. This works out so perfectly that you have to suspect it was planned in advance. Hmmm.

**One 'watch' = millennium method**

Psalm 90:4 says further that 1000 years are "as a watch in the night". The Jewish day and night are divided into four watches each. The night, averaging winter and summer, starts nominally at 6:00 PM and a new watch starts every three hours until 6:00 AM. Thus, 12:00 midnight is literally the middle of the night. Similarly, 12:00 noon is midday. There is good internal evidence for a watch/age theory as well as a day/age theory.

Consider Job 38:4-7 which tells us that at the creation the morning stars all sang together. If creation occurred at 6:00 AM of the first watch of the day, and Jesus came 4000 years later, His coming would correspond to 6:00 PM or suppertime. Now look at the parable in Luke 14:16-24 where Jesus offers the kingdom to the Jews. Notice that this indeed occurs at supper time, but that supper must be held up until different people can be invited in two forays. If it took two more watches (6 hours or 2000 years) to collect the new invitees, the supper would finally be eaten at midnight. This corresponds to the parable of Jesus' second coming in Matt. 25:1-13 in which the bridegroom comes at midnight. According to the book of Revelation, the marriage supper occurs just before the millennium and shortly after the final rapture of the Elect (Rev 19:6-11).

In John 9:4-5 Jesus said:

*Joh 9:4 I must work the works of him that sent me, while it is day: the night cometh, when no man can work.*
*5 As long as I am in the world, I am the light of the world.*

Jesus indicated that it was still daytime when He was here because He is the light of the world. According to Malachi 4:2, Jesus is the SUN of righteousness. Jesus went on to explain that no man can work (that is please God by obeying the system of law) in the coming night. The Church Age is the age where the final all sufficient sacrifice has already been made once for all time. Thus, we can see that the current age when works of the law are no longer required is the night that Jesus spoke of. Using this system, we see that this age would end after two watches or 2000 years at midnight. Thus, according to the watch/age theory Jesus returns after 6000 total years of history, and 2000 years after His first advent.

The takeaway? The pre-trib rapture is almost here!

These two ideas are by no means incontrovertible doctrine. They are interesting, however, in that both seem to indicate 6000 years of history before Christ's millennial reign. There is plenty of indication that this is an intentional code in the scripture.

**The three appearances of God in the flesh.**

Another way to look at the division of the ages can be found in the appearances of God in the flesh upon the Earth. These appearances all come at the beginning of a significant change in God's dealings with man. They mark the eras from creation to Abraham, from Abraham to the first coming of Jesus Christ, and from Jesus' first coming to His second coming. The first two periods each lasted 2000 years and it seems very likely that the last period will end after about 2000 years. This is yet another indication of 6000 years of history before Christ's millennial reign. Consider the following:

God is a tripartite Being and the number three can almost be viewed as the signature of God on the masterpiece of creation. The Godhead is composed of the Father, the

Son, and the Holy Ghost.  We, being made in His image are composed of a body, a soul and a spirit.  In fact, God Himself is composed of a Body, a Soul, and a Spirit where the Body is associated with the Son, the Spirit is associated with the Holy Ghost, and the Soul is associated with God the Father.  God is also described as being omnipotent, omniscient, and omnipresent.

God's signature can be seen in creation.  To review, the universe is composed of space, matter, and time.  Space is further described by three dimensions - length, width, and height.  Matter is further composed of solids, liquids, and gases.  Finally, time is further reckoned as past, present, and future.

God's signature can also be seen in His dealings with man.  He ordained three offices by which He dealt with His people Israel.  He chose their prophets, their priests, and their kings.  When our Lord reigns in the flesh through the millennium, He will hold every one of these offices and thus have no legal need to defer to others in executing every office of government.  We will here discover how He will come to obtain these three offices.

About 2000 years ago, God sent His only begotten Son into the world as the Prophet of Nazareth named Jesus.  If you are a Bible literalist, you will have to place this event at about 4000 years after creation.  Moses prophesied that He would come as a Prophet in Deut. 18:18, and Jesus Himself confirmed that He was indeed a prophet in Matt. 13:37.

It was prophesied that he also would be a high priest forever after the order of Melchizedek in Psalm 110:4 and confirmed in Hebrews 6:20:

*"Whither the forerunner is for us entered, even Jesus, made an high priest forever after the order of Melchisedec."*

This raises some very interesting questions. Who was Melchizedek and what was so special about him that our Lord would take His priesthood after him? Melchizedek was first mentioned in the Bible in Genesis 14:18-20. After Abraham had rescued Lot from Chederlaomer and his allies, he gave tithes of all he recovered to Melchizedek who was king of Salem and the priest of the most high God. Interestingly, Melchizedek brought forth bread and wine – the very elements by which we remember our Lord's body and blood in the ordinance of the Lord's Supper. Another interesting tidbit is that Salem is generally believed to be the same city as Jerusalem. Melchizedek is mentioned only one more time in the Old Testament in the prophecy of Psalm 110:4.

If this were the last mention of Melchizedek, he would have to be classified as a minor character indeed. However, the book of Hebrews devotes the better part of two chapters comparing him to Christ and makes some very intriguing comments about him. Melchisedec turns out to be a very enigmatic character. Let's look at Hebrews 5:5-11:

*Heb 5:5 So also Christ glorified not himself to be made an high priest; but he that said unto him, Thou art my Son, to day have I begotten thee.*

*6 As he saith also in another place, Thou art a priest for ever after the order of Melchisedec.
7 Who in the days of his flesh, when he had offered up prayers and supplications with strong crying and tears unto him that was able to save him from death, and was heard in that he feared;
8 Though he were a Son, yet learned he obedience by the things which he suffered;
9 And being made perfect, he became the author of eternal salvation unto all them that obey him;
10 Called of God an high priest after the order of Melchisedec.
11 Of whom we have many things to say, and hard to be uttered, seeing ye are dull of hearing.*

Notice that after being proven perfect in obedience in verse 9 Christ was 'promoted' to high priest in verse 10. This was necessary because according to Exo. 30:10, Heb. 2:17, and Heb. 9:7, only the high priest can make the sin offering for all the people. In verse 11 we begin to see that there is more to Melchisedec than meets the eye.

In Hebrews 7:1-4a we begin to get an even clearer picture of Melchisedec:

*Heb 7:1 For this Melchisedec, king of Salem, priest of the most high God, who met Abraham returning from the slaughter of the kings, and blessed him;
2 To whom also Abraham gave a tenth part of all; first being by interpretation King of righteousness, and after that also King of Salem, which is, King of peace;
3 Without father, without mother, without descent, having neither beginning of days, nor end of life; but made like unto the Son of God; abideth a priest continually.
4 Now consider how great this man was,*

Since God instructs us to consider how great this man was, we will obediently do that now. Looking at verse 3, we find that there are several amazing facts about this man.

He had NO FATHER;

He had NO MOTHER;

He had NO DESCENT;

He had NO BEGINNING OF DAYS – he was immortal;

He had NO END OF LIFE – he is immortal;

He was made LIKE UNTO THE SON OF GOD – he has the same attributes as the Lord Jesus Christ.

Hebrews chapter 7 goes on to explain in verses 11-28 that Jesus could not possibly take His Priesthood from the Aaronic line because those priests were weak and imperfect, and they administered an imperfect system. God can never be associated with imperfection and still maintain His Godhood. God's Priesthood must come from a perfect line and therefore Melchisedec had to be perfect. God could not take His Priesthood from a lesser or inferior being either. That would cheapen the Godhead as well. THEREFORE, WE MUST CONCLUDE THAT MELCHISEDEC WAS GOD HIMSELF, COME IN THE FLESH!!

The verses we looked at above stress that Melchisedec is eternal. Since God above claims to be one God (in three persons) and the only eternal being, we are left with no choice other than to assign to Melchisedec one of the persons of the Godhead. And, as the physical representation of the Godhead, that person can be none other than the Son of God, Jesus Christ. This is disputed by many in the Church, but the scriptures allow for no other possibility. At this point, I want to insert a couple passages where JEHOVAH Himself speaks to His uniqueness. Not because we need further proof, but just because they are fascinating to contemplate.

*Isa 44:6 Thus saith the LORD the King of Israel, and his redeemer the LORD of hosts; I am the first, and I am the last; and beside me there is no God.*

*7 And who, as I, shall call, and shall declare it, and set it in order for me, since I appointed the ancient people? and the things that are coming, and shall come, let them shew unto them.*

*8 Fear ye not, neither be afraid: have not I told thee from that time, and have declared it? ye are even my witnesses.* **Is there a God beside me? yea, there is no God; I know not any.**

*Isa 43:10 Ye are my witnesses, saith the LORD, and my servant whom I have chosen: that ye may know and believe me, and understand that I am he:* **before me there was no God formed, neither shall there be after me.**

*11 I, even I, am the LORD; and beside me there is no saviour.*

One more important fact to point out about Melchisedec is that, as a contemporary of Abraham, he would have been living on Earth at about the 2000-year point from creation. This would have been about 2000 years before the advent of Jesus Christ. The Apostle John, in his gospel, reported Jesus' words:

*Joh 8:56 Your father Abraham rejoiced to see my day: and he saw it, and was glad.*
*57 Then said the Jews unto him, Thou art not yet fifty years old, and hast thou seen Abraham?*
*58 Jesus said unto them, Verily, verily, I say unto you, Before Abraham was, I am.*

Abraham did indeed rejoice to see the Lord's Day. He saw Him in the flesh as Melchizedek and paid tithes to Him on his spoils of war.

We see then, that our Lord has lived among us and earned the titles of Prophet and High Priest. According to the prophecy of Rev. 19:11-13, 16, He is coming again with the title of King of kings:

*Rev 19:11 And I saw heaven opened, and behold a white horse; and he that sat upon him was called Faithful and True, and in righteousness he doth judge and make war.*
*12 His eyes were as a flame of fire, and on his head were many crowns; and he had a name written, that no man knew, but he himself.*
*13 And he was clothed with a vesture dipped in blood: and his name is called The Word of God.*

*Rev 19:16 And he hath on his vesture and on his thigh a name written, KING OF KINGS, AND LORD OF LORDS.*

You should note in verse 12 that He has a name that, up to that point, no man knew. It is after this appearance that our Lord will set up His Final Kingdom and literally and bodily reign as King over all the Earth. From this point on, He will dwell among His people.

So, we see that God has a program that includes living among men in the flesh on three occasions. He came the first time at 2000 years from creation as a man named Melchizedec and obtained the office of High Priest. He came the second time at 4000 years from creation as a man named Jesus at which time, He obtained the office of Prophet. He's coming one more time at ???? years from creation under a name that no man yet knows, at which time He will obtain the office of King of kings and set up an everlasting Kingdom of righteousness and peace and joy in the Holy Ghost.

Our takeaway? We have arrived at the pre-trib rapture!

God's signature on creation is in the number three. To this point, our Lord has come twice at 2000-year intervals, taking us up to 4000 years from creation. If He were to continue that progression, then we should see His third appearance in the flesh at the 6000-year mark from creation. That means we should then expect His coming very soon - probably in the next few months or years.

So, we have yet another internal biblical indication that the time of the Thief rapture is at hand. In chapter 5 and verse 8 of his epistle James wrote: **"Be ye also patient; stablish your hearts: for the coming of the Lord draweth nigh."**

If His coming was close 2000 years ago, where are we now? You may only have a short time to make a difference in the growth of the Kingdom of God. What will you do about it?

To this point, we have dealt with several interesting but quite general indicators of the timeframe we find ourselves in. In the next section, we will drill down a little more by examining the relationships between Israel and the nations in the last days.

First, there is a very important point to make in this discussion. It has become very fashionable to tie every detail of prophecy to Jewish feast days. This has come about because many Messianic Jews have succeeded in convincing both Jew and Christian that, having been raised in the Jewish tradition and familiarity with the Hebrew language, gives them a distinct advantage. They have been able to, in many cases, intimidate other Christians with their special knowledge and understanding. Thus, they have been able to draw many admirers and followers using a fortuitous circumstance. However, I would hearken back to a famous Jew, Peter the Apostle, who wrote:

*2Pe 1:20 Knowing this first, that no prophecy of the scripture is of any private interpretation.*

So, here are a couple questions. Which feast day was Jesus born on? Which feast day did Jesus begin His public ministry on? If you offer one, do you have proof? This could go on for a while. Folks, everything isn't tied to a feast day. In fact, when Jesus came the first time, his coming was tied to a **secular** event. Daniel was told Messiah would appear 483 years after a future decree to restore and build Jerusalem. This turned out to be the decree of Artaxerxes to Ezra. It was not tied to anything peculiarly Jewish at all, although it impacted the Jewish people. Likewise, His second coming seems to be tied to a **secular**, United Nations, decree to legally and formally reinstitute the nation by May 14, 1948 (5 Lyyar, 5708 at midnight on the Jewish calendar)!

Those of us who will be taken in the pre-tribulation rapture may not be concerned with Israel beyond that point, but it would be helpful to know what to watch for up to that point in time. We will confine the rest of this chapter mostly to events we may be privileged to watch.

### The prophesied end-times characters and alliances are now taking their places.

It is the belief of this author that all these things point to the Thief rapture within just a very few years or months. If that is true, then many of the end-times characters are likely already in place. Thus, we can legitimately begin to wonder: Is Vladimir Putin of Russia, Gog? Is el-Sisi in Egypt the king of the south, the final Pharaoh? Is Ayatollah Khamenei in Iran the final king of the north as well as the latter-day Nebuchadnezzar? Only time will tell, but such considerations are now legitimate. So, next I will enumerate several prophesied events and then present the scriptural support for them. I hope you will look it up or take my word for it that every passage has internal indications that they are dealing with end-times events although they may not appear in the quoted text.

Here is a quick rundown of the events we will look at next. Immediately after the defeat of Gog, another leader will rise up and conquer many nations. This leader is variously referred to as the king of the north, or the last days Nebuchadnezzar, or the king of Babylon. He is almost assuredly a Shiite Muslim and probably intent on setting up a worldwide Muslim Caliphate. Egypt will eventually oppose him and begin marching toward his land. The king of the north will meet the last days Pharaoh in the land of Israel and totally destroy him. In addition, he will destroy the Sunni Muslim land of Egypt with nuclear weapons such that the foot of neither man nor beast will be able to pass through the land for 40 years. (Ezekiel chap. 29).

This last days Nebuchadnezzar will not further attack Israel nor will he try to take the lands that Israel has won but he will treat them as his possessions. He will set the tabernacle of his palaces in the temple mount and will commit a transgression of desolation there. He may only last a little over seven months into the tribulation before he is killed. This information can be gleaned from Daniel chapters 8 and 11. With that brief overview, we can turn our attention to what will occur between the present and the Gog attack.

Since 1948 there have been many attacks on Israel. They have all ended badly for the attacker just as it will for Gog. These wars are all well documented and most amazing for how quickly and completely Israel overcame huge odds time and again to win each conflict. Israel has captured land from the aggressors in these wars and used some of this land to make for more defensible borders. This practice will greatly increase prior to the tribulation.

It seems likely that the next territories Israel will annex are those of the present-day Palestinians. The present-day

Palestinians currently occupy lands formerly held by the Canaanites and the Philistines, sometimes called the Cherethites, and other peoples and tribes. They included such cities as Gaza, Ashkelon, Ekron, Ashdod, and Gath. These names are all used in various prophecies to identify the Palestinians of our day.

At the same time, Israel will capture the West Bank and most of present-day Jordan. The national names for the ancient nations found in Jordan are (from south to north) Edom, sometimes denoted as Idumea, Moab, and Ammon. In His foreknowledge, God has grouped these three ancient nations together in many passages. The very ground itself will sometimes be destroyed in these lands. The descriptions in the Bible include terminology such as "the breeding of nettles, and saltpits, and a perpetual desolation".

Also, at this time, Lebanon will be captured including the cities of Tyre and Sidon. We see then that most of the nations that directly border Israel will be defeated and their land claimed by Israel. This will amount to a huge land grab and will infuriate many of the rest of the nations of the world. All of these nations currently have high hopes that Israel will one day be wiped off the face of the Earth or driven into the sea. Here's how God says it will go:

*Mic 4:11 Now also many nations are gathered against thee, that say, Let her be defiled, and let our eye look upon Zion.*
*12 But they know not the thoughts of the LORD, neither understand they his counsel: for he shall gather them as the sheaves into the floor.*

*13 Arise and thresh, O daughter of Zion: for I will make thine horn iron, and I will make thy hoofs brass: and thou shalt beat in pieces many people: and I will consecrate their gain unto the LORD, and their substance unto the Lord of the whole earth.*

We will examine several prophecies that lock down the timeframe for this campaign. In several cases, the language of the passage indicates that it occurs when the Day of the Lord is very close. We have already established that there will be a pre-tribulation rapture for the church which will not occur until immediately prior to, or concurrent with, the start of the tribulation. Therefore, the church will be around to see these next events take place. We will start with Obadiah's account:

*Oba 1:15 For the day of the LORD is near upon all the heathen: as thou hast done, it shall be done unto thee: thy reward shall return upon thine own head.*
*16 For as ye have drunk upon my holy mountain, so shall all the heathen drink continually, yea, they shall drink, and they shall swallow down, and they shall be as though they had not been.*
*17 But upon mount Zion shall be deliverance, and there shall be holiness; and the house of Jacob shall possess their possessions.*
*18 And the house of Jacob shall be a fire, and the house of Joseph a flame, and the house of Esau for stubble, and they shall kindle in them, and devour them; and there shall not be any remaining of the house of Esau; for the LORD hath spoken it.*
*19 And they of the south shall possess the mount of Esau; and they of the plain the Philistines: and they shall possess the fields of Ephraim, and the fields of Samaria: and Benjamin shall possess Gilead.*

*20 And the captivity of this host of the children of Israel shall possess that of the Canaanites, even unto Zarephath; and the captivity of Jerusalem, which is in Sepharad, shall possess the cities of the south.*

Less than half of the Jews in the world now live in Israel. Scriptures declare in many passages that all Jews will return to their ancient homeland over time. As the passage indicates, these campaigns will open up more land area to support the return of the Jewish people. Anti-Semitism is growing worldwide at an alarming rate, even, and maybe especially, in the more liberal wing of the Church. Although many terrible events will occur to Israel, it is likely that a Jew will still be safer in his God-given land than anywhere else in the world. We can garner much more from the prophet Zephaniah's account:

*Zep 1:14 The great day of the LORD is near, it is near, and hasteth greatly, even the voice of the day of the LORD: the mighty man shall cry there bitterly.*

*Zep 2:1 Gather yourselves together, yea, gather together, O nation not desired;*
*2 Before the decree bring forth, before the day pass as the chaff, before the fierce anger of the LORD come upon you, before the day of the LORD'S anger come upon you.*
*3 Seek ye the LORD, all ye meek of the earth, which have wrought his judgment; seek righteousness, seek meekness: it may be ye shall be hid in the day of the LORD'S anger.*

This portion of the passage implores the nation not desired, Israel, to return to the homeland before the day of the Lord starts. It then makes an appeal to all the meek of the Earth to seek righteousness and meekness. The reward is a possibility of being hid in the day of the Lord's anger. This part of the appeal is not to Jews only, but to all the Earth. This is the event we call the pre-tribulation rapture. Next, the passage describes the state of many of the nations we are presently discussing. As you can see, Israel has already crushed these nations by the time this rapture occurs.

*Zep 2:4 For Gaza shall be forsaken, and Ashkelon a desolation: they shall drive out Ashdod at the noon day, and Ekron shall be rooted up.*
*5 Woe unto the inhabitants of the sea coast, the nation of the Cherethites! the word of the LORD is against you; O Canaan, the land of the Philistines, I will even destroy thee, that there shall be no inhabitant.*
*6 And the sea coast shall be dwellings and cottages for shepherds, and folds for flocks.*
*7 And the coast shall be for the remnant of the house of Judah; they shall feed thereupon: in the houses of Ashkelon shall they lie down in the evening: for the LORD their God shall visit them, and turn away their captivity.*
*8 I have heard the reproach of Moab, and the revilings of the children of Ammon, whereby they have reproached my people, and magnified themselves against their border.*
*9 Therefore as I live, saith the LORD of hosts, the God of Israel, Surely Moab shall be as Sodom, and the children of Ammon as Gomorrah, even the breeding of nettles, and saltpits, and a perpetual desolation: the residue of my people shall spoil them, and the remnant of my people shall possess them.*

According to verse 5 above, the Philistines, or Palestinians of today, will be completely driven out or killed. The land will be available for population as Jews continue to return to the homeland into the tribulation according to verse 6 and 7. Zechariah 10:6-10 makes a very similar statement and references Gilead in Jordan and Lebanon to the lands that Israel will conquer as more Jews return. The following passage also establishes that Lebanon will fall at the same time that the Palestinians are destroyed:

*Jer 47:4 Because of the day that cometh to spoil all the Philistines, and to cut off from Tyrus and Zidon every helper that remaineth: for the LORD will spoil the Philistines, the remnant of the country of Caphtor.*
*5 Baldness is come upon Gaza; Ashkelon is cut off with the remnant of their valley: how long wilt thou cut thyself?*
*6 O thou sword of the LORD, how long will it be ere thou be quiet? put up thyself into thy scabbard, rest, and be still.*
*7 How can it be quiet, seeing the LORD hath given it a charge against Ashkelon, and against the sea shore? there hath he appointed it.*

**The Lake of Fire will break through the surface of the Earth.**

A fascinating special case is made for Edom, sometimes identified with the land of Idumea. Some of the major cities cited in these lands were Bozrah, Sela (Petra), and Teman. The descriptions of this area into eternity are very reminiscent of the Lake of Fire. This possibility has been brought forth by others but is worthy of discussion here in light of what we may infer from this about our final state. This area will ultimately include much of Iraq and Jordan

It is not hard to imagine a scenario that could trigger the Lake of Fire coming to the surface. We will establish in this chapter that the latter days king of the north will almost certainly have nuclear weapons. Also, it is very possible that this latter-day Nebuchadnezzar will rule Iran. So, if Iran fires a nuclear tipped missile at Israel and misses or it is deflected, it just might land in present-day southern Jordan. It is possible there could be a topographic situation there that would split open the crust of the Earth and allow a lake of magma to rise to the surface. I can't speak to the nuclear fallout issue, but maybe something can be figured out for that.

There is one more possibility of note. Consider this fascinating passage:

*Isa 63:1 Who is this that cometh from Edom, with dyed garments from Bozrah? this that is glorious in his apparel, travelling in the greatness of his strength? I that speak in righteousness, mighty to save.*

*2 Wherefore art thou red in thine apparel, and thy garments like him that treadeth in the winefat?*

*3 I have trodden the winepress alone; and of the people there was none with me: for I will tread them in mine anger, and trample them in my fury; and their blood shall be sprinkled upon my garments, and I will stain all my raiment.*

*4 For the day of vengeance is in mine heart, and the year of my redeemed is come.*

In this passage we find the Lord asking and answering His own questions. It appears here that He will, at some point, personally come to Bozrah and turn that area into perpetual wastes. So, that might be the simplest explanation as to how the Lake of Fire will be brought to the surface of the earth! This possibility is further strengthened by the statement: *"For the day of vengeance is in mine heart, and the year of my redeemed is come"*. This is the day of the LORD! (See, for instance, Jer. 46:10.) So, we see that no matter what we see from our perspective, The Lord Himself will make the Lake of Fire happen in a very personal way when the day of the LORD is at hand, or near.

The following passage is long, but it has much to say about this matter:

*Isa 34:5 For my sword shall be bathed in heaven: behold, it shall come down upon Idumea, and upon the people of my curse, to judgment.*
*6 The sword of the LORD is filled with blood, it is made fat with fatness, and with the blood of lambs and goats, with the fat of the kidneys of rams: for the LORD hath a sacrifice in Bozrah, and a great slaughter in the land of Idumea.*
*7 And the unicorns shall come down with them, and the bullocks with the bulls; and their land shall be soaked with blood, and their dust made fat with fatness.*
*8 For it is the day of the LORD'S vengeance, and the year of recompences for the controversy of Zion.*
*9 And the streams thereof shall be turned into pitch, and the dust thereof into brimstone, and the land thereof shall become burning pitch.*
*10* **It shall not be quenched night nor day; the smoke thereof shall go up for ever***: from generation to generation it shall lie waste; none shall pass through it for ever and ever.*

Verses 9 and 10 here are reminiscent of several verses in Mark chapter 9:

Mar 9:43 *And if thy hand offend thee, cut it off: it is better for thee to enter into life maimed, than having two hands to go into hell, into **the fire that never shall be quenched**:*
*44 Where their worm dieth not, and the fire is not quenched.*

Continuing:

*Isa 34:11 But the cormorant and the bittern shall possess it; the owl also and the raven shall dwell in it: and he shall stretch out upon it the line of confusion, and the stones of emptiness.*
*12 They shall call the nobles thereof to the kingdom, but none shall be there, and all her princes shall be nothing.*
*13 And thorns shall come up in her palaces, nettles and brambles in the fortresses thereof: and it shall be an habitation of dragons, and a court for owls.*
*14 The wild beasts of the desert shall also meet with the wild beasts of the island, and the satyr shall cry to his fellow; the screech owl also shall rest there, and find for herself a place of rest.*
*15 There shall the great owl make her nest, and lay, and hatch, and gather under her shadow: there shall the vultures also be gathered, every one with her mate.*
*16 Seek ye out of the book of the LORD, and read: no one of these shall fail, none shall want her mate: for my mouth it hath commanded, and his spirit it hath gathered them.*
*17 And he hath cast the lot for them, and his hand hath divided it unto them by line: they shall possess it for ever, from generation to generation shall they dwell therein.*

Many of the animals mentioned in this passage are strongly associated with devils and servants of Satan. In fact, the satyr is a demi-god in mythology and doubtless a creation of Satan.

Most interestingly, there is such an area mentioned in proximity to the New Jerusalem on the eternal New Earth:

*Isa 66:22 For as the new heavens and the new earth, which I will make, shall remain before me, saith the LORD, so shall your seed and your name remain.
23 And it shall come to pass, that from one new moon to another, and from one sabbath to another, shall all flesh come to worship before me, saith the LORD.
24 And they shall go forth, and look upon the carcases of the men that have transgressed against me: for their worm shall not die, neither shall their fire be quenched; and they shall be an abhorring unto all flesh.*

In both the passage in Mark and this one in Isaiah, men in hell are likened to worms. This may be verified from a curious parable of Jesus:

*Mat 22:11 And when the king came in to see the guests, he saw there a man which had not on a wedding garment:
12 And he saith unto him, Friend, how camest thou in hither not having a wedding garment? And he was speechless.
13 Then said the king to the servants, Bind him hand and foot, and take him away, and cast him into outer darkness; there shall be weeping and gnashing of teeth.*

Here, a man is bound hand and foot before he is cast into hell. Now imagine billions of people bound hand and foot in a fluid medium. As they wriggle and writhe around would they not look like so many maggots or worms when seen from a height? I don't know at what level men will go forth from the New Jerusalem, but you should understand that, according to its description in the Bible, New Jerusalem will extend from the ground upwards for 1500 miles. You read that right. That's about 6 times higher than the International Space Station and about 1000 miles into the current Van Allen radiation belt. Finally, in the Revelation we find that sinners are outside the New Jerusalem on the re-created Earth.

*Rev 22:14 Blessed are they that do his commandments, that they may have right to the tree of life, and may enter in through the gates into the city.*
*15 For without are dogs, and sorcerers, and whoremongers, and murderers, and idolaters, and whosoever loveth and maketh a lie.*

Putting these verses together we see a distinct possibility that the lands of Idumea and Edom, and especially the city of Bozrah, along with much of Jordan and Iraq, may be the eternal site of the Lake of Fire. If you argue here that this seems a trivial exercise, you should consider how this vividly demonstrates the actuality of the doctrine of eternal damnation. Every word in His Book is given for a reason. There are no superfluous words in God's Book.

*Jer 49:13 For I have sworn by myself, saith the LORD, that Bozrah shall become a desolation, a reproach, a waste, and a curse; and all the cities thereof shall be perpetual wastes.*

*Jer 49:17 Also Edom shall be a desolation: every one that goeth by it shall be astonished, and shall hiss at all the plagues thereof.*
*18 As in the overthrow of Sodom and Gomorrah and the neighbour cities thereof, saith the LORD, no man shall abide there, neither shall a son of man dwell in it.*

In summary, this massive annexation of other lands into the nation of Israel will most likely occur just prior to the

Gog attack and probably, as we noted, be a primary driver for the Gog war. That war has the earmarks of a police action by the rest of the world for Israel's audacity. If the fig tree analogy is true, then these events should occur in the very near future. It is fascinating to watch as the current situation in each of these nations seems to be unfolding exactly according to Bible prophecies right before our eyes today.

There is another end-times prophecy that may have been unfolding before our eyes right now. This one has to do with the rise of the Daniel chapter 11's last days king of the south. We will demonstrate his rise to power prior to the tribulation here in order to tie all this together.

*Isa 19:1 The burden of Egypt. Behold, the LORD rideth upon a swift cloud, and shall come into Egypt: and the idols of Egypt shall be moved at his presence, and the heart of Egypt shall melt in the midst of it.*
*2 And I will set the Egyptians against the Egyptians: and they shall fight every one against his brother, and every one against his neighbour; city against city, and kingdom against kingdom.*
*3 And the spirit of Egypt shall fail in the midst thereof; and I will destroy the counsel thereof: and they shall seek to the idols, and to the charmers, and to them that have familiar spirits, and to the wizards.*
*4 And the Egyptians will I give over into the hand of a cruel lord; and a fierce king shall rule over them, saith the Lord, the LORD of hosts.*

Chapter 19 of Isaiah starts with the rise of the final king or Pharaoh of Egypt and ends with the healing of the land after nuclear destruction. Here is corroboration by Ezekiel.

*Eze 29:9 And the land of Egypt shall be desolate and waste; and they shall know that I am the LORD: because he hath said, The river is mine, and I have made it.*

*10 Behold, therefore I am against thee, and against thy rivers, and I will make the land of Egypt utterly waste and desolate, from the tower of Syene even unto the border of Ethiopia.*

*11 No foot of man shall pass through it, nor foot of beast shall pass through it, neither shall it be inhabited forty years.*

*12 And I will make the land of Egypt desolate in the midst of the countries that are desolate, and her cities among the cities that are laid waste shall be desolate forty years: and I will scatter the Egyptians among the nations, and will disperse them through the countries.*

*13 Yet thus saith the Lord GOD; At the end of forty years will I gather the Egyptians from the people whither they were scattered:*

*14 And I will bring again the captivity of Egypt, and will cause them to return into the land of Pathros, into the land of their habitation; and they shall be there a base kingdom.*

This will take until about 33 years into the millennial reign of Christ. In these first four verses of Isa. 19, we find civil unrest in the land that ends with the rise of a cruel and fierce king.

The overthrow of long-time strongman Hosni Mubarak and the events following the Arab Spring uprising in 2011 could possibly qualify as this event. Elections were held and a man named Mohammad Morsi was elected president. He then quickly changed leadership in his military to men he felt would be loyal to him. But his chief of staff, Abdel Fattah Saeed Hussein Khalil el-Sisi, ousted him in a bloody uprising and questionable election that left 1400 dead and 16,000 detained. Is this the civil unrest spoken of or is there a greater civil war to come in Egypt?

**Some guesses about how it will all happen.**

Putting it all together, and taking a few liberties of personal viewpoint, here is a possible scenario for the time between now and the start of the tribulation. We will start in Egypt where it is possible that the prophesied civil unrest has played out in the Arab Spring uprising that eventually led to a bloody coup. If this is the case, the final king of the South per Daniel chapter 11 would be el-Sisi.

It is quite obvious that the most powerful nation on Earth at this time, the United States of America, will be a non-factor in the biblically prophesied end-times events. Many theories have been put forth in an attempt to identify the US in prophecy, but none have really taken hold because the evidence presented has simply been weak and unconvincing. The US is currently an imperialist or empire building nation with a penchant for meddling and involving itself in every other nations' business on almost any pretense. There is no way that it would not be involved in at least some of the prophesied events if it were able. We must therefore assume that it will not be able to get involved.

It is reasonable to assume that the US will soon cease to be an international factor in this world. There are at present many ways that this could come about. For instance, the US has the oldest and least hardened power grid in the world. A bill was proposed years ago in congress to harden the grid to solar flare and EMP damage at a relatively inexpensive price tag. The bill has not moved forward for several years. Because the grid is so interconnected, damage to a portion of it could bring it down in its entirety. A shutdown of that proportion would result in the starvation of the majority of the population within months and take decades to repair. Could this be just the foolishness of our leadership or is it the hand of God at work to remove the US from the last days equation? Alternatively, there could be a cyberattack that would cause as much damage. This has become a growing concern for all western nations.

In another plausible scenario, there could be a devastating economic collapse. The US is currently deeper in debt than any nation in the entire history of the world. It has been estimated that between the public debt and personal or private debt, that every American family is over 875,000 dollars in debt. What percentage of families do you think can ever hope to pay off that much debt? The US is far beyond flat broke. Her only two ways out would seem to be overt default or hyperinflation. Either way would devastate our economy, destroy the wealth of almost all our citizens and leave a dirt poor third world nation in its wake. We would cease to be a credible factor on the world stage.

There are other highly plausible scenarios such as having computer systems in our banking, military, infrastructure and other systems compromised. A successful attack on any of these could cripple us for many years to come. Then there are possible biological or chemical attacks or plagues that could, if strategically placed, cause enough damage to cripple the nation. With the explosion of drone technology, delivery of deadly devices is no longer much of a challenge. There are many other such scenarios that could be mentioned or dreamed up. The point here is that although we feel secure and in charge right now, peace and safety can never really be taken for granted. The Bible tells us that this is especially true of the last days:

*1Th 5:1 But of the times and the seasons, brethren, ye have no need that I write unto you.*
*2 For yourselves know perfectly that the day of the Lord so cometh as a thief in the night.*
*3 For when they shall say, Peace and safety; then* **sudden** *destruction cometh upon them, as travail upon a woman with child; and they shall not escape.*

With the United States removed from the equation, the balance of power in the world would quickly shift from west to east. Already we see Europe fading and China and India rising in the world economic system. Russia has come a long way back from her economic collapse in the Reagan era and is eagerly reasserting herself on the world scene. Russia is allying itself with Iran/Persia, Syria, Turkey, and other middle east and Muslim nations with the notable exceptions of Egypt and Saudi Arabia. She is currently, as we saw, significantly fulfilling the alliances of Ezekiel 38-39. Considering the lateness of the hour, this is no accident. The hand of God is clearly visible in this matter to those with enough biblical knowledge to recognize it.

We have seen that Israel will commit a degree of genocide on the Palestinian people as well as conquer Lebanon and

Jordan in the near future and prior to the tribulation. The question arises as to the possible motivation for such an extreme move. It seems the answer is to be found in Israel's concern with Iran's nuclear ambitions.

Israel is convinced that Iran is working to develop nuclear weaponry and is in fact quite far along in that effort. A student of biblical prophecy should know that Daniel 11's final king of the north will have this capability, so if Iran produces this last-days king of Babylon, then Iran will get nuclear weaponry. The scripture says this on the subject:

*Eze 30:24 And I will strengthen the arms of the king of Babylon, and put my sword in his hand: but I will break Pharaoh's arms, and he shall groan before him with the groanings of a deadly wounded man.*
*25 But I will strengthen the arms of the king of Babylon, and the arms of Pharaoh shall fall down; and they shall know that I am the LORD, when I shall put my sword into the hand of the king of Babylon, and he shall stretch it out upon the land of Egypt.*

This passage deals with the final battle between the kings of the north and south which ends in the nuclear devastation of Egypt. According to this passage, the Lord will personally see to it that someone in the land of ancient Babylonia/Persia will attain nuclear weaponry.

Israel, for many years now, has been considering a preemptive strike to destroy Iran's nuclear facilities. It would seem that she will wait too long or else fail in that objective. Iran, on the other hand, may conduct a preemptive strike on Israel to destroy her ability to strike.

At the same time, Hezbollah in Lebanon is waiting for an opportunity to attack Israel with a reported 100,000 plus rockets and missiles aimed at targets all over the land of Israel. They are constantly upgrading to more powerful ones, as well. Hamas and the Islamic Jihad in Gaza have a reported 10,000-20,000 more rockets and missiles aimed at targets all throughout Israel. In addition, there are militant groups and terrorists on the Sinai border and more in the West Bank and Jordan.

In Syria, Russia has an airport some 70 miles from the border with Israel as well as a seaport in Syria. There is an uneasy truce with Israel, but with all the different groups flying bombing missions, and especially with Israel bombing Iranian targets almost at will in Syria, toes are likely to get stepped on. The situation is entirely untenable and only bad things can come of it. There is a strong possibility that a very large war could come of it.

To Israel's east, the usually stable nation of Jordan has been getting more belligerent. Jordan has jurisdiction on the Temple Mount, but the conservative and religious Jews are about fed up with that situation. Israel is hinting at taking some of that authority to herself.

All of these forces are just waiting for a trigger event to launch on Israel. The moment Israel is engaged in any kind of major military action, she will be immediately attacked from all these fronts. Psalm 83 has much to say on this subject. Her only chance of survival would seem to be a quick, concurrent, no holds barred assault on these enemies before they have a chance to launch too many missiles. The attack would have to thoroughly decimate the enemy forces in a very short time. Such an attack would necessarily have a high collateral mortality rate on the civilian populations meeting the biblical standards of genocide on the native populations.

Whether Israel succeeds or fails in her mission against Iran, she will surely succeed against her neighboring nations. This, in all likelihood, will not be acceptable to the rest of the world. A police action of sorts will be decreed against Israel and Russia will be selected to lead a confederation of nations against Israel to take the conquered territories back. This will be the Gog war described in Ezekiel 38-39 which will take us up to the start of the tribulation.

This may not be the actual way everything plays out, but we can know one thing for certain. Whenever Gog attacks Israel, it is time to look up.

*Luk 21:28 And when these things begin to come to pass, then look up, and lift up your heads; for your redemption draweth nigh.*

So now we have some powerful tools in our watcher's toolbox. Especially with respect to watching for Gog. Never forget the overarching reason for watching. We want to be taken in the pre-trib rapture. For that to happen, **we must be found watching and living in righteousness** when the Lord comes for us.

### Eleven ways to watch for the pre-trib rapture

The following is just a handy reference list for the events and ideas we have presented throughout this work to help us see that day approaching. It generally goes from less specific to more specific.

- ✓ The offices of Priest, Prophet, and King attained at 2000-year intervals.
- ✓ The day/millennium code at 1000 years per day of creation.
- ✓ The watch/millennium code at 3 hours per millennium for one day starting at sunrise.
- ✓ Hebrews 9:26 assertion that we have been "in the end of the world" for 2000 years now.
- ✓ Daniel 9:27 statement that the city and the sanctuary would be desolate until the consummation of the prophecy of seventy weeks.
- ✓ Jesus' statement in Luke 21:24 that Jerusalem would be trodden down of the Gentiles until the times of the Gentiles be fulfilled.
- ✓ The parable of the Fig tree which allows one generation from its leafing out.
- ✓ The last days wars of Israel which include near genocide of the Palestinians and the desolation of Jordan and the conquest of Lebanon.
- ✓ The Lake of Fire breaking through the surface of the Earth in some manner.
- ✓ The Russian invasion of Israel and entering of Jerusalem.
- ✓ The ministry of Elijah in the person of a mighty, date-setting preacher in the waning months or days of the pre-trib age.

## How to live in the face of this awesome understanding

OK. So, now we know what to look for and a little bit about when to watch more carefully. What then, does that mean with regard to our day-to-day life? I'm glad I asked. The first and most important point I would like to make in regard to this question is that we must do exactly what the Savior told us to do. Naturally, He foresaw this situation as a problem for many and gave us instructions.

*Luk 19:12 He said therefore, A certain nobleman went into a far country to receive for himself a kingdom, and to return.*

*13 And he called his ten servants, and delivered them ten pounds, and said unto them, Occupy till I come.*

*14 But his citizens hated him, and sent a message after him, saying, We will not have this man to reign over us.*

In this parable we find citizens and servants. The citizens are the Jews who rejected Him, while the servants are the Church Age saints. The pounds are gifts for ministry as found listed in 1Cor. 12:1-11 and 12-27 and 28-31. Also, study Eph. 4:11-16. The number one thing to do is occupy until He comes. That means keep doing whatever it is you are doing right in your life. It doesn't mean quit your job, or go wait on the top of a mountain, or sell your house, or any of the many other foolish things Christians have done in the past. Also, understand that despite prevailing Baptist theology, everybody can't do everything **but** be a pastor. My advice is to stay within your gifts.

Paul also gave some advice on the subject:

*1Co 7:20 Let every man abide in the same calling wherein he was called.*

However, and there is always a however, there are things you can do to be proactive in the face of this special knowledge.  If you are well off financially, you might up your giving a bit.  You're not going to need one cent in heaven and yet you can send some money ahead to purchase greater rewards at the judgment seat of Christ.  If you have extra time, you might spend a little more time in intercessory prayer for lost friends and loved ones.  Time has never been more precious for them than it is right now.  Above all though, find out what your special ministry gift or gifts from God is/are and do that with your whole heart.  That is the best way to occupy until He comes.

Finally, don't be fearful, or apprehensive, or nervous.  If you are not being openly rebellious, or living in gross sin, and if you truly want to be with your Savior, that's where you will be when He comes.  He also longs to be with you and welcome you into His home in glory.  I can only imagine the great sense of peace and joy and love that will flood over all of us the moment He calls us home.  But it is a good imagining.

*Joh 17:24  Father, I will that they also, whom thou hast given me, be with me where I am; that they may behold my glory, which thou hast given me: for thou lovedst me before the foundation of the world.*

## How to become eligible for the pre-trib rapture of the Church

Before any of this study even matters, we must be part of the family of God. Let's look at what the scriptures say about attaining that prize.

When God created this present world, He was very pleased with His work. He had this to say about it:

*Gen 1:31 And God saw every thing that he had made, and, behold, it was very good. And the evening and the morning were the sixth day.*

God created Adam and Eve and gave them a set of instructions. He also gave them a penalty of death if they willfully disobeyed Him. As we all know, they failed miserably and brought death upon themselves and all their descendants. This went beyond physical death. It was to be eternal death in the Lake of Fire where the worm (body) dieth not and the fire is not quenched.

But God did not want to lose His creation entirely, so He introduced a plan of redemption. By shedding one's own blood, mankind could pay for sin and be restored, but would be restricted to the soulish state. That would work out OK if there was only one sin to pay for. But as soon as there was more than one sin, there was a problem. There was no more blood to shed for the second sin. So, God instituted His great plan of redemption to restore back to Himself all those who would freely choose to return to Him.

This plan of redemption was very costly to God. It involved coming into a sin filled world, living a sinless life and then shedding the very blood of God on a cruel cross. He sent His only begotten Son, Jesus to accomplish that mission. The death on the cross was very bad, but the real pain Jesus experienced was becoming guilty of every sin ever committed by those who would accept His payment for their sins. The blood of God is so powerful that it can do that.

That is the story behind the verse that follows.

*Joh 3:16 For God so loved the world, that he gave his only begotten Son, that whosoever believeth in him should not perish, but have everlasting life.*

Jesus made this great sacrifice for every person who ever has lived or ever will be born into this evil world. That is because:

*Rom 3:23 For all have sinned, and come short of the glory of God;*

This was the ONLY way a sinful man or woman could be saved for an eternity with God. The Bible makes the alternative very plain:

*Rev 20:15 And whosoever was not found written in the book of life was cast into the lake of fire.*

God realized that man could never make the sin payment for himself, so He sent Jesus to make the payment for us. That would make our eternity with God a free gift.

*Rom 6:23 For the wages of sin is death; but the gift of God is eternal life through Jesus Christ our Lord.*

There is a condition, however, to receiving the free gift. That is to voluntarily restore ourselves to the original plan and will of God for our lives. This means we must learn His ways for us and seek to live them. That is called repentance. We must realize that living our way is full of emptiness and sorrow and turn to His way of peace and joy.

*2Co 7:10 For godly sorrow worketh repentance to salvation not to be repented of: but the sorrow of the world worketh death.*

Now, we have an enemy army fighting within the spirit world to keep us from doing this. That is Satan along with his angels. He plants tremendous doubt in our minds to keep us from truly believing this story of redemption is true. So, we need one more thing from God:

*Eph 2:8 For by grace are ye saved through faith; and that not of yourselves: it is the gift of God:*
*9 Not of works, lest any man should boast.*

God gives us the very faith to be saved at just the time we are ready to accept Him. It is very important not to turn away when this great gift is being offered to us. It may not always be there. So, how do we accept this gift?

*Rom 10:9 That if thou shalt confess with thy mouth the Lord Jesus, and shalt believe in thine heart that God hath raised him from the dead, thou shalt be saved.*
*10 For with the heart man believeth unto righteousness; and with the mouth confession is made unto salvation.*
*Rom 10:13 For whosoever shall call upon the name of the*

*Lord shall be saved.*

We make confession unto salvation with our mouth. In other words, we must physically and intentionally and purposefully ask God to forgive our sins against Him and save us.

Putting this all together and remembering that we must fully intend to show repentance as we discussed above, meaning we intend to give our will over to God's will and live in His light and truth for eternity, we simply ask at this point. You should be ready to pray a prayer to God the Father that goes something like this:

**Most gracious heavenly Father, I realize I am lost in sin and on my way to eternity in the Lake of Fire. I repent of my sins and my separation from You. Based on Your promises in the scriptures and the shed blood of Jesus Christ, I ask for the salvation Your redemption brings. Let Jesus come into my heart and be Lord of my life to guide me into your ways forever. Thank you for saving me through this simple act of asking. I make this prayer with complete confidence in Jesus' name, amen.**

If you have prayed this prayer with sincerity and if God has saved your body and soul for eternity, you should be very careful and very sure to tell those who are dearest to you about the change in direction you have made in your life. This is the greatest moment of your life. You have made the decision God has kept you alive for up to this point in your life. You have just gone from being an utter failure to an unqualified success in life! Now you must learn His ways and begin living your life for His great honor and glory. Just to get you started, let me show you just one of the great new differences in your life now:

*Rom 8:14 For as many as are led by the Spirit of God, they are the sons of God.*

*15 For ye have not received the spirit of bondage again to fear; but ye have received the Spirit of adoption, whereby we cry, Abba, Father.*

*16 The Spirit itself beareth witness with our spirit, that we are the children of God:*

*17 And if children, then heirs; heirs of God, and joint-heirs with Christ; if so be that we suffer with him, that we may be also glorified together.*

Printed in Great Britain
by Amazon